The City Is the Frontier

Other Books by Charles Abrams

Revolution in Land

The Future of Housing

Forbidden Neighbors

Man's Struggle for Shelter in an Urbanizing World

The
City
Is
The
Frontier

By CHARLES ABRAMS

HARPER & ROW 18 17 PUBLISHERS
NEW YORK

FIRST EDITION

LIBRARY OF CONGRESS CATALOG CARD NUMBER: 64-25145

I-P

Contents

[v

PART II. THE PRESCRIPTION—URBAN RENEWAL

Preface

In 1960, the Ford Foundation requested that I undertake a study of the urban renewal program in the United States and made the grant to the Joint Center for Urban Studies of the Massachusetts Institute of Technology and Harvard University that made it possible. Though I had been associated with the housing program in the United States since its inception in 1933, a considerable part of my time after 1954 had been devoted to the problems of underdeveloped areas. But my interest in the American housing problem had never abated and my four years of service in New York State as a member of Governor Averell Harriman's cabinet as well as my work as chief consultant to the Governor's Advisory Commission on Housing Problems in California in 1962 helped keep me close to the American scene and its problems. The Ford Foundation assignment provided me with a welcome opportunity to assess a program that was not only one of the most novel but which had become one of the most controversial among the many efforts to improve the housing conditions of the American people.

A mission under the auspices of the United Nations to Ireland in 1960 and another to Singapore in 1963, both of which countries were planning urban renewal programs, had, moreover, made me aware that the urban renewal concept was of more than domestic concern. But despite the influence it had generated abroad, the program seemed to have gained few advocates at home, except perhaps among the officials who were administering it. This should not have been surprising, for the program had had a slow start; it had been laboring under many impediments inherent in its basic legislation; the dislocation of thousands of poorer families from their homes and the assignment of their sites to higher income families had exposed it to ethical challenge. Its critics kept highlighting its faults more often than its virtues, and it had become almost fashionable for the intellectuals in the planning schools to be classed among the program's most eloquent foes.

In the last few years, however, more of the program's contributions and potentials have been coming into focus. It is still a program in flux and some of its deficiencies persist, but to urge its repeal, as some of its critics have been doing, instead of pressing for its supplementation with the programs it needs to make it viable makes little political sense, if indeed it makes any sort of sense at all. The renewal program was not conceived as a means of solving the problems of cities, and only in recent years has its purpose been involved with the improvement of cities at all. Though it was spawned primarily as a housing device, it still lacks an adequate housing program for the people it displaces. It still fails to address itself to some of the main troubles facing cities, which are in a state of physical decay, in social strife, and in economic crisis. The middle- and upper-income families have been taking flight from them; trade, manufacture, and commerce have been shifting to their outskirts; urban debt and taxation have been increasing almost to the limits of the city's capacity. The states are no longer able to help nor are they disposed to do so politically. All this has been happening at a time when the national economy is at the height of its prosperity, and, odder still, when we have become a predominantly urban society.

Though the federal government had been empowered since 1936 to deal with the nation's general welfare, and although general welfare is now involved with the welfare of an urban people, the real weakness in all federal programs bearing on city problems is that they lack a clear objective and are harnessed to no identifiable purpose.

Housing and renewal projects have mushroomed since 1933 and there is some incipient aid to urban transportation as well as a federally financed poverty program, but the total benefits they give to the cities are trifling compared to what the cities require for their survival and regeneration. Although Congressional legislation has promised "a decent home in a suitable environment for every American citizen," there is no adequate program to implement the promise, and President Johnson's prospectus for the "Great Society" will remain more hope than reality without a radical change in federal and state responsibilities as well as a recasting of the power, debt, and tax structures at all three levels of government.

For these reasons, I have made the urban renewal program a take-off point for a more general study of America's urban problems. The renewal program is only one device to aid cities, the housing program a second, the transportation and poverty programs are others, but they are not enough in themselves to grapple with the city's growing predicaments.

More recently, the renewal program has generated a new interest in cities by the local citizenry, and some better recognition of the needs of cities has also become noticeable at the federal level. Direct rent supplements to families to accompany a public housing program, which seemed inconceivable seven years ago,[1] has won support, if only as a token program. While we are not yet ready to authorize the building of government-initiated new towns, the idea did at least gain executive blessing in 1965. Federal loans at low interest rates for nonprofit housing is accepted. All this promises some hope for the future, but the main gap must still be bridged, i.e., there must be a change in the national attitude toward our central cities that will spur the assumption by the federal government of responsibility for building and rebuilding an urban America consistent with our wealth, our leadership, and our stature in the world. It is primarily to this theme that federal policy must still address itself.

A few words of gratitude are due to people who have been helpful

[1] Charles Abrams, *U.S. Housing, A New Program*, New York, Tamiment Institute, 1958.

to me in the preparation of this study: Lloyd Rodwin of the Joint
Center for Urban Studies, Martin Meyerson, its former codirector,
and James Q. Wilson, his successor, for helping to make the study
possible; Paul Ylvisaker of the Ford Foundation for his faith that I
would complete it and that it would be useful; Robert C. Weaver for
reading the galleys despite the pressures of his other duties; Louis
Winnick, Bernard Frieden, Ralph Taylor, Joseph Wershba, Marshall
Kaplan, Roma Connable, Frank Kristof, Kenneth Platnick and
Aryeh Cooperstock for reading all or part of the manuscript and
making valuable suggestions; Alexander Crosby for editing a first
draft and for his encouraging comments; Bruce Smith and John Dickie
for checking the material and citations in the galley and page proofs,
and Peggy Andre for her clerical assistance; William Slayton for his
frank discussion of the program in the early stages of the writing; and
the National Association of Housing and Redevelopment Officials for
arranging a meeting with fifteen directors of local urban renewal
agencies with whom I was able to discuss my preliminary conclu-
sions. I am grateful above all to my wife, Ruth Abrams, for her
patience during the many months I was writing this book.

—CHARLES ABRAMS

New York City
June 14, 1965

Part

I

URBAN PROBLEMS

IN

OUR URBAN AGE

Chapter

1

The City at Bay

THE HISTORY OF CIVILIZATION from Memphis, Egypt, to Memphis, Tennessee, is recorded in the rise or demise of cities. It is the story of Rome and its million people in the first century reduced to a city of 17,000 in the fourteenth; of the scourges and famines of Paris and the Renaissance that made it the intellectual capital of Europe; of the heap of ruins that was London fifty years after the Roman evacuation, its rise under mercantilism, its desolation by war, and its resurgence to the London of today.

In our own era, the world's cities are witnessing their greatest surge in man's history. Everywhere, hordes of people are leaving the hinterlands in quest of the city's opportunities, its excitements, and its way of life. From 1800 to 1950, the proportion of people living in cities with more than 20,000 people leaped from 2.4 per cent to 21 per cent. Our civilization is becoming urban, and the advance into cities is one of the most spectacular social phenomena of our time. The city has become the frontier.

The United States is also experiencing the impact of urbanization. Whether they live in the city proper or a few miles from its borders, the nation's people are becoming an urban people. But while 70 per cent of the nation's population now lives in urban areas, most of its great cities, which are the cores of these areas, have been declining both in population and influence. This, too, is a phenomenon, and no other country in our time or at any time has experienced a similar contradiction.

In 1937, Congress authorized a small public housing program, and in 1949, it supplemented this with a program aimed at renewing its cities. These were the first real signs of a federal responsibility for the improvement of America's urban environments. In terms of money, the two programs were of minor significance. But in political terms, they were revolutionary, for under the nation's unique political system, cities were always the creatures of the states, and for the federal government to deal directly with their problems—even if undertaken with the states' technical consent—was an innovation and a significant exercise of the federal government's new and still undefined welfare power.

That the urban renewal program, moreover, should have gained both its name and its current impetus in the United States is an anomaly, for the attitudes toward cities that prevail in the Old World had never expressed themselves in the American story. Almost from its beginnings as a nation, America's cities fell into low esteem. Thomas Jefferson feared they would harbor Europe's rabble and become "pestilential to the morals, the health and the liberties of man." During the century that followed Jefferson's death, cities and political corruption were held to be virtually synonymous. It was in the cities that nativism and anti-alien movements rose with each immigrant influx. The farmer inveighed against the city's rising power, while the fledgling West blasted the city's capitalists as the enemies of American progress.

Nor had our cities won more honor in our own era. An O. Henry or an E. B. White might be sensitive to the city's values, Carl Sandburg might chant of Chicago as the city with the big shoulders, while H. L. Mencken could see New York as "the icing on the pie called Christian civilization." But they have been a small voice[1] in the anticity clamor—and as new minorities keep pouring into the central

[1] Compared to the anticity sentiments of intellectuals such as Emerson, Hawthorne, Poe, Thoreau, Henry James, Henry Adams, and William Dean Howells, among others. See Morton and Lucia White, *The Intellectual Versus the City*, New American Library, 1962.

cities, they are again being defamed as the nests of mobs, the seats of slums, and the dens of crime. The important role they played in the nation's development and the role they still play in its progress are being obscured as the strong undercurrents generated by the racial problem are making themselves felt.

The American attitude toward cities contrasts sharply with attitudes in the Old World. For thousands of years, man had built cities and idealized them. Aristotle could find the common life for the noble end only in Athens, and Socrates would never leave it for the trees. Voltaire could see the London of his time as the rival of ancient Athens. Europe's culture and progress continue to this day to be reflected in its Paris, Rome, Geneva, Amsterdam, and Vienna. Urbanity was always associated with urban life, while suburban and suburbanity were contemptuous slams at the inferior ways of the provinces.[2] But the flight to suburbia in America has taken on the semblance of a flight from scourge.

This contrast in attitudes toward cities between the Old World and the New might be partly explained by the existence of a European urban culture that had been well rooted long before the industrial revolution had blemished it. The words city, civility, and civilization shared a common root. Antiquity and tradition in Europe stood their ground against the contaminations of industrialization, and when social problems festered, they were met by social reforms, not flight. People from all walks of life shared the adventure of living in the city and continued seeing its virtues above its blight, its surviving grace over its rising slums. Similar traditions and cultural ties to a past never gained root in an America whose cities were springing up almost overnight. Most of its buildings are of recent origin and were built for speculation, not use. For more than a century, the city's elite had been terrified by the ever-flowing hordes of foreigners who kept edging toward their moorings. A lasting pride in place could not exist for long in a country constantly washed by massive waves of an unwelcome poor and by a society on the move.

[2] According to the *Oxford Dictionary*, suburban also meant "having the inferior manners, the narrowness of view, etc., attributed to residents in suburbs."

What, therefore, are the reasons behind the current effort to renew American cities? Are they earning a new acknowledgment of their values comparable to those of London or Paris? Can the current urban renewal effort salvage them? Or is it just another passing flare in the political spectacle, to be forgotten when it has run its course?[3]

American cities embrace a variety of categories. They are large and small, trade centers and industrial centers, rich and poor. They are as heterogeneous as the people who inhabit them. In assessing the state and fate of American cities, one should distinguish between polymorphic cities like New York or Chicago and cities like Gary, Detroit, Grand Rapids, or Fall River that owe their lives mainly to one or two industries and might die with their departure. There are American capital cities that never change anything but their governors, cities that are no more than languid milltowns, cities that have more cows than people, cities dominated by the aging, cities with most of their houses on wheels, cities like Los Angeles that spread for miles and are still spreading, and one city in California that supports its quick on the burial fees of its dead.

The Declining Central City

There are, however, a large number of cities in the United States that are more or less similar in their troubles. They are principally the older central cities that grew up in the first flush of America's industrial revolution, have now aged, and are being challenged by the suburban

[3] It should be prefaced that those who talk for and against cities have not always been talking about the same thing. Aristotle and Socrates were referring to a city-state and Jefferson to the sordid, dirty, and explosive cities of eighteenth-century Paris and London. Many Americans who currently prize city life think mostly of New York (Washington Square and the posh East Sixties) or San Francisco (the Top of the Mark or its Montmartre at the bottom of the hill). The British city of the historian may have been only a cathedral town or a little district north of the Thames; Bethlehem was no more than a village, while Nazareth only recently began taking on the appearance of a city when Israel added factories on the highland overlooking the sleepy Arab community. In an entirely unprecedented definition of a city, President Johnson in a footnote to his message to Congress on March 2, 1965, defined a city as "the entire urban area—the central city and its suburbs."

push on their peripheries. They are seeing the emigration of some of their industries, their more affluent taxpayers, and their institutions. Together they are still the pulse of America but a pulse that falters. These cities include not only New York, Baltimore, Cleveland, Chicago, San Francisco, Boston, Cincinnati, St. Louis, and Philadelphia, but also hundreds of smaller cities such as Newark, New Haven, Trenton, Norfolk, and Knoxville. They represent billions in investment and are still the centers around which the surrounding populations and their new communities are polarized.

For more than a century, these older cities were able to hold their own against the invasion of Europe's poor, the anticity propaganda, the shift of population to the west, and the gathering flesh on their peripheries. They were small compact units, geared to foot and hoof, which happened to be the only means of bringing people together. Immigration and births met their labor needs and fed them more recruits than they lost by exodus. Class patterns in these cities were not only buoyant but ebullient; while the slum was disdained, the slum dweller was no captive to his environment, and the Horatio Alger stories were not all fiction—a slum immigrant or his boy, by taking an American haircut and learning the language, could rise in a single generation from bootblack to owner of the shoe company. Indeed, many did. Despite anti-alien movements, graft, and corruption, these cities spawned the brain and brawn of the country. The streak of vibrant land from Boston to Chicago not only became the haven for the oppressed and hungry of Europe but America's great belt-line that carried the fruits of its minds and machines to the world's four corners.

The dawn of the twentieth century saw these cities spreading outward to accommodate their swelling complement of rich and poor. The slums which housed their poor were not always isolated from the main stream of city life; and some, in fact, were at the city's center where the poor could more conveniently serve their betters—fire their furnaces, launder their cuffs, and fix their plumbing. Others were an hour or more from work, the slum dweller paying the penalty of distance for his poverty. City life contrasted sharply with the rural and village life in America's hinterlands and with the peasant environment from which most immigrants came. Its impersonality was now a characteristic of the American milieu both in the city's center and on the fringe. Lord Bryce in 1921 described the American city as:

. . . a huge space of ground covered with houses, two or three square miles appropriated by the richer sort, fifteen or twenty, stretching out into the suburbs, filled with the dwellings of the poorer. . . . They [the poorer] were not members of a community, but an aggregation of human atoms, like grains of desert sand, which the wind sweeps hither and thither.[4]

The Effluent Society

The shift from reins to ignition had sparked more than the spark plug. As roads were cut into the farmlands, the peripheries overreached the poorer settlements on the outer precincts. Cities changed from self-contained trade centers into the cores of ever-expanding regions girded by independent suburban formations which the city could no longer swallow up. These outer areas were soon occupied by the burgeoning middle- and upper-income classes who sought its more open spaces, its free-standing houses, and its new life-styles. Forty years after Bryce's description, population in the suburban areas was increasing almost five times faster than in the central cities; and from 1950 to 1960, more than three-fourths of metropolitan growth had taken place outside the central areas. But forty-one out of sixty-two northeastern central cities had lost population, with fourteen of them losing more than 10 per cent. Among those losing population were nine central cities in the nation's eleven largest metropolitan areas. In the single decade 1950–1960, metropolitan counties outside such central cities showed a population increase of 61.7 per cent, while the central cities showed a population growth of only 1.5 per cent.[5] It was apparent that the nation had become urban-suburban. It was apparent also that the central cities were becoming urban islands in

4 *Modern Democracies*, Macmillan, 1921, II, 108.
5 Warren Jay Vinton, "The Census of 1960," *Housing Yearbook*, National Housing Conference, 1961, p. 2.

an ever-expanding sea of suburban satellites. This spread of living areas and work locations is only an extension of a trend that started and accelerated with urbanization itself. It takes no longer to travel from the old city to the new suburb today than it once took to cover the distance between the city's central business district and some of its residential areas. But the disorganized pattern of the many small, political jurisdictions that surround the central cities is a relatively new and perplexing complication. Though dependent on the city, these formations have developed their own government apparatus and have been isolating themselves from the stream of problems that beset the region of which they are a part.

As the suburbs continued fanning out, some industries began to follow the population trend by settling where land was cheaper and where efficient one-story factories could be built. Skilled and white-collar workers bought homes there; the air was cleaner, and the surroundings better. Soon churches followed their parishioners, discount houses hawked their bargains on the freeways, and department stores moved into huge regional shopping centers on the roadsides, where a housewife could buy all her goods and gadgets with a minimum tax on her energies.

In the population reshuffle, some among the rich have preferred to remain ensconced in their urban mansions or in expensive new apartments safely insulated against unwelcome intrusions. The old big city also continued to harbor the elderly, the slum tenant, the single person, the widowed, the confirmed city dweller, the reclaimed exurbanite, and the atypical folk. In general, however, a new class formation had begun to transform America's social pattern. With few exceptions, Lord Bryce's generalization of the richer sort inhabiting the city and the poorer the outskirts was no longer true. The poor now live predominantly in the central city areas left behind by the once poor, the rising middle class, or the more opulent. Their ranks are being swelled by hordes of minorities, particularly Negroes, in quest of haven and a better break in life.

Other Causes of Central City Decline

The central cities are the products of the burgeoning system of private enterprise. Profit conditioned planning and housing standards; whatever city planning there was, was geared to the speculation urge. (The gridiron plan for New York City, which still dominates it more than 150 years later, had been chosen because "straight-sided and right-angled houses are the most cheap to build.") What the private builder built also had to fit the immigrant's purse, which meant crowding the land, providing no heat and only a single toilet for a whole tenement. But as higher standards were imposed in response to social pressures, the costs of new buildings rose, too; and the older run-down houses hung on because they were the only shelter the poor could afford. As for recreational facilities, a swath might be cut out here or there for a park or play space after private developments and people had already established their crude settlements.

The central cities had also been built for limited populations and services. The same three-man commission that had been set up in 1807 to plan New York City, for example, had thought it would be a "source of merriment" that it had planned for a "greater population than is collected on any spot on this side of China"; but only forty years later, the city's population had already doubled the estimate.

In laying out the cities, lots had been divided into small parcels of 20 or 25 by 100 feet. But with the advent of steel construction and the need for larger plots, assembling land for an economic parcel became a costly exercise in patience, luck, and cunning. It is no surprise, therefore, that the million or more acres being added to the urbanizing areas every year for homes and new settlements are mostly outside the central cities. There, a developer can more easily acquire 50 suburban acres from a single farmer-owner and develop his land as a unit. He might also build without more costly union labor, offer better mortgage terms, and find a ready market for the middle and upper class fleeing the cities.

There are a number of other problems that intensify the quest for the suburban alternative. Cities handle a daytime population 30 to 50 per cent greater than their residential population.[6] During the rush hours, the automobile flow is often slowed down on the old city streets to the pace of the horse and sometimes the snail. Traffic snarls, lack of parking space, difficulties in loading and unloading, and lack of storage facilities add to business and personal frustrations. One estimate puts the cost of traffic jams at $5 billion annually in time and wages lost, in extra fuel consumption and vehicle depreciation, and in lower tax yields and other costs.[7] Besides being troublesome to business, traffic has also accentuated the fear of accidents to children. Sidewalks that were always inadequate for play are being narrowed to make room for the car, and the child tends dangerously to share its assigned preserve. The long distance to a safe recreational area, the trek to the local school past automobiles, and the specter of a child under a truck are enough to speed the exodus to the cul-de-sacs of suburbia.

It is, however, the influx of Negroes and other minorities into cities that has added a dimension to the problem which cannot be reckoned with easily. The Negro concentration in central cities is changing their social atmosphere and altering the racial composition in public schools. The white child is often a minority in the classroom, and the quality of teaching is not keeping pace with the growing imperatives. The increase in breakins, muggings, and rioting and the failure of police action to cope with them has made more sections of the city unsafe, particularly at night. Other fears also play a part in the changing compositions of population and the flight from cities—fear of loss of social status, of neighborhood associations, and of property values.

Meanwhile the Hegira to the suburbs has drained from the city some desperately needed civic leadership, the presence of which had not only stabilized neighborhoods but had brought essential pressures on officialdom for reform. With continued inmigration of the less privileged, mediocrity and corruption are again fixing their holds on

---

[6] *Guiding Metropolitan Growth*, Committee for Economic Development, 1960, p. 19.

[7] *Report, on H. R. 11158,* House Committee on Banking and Currency, 87th Cong., 2nd Sess., July 3, 1962.

some of the political apparatus; the poorer and the in-migrant are again becoming fair game for the opportunist.

While the city's social problems and its educational needs, pensions, and payrolls are rising, its springs of revenue are drying up. Only a generation ago, municipalities were collecting more taxes than the national and state governments combined. Their take, 52 per cent of the total in 1932, had dropped to 7.3 per cent by 1962. The capacity of the city's real estate to support the rising costs is becoming more limited with the outflow to the suburbs. From 1930 to 1963, for example, Boston raised its tax rate from $31 per thousand dollars of real estate assessment to almost $100, but in the same period, its real estate valuations had shrunk from $1.8 billion to $1.3 billion. A sharp rise in the real estate tax brings proportionate diminutions in value, while local sales taxes required to supplement property levies take about a billion dollars a year from taxpayers. Retail sales in the core of New York dropped from 69 per cent of the New York region in 1929 to 55 per cent in 1954.[8] Suburban competition is a main reason, but the difference of $80 on a car or $12 on an air conditioner is not overlooked by the shopper. Limited in their capacity to tax, the cities are borrowing heavily, and thanks to the federal tax exemptions extended to the bond buyers, the volume of borrowings has soared.

The Fabulous Invalid

With all its troubles, the ailing central city is anything but dead. Some suffer more than others, while big cities like New York, San Francisco, Atlanta, or Chicago can take a beating and still show re-markable staying power. Although eight out of ten people are electing to settle on the fringe, some dwellings continue to rise in the center, and despite its troubles, New York City even experienced a spurt in apartment building in the 1960s; hotels, factories, executive offices, and new enterprises still see the central city's special advantages. The central city is changing, losing retail trade and manufactures; but it

[8] *Guiding Metropolitan Growth*, p. 17.

is still the primary source of skills, the main market for goods and ideas.[9] It is the seat of business services, can still boast a large built-in consumer market, is a magnet for visitors, salesmen, and buyers; it provides a central place for banking, subcontractors, bargains, and for the spare parts without which the machine wheezes and goes dead. In an era of expanded government intervention, it provides more intimate contact with officials, proximity to import and export licenses, consuls, lawyers, banks, and accountants. Life insurance companies, wholesale trade, and newspapers continue in the city, and not all industries can afford to pull up stakes, move costly machinery, and gamble on recruiting talents in their new surroundings.

If the central city no longer attracts most of the newcomers, it serves a vital function for some of them and for many others. It has lights as well as shadows, savants as well as bums, and a host of attractions that include not only cabarets, twist emporia, and race tracks but opera, coffee houses, and theaters. The universities, fixed to the city, provide a cache of research and brain power. The museums, art galleries, and the central library are there, too. Though the sumptuous roadside inn is offering challenge, some talented chefs still practice their alchemy on the main streets. Many a fringe-dweller still looks to the central city for his job, and the variety of jobs in cities adds to his sense of confidence and independence. The rising young housewife turns to the city when she needs old andirons or a painting; and for the curious, a ramble past a Victorian mansion or an old Greek Revival loft may call up richer conversation than the best recipe for suburban icebox cake. Though age in America is still equated with obsolescence, some city sections are still capable of aging gracefully, if given the chance.

If the city's chaos is part of its planlessness, its contrasts and variety

[9] Thirteen of the largest cities still hold 19 per cent of the nation's nonfarm population and provide 23 per cent of its nonagricultural employment (Raymond Vernon, *The Changing Economic Function of the Central City*, Committee for Economic Development, January 1959, p. 14). Twenty of the fifty largest cities which lost population from 1950 to 1960 held about 25 million people, or 14 per cent of total population, in 1960; while their metropolitan areas held about 49 million people, or 27 per cent of the total population.

still offer relief from the sameness of suburbia and its greater exposure of one's personal life and idiosyncrasies. People still seek escape to the metropolises, crave contrast, look for occasional anonymity, and want to see more people without being seen. They do not get all this at three families to the acre, and there is a limit to what a round of cocktail parties can do for the suburban spirit. If the nation was just one sprawling network of suburbias, it would be a bore.

Fringe living does offer many advantages for families—home ownership, better air, more play space, and fewer tensions. But it is not so free of infirmities as to offer a lasting guarantee that the confirmed exurbanite may never return. The American family likes to move about and moving is not always the one-way trip suburbanward. The commuter railroad, with its waning schedules and service, is turning many an out-dweller inward; while toll bridges, highways, tunnels, and parking problems have become a heavier drag on him than on the city dweller, and if it is still tolerable today, it may be intolerable by 1975 when more than 225 million people will be weaving in and out of our urban areas in some 80 million automobiles. Add the dearth of maids and day laborers to make life easier (a by-product of suburban exclusion devices) and the housewife may yet be driven back to the city after the child is off to college or boarding school and the seven-room split-level has become a splitting headache. There is already some evidence that this is happening in a few of our larger cities.

Many a suburb, moreover, has still to pay for its new schools and services, and a suburbanite may give up the lawn in despair after looking at the tax bill. Nor are suburbanites immune against the social distortions and infiltrations of the very minorities who have driven them out of the city. They will try hard to remain exclusive but the availability of jobs for minorities in the suburbs, their yearning for home ownership, and the improvement in their incomes may well make the minority problem a factor in some suburbs as it is now a factor in the cities. The urbanization of the suburb may, therefore, bring some of the city's vexations to it without the compensations of the central city and its greater ability to take social challenges in stride.[10]

In thirty-five years, 160 million people will be added to the population, and most of them will probably try to stake out a niche in the suburbs. Our urban and suburban population will double, and the land it occupies will double too. But the time is not far off when travel will have reached the maximum of human endurance, when a multiple dwelling may be all that is offered, and when many a suburb will be just another city with all of its headaches.

The pace of the continued drift outward will also hinge on whether each suburb can retain its exclusiveness, continue building good schools, hold its taxes down and provide good services, and social advantages. It will also depend on whether the fringe can provide enough of the amenities and interests the central city offers—theaters, efficiency units, more interesting people, more relief from dullness, and a larger sense of anonymity when one needs it. In short, the future of the fringe may depend on whether it can itself acquire some of the amenities of the core city or itself produce a big city replica that can cope with some of the same problems the big city faces. Thus, the core city, new or existing, will be on hand—to house the menials and the poor (if there will still be any), the migrant and the transient, the city's working mothers, the nondrivers and walkers, and the millions of nonconformists and nonaverage folk who live in the cities today and will have nothing else.

The salvation of the existing core cities, in turn, will depend on whether they can provide better schools, make their own environments healthier, more interesting, more recreational, more suitable for children and the family, more useful and more opportune for a job. This,

[10] Darien, Connecticut, a commuter town of 18,000, for example, found that its boys and girls of all ages were stealing anything from candy bars to automobiles—in fact, a club at the high school required stealing for membership. School windows were broken "all the time," 85 per cent of the children were drinkers, according to a senior, and for a teenager, "accepting a date to the drive-in movie is like accepting a date for sexual relations" (*New York Times,* May 17, 1963, p. 56). In serious crimes, the rate of increase in suburbs in 1964 equaled or surpassed that of cities.

too, will depend on the American will to keep the central city among the electives available to its people, and on whether we are willing to pay the price of making the city a sound component of the nation's social structure. In an era in which life is becoming urban and human behavior becoming the behavior of people in an urban setting, we may be producing the most ingenious machines but computing and commuting are routines, not civilization. If we lack the capacity for creating the social ideas for the new life and the variety of environments and opportunities which human beings need for human progress, we may decline as a nation.

Despite its setbacks and its new concentrations of minority families, the central city is still the heart of American life and still shapes its more vital institutions. It is still the confluence of diversities, and when a nation has many cities and many types of cities, the diversities and alternatives are multiplied. It is still the precinct of many faces, the vast mobile in an ever-shifting human landscape. If it brings loneliness to some, it guarantees privacy for others. It has maintained its ancient role as a refuge for the oppressed. It is even the unspoken refuge of those who try to escape from the city to the outskirts—for they are within its magnetic field though not at its pole. If the city is presently the seat of new social conflicts and new group tensions, it continues to be the melting pot in which ways of life are blended, the training ground of the poor in search of a better life, the crucible in which will be tested our ability to endure the fatigue which democracy exacts.

A city, even an American city, is the pulsating product of the human hand and mind, reflecting man's history, his struggle for freedom, his creativity, his genius—and his selfishness and errors. It is the palimpsest on which man's story is written, the record of those who built a skyscraper or a picture window, fought a pitched battle for a play street, created a bookshop or bakeshop that mattered. It is a composite of trials and defeats, of settlement houses, churches, and schoolhouses, of aspirations, images, and memories. A city has values as well as slums, excitement as well as conflict; it has a personality that has not yet been obliterated by its highways and gas stations; it has a spirit as well as a set of arteries and a voice that speaks the hopes as well as the disappointments of its people.

If American cities do not bear the mark of the generations of craftsmen who built Europe's churches and works, most of them, barring atomic destruction, are destined to last as long—for better or worse. If it is to be for the better, there must be a national will to make it so. For the nation's strength is that we are a nation of diverse people—35 million of us move annually from and into cities, suburbs, farms, villages, mobile parks, warm and cold climates, and every variety of house and environment. Much of the nation's strength and freedom exist because of the concentration of job choices in cities; the variety of places in which people live or may choose to live—those who seek the fringes and those who will settle for nothing less than the collision of minds in an ever-changing medley of faces and people.

The physical patterns available to people, however, and the existence of alternatives no longer rest exclusively on the decisions of private industry or of individuals. For in our time, public policy has become one of the most important forces in determining whether the city improves or wanes, the suburb stagnates or grows, the farm survives or disappears. Public policy for slum clearance, housing, race discrimination, zoning, road building, community facilities, transportation, suburban development, recreation, relief of poverty, and for spending and taxation is a main lever in manipulating the patterns of the society and the choices available to its members.

If we are to be committed to retaining the city as one of the choices in our national life, real urban renewal therefore calls for something more than tearing down a few slums, putting up another string of public projects, or another row of apartment houses. It will entail more than a few isolated and unintegrated programs hailed as a war on poverty or a token federal appropriation for a skirmish against ignorance or an unimplemented declaration of the need for equal opportunity. It will hinge also on whether the central city with all its problems is acknowledged as one of the vital options in American life.

It is only if the national purpose is known and defined that the value of the present renewal effort and the other federal programs directed toward achieving a great society can be measured. It is only if the central city is accepted as one of the living forces in the American scene and the problems of the people who live in it become part of the nation's concern, that meaningful specifications can be framed for the city's regeneration.

Chapter 2

The Slum

THE SLUM, which has been called the shame of the cities, is also the sperm of the public housing and urban renewal concepts. It is as distasteful a four-letter word as any in the dictionary. The word is a piece of cant of uncertain origin, little more than a century old.[1] The *Encyclopedia of Social Reform*[2] suggested that it was a corruption of "slump," meaning swamp, but there are indications that it is cousin to slime, which in turn is derived from "lime," meaning mud. It links both slop[3] and scum and also has the cadence of slush, slovenly, slut, slump, slug, slubber, slob, slub, sludge, slummock, slutch, and slutterly. Slum gives its meaning the moment it is uttered.

Since a word can be a repellent as well as a persuader, and since slum is both, it has spurred emotions on the hustings, the pulpit, and the bench. Unlike words such as substandard, tenement, and insanitary housing, it is short, electric, and suited to newspaper headlines. From the day slum entered the language of social reform, its mere mention was enough to revolt the good citizen, win the support of the crusading press, and dedicate official action to its extinction.

[1] Thus the *Oxford Dictionary* cites an 1828 usage from the History of Gaming (p. 28): "Regaling in the back-parlour (vulgo *slum*) of an extremely low-bred Irish widow."
[2] Funk and Wagnalls, 1897, p. 1260.
[3] It was Middle English *cousloppe* that gave us slop and sloppy. A cowslip is a flower that grows in cowslop.

The slum, however, is easier to revile than to remedy. During England's industrializing period some of its luminaries implied that the slum dweller was to blame. They defined slums as the dirty back streets or alleys shared by the poor and criminal classes. If the all too fertile slumdwellers could be exhorted to be more chaste (chastity would hold down their numbers), shun whiskey (giving up drink would make them more frugal), and fear God (piety would keep them honest, peaceful, and clean), slums would disappear. The filthy habits of the slum dweller himself were also held to be the cause of slums in America.[4]

Other reformers blamed the landlord.[5] His rents were seen as swallowing up all profit and unless something was done to check him, it was feared he would soon rule the world.

A whole series of laws were enacted both in England and America aimed at compelling landlords to improve their dwellings. But the slum dweller never fully escaped reproach and, in fact, association of the criminal classes with slums still colored the slum definition in the 1934 edition of *Webster's New International Dictionary*.

In the 1920s, writers like Edith Elmer Wood,[6] taking their cue from the more recent and more enlightened programs of England and the continent, began to highlight the disparity between income and shelter cost as a main factor responsible for slum life. The building industry, it was contended, was not producing houses at costs the slum people could afford. At first, nonprofit housing built by government was advocated,[7] but it was soon concluded that only if the housing were subsidized would rents be low enough for the poor to afford them.

The argument made no impression until the depression period, when three circumstances conspired to make subsidized housing po-

[4] *Health Department* v. *Dassori*, 21 App. Div. 348, 47 N.Y.S. 641 (October 15, 1897).

[5] The landlord in the United States was accused as far back as 1817 when Gerritt Forbes, New York City Inspector of Health, wrote: "And we have serious cause to regret that there are in our city so many mercenary landlords who only contrive in what manner they can stow the greatest number of human beings in the smallest space" (Robert W. DeForest and Lawrence Veiller, *The Tenement House Problem*, Macmillan, 1903, II, p. 69).

[6] *The Housing of the Unskilled Wage-Earner*, Macmillan, 1919.

[7] *Ibid.*, p. 259.

litically palatable. When many among the 13 million unemployed in the 1930s found themselves homeless or crowded into slum flats, it seemed illogical as well as impolitic to assert that all these people could be criminal, filthy, and inebriated. The second factor was the stagnant state of the building industry, which, it was felt, was holding back an economic recovery. Tearing down slums and building new housing would employ workers. The third factor was the experimental mood of the New Dealers who were willing to try anything as a pilot effort that would stimulate purchasing power. Public housing seemed to offer the dual prospects of economic and social amelioration in a single package.

After a number of pilot housing operations, the federal government in 1937 officially redefined the slum to encompass the physical condition of the buildings, the absence of amenities, and the overcrowding of the land. This new emphasis on structure made society partly to blame and imposed upon government the obligation to eradicate slums. They would be demolished by local housing authorities set up by the cities, which would build good housing on the sites and let it to the slum dwellers at rents within their means. The federal government would provide the necessary annual subsidies. Fortunately, there was a slum surplus in those days, and as slum dwellers were ordered out of their homes to make way for their own social progress, a few moved into the new public housing built for them, while the rest drifted into other available slums or emigrated to farms or to other cities.

As economic conditions improved, however, slum vacancies began to fill up. A number of cities began to experience a shortage of both higher-priced dwellings as well as slums.[8] When, for example, a few slum blocks were razed to make way for the Triborough Bridge approach in New York City, slum rents in the area went up by 25 per cent. Overcrowding within dwellings and ransom rents—not the

[8] From March to October 1936, vacancies were cut in half in New York City, while the median vacancy rate in all types of residential structures in cities showed a decline of vacancies from 7.3 per cent in 1933 to 2 per cent in 1936 (*Report on Living and Housing Conditions to Mayor Fiorello H. La-Guardia,* New York City Housing Authority, January 25, 1937, p. 16).

physical condition of buildings—became the more painful aspects of slum life. Slum demolition should have stopped, and vacant or under-occupied land should have been selected for low-rent projects so as to increase the housing supply for the less privileged.[9] But slum clearance had already gained a political momentum which could not be stayed. Politicians eager for a headline were busily competing for a place on the steam shovels. Social workers and reformers were highlighting the crime, disease, and delinquency in slums, while courts were incorporating their statistics into eloquent opinions that made the evils of slum life *res adjudicata*. Slum clearance was now not only a lawful undertaking by government but a moral obligation as well.

Under the federal public housing program, nearly 200,000 sub-standard dwellings were eliminated by June 30, 1953; and of all the housing units built under the Housing Act of 1937, 89 per cent were on slum sites, only 11 per cent on vacant land. As other slums went down due to private demolitions, code enforcement, and highways, the slum supply shrank further. The net housing supply available to the low-income family was thus steadily diminished as one slum after another was consigned to the wrecking crew.

The Newtonian and Darwinian Laws of Social Reform

One reason for the continued accent on slum clearance, even during a housing shortage, is that in politics as in physics, a law in motion tends to continue in motion, acquiring additional momentum from the interests and the pressure groups (*pro bono publico ut pro sese*) who draw its perquisites. Urban renewal's unremitting emphasis on slum clearance and relocation within the city is part of the same process. So is the persistence of the old formula under which the fed-eral government keeps the poor in the cities by subsidizing their housing, while providing no formula to enable them to move else-where after they are evicted from their slums. For reasons not mer-

[9] See Charles Abrams, *Shelter* (1939), reprinted in M. B. Schnapper, *Public Housing in America*, H. W. Wilson, 1939, p. 88.

cenary, these laws of social reform operate for the public official out to protect his public image as effectively as they do for a realtor out to protect his private dollar. The local public officials are managing programs that have taken years to put through. The public has had to be educated, the legislation fought through the Congress, and the enabling acts won in the state and local legislatures. Once the public has been indoctrinated, moreover, it is not easy to confess that the whole approach was wrong from the beginning, or that supervening circumstances have made it senseless to continue digging into the same hole.

The housing reformer is no more happily situated. He has committed himself to a position. Even if he has not been impressed into officialdom (as so many of the faithful have been), he is not prone to concede that all has not worked out for the best. His old speeches and writings remain to plague him; he has won over the good citizen and the press to his arguments (editorial positions are almost as sacred as judicial opinions, at least until they have faded from the public memory).

A somewhat similar reluctance paralyzes legislatures. The senator who has valiantly led the long fight for better housing has educated his fellows by debate. Having finally won a substantial part of his aims, a confession to his program's errors would be impractical, if not foolhardy, particularly since the unrelenting record of his remarks is at his opponent's elbow. "Keep what you have won and try to add the new bit by bit" is viewed as more sensible. The antiquated must be reverenced while the slow transition to reality is achieved—if at all.

The result is a gaping ideological lag between what is and what ought to be. Vested errors command respectability because they are defended by the respectable people. The protagonist of change is viewed as a turncoat or a pharisee.

Both public housing and the urban renewal program are products of the educational crusading against slums and for their clearance. They re-echo the old dictum about slum evils, but the public housing feature that was once an inseparable concomitant of slum clearance and which should be a concomitant of urban renewal clearance has been held down to a shell. Urban renewal tears down slums to make way for higher-rental projects while the slum dweller is relegated to the residual supply and forced to pay higher rents. Renewers and their professional advisers now press for benefits in the name of slum elimination and social progress. They have been joined by department store owners with heavy fixed investments and by owners of real estate threatened by encroaching blight. City officials now inveigh freely against slumlords while simultaneously looking to the urban renewal projects for the new revenues with which to pay the growing costs of local government; taxpayers viewing once-prime sections being taken over by home-hungry minorities see the slum clearance and renewal processes as the only means of retenanting the sites with white, taxpaying citizens. The evils of the slum are still cited, but the aim is no longer to improve the conditions of the poor. The less privileged for whom slum clearance was first devised are no longer the prime beneficiaries—often, in fact, they are the prime victims as they scurry about from one slum to another within the city.

The vested fictions that have enveloped slum clearance beleaguer the public housing formula as well. Subsidized housing in some form is needed as much as ever, but it need not be mainly or exclusively public housing or be confined to the cities to the exclusion of the suburbs. Existing programs, however, continue substantially unchanged despite their failure to meet the need for which they were devised.

The Persistent Fictions

The fictions that underlie the present housing and urban renewal programs are:

Fiction I: The housing of low-income families can be solved by tearing down the slums in which they live. People live in slums primarily because they can afford nothing better. Nothing better is built for them because it does not pay to build it at the rents they can pay. For 1962, the Bureau of the Census reported the breakdown of incomes shown in Table 1, to which has been added an estimate of the maximum housing outlay for each category:

TABLE 1

Income	Per cent of All Families	Maximum Monthly Housing Expense[a]
Less than $2,000	11.6	$ 33.00
Less than $3,000	19.9	50.00
Less than $4,000	29.1	67.00
Less than $5,000	39.0	83.00
Less than $6,000	50.5	100.00

[a] Maximum monthly housing expense is estimated on the assumption that no more than one-fifth of income should go for housing, including heat and utilities.

Standard houses or apartments with three bedrooms costing no more than $83 with all utilities are hard to find in most parts of the United States. Even at $100 rent there will be few offerings in the cities and suburbs of the East, North, and West.

Rising real incomes are one way of bridging the rent-income gap as well as improving housing conditions, and between 1950–1960 there was a general improvement in these conditions and a reduction in overcrowding. While in 1950 only 61 per cent of all units were not dilapidated and had all plumbing facilities, the census in 1960 set the figure at 82 per cent.[10] The 1960 census showed that four-fifths of our households enjoyed structurally sound units. The worst conditions were in rented quarters outside of metropolitan areas. Less than half of these renters lived in structurally sound units with all basic plumbing facilities.

From the total housing inventory of 58 million units for 1960, 15.7 million dwellings were listed as substandard (either dilapidated or lacking a private inside bath or hot and cold running water) or located in slum areas where "they will soon deteriorate into the

[10] The census figures which indicate improvements in housing conditions in 1960 are on the optimistic side because of the addition of a new housing quality category, e.g., "deteriorating." "Standard" housing also included deteriorating housing if it had plumbing facilities. Thus what is called standard by the census takers of 1960 may hardly be good housing.

substandard category." About 47 million people were living in these units. The main victims of slum life were the minorities.[11] Low income and slums went together: 85 per cent of the nonwhite slum occupants in 1960 had less than $4,000 per year, 58 per cent less than $2,000. Overcrowding was also more prevalent in these areas.

The words "slum" and "substandard housing" are, however, misleading, even if the more recent definitions of what is "standard" are accepted. One might live in a structurally sound house and be paying 35 per cent of his income for rent, as many do. He may be living in a sound house but be paying a ransom for transportation to work. There may be fewer leaks in the roof, but the neighborhood may have become unbearable. In these instances, he is living under "substandard conditions," but there are no figures that tell the real story. In these respects, the housing situation may be far more serious and the improvement in living conditions far less substantial than indicated by the census.

In many cities, particularly the larger ones, the substandard house includes a diversity of types. Some are physical slums which should be torn down. Others are physically sound but the families are living in them under oppressive conditions rather than in structural slums. Those in the physical slum classifications are:

1. Decayed buildings that were once sound

2. Structurally unsafe buildings

3. Converted basements and cellars which, though illegal, continue to be occupied

4. Improvised shelter, put together from scrap or makeshift materials

5. Sordid flophouses that shelter not only the skidrower or the wayfarer but the permanent single person who can afford nothing better

6. Decrepit trailers purchased for $1,000 or less and placed on cheaply rented lots.

[11] The proportion of households in dilapidated dwellings or those without adequate plumbing was 13 per cent in 1960 for whites compared to 44 per cent for minorities. While three-fourths of American households were living in "standard" structures with essential plumbing, only 44 per cent of minority families occupied such structures.

Those which may not be physically slums but in which families live under slum or substandard conditions are:

1. One-room units into which whole families are herded
2. Furnished rooms once reserved for bachelors and transients, but which now house entire families. These may include fictitious "hotels" which are really rooming houses but have none of the services required for family living.
3. Stores or lofts not built for residence and lacking toilet facilities
4. Subdivided apartments intended for one family but now housing four or five families
5. Bungalows built for warm weather only, pressed into use for year-round rental.

The 15.7 million dwelling units still classed as substandard in 1960 do not reflect the poor housing conditions under which American families live, though they do reflect the hard core slums and many of the houses targeted for clearance in current programs. But the prospects for providing alternative shelter for those who need better housing are becoming dimmer as demolition or decay continue.

Nor are slums confined to the cities for which public housing and urban renewal are designed. A survey of six communities by the State Division of Housing of California[12] shows that:

• More than 80 per cent of farm worker families live in dwellings which violate standards of health, safety, and comfort
• Nearly 65 per cent of the dwellings occupied by general field workers are dilapidated or deteriorated
• Pit privies still serve 33 per cent of the dwellings occupied by general field workers
• Thirty per cent of the dwellings have no bathing facilities and 25 per cent lack even a kitchen sink with running water.

The most serious aspect of slum life is overcrowding, and overcrowding is increased, not reduced, when the number of dwellings for low-income families is continuously reduced. Since two of the

[12] Oliver McMillan, *Housing Deficiencies of Agricultural Workers and Other Low Income Groups in Rural and Urban-Fringe Communities*, Division of Housing, California Department of Industrial Relations, 1962 (prepared for the Governor's Advisory Commission on Housing Problems).

factors contributing to tuberculosis are overcrowding and poor nutrition, a continued slum clearance program which curtails living space and enables owners of remaining slums to jack up rents can actually increase tuberculosis. When rents go up, there is less money for food; and when four people share a room, more chance of contagion. Clearance of a slum should mean clearance of bad conditions (in the same sense as clearing one's throat—one eliminates the condition but does not throw out the throat). Clearance may be achieved not only by better housing but by better income, better neighborhoods, and better opportunities in life. It should mean more space and more choice of dwellings from a varied inventory, not less. Slum demolition is authorized only when there is a substantial surplus of cheap housing and when it will not aggravate slum conditions.

Fiction II: Slums inevitably cause crime, delinquency, disease, and other morbidities. This is a generalization with some truths, some half-truths and some nontruths. The causes of crime are numerous and complex, and it is doubtful that a man's house always converts him into a lawbreaker—or that decent housing smothers any inclinations toward mayhem and larceny. Some of the misguided executives who served time for violating the income tax or antitrust laws were not from the slums, and some of the most sensational juvenile delinquents have been boys and girls from the very best neighborhoods. Poor housing is nevertheless demoralizing, and family life in a single room of a fifth-floor tenement is hardly conducive to proper parental controls. What increases the incidence of delinquency is less the structural condition of the house than the sordid conditions of the neighborhood, its lack of amenities, and the obliviousness of society to its needs.

A similar logic applies to the incidence of poor housing on health. Lack of sun, dampness, filth, poor water, and decay impair not only health but the human spirit. But the slums are not the only cause. In 1933 the Slum Clearance Committee of New York studied tuberculosis rates in the Lower East Side, long a target of reformers and slum-sisters. Thirty years earlier, Robert W. DeForest and Lawrence Veiller reported there was "hardly a tenement house in the area that had not had at least one case of pulmonary tuberculosis in the preceding five years, and in some houses there has been as great a number as twenty-two different cases of this terrible disease."[13] Yet in 1933 the Slum Clearance Committee found tuberculosis rates in the Lower East Side slums among the lowest in the city (50 to 74 deaths per 100,000 persons, compared to the national rate of 71 in 1930). The astonished committee, after considerable thought, concluded that "conditions are best where the service institutions are most frequent and at their worst where practically none of the listed agencies are found."[14]

This lesson from 1933 is tremendously significant. Slum dwellers are not inherently evil or sickly. But the vast majority are poor, and a considerable number are desperately poor. People who cannot afford good food and adequate education are headed for trouble. And they will get into trouble unless the community acts to help them. When the social agencies got busy on the East Side between 1903 and 1930, the tuberculosis rate settled down to normal.

So, too, overcrowding, whether in a good or a bad dwelling, can be more dangerous and more demoralizing than the physical condition of the building. Equally exacting are high rents that leave little for other family necessities.

Environment is not only physical environment but a complex of physical, economic, social, parental, and other factors which combine to make life unbearable for the parent as well as the child. Yet this broader concept of environment has been slurred over in the slum clearance and housing programs. The emphasis has been on zoning, project living, and demolition. "Neighborhood conservation" has focused on patching up structures rather than conserving people. Too often, "urban renewal" has subordinated the moral and spiritual renewal of the people whose homes have been taken from them, so the land can be used for the more prosperous. "Slum reclamation" and "neighborhood rehabilitation" have shown scant concern with the rehabilitation of teenagers. Almost every aspect of city rebuilding

[13] *The Tenement House Problem,* Macmillan, 1903, I, 10.
[14] *Report of Slum Clearance Committee,* New York, 1933–1934, Charts 14 and 16. See also Appendix A of the report.

has emphasized the physical, while the social aspects have been viewed as incidental or have been overlooked entirely. Not until the recent poverty program have the social aspects of neighborhoods received even mention in federal programs.

The existence of slums in the world's richest nation is a national disgrace, and the day must come when they will be removed from America's horizons. But the removal of slums with nothing more is worse than leaving them alone. In a number of cities, there is a shortage of cheap apartments and in such cities, there is nothing that wholesale removal of slums can accomplish that cannot be done better by an earthquake. An earthquake, in fact, would arouse a sympathetic response and an immediate movement to rebuild with something better than what was lost.

Fiction III: The poor deserve only minimum accommodations. The federal public housing law banned "extravagant" or "elaborate" design for public housing projects. Cost limitations were originally fixed at $4,000 per unit or $1,000 per room (and somewhat higher in areas where building costs were higher) but were raised periodically and often belatedly as costs rose. The limitations were continually geared to minima in design and specifications. As building costs rose, the housing authorities often had no alternative but to reduce standards even more.

Most of the projects have unhappily reflected the Congressional economies. In a few areas where land and building costs were low and the climate clement, authorities have built low-rise dwellings that look like homes. The usual product, in the big city, however, has a sameness of look which labels it as "the project." Irrespective of an architect's genius or his passion for originality, he could not create either a private or an individual appearance. Towering and prophylactic, these structures often overwhelm the mortals who live in them. Mothers lose contact with children who go out to play. They worry, too, lest a small child might try to emulate Superman and take wing from the tenth floor. Indeed some do so, without success. Sometimes even the most thoroughly toilet-trained youngster cannot make it from playlot to bathroom—which does not help the elevator. Yet, after thirty years of experience, the New York City Housing Authority announced in 1963 that it will build on the Polo Grounds site, where the Giants once played, two giant public housing towers of thirty stories each for 1,600 families.

Economy in the short run is not necessarily economy in the long run. The huge steel and concrete projects will stand for generations, long after the bonds that financed them have been paid. A smaller, cheaper building is dispensable when the time for the second round of urban renewal arrives. But a sixteen- to thirty-story structure will last a century if not more (even New York's old-law tenements have survived almost that long and give promise of living on). It would be wiser economy to build low-rise buildings to such minimum standards but impose maximum standards on long-life investments. Projects might include a varied design with taller structures for the childless couples and smaller buildings for families with children. It is not inconceivable, moreover, that projects tenanted by low-income families might ultimately include occupants from all economic strata. The social and economic fluidity of American life denies the continued prevalence of a permanent low-income class settled everlastingly in a given project or in the central city. By building better houses from the beginning (which would be possible if cost limitations were more realistic or if rents were raised as the incomes of tenants improved), the projects might then be pleasing additions to the gruesome urban horizons; the tenancy would be more stable; the projects would be viewed as homes instead of way stations; a larger proportion of urban renewal displacees might apply for tenancy, too. But this type of thinking would run afoul of another federal requirement later discussed, i.e., income limitations on occupancy.

Fiction IV: The poor live only in rented dwellings. By 1963 almost two-thirds of the nation's families were homeowners. The yearning of poorer families for ownership is no less and often greater than the desire of the middle class or the rich. Possessing other assets, the more affluent can enjoy the feeling of security with or without a freehold but "the roof over our head" is the poor family's highest aspiration. Yet although billions have been extended in housing credits and subsidies, no device has even been framed to give poorer people the home-owning opportunity. The bulldozer in urban renewal and road programs razes an owned home or a rented one with an equal thrust, and if the occupant is offered any alternative at all, it is usually tenancy. Yet slums are both owned and rented, and a slum one can call his own may be a more precious thing than a rented apartment. Even the elderly poor, whom many experts think should live in rented units only, often prefer ownership. In California, for example, 25 per cent of the elderly homeowners had incomes up to $1,000 a year; and another 20 per cent, from $1,000 to $2,000. The incomes of many are so low they could not qualify for public housing. Yet home ownership appears to be most desired even by these people.[15]

Fiction VI: The housing problem can be solved by replacing slums with better buildings. This notion again assumes that the slum's evils are all structural. Replacement may be a good thing for the community and may give it a better appearance and more revenues. But the apartments going up under urban renewal exact as much as four times the rental the evictees had been paying. Where there is no large supply of vacancies at the rents that were charged in the demolished dwellings, the reduction in the slum supply is apt to raise the rents of the residual slums. In such cases, replacement of slums without a fresh supply of good dwellings which the evicted families can afford may do them and the community more harm than good.

Fiction VII: Housing projects in slum areas must be self-contained and large enough to create their own environment. This theory sprang from the fear that a small project in an existing slum would soon be overwhelmed by the "creeping blight" of the surrounding slums. It has prevailed from the time public housing projects were first built, and has also been the theme of new-town planners. A large project, it was thought, would have an "increased chance of maintaining its distinctive character because its very size helps it to dominate the neighborhood and discourages regression." In a smaller project, i.e., covering one or two blocks, the "project may slip back

[15] Wallace F. Smith, *Housing for the Elderly*, Institute of Business and Economic Research, University of California, 1961, p. 2.

and show evidences of being overpowered by the surrounding conditions instead of acting as an improving influence."[16] This led to acquisition of extensive acreage in the slum areas as well as to a search for cemeteries, waterways, bridges, and other barriers that would keep blight in its place.

The first site in New York City was First Houses on Avenue A and East Third Street, in the heart of a distinguished slum, and it was no larger than a half-square block. It accommodates 121 families in five-story remodeled walk-ups. When the project was first broached, architects berated it; when it was approved, the authority's chief architect said it was worth doing only to prove that it was wholly impractical. Yet First Houses stands in the midst of its slum today and is still one of the best housing efforts. It has not been overwhelmed by the surrounding blight but has in fact helped improve the adjoining section. It looks as though it belonged to the neighborhood. Its human dimensions give tenants a satisfaction never found in a huge project.

Harlem River Houses, an early four-story walk-up project in East Harlem, was built like a compound on two blocks. Children play in its open center under the eye of parents or neighbors. Although vandalism is seen everywhere in large projects, the trees have remained unharmed. Housing experts from ten nations toured New York City projects during a United Nations conference in 1962. All of them told me they were impressed by the human feeling at Harlem River Houses, and by the contrast in attitudes of the tenants and the children when compared with the bigger projects they visited. Noteworthy was the tenants' obvious pride in the project and their feeling of belonging to it.

Fiction VIII: Public housing is the happy alternative for those displaced from slums. This theory was the original basis for coupling public housing with slum clearance. As Housing and Home Finance Administrator Raymond Foley told Congress:

I want to emphasize again that the mere tearing down of bad houses will not solve the problem of the families who live in them, any more than war-caused destruction of the slums in London solved the problem of

[16] James Ford, *Slums and Housing*, Harvard University Press, 1936, II, 774, 775. This fine study simply re-echoed what no planner or official of the period would deny. It was a firm part of the planning folklore.

the bombed-out families. . . . If we are to make real progress in clearing slums, there must be adequate provision for the low income families who live in them.[17]

Foley urged that 1,050,000 additional low-rent dwellings be built over a seven-year period. Displaced low-income families were to have first preference as tenants.

Public housing was a momentous acknowledgement by government of a public responsibility to provide better housing for its forgotten poor. It created the first agencies for building such housing and made frontier demonstrations in land assemblage techniques, public financing, and management. It continues to have a place as one of the choices available, but a limited place, in what should be a total effort to rehouse the low-income family.

There are, however, a number of things wrong with the present program as a device for rehousing slum dwellers evicted by urban renewal and other public action. By the time the public housing has been completed, many who had been forced to leave their homes are no longer to be found. Some public housing authorities have become chary of accepting displacees because of the high percentage of problem families. Nor is the program broad enough to shelter the bulk of evictees. In 1962, only 100,000 units of new public housing were authorized for the whole country. During that year only 28,633 units were completed; 39,725 were "under reservation."

Successive roadblocks have beleaguered the program, small as it always has been. For example, when Congress authorized 150,000 additional units in 1959, the bill was vetoed. Finally, only 37,000 units were authorized. Meanwhile, as the public housing appropriations were being scuttled, the urban renewal authorizations and evictions for code enforcement and highways proceeded without diminution. In many communities with urban renewal programs, moreover, public housing was nonexistent. In California, local referendums are required for proposed public housing projects, and defeats are common. No referendum, however, is required for displacement.

[17] Hearings before the House Committee on Banking and Currency, 81st Cong., 1st Sess., on H. R. 4009, April 7, 1949, p. 47.

Even where public housing was being built, it was no longer serving its intended function as the harbor for urban renewal displacees. Many have incomes too low or too high to qualify. (Families admitted to projects averaged a weekly income of only $46 in 1962.) In Fort Worth, 11 per cent of the displacees had incomes too low for the minimum rents in public housing. Of the nation's families scheduled for displacement, less than a fifth moved into public housing in 1963. In Philadelphia, where 80 per cent of the dislocated families qualified for public housing and 67 per cent were actually referred for occupancy, less than 15 per cent moved in.[18] In New York City's West Side renewal area, only 16 per cent of the 68 per cent found eligible said they would live in a project.[19] Only 3 per cent of the site dwellers in one Detroit renewal area entered public housing—most preferred the slums. In a large renewal area in Los Angeles, less than 1 per cent of the inhabitants were willing to occupy public housing.[20]

Public housing, in short, has ceased to be the slum dweller's dreamland. Some like it, and some do not. Some families consider it a stigma to live in a project, which they look upon as an institution. And there is no concealing of the family's substandard income from outsiders and snooper neighbors. A great many families object to public housing because they want to stay in their old neighborhoods, free of the rules and regulations laid down by a government landlord. A number in the slums are homeowners or want to be, and many would head for the suburbs, if a subsidized program made it possible. The low income limitations, moreover, have headed too many of the projects toward a heavy percentage of nonwhite tenants so that white families often shun such projects, while some Negroes object to projects that have become predominantly Negro.

A fact public housing agencies have not fully accepted is that people who live in slums, like people elsewhere, defy all classifications. Some sentimental families have balked because they had cats or dogs which, while not counted as wage earners in computing income,

[18] *Relocation in Philadelphia,* Philadelphia Housing Association, 1958.

[19] Citizens Housing and Planning Council of New York, Committee on Urban Redevelopment, *Toward a Better New York,* 1960.

[20] This figure was obtained from local officials in the area.

rendered their masters unqualified. At least one sizeable housing authority forbids ownership of an automobile by any tenant. Slum dwellers lack wealth but not pride. Some live out of wedlock without living in sin; it may be a matter of custom or convenience or because of higher social security payments, but housing authorities insist upon the marriage bond. Some slum dwellers are alcoholics, skidrowers, mental cases, or chronic lawbreakers, all of whom are not wanted in public housing. Others who shun public housing or are shunned are faithful churchgoers who practice their religion every day of the week.

Slum dwellers are not simpletons. They know there is a big difference between life in a vast housing project, where the nearest store may be three or four blocks away, and a friendly slum neighborhood where a loaf of bread or a glass of beer may be had just around the corner. An old person may wish to live in a furnished room under a watchful landlady, rather than be isolated in a project, and a parent may have valid prejudices against the school serving a public housing project.

The presumption that an offer of public housing to a displaced family automatically satisfies the redevelopment agency's obligation to relocate is an arrogance that disregards the independent spirit still found among the nation's humble. The irony is that while public housing prescribes all sorts of conditions for acceptance, urban renewal and other public undertakings displace with an even hand, demonstrating what Anatole France in another context called the law's "majestic equality": it allows both rich and poor to be put out on the streets without discrimination. As all laws should be, those authorizing eviction are blind; as no law should be, they have too often been ruthless.

Fiction IX: When tenants in public housing projects improve their incomes, they should be ousted. One of the main defects of the federal law is its requirement that public housing be available only to those in the lowest income group. The income limits for admission vary among cities, and tenants whose incomes go beyond the limits for continued occupancy must look for quarters elsewhere. The median family income in 1963 was $2,464.

The law requires a 20 per cent gap between public housing rentals and the lowest rent for standard private housing in the area. In the case of families displaced by government action, the gap may be only 5 per cent.

Income limitations in public housing have brought no end of troubles. Some tenants have concealed their incomes, some have refused to work overtime, and some have even turned down better-paying jobs. A child reaching working age may disqualify the family for continued occupancy unless he moves out. Where the American family normally boasts of financial improvement, a public housing tenant may find it the prelude to an eviction notice. The more successful occupants who could give leadership to the community are usually those forced to go. Since Negroes earn considerably less than whites, fewer Negroes are evicted and more Negro families than whites qualify for the vacancies. Departure of the whites brings Negro segregation into local schools and destroys the integrated aspect of projects, schools, and neighborhoods. Departure of the better wage earners, white and Negro, also tends to stamp the project as the haven of the poor.

Public housing was designed partly to help families do better, not to penalize a man for getting a raise. If incomes go beyond the limits, the rent should be increased proportionately. The subsidies would thereby be reduced, and many families would not be forced to go back to slums.

Ireland has a more sensible formula. An economic rent is fixed on each dwelling unit. Rents are then adjusted to a family's income and raised when earnings increase. No tenant, however, is forced to reveal what he earns; he may, if he chooses, simply pay the economic rent. He then continues occupying his house as an unsubsidized tenant. The procedure has not interfered with private housing operations and no tenant considers it a stigma to live in a project.

Fiction X: Public housing must be owned by the city forever. This notion had its roots in the early *laissez faire* theory that there is a clear dividing line between the public and private sectors. It re-echoes Adam Smith's contention that private enterprise should have the main field to itself while public operations should be confined to those areas which are not profitable and in which only the public sector can function (schools, parks, etc.) What the public sponsored or built, the public also owned and operated. Since Adam Smith's day, however, not only has the public sector grown immensely, but the interests of government and entrepreneur have become interlaced. The public purpose in urban renewal, for example, is clearing slums; building the houses is left to the entrepreneur.

As long as public ownership continues to be the sole formula, public housing will never be more than a token program. For if public housing were to continue until every slum were cleared, the project type of housing would be the only type available to one-fifth of the population—assuming that all would be accepted. The government would be the only landlord to whom low-income families could apply for shelter. And if the authorities persist in accepting only the qualified poor, what choice would there be for the breadwinner with a jail record? the family with a delinquent child? the noncitizen or the alleged Communist? Monolithic landlordism is inconsistent with the American theme. The normal diversity of ownership—even including slum ownership—affords a variety of choices in dwelling types, in landlords, and in form of tenure, and a diversity of ownerships should be sought for projects in which poor people may live.

The prospect is even more serious under the whip of continued slum clearance. While families can be driven from one slum to another, they can be barred from public housing if they fail to meet its specifications. If clearances go on and the sinful among us are afforded no alternate haven, it would not be unlikely that the slum supply (if one remains) would become the concentrated retreats of the social outcasts, the dregs, the families with delinquent children, the poor alien, the ex-prostitute, the common-law couples—probably the saddest and bitterest assemblage of mortals ever permitted a foothold on earth.

It is for these reasons that public housing can be only *one* form of shelter—not *the* form. When it had cleared a prescribed number of projects and produced a stated number of units, it would have to come to a stop. If it is to be built in greater volume, its ownership—or at least its management—should be deconcentrated. The restrictions imposed upon it by Congress as to income limits, construction costs, standards, and equivalent elimination must be removed. Finally, parallel programs under which poorer families can live, in private as well as public projects at subsidized rentals, must be devised at the same time as public housing programs are expanded.

Chapter

3

The Housing Problem

THE HOUSING PROBLEM is more than the slum and more than the predicament of the low-income family. It spurs migrations from cities and deters movements into them. It is the source of many discontents among the millions of mishoused or dishoused families yearning to be rehoused. It affects family budgets, security, happiness, and stability. It is tied into the issues of segregation and neighborhood decay. Though the federal government looks upon housing shortage and other imperfections of the housing market as factors in national employment and economic activity, few other problems have more serious impacts on the economic well-being of cities and the social well-being of their citizens.

The Pathology of Housing

The diseases of housing rival those in pathology. They include irritations over spatial, physical, and financial limitations. They are involved with neighborhood tensions, the shortcomings of neighborhood schools, transportation, and police protection; lack of proper playgrounds, parks, and open spaces; noise, smoke, smells, smog, drafts, dirt, insects, and vermin. The personal vexations of the housing problem are not only multiple and complex but they defy categorization.

40]

Over a period of twenty-five years of teaching in both graduate and adult education classes, I have asked some 2,500 people to list their housing complaints. The answers have been a variety of cravings and disaffections which go far beyond anything revealed by the Census and beyond anything that has been resolved by the Federal Housing Administration, Veterans Administration, or the wrecking-crew prescriptions of the housing acts. Complaints have survived the recent spurt in repairs and the increase in the number of homeowners. They would survive even if we knocked down every hovel, built a bold surplus of public housing, and stepped up FHA-aided projects to validate the most optimistic home-building predictions.

The trials of central city life bring out a diversity of protests, which include troubles with landlords and rent hikes, influxes of minority groups and school problems, air pollution, odors, neighborhood deterioration and disrepair, the long journey to work and up the stairs.

The first wail announcing the baby's presence accents the house's intractability, and each year of the baby's growth points up some unanticipated failing in structure or surroundings. Lack of space comes first, followed by a myriad of agitations—overexertion, the pressure of rent, the complaints of a neighbor, the annoyances of the stairs, or of a knocking radiator once taken in stride. With each year that passes, house and neighborhood become more distressingly interlinked, emphasizing inadequacies or disappointments—in school, play space, or street. The drive is then for a more suitable house in a more suitable neighborhood (usually suburban), but it may distort the budget, stretch the distance to the job, impose the added burden of an automobile or two, and make the father's presence in the household more like that of a visiting relative.

Other special problems include a landlord's prohibition of pets which brings heartbreak, particularly to the very old and the very young. Since the automobile, contact with animals has all but disappeared from urban life, and the popularity of Westerns on television may be ascribed at least partly to the nostalgia for the horse. When the Cambridge (Massachusetts) Housing Authority tried to enforce a regulation against dogs or cats, tenant protests made front-page news for days and finally forced a concession. A *New York Times* copyreader, sued by his landlord for keeping two Siamese cats alleged to be a nuisance, made a test case and won. But usually the landlord triumphs in the encounter. The pet must go.

Spatial shortage is one of the more frequent complaints. To get the space they need, families may pay rents beyond their means, live too far from school or work, or in neighborhoods and homes unsuited to their requirements. Yet in 212 metropolitan areas, more than 2.8 million households or 20 per cent of all renters paid 35 per cent or more of their income for shelter. Almost all of these families paying such rentals earned less than $4,000 a year. Twenty or at most 25 per cent for shelter is regarded as the maximum, but this proportion is a hardship for poorer families who would have barely enough for life's necessities even if they paid nothing for rent.

The distribution of families by their total money income in 1962 as reported by the Bureau of the Census is given in Table 2.

TABLE 2

Total Money Income of Families	Number of Families (Thousands)	Per Cent
Under $1,000	1,950	4.2
$1,000 to $1,999	3,469	7.4
$2,000 to $2,999	3,901	8.3
$3,000 to $3,999	4,325	9.2
$4,000 to $4,999	4,669	9.9
$5,000 to $5,999	5,424	11.5
$6,000 to $6,999	5,100	10.9
$7,000 to $7,999	4,023	8.6
$8,000 to $9,999	5,804	12.3
$10,000 to $14,999	6,019	12.8
$15,000 and over	2,314	4.9
Total	46,998	100.0

In other words, more than half the American families earned less than $6,000 and a fifth had less than $3,000. The cost of new private single-family homes in 1963 averaged $18,000, a figure far beyond the reach of lower-income families.

The Displaced and Evicted

Involuntary removals, including those necessitated by job changes and evictions, have shown a marked increase in recent years. The causes include not only public projects but industrial movements, or an order by the Defense Department to close military installations. A decision by the Reynolds Metals Company to leave Louisville, Kentucky, put six hundred houses on the market all at once and depressed values. The poor labor relations of a large firm in Stamford, Connecticut, led to its removal from the area with a similar impact on the housing market. A few companies, upon withdrawing from an area, have generously taken over their employee's houses and offered them for resale, but they have found that too much capital was tied up for too long. Most companies are not generous, except to those whose talents are indispensable.

Eviction because of public works, code enforcement, or urban renewal (not to mention private developments) are among the other aggravations. Before 1934, evictions to make way for public improvements were confined to traditional needs such as school sites, roads, and public buildings. The road program was much smaller, code enforcement was minimal, and urban renewal nonexistent. The demolition of a city's workshops and stores or the eviction of 8,000 families from a single site, as in New York's West Side renewal area, would have been unthinkable.

Following 1934, major land operations covering 10 to 30 acres per project arrived with public housing and expanded with public works programs and urban renewal. The more extensive public operations such as freeways, renewal operations, toll roads, parking lots, airports, and other enterprises, played an important part in the increase of demolition. The net losses from the housing inventory during the 1950–1956 period was more than 200,000 units a year.

During the 1957–1959 period it had leaped to 475,000 a year.

In California, with its newer stock of houses, no less than 359,000 units—10 per cent of the 1950 inventory—had been erased by 1960 through private action, highway programs, code enforcement, urban renewal, or the elements.[1]

The emphasis on demolition and evictions has made life for many families an unending trek from one slum or furnished room to another. Building a stable life within a context of rootless living is virtually impossible. Children are uprooted from schools, parents separated from friends, and rootlessness ultimately gives way to hopelessness.

The Aged

The aged are the most numerous among those neglected by the housing industry. The passage of two decades has seen the aged grow both in numbers and in the severity of their housing problems. From 1950 to 1960, the general population increased by only 19 per cent, but the older population grew by 35 per cent.[2] People 62 years of age or over number 21 million, and by 1980 they are expected to number 30 million. Older people are more prone to have special problems—8 out of 10 have chronic illnesses; they spend twice as many hours in hospitals as those under 65. Proximity to doctors and institutional facilities is therefore essential.

They also have rent and income problems, for their median income is about half of those under 65. Half have less than $3,000 annually, a third less than $2,000 annually, while half the single persons have less than $1,050 a year.[3] About half are in another special group—

[1] In California, the proportion of families scheduled to be displaced by urban renewal in the two years from July 1962 was 44 per cent for urban renewal and 56 per cent for code enforcement, highways, and other causes. In programs awaiting certification, the proportions were 31 per cent for urban renewal, 14 per cent for highways, 48 per cent for code enforcement, and 7 per cent for other causes.

[2] The age group 85 and over grew by more than 61 per cent.

[3] *Report on Housing for Senior Citizens*, Subcommittee on Housing, Senate Committee on Banking and Currency, 87th Cong., 2nd. Sess., June 15, 1962, p. VII.

they are either widowed, divorced, separated, or single. There are 8 million of these elderly people living alone.

The housing problem of the older person is both unique and difficult. Some are sensitive to the harder climates, are more exposed to the dangers of home and street accidents, and are less poised to grapple with the demands of the 5–7 room house. Two-thirds live in their own homes, generally bought in earlier years, and many of these are now ill-suited to their needs.

A study by the Cornell University Center for Housing and Environmental Studies showed that the poorest in health tended to occupy the poorest housing. About 45 per cent of all aged households were classified as in need of better accommodations.[4]

A California study in 1961[5] concluded that living with relatives was a distasteful alternative for most elderly people. Most want housekeeping arrangements, most would like to own their homes (but rooming house life is more acceptable to men than women). Though public housing offers the cheapest accommodations (average rent is $32 and median income $1,500) it provides for only a tiny fraction of the elderly. If, for example, only 10 per cent of California's aged who were living in 1962 with relatives or in rooming houses were to apply for public housing, their number would exceed the total of the state's public housing units for families of all ages. FHA-insured loans (under Section 231 of the Housing Act) resulted in median monthly rents in 1963 of $118. Federal direct loans below market interest rates accommodate those with incomes well above $3,500 per year, and in any event as of December 1964, the number of projects in process was small, and funds were reserved for less than 19,000 units. Federal aid to nonprofit groups has produced dwellings mostly for the higher-income families among the elderly—median monthly rent of completed units in 1963 was about $87. The nursing home program is also for those with higher incomes.

In short, no federal program is serving any substantial number of

---

[4] *Ibid.*, p. VIII.
[5] Wallace F. Smith, *Housing for the Elderly,* Institute of Business and Economic Research, University of California, 1961.

the low-income elderly. Because many of these people live in old housing, they are also among the first victims of demolition through urban renewal, public works, or code enforcement. What should be the cocktail hour of life becomes their bitter evening.

The Misfits

A contributing factor to the housing troubles of families is the inability of the building market to meet their real needs. The housing industry is geared to meeting effective demand, not need, and the most effective market is for the "average family." This average family is composed of a husband, a wife, one to three children, and an occasional relative. In the 1940s such families made up less than half of all families occupying dwelling units; and, except for some token programs, the housing produced today is still unsuited to the needs of most American households. Occasionally, housing is built to suit the well-to-do husband and wife with no children but little is produced to suit the needs of the atypical families, particularly those with low or moderate incomes as well as the person living alone, two males or females living together (including the elderly), large families of seven or more persons, widowers with children, the physically limited, and other groups. These groups must pay the penalty for their antistatistical behavior.

There are also the families with atypical occupational patterns, a large group of which comprises those with both husband and wife working. Neither the home nor the neighborhood is set up to lighten the chores of the working females, particularly the mothers, many of whom prefer to go on relief or collect unemployment insurance instead of paying a nursemaid two-thirds of their earnings. By contrast, Sweden's school children are called for during the mother's working hours at no cost. Some of the Swedish projects have cooperative kitchens and cooperative cleaning services especially designed for working mothers. But this sort of thinking has not yet entered into the calculations of officialdom.

Other neglected housing problems are those of professional persons who work at home, families whose shop is in the home, married graduate and undergraduate students, and migrant laborers and seamen.

Skid Row

Perhaps the most dramatic of those among the housing misfits is the skidrower, whose "home" is found in every big city from Boston to San Francisco. Cities look upon him as dispensable if not undesirable. Because skid rows are mostly in or near the city centers, they have become a main target of the bulldozer.

Skidrowers occupy old flop houses in which finding a bed is a daily gamble. Some sleep on the streets or in hallways or pile up on the floors of a city shelter—if there is one.

The skidrowers are a miscellaneous lot—semisettled or settled panhandlers, homeless workingmen, chronic alcoholics and criminals, the elderly, the disabled, and the unemployed.[6]

Many pensioners and ordinary workers find in skid row the cheapest and often the only accommodations available. Though skid rows are generally looked upon as the most sterile and extinguishable parts of town, they are often labor centers for agricultural, unskilled, and semi-skilled workers who can be recruited for work away from their "homes." (Automation, however, is cutting down on their work apportunities.) In skid row, the sensitive poor can spend least for clothing and care without social embarrassment. Welfare and social agencies can send older or disabled clients to skid row because lodgings are cheaper. They are cheaper because they are cramped, deteriorated, and often vermin-infested; many are firetraps.[7]

The sidewalks of New York City's Bowery and the vestibules of nearby stores are the beds of many who shun the city-owned flophouse on East Third Street. Behind its grim façade are hundreds of old, handicapped men, some legless, with ill-fitting artificial limbs—most of them a premature step from the grave.

[6] *The Homeless Man on Skid Row,* Chicago Relocation Bureau, September 1961.
[7] *Ibid.,* p. 13.

On one rainy day I visited the boiler room of the flophouse, thirteen feet below street level. Thirty infirm or crippled men, mostly elderly, were sitting on wooden backless benches; and in the adjacent storeroom were ninety others, many leaning on crutches. The room stank of sweat and disinfectant. A large sign on the cellar wall read, "Check All Your Valuables. The City of New York is Not Responsible . . ."

The situation was hardly better for the homeless younger men. About 40 per cent in New York's Bowery flophouse might have become useful citizens if they had a home or were given a chance. But New York is a big, busy city in which most people do not look, do not know, or do not care.

No big city has even ventured a solution for its skidrow problem or for the homeless, though one or two are playing with the idea. Most cities do not have even a flophouse for their skidrowers; they either look to urban renewal as the way of "solving" the problem or press the skidrower to move to some other city. If the skid rows are destroyed, some occupants will drift to those in the other cities; many others will remain—deprived of the only shelters they had, miserable as they were.

The Overmortgaged Society

That the housing situation is thorny for the city dweller does not mean that the quarter-acre is clover for the suburbanite. The growth of the suburb has widened the choices for the middle- and upper-income family. It provides the breadwinner with more open space, a touch of the green instead of the grey, an escape from the city's afflictions, an opportunity to do some week-end tinkering, and the feeling, right or wrong, that the downpayment now guarantees him a home he can call his own. The suburb, in short, does provide a new housing alternative.[8] But many choose the alternative, less because it is the answer to the family's prayer than because it is their only escape from an environ-

[8] For an interesting study of the virtues and problems of the move to suburbia see Herbert J. Gans in *The Urban Condition,* ed. Leonard J. Duhl, Basic Books, 1963, p. 184.

ment that has become ill-suited or unbearable for them. Others move because of the city's poorer schools. The choice of the suburb carries with it the commuting problem and the installment payments on the automobile. If the job is in the city and the commutation is long, the father is unable to see his children or aging parents as often as he should.

Not the least of the problems confronting the suburban home owner is that buying a home and furnishing it raises the proportion of income he should normally pay for shelter, and while the long-term FHA mortgage makes the monthly payments smaller, it also prolongs the duration of the personal obligation and the risk. The average bread-winner buying a home under the 90 per cent mortgage generally commits himself to the maximum he can afford, and if he loses his job, suffers a salary cut, or binds himself to an extra car, he may find his mortgage jeopardizing his tenure. For the first dozen years or so, amortization of the mortgage just about parallels the depreciation rate. As long as the price level continued pointing upward, the home buyer was lucky. The price level on homes bought from the time of the deep depression up to 1957 has been accommodating for most buyers and helped many to build up substantial equities.

At the close of 1960, however, the total outstanding residential mortgage debt had soared to $160 billion. About 88 per cent of the total was on one- to four-family houses, and this was steadily on the increase. With the 80–100 per cent mortgage, we have become a nation of debtors; the value of our homes has been fluctuating with the value of the dollar. When values fall or depression hits a particular area, foreclosures mount. An owner in a depressed area might tighten his belt or turn back his television set, but the mortgage lender is unyielding—particularly since the FHA arrangement allows him the option of foreclosing or demanding government bonds for his defaulted mortgage. No mechanism exists to insure the owner against loss of his home for a default due to temporary embarrassment. Failure to make a single payment during the mortgage term brings foreclosure and sometimes a judgment against the owner to boot.

In the 1960s, foreclosures hit their highest point since the deep depression. Defaults on home mortgages increased fivefold—from about 10,000 in 1957 to 52,000 as of December 1963. According to FHA, the "weakest link" has been the poor credit characteristics of the individual borrower.[9]

Nor does today's family enjoy that old feeling of warmth that comes with the burning of the mortgage. Modern mortgages are fireproof for the mortgagee (thanks to fire insurance) but not foreclosure-proof for the owner. To tap a larger market, Congress, instead of lowering mortgage interest, periodically authorized smaller downpayments and longer mortgage periods. These liberalizations resulted in higher outstanding balances throughout the life of the mortgage. As long as property values were rising, the home owner stayed ahead in the race for home security, and if he found it hard to maintain his mortgage he could sell. But after 1957 supply and demand came more nearly into balance, and easy sales became tougher. As the FHA Administrator conceded, it is important to keep in mind ". . . that from 1934 until recent years . . . FHA insuring operations have been carried on under most favorable market conditions. It is almost axiomatic that no serious error in mortgage finance can come to light in periods of rising prices."[10] But the error does come to light when the element of speculative increase no longer functions to vindicate misjudgments.

Housing Inflexibility

Neither family composition nor housing needs are constants. They vary with the life cycle, the birth and growth of children, the health, age, changing fortunes, and death of people. They vary also with the decisions of industry, job locations, building costs, and land availability. About 40 per cent of all housing is more than forty years old. As the needs of families change, they must look not only to the new, mostly on the fringes, but also to the old, mostly in the cities.

Some 58.3 million dwelling units, good and bad, are available to 53

[9] Neal J. Hardy, FHA Administrator, in *Progress Report on Federal Housing Programs,* Subcommittee on Housing, Senate Committee on Banking and Currency, 87th Cong., 2nd Sess., August 29, 1962, p. 6.
[10] Hardy, p. 7.

million American households. The older housing in the inventory includes both the dispensable and the salvageable. The salvageable is also more adaptable to change. The newer stock is generally less alterable either because zoning forbids substantial changes or because it does not lend itself to major alteration. It has been built to meet the requirements of the average family and none other. The median size of new homes financed with FHA-insured Section 203 loans was 1,182 square feet, representing a 22 per cent increase over the comparable FHA figure fifteen years earlier. Most had three bedrooms and 75 per cent were bought by people in the upper 50 per cent income group. A hundred thousand houses are sold annually as incomplete or "shell houses" to be finished when the owner can afford it. (The South is one of the best customers.) In 1963, another 151,000 living spaces were sold as mobile units, some of which are placed on permanent foundations.

Despite its age or obsolescence, a fair proportion of the city's older stock, though worn and seedy, has more space and height than those built after zoning was known, before building standards were elevated, and before power tools, paint spray guns, and pneumatic hammers came on the scene. They can also be altered, enlarged, or reduced in size to fit special needs or changing requirements of the life cycle. However one might scoff at the city's Baroque revivals or Kensington classics with their high stoops and ceilings, many can meet changing needs better than the latest split-level or economy house. Even New York's excoriated old-law tenements, built for the European immigrant at the lowest standards possible often had five rooms; and some are being turned into two-room efficiency units and studios for the intelligentsia of Greenwich Village and the Lower East Side. An air-conditioner makes even its windowless room serviceable.

The new suburban houses, however, will continue to exercise a tyranny that will not bend easily to the changing requirements of America's metamorphic families. These families can look ahead not only to a housing plant of less flexible units, but to a diminution of the older supply in the cities through slum clearance, highways, fire, obsolescence, or structural decay. Thus, the new houses in the city or suburb may suit the present but not the future. The old houses that might still serve the future are gradually disappearing.

Congress has belatedly acknowledged the importance of preserving as well as destroying the old crop. Age of a building is no longer disparaged, and terms for rehabilitation have been liberalized. But diversification of housing types is infrequent and the preservation of what exists has hardly gotten off the ground. The good alterable stock is being steadily reduced in the cities, while the suburb continues to be headed toward a rigid, tedious uniformity and an early obsolescence.

If, thanks to rising incomes, housing conditions have improved for some in recent years, the central city has reaped few of the dividends. Since much of its housing is frayed and therefore cheaper, it has become host to the poor as well as heir to their social problems. Much of what was sound and salvageable is being cut up or crowded with poorer people to conform to their meager budgets. Because the city is not poised to assume the increased costs of policing and servicing the deteriorating areas properly, or financing the improvement of its housing and neighborhoods, the exodus to suburbia continues to accelerate.

Slum properties were once considered good investments because they were always sure to be filled by immigrants from Europe and because they called for minimum maintenance charges—almost all the gross rent, after taxes, insurance, and loan charges, was net profit.

As the cities advanced toward stricter law enforcement, the old crop of landlords, facing the prospects of fines and even jail sentences, sold out. Simultaneously institutional mortgage lenders ceased lending on the properties. (In New York City these institutions had liquidated such holdings as far back as 1937.)

Many of the slum properties have been sold in recent years at liquidation prices to a new type of slum specialist. Simultaneously, a new crop of speculative mortgage lenders appeared who have been willing to take the risks of default in return for discounts ranging from 30 per cent of the face amount of first mortgages to as high as 50 per cent for the seconds.

Contrary to general belief, the new specialists are not tycoons but mostly small-scale operators looking for large profits with small stakes.

The profits compensate them for troublesome management and for the collection of weekly rents from people, many of whom are unemployed, and for the growing risks of ownership. The values of these properties fluctuate not only with the imposition of more rigid standards and penalties but with the prospect of acquisition by the cities. Thus a sharp drop in prices occurred in New York City when a Brooklyn landlady was convicted of manslaughter after a fire consumed her tenants, and they rose with each prospect that the area might be designated for urban renewal or a housing project.

As the poorer people move to other parts of cities vacated by the middle class, repairs and improvements decline and more buildings become candidates for ultimate demolition.

The housing problem of the central cities will be solved only by expanding the supply and varieties of decent housing for all families at prices they can afford. This might help make the city more competitive with the suburb. Simultaneously the suburb must share the responsibility for housing those who require subsidies. Only with such a policy will the housing problem besetting American families approach solution and the cities have better than an even chance to survive.

The Racial Upheaval in Cities

THE REMARKABLE ADVANCE of the United States from a frontier land to the world's most majestic industrial power has been speeded by the swelling wave of labor that began pouring in after 1830 and continued unchecked for almost a century thereafter. These immigrants provided America's menials, miners, tracklayers, and boilermakers as well as the geniuses and their sons who designed its automobiles, rockets, and computers.

When foreign immigration was virtually halted in the 1920s, the unexpected demand for cheap hands released the pool of Negro labor that had been stagnating in the backward South. Though the Negro was not city-bred, he generally headed for the city where there was work, shelter upon arrival, and a ghetto where he might find a friend who had already made the journey.

The Negro migration, which was no more than a trickle at the turn of the century, soon took on the semblance of a stampede. Negro population outside the South has grown sixfold since 1910 and more than doubled since 1940.[1] By 1960 the central cities of the twelve largest metropolitan areas accounted for 24 per cent of all U.S. Negroes. The migration saw Negroes become 29 per cent of Detroit's and Cleveland's population, 35 per cent of Baltimore's, a quarter of

---

[1] The words "Negro" and "nonwhite" are used interchangeably. Actually, the Negro constitutes 92 per cent of the total nonwhite population.

Philadelphia's, 34 per cent of Newark's, and 55 per cent of Washington, D.C.'s. New York City's Negro population held to 15 per cent of total in 1960, largely because of the in-migration of Puerto Ricans, who began pouring in after 1940 and competed with the Negro for the available jobs.

Some 10.3 million or more than half the nonwhite population lived in the central cities in 1960; this represented a gain of 63 per cent in a decade. The whites, on the other hand, continued shifting to the suburbs so that by 1960, less than a third of the urban–suburban white population were living in central cities. In the nation's 212 standard metropolitan areas, 52 per cent of the whites lived outside the central cities, while 78 per cent of the nonwhites lived in the central cities. (Only in the Southern region do more whites live in the central cities than in the suburbs.)

As long as the Negro had been a small and docile minority in the North, it was the European immigrant, not the Negro, against whom the established whites would spend their resentments. "Where the Negro pitches his tent," wrote Jacob Riis in 1902, "he pays more rent than his white neighbor next door, and is a better tenant."[2] A half century later, the Negro might still be paying more rent but he was no longer considered a better tenant. As he kept pouring into the cities, both the established urban Northerner and the more recent immigrant soon found common cause in a common realization that the Negro was altering the composition of their neighborhoods, their schools, and their institutions. As he became urbanized, moreover, the Negro was no longer docile but demanding his rights as a citizen.

During the period when the upper and middle classes in the North were being challenged by the mass in-migration of European immigrants, they could shift their locations to some other areas within the city. If the new section was just outside the city, the city was still politically strong enough to annex it. But with the Negro challenge and the growth of politically independent suburbias, the whites now moved in greater numbers outside the city's reach. The independent all-white suburb soon became an established part of the American scene.

[2] Jacob Riis, *The Battle with the Slum*, Macmillan, 1902, p. 110.

As millions of Negroes moved into houses previously occupied by whites, their ghettos soon spread to other white sections; white parents seeing classrooms fill up with Negro children scurried about for other neighborhoods, sent their children to white private schools, or speeded their move to the suburbs. Washington, D.C.'s schools were more than 85 per cent Negro in 1965, while in Manhattan, New York City, more than 70 per cent were Negro or Puerto Rican.

The Negro is not so dominant a percentage of the nation's population as to threaten overshadowing the white man. At the time of the Confederacy, three Southern states had a Negro majority or near majority—there are no such states today. Negroes formed 14 per cent of total population at the time of the American Revolution; today they are only 11 per cent. Since about half the Negroes are still in the South, their presence would hardly be noticeable in the North and West if they were more widely distributed within the metropolitan areas. Their concentrations in the central cities, however, spark fears that they will overtake the whites everywhere, invade suburbia as well, attack its social status, and challenge the financial soundness of its real estate.

The Negro has thus become a factor in cities far more significant than his numbers would indicate. He was not the initial cause of suburbia or the main reason for its spread. But in accelerating the outward movement of whites, he also accelerated the suburban formations and made them race conscious; he has materially affected the city's social structure, changed the composition of its schools and placed upon the cities social and economic burdens which they are unable to sustain.

Negro Economic Status and Discrimination

Though a latecomer in the competition for jobs, the Negro has made important breakthroughs in department store employment, clerical jobs, and transportation. It is no longer unusual to see a Negro register at a Northern hotel, eat in a first-class restaurant, or appear behind a bank teller's window. Median income of Negro families has gone up from 37 per cent of white income in 1939 to 53 per cent in 1963.

Yet Negro family income continues at a low level—the median was $3,465 a year in 1963 as against $6,548 for white families. The Negro is still the last to be hired and the first to be fired. His unemployment rate is about twice that of the white worker. Because he continues to hold the menial jobs, he has earned menial status in the social structure—the proportion of nonwhites in the service industries was nearly three times that of whites. Only 17 per cent of all employed nonwhites were in white collar occupations, compared with 47 per cent of white workers. One reason for his low economic position is his lower educational status—in 1960, 47 per cent of Negroes more than twenty-five years old had less than an eighth-grade education compared to 20 per cent for whites.

A number of theories have been propounded for the Negro's lower status, and some include forecasts of his prospects. There is the theory of the preordained breakthrough, which holds that the same sequence of struggle, advance, and social assimilation will ultimately follow in the Negro's case as with the immigrants who preceded them. A second theory sees the Negro progressing to the white level but on a "separate but equal" basis. A third theory is that the prejudice that holds the Negro to a low estate is a social attitude propagated by the white ruling class to stigmatize the Negro as inferior so that he can continue to be exploited for the white man's benefit. A fourth theory is that poverty[3] is the ineluctable fate of a particular social or economic group due to its low-born status, misdoings, or its inherent inability to rise over its obstacles. Laziness, inferiority, drink, a propensity toward crime, or some other implanted trait is said to affect most of the members of the group and is responsible for its predicament. A fifth theory holds that prejudice and its social and economic by-products will disappear only with intermarriage with whites. A sixth theory, and one esteemed by current intellectuals, argues that white prejudice and fear are fixed in the recesses of the white soul; Negroes have been too long held

[3] In the sixty-eight cities studied by the Census, the proportion of Negro families with an annual income below the "poverty line" figure of $3,000 ranged from 15 to 62 per cent (*New York Times,* November 16, 1964, p. 21).

down and have been taught to despise themselves; they are unable or
unwilling to compete because of an ingrained "anomie" that destroys
and distorts their lives. The only way out is to give the Negro the
means and the spirit to help himself; he must find self-reliance and
assert himself; only then will the ingrained anomie dissolve.

The merits of any one of these theories are outside the scope of
this study. There is, however, one important development all of them
have ignored, i.e., the recent ascent of government as a factor in human
environment and as a force for perpetuating or advancing status and
opportunity.

In the *laissez faire* economy, individual conduct had been governed
by the rules "I am not my brother's keeper" and "Let the devil take
the hindmost." In that universe, the Negro's condition and the white
man's discriminatory impositions were their own affairs. But government today is a more dynamic government than it was in the 1920s.
Since the New Deal, the federal government has assumed the power
to control and even create the environment in which people live and
children grow. It can help the cities relieve poverty or suffer it to
continue. It can elect to train and retrain, educate well or badly, and
with segregation or desegregation as the pattern. It can help provide
good houses for everyone in a good environment or confine its benefits
to the more affluent whites. It can compel enterprise to hire on an
equal basis and can condition its vast aids on their doing so. Through
its housing policies, it can limit residential mobility and encourage
school segregation or help break the barriers that restrict free movement. It can restrain state and local majorities from discriminatory
conduct or wink at their oppressions under the cover of decentralization or local autonomy. It has, in short, not only acquired the power
to aid a particularly depressed group but it has also become the main
influence in setting the ethical standard; and, in this respect, it can
either cotton to the majority and sanction its unfair customs and
practices, or it can follow the higher ethic as implied in its constitution
and in the moral law.

Whatever have been the theories of class poverty and race discrimination in the past, they applied to an era that is gone, an era that

gave the Negro emancipation but not full freedom. The Negro may, in the years to come, fail to rise above his impediments, but if physical and cultural environment influence the structure and behavior of men, and if government may now create and induce the physical and cultural content of that environment, it must share with the Negro the responsibility for the result and be judged in any future assessment by its omissions as well as its commissions. It is similarly culpable if it stands idly by as the Negro is denied equal access to any of life's essentials.

The Negro's Housing Problem

The Negro's housing and the neighborhoods to which he is relegated play and will play an important part in shaping the environment that conditions his prospects. The housing available to Negroes is inferior in quality compared to the housing of whites; both the housing and neighborhoods in which he lives show signs of greater deterioration; there are fewer amenities; mortgages are more difficult to obtain; there is little or no private investment in new buildings for Negroes; tax arrears are higher in their neighborhoods and public interest in maintenance is lower; real estate values are lower in relation to net income; overcrowding is more intense; schools, hospitals, and recreation are inferior; and the Negro usually gets less housing value per dollar he pays.

While the white move to the suburbs has provided the Negro with a wider choice among the leavings, overcrowding and high rents are among the more serious aspects of his slum life. A census survey in March 1965 in the renewal areas of 132 cities showed 36 per cent of the nonwhites paying 35 per cent or more of their incomes for rent. As the Negro migration into the cities continues, suburban resistance to Negro intrusion is stiffening, and new devices are being fashioned to make the suburb impregnable.

The poor housing conditions under which the Negro lives affect his employment opportunities, his income, his education, and his training. Lack of training and equipment, combined with prejudice, are responsible for his low income. Low income enforces slum life. Slum life, low income, and a lower level of training and education reinforce the stereotype that he is less fitted for jobs; they also generate and regenerate biases among whites.[4] Whenever the Negro improves his earnings and competes for a better house, he challenges the social status of neighborhoods, sparks more fears and resentments, and intensifies efforts to keep him out. As more industries head for the outlying areas, either the industry is reluctant to hire him because of community strictures or his journey to work from the city is made more onerous. Restriction in residence thus means restriction of opportunity.

When, as chairman of the New York State Commission Against Discrimination, I called together the nation's airline officials in an effort to have them hire Negro hostesses, one of their main contentions was that the hostesses would run into difficulties in finding suitable housing near the airports. The president of the Mohawk Airlines, which was the first airline in the country to hire a Negro hostess voluntarily, conceded that when it changed its main office from Ithaca to Utica, two competent Negro employees had been compelled to quit their jobs because they could find no housing in Utica. A study made for the commission showed that when a large industrial corporation hired four Negro engineers for its Syracuse office, three of the four asked for a transfer after being turned down by one landlord after another. A top executive said he would not hire a Negro secretary because the community in which the factory was located does not want Negroes living there.[5]

The same study also showed, however, that in two cities in which the Negro population had not experienced substantial Southern inmigration, the over all differences between Negro and white students were few. The Negro students did as well if not better than the whites; there were fewer dropouts among the Negroes; and of those who had graduated, more went to college.[6] There was no evidence of any innate inferiority because of color.

[4] For specific examples see Charles Abrams *et al.* in *Discrimination and Low Income,* New York State Commission Against Discrimination, 1959.
[5] *Ibid.,* p. 25.
[6] *Ibid.,* p. 31.

Thanks to the white exodus and the Negro's improved income, more housing has become available in the larger cities, although it has often come hard. But barely 4 per cent of the total suburban population of metropolitan areas with a population of half a million or more are Negroes, and a substantial portion of this number live in little fringe ghettos or in old Negro pockets that have precariously survived suburban expansion.

One reason for the widespread suburban bias against Negroes is that for fifteen years, government housing programs and Negro exclusion had proceeded apace. From 1935 to 1950, the federal government insisted upon discriminatory practices as a prerequisite to government housing aid.[7] The Federal Housing Administration's official manuals cautioned against "infiltration of inharmonious racial and national groups," "a lower class of inhabitants," or the "presence of incompatible racial elements" in the new neighborhoods. "The social class of the parents of children at the schools" was declared to have a vital bearing on whether a neighborhood was "stable." A neighborhood was to be considered less desirable if inhabited by "a lower level of society." (FHA added, however, that this could be remedied by having the children "attend another school with pupils of their same social class.") Stables and pigpens were put by FHA into the same category as a section occupied by the "wrong" race. Zoning was advocated as a device for exclusion, and the use was urged of a racial covenant (prepared by FHA itself) with a space left blank for the prohibited races and religions, to be filled in by the builder as occasion required.[8] The Home Loan Bank System—the federal agency which regulates savings and loan associations—urged similar practices.

[7] The late Herbert U. Nelson, the Executive Vice President of the National Association of Real Estate Boards, told a Senate committee in 1950: "We put several hundred of our people, whom we found and persuaded to go into government service, into positions where they could give their services." This was one of the reasons for the inclusion of racial restrictions in government manuals.

[8] The sections of the official FHA manual in which these provisions appeared were Sections 927, 310, 315, 307, 229, 330, and 255 of the 1935 manual; 228, 252, 266, 210d, 284, and 229 of the 1936 manual; 233, 935, 937, and 951 of the 1938 manual; and 207 and 217 of the 1940 manual.

For some sixteen years, then—a period in which more than 11 million homes were built—federal housing agencies pursued a concerted, relentless, and officially sanctioned drive to keep people living only with their own kind and to get them to oppose intrusions by anybody who was different. Federally approved racial covenants soon covered the greater part of suburbia; neighborhoods were divided into those of the desirables and the unwanted; intolerance gained such rapid headway that men in high national office now saw nothing wrong in signing such covenants, one of the most popular of which barred not only Negroes, but Jews, Armenians, Persians, and Syrians.[9]

As the Negro kept increasing his numbers he became the main target of the exclusionary practices. Virtually all the vacant land in suburbs and cities was barred to him—estimates ranged up to 80 per cent in Chicago and Los Angeles. In the New York City suburbs, five-sixths of the subdivisions were racially restricted; and in a sample survey of 315 developments in the area, 56 per cent of all homes were forbidden to Negroes.[10]

The general acceptance of such covenants, even by those in high office, was disclosed in the 1952 presidential campaign, when it was discovered that Richard M. Nixon, the Republican nominee, had executed a racial covenant against Negroes (as well as Jews, Armenians, Persians, and Syrians). The issue was not publicized because it was discovered that John Sparkman, the Democratic nominee, had bought his house subject to an anti-Negro covenant. In the Presidential campaign of 1964, William E. Miller, the Republican nominee for vice president, charged that President Lyndon B. Johnson had executed an anti-Negro covenant in 1946 on his Texas property, only to be confronted by a disclosure that Mr. Miller himself had lived in a house subject to a similar covenant.

A break in the tide of discrimination came when the Supreme Court in 1948 held the covenants unenforceable; when President Truman

[9] As recently as 1961, Secretary of State Dean Rusk was confronted with such a covenant in the purchase of a Spring Valley house. He refused. But many other high public officials in previous years did not hesitate to sign such covenants in the Washington area and elsewhere.

[10] Abrams, *Forbidden Neighbors,* pp. 218ff.

thereafter ordered FHA to change its manual, it did so reluctantly and grudgingly. Thirty-seven major civic and religious organizations thereafter joined together in the National Committee Against Discrimination in Housing to outlaw housing discrimination at the federal level and in states and cities. In 1962, President Kennedy signed an executive order outlawing discrimination in federally aided housing; and by that time, seventeen states, the Virgin Islands, and fifty-six cities had passed antidiscrimination laws or resolutions. Twelve of the states even banned discrimination in private housing. Altogether, the laws and resolutions embraced some 65 million people. But the victory against housing bias was far from assured. While the laws helped widen housing opportunities in the cities in which Negroes already lived, it did little to break down discrimination in the suburbs, where there was either no antibias laws or no enforcement of the law.[11]

The Semantics of Reform

While antibias laws have helped break down some segregated patterns, the development of the essential techniques for effecting greater progress has lagged. A reformer who ventures a constructive suggestion may be shunned for using a word alien to the accepted vernacular. One who opposes wholesale eviction of Negroes from slums may be accused of opposing slum clearance and public housing. A housing agency that seeks in good faith to maintain a racial balance in a project so as to keep the local public school from becoming segregated, will be accused of practicing a "quota system." To favor higher income limits for public housing, so as to encourage white as

[11] The executive order was a compromise limited mainly to future mortgages insured or aided by federal agencies and to properties owned by the government. Nor did it apply to savings and loan associations, though they were beneficiaries of federal deposit insurance and of extensive federal low-interest credit. Less than 23 per cent of all new housing construction was embraced by the order, and since half of these dwellings were already covered by state and local laws or resolutions, it affected only 13 per cent of new housing at best. Neither the state and local laws nor the executive order were enough to crack the vitrified prejudices and fears achieved during the decade and a half of federal anti-Negro policy.

well as Negro occupancy, is equivalent to opposing tenant selection
based on need. It is apparent that a re-examination of existing shibboleths is long overdue.

Segregation, a much-abused term in the dictionary of social reform,
is not always as bad as it sounds. Every ethnic and immigrant group
lived at first with its own people, where it felt it could build a greater
sense of security, create its own institutions, and raise its members
without fear and with dignity. Harlem is a ghetto, but it is an exaggera-
tion to assert that it is an enforced ghetto for all Negroes, or that it
completely lacks a culture, or that if it were torn down and its Negro
population were allowed to live wherever it chose, the same voluntary
racial agglomerations would not form in other sections.

The test is not whether a group is segregated but whether there are
elements of compulsion which keep its members in place when they are
ready, willing, and able to live elsewhere. In the case of the Negro,
all the compulsory elements—social, political, and economic—are
present, particularly on the outskirts of the central cities where eight
of every ten new houses are being built. The central cities are performing their historic role of the refuge; but even in some of these older and
larger cities, there are still forces at work to confine the Negro to
segregated sections or oust him, ostensibly to make way for public
improvements. In some of the newer cities, there is not a single Negro
family, and in Dearborn, Michigan, a city of over 100,000 population,
the mayor won election on his boast that he kept Negroes out of his
city. That from 60 to 72 per cent of those displaced from their homes
by urban renewal have been Negroes has been one of the least com-
mendable aspects of the renewal program.

A similar ambiguity obscures the meaning of "housing discrimination." It is generally used to signify only exclusion from housing, but
it should also embrace the unnecessary displacement of minorities
from housing they already occupy; failure to open the mortgage market
to minorities; failure to provide publicly assisted housing for them
when it is the only type of housing they can afford; exclusion of
minorities from housing already available to other groups; and enforced segregation in housing.

Bias is also being practiced in suburbs by discriminatory devices legal on their face, such as rigid zoning or building laws that are relaxed for builders of white developments and rigidly adhered to for others. Approval of membership in the community club may be a requirement for home purchase with an understanding among members that a Negro is unwelcome. Condemnation for a park, school, or street may be voted for an area in which Negroes have established a foothold; and inspectors, school officials, or police skilled in the techniques of making life intolerable for the unwanted may aim a myriad of other subtle harassments against Negroes who venture into a white area.

In the 1960s ominous signs of a "white sidelash" appeared, which threatened to end whatever progress was being made. In Berkeley, California, and Seattle, Washington, efforts to enact antidiscrimination laws in housing were defeated. Worse still, in 1964 the National Association of Real Estate Boards launched a well-financed national campaign to halt the spread of antibias housing laws. It made its first important test in California by putting a proposition on the ballot which would ban antidiscrimination laws in housing by constitutional prohibition. The proposition won by a 2 to 1 vote. Detroit, Michigan, and Akron, Ohio, passed similar laws.

The experience in California, Detroit, and Akron suggests that while people might acquiesce in the passage of antibias laws by their legislators, or in the issuance of a Presidential order banning discrimination in publicly-assisted housing, they will put their own property rights above the rights of minorities when asked to voice their views directly. If these laws are sustained by the courts, the threat of a "tyranny of the majority" looms, not only in housing but in other areas of civil rights.

Freedom and Welfare

The growth of federal powers and of federal expenditures has brought great benefits and promised new varieties of freedoms—a new "freedom from want" and freedom from slums, a freedom from fear of unemployment, and from the hazards of insecurity, illness, and old age. It promises greater access to home ownership, to education, and to other advances. Many have benefited among the rank and file, and some of the benefits have trickled down to the lowliest. The real test of democracy, however, is not that it has benefited a majority—it is not democracy if it bans some from the same opportunities it offers others.

When a political or economic system changes as the American system has done in the last three decades, there is always the risk that the established values and protections of the old system may be lost and that expanded power will be used to oppress rather than to help a group that needs help. Here Rousseau's claim that it is the tendency of all governments to degenerate takes on grim reality. In a society in which housing and other aspects of the market process become involved with government, respecting the will of the majority in the dispensation or restriction of public benefits to one class or race threatens the democratic concept.

The great Negro protest of the 1960s has won more political rights for the Negro, particularly in the South. But as more rights are won, the Negro must be ready, willing, and able to compete for the opportunities he has gained. Winning the right to a home in a white suburb is meaningless unless he can afford it—this means that he must either improve his income or be subsidized together with other low-income families in his housing. Winning the right to a union membership and to skilled work will not get him the job if he lacks the education to qualify—this implies better access to better education and to a better environment. It also calls for the right to live near that job. Winning the right to vote is important, but the Negro must be sufficiently instructed to distinguish between the meaningless promises of politicians seeking his favor and the reforms that can help gain for him a real equality. There is thus an interplay between what government does for the Negro and what the Negro does for himself to enable him to compete more effectively in a competitive society.

One thing is clear. Without access to land the right to home ownership will not exist. Without equal access to a home the Negro can afford, there will be no equal access to opportunity; nor can there be real freedom of movement, equal use of recreation and leisure, or the equal protection and privileges of the laws. However diligently the courts may strike at segregation in schools, school segregation will continue when there is compulsory segregation in neighborhoods. Indeed, enforced neighborhood segregation will tend to become the new vehicle for achieving indirectly what the courts have outlawed directly.

Thus "Land and Freedom" may become as commanding an issue as it was in the last century. The people of the cities will claim their freedoms are being threatened by suburban exclusion; the suburbs will argue that their right of self-determination is being invaded. Socially minded citizens will ask for state action to open up peripheral land to people of all races, while the suburbs will resist it in the name of local autonomy and home rule, or by contriving some new planning device out of a swelling catalogue.

The problems faced by the city are problems in many respects similar to those facing the Negro. The more Negroes move into the city, the more concerted will be the effort to have the city continue bearing the exclusive burden of the Negro's segregation, his child's school problems, his poverty, and his social and economic handicaps. The more the suburbs grow, the stronger will become their influence at the state and federal levels. Reapportionment may help a few cities, but in the long run, the power will go to the rising suburban vote.

Neither antibias laws nor Supreme Court decisions will be enough to ease the plight of the central city or give its Negroes better housing and a better environment. For even if suburbia were opened to the Negroes, most could not afford the housing offered them. The most subtle and most effective form of housing discrimination is therefore the failure of the federal government to provide a realistic program of subsidized housing in suburb as well as city at costs the Negro can afford. Such a program must include access to ownership as well as rental. If private builders or the state and local governments refuse to build the housing, then the federal government must do so. Only with such a policy can one of the most stubborn links to poverty and inequality be disengaged and the bonds of repression broken.

THE PRESCRIPTION

—URBAN RENEWAL

Chapter

5

The Federal Role in Housing and Urban Renewal

IN THE DEPRESSION of the 1930s, when the central cities were wincing under the spasms of economic crisis, some of the New Deal experimenters milling in and out of the White House calculated that spending for public works and propping up the house-building industry were two good ways of lubricating the ailing economy. Their main interest was centered on helping the private builder and mortgagee. Though the time was also opportune for a major program of city rebuilding, the only interest in this sort of proposal was shown by Secretary of Labor Frances Perkins, who suggested that the clearance of slums might perform the dual purpose of stirring up building activity while incidentally improving the living conditions of the city's poor. Public housing thereafter gained a small experimental appropriation as a part of a huge public works program.

The interest in reviving the building industry was not hard to understand. It had long been the bellwether of economic activity. When buildings go up, so do employment, purchasing power, and local revenues. When construction dwindles, the economy suffers.

One trouble with the effort to help the building industry was that home building was then generated by a disparate and undercapitalized group of little builders who put up—on the average—only about four houses a year. But though they were small fry in the big pool of American enterprise, it was their small-fry operations that fortified local economies and started things moving in the bigger workshops and rolling mills of America. Some means had to be found, therefore, to expand their operations into the larger-scale deals that would be economically meaningful.

House-building was then a creature of the market in which this little builder put up the equity money and took the risks until a customer accepted his product. The builder needed capital that could be frozen for long periods, and lending institutions were chary of advancing more than two-thirds of the building value. He therefore built cheaper or costlier buildings, bad or better ones, depending on what his customers could afford and how much capital he could raise to finance his operations.

The federal government could have spurred the builder's operations either in the cities or on their fringes. But if building operations were activated in the cities, it would have been necessary to acquire contiguous sections of land, and this could be done on a large scale only through compulsory land acquisitions, which could be undertaken only by public agencies for clearly public purposes. It seemed simpler to help expand private building operations on open land. While a trickle of building found its way into the still-vacant land of cities, most of the building thereafter went to the suburbs.

To stimulate the small builder and help him finance larger operations, the Federal Housing Administration undertook to insure mortgages up to 90 per cent of the cost of land and building. At first, FHA's emphasis was on small homes, but it was not long before it embraced speculative multiple dwellings as well. Not only would the builder now require only a nominal investment in the operation—about equal to his building fee—but the government-insured lenders, it was thought, would no longer hesitate to advance all the money he needed for his larger undertakings. To stem the mounting foreclosures, but also to provide the lending institutions with added capital, the government set up the Home Owners Loan Corporation, which bailed the institutions out of their sour mortgages to the extent of more than $3 billion.

Once started on its course, federal ministrations to the building industry continued even after a full recovery had begun to set in. The government scattered its credit assistance over a widening terrain, and as it did so, the number of fresh claimants upon its generosity grew. Not only were builders and lenders now the beneficiaries but also home buyers and the new suburban jurisdictions in which they settled. Soon army personnel, war veterans, nursing home operators, prefabricators, cooperatives, farmers, the mobile homes industry, middle-class families, and colleges in need of dormitories also filed their claims and Congress sought to satisfy them too. After the initial public housing experiment, Congress in 1937 also passed a United States Housing Act under which it provided loans and subsidies to help cities house their low-income families. By 1950, hardly a phase of home building and improvement remained unaided. The little builder gradually became a bigger-time operator who could swing a million-dollar deal with no more than a little front money. The federal government became the shaft and spoke of the building wheel, the brace of the mortgage business, the buttress of home ownership, and the prop under new rental housing. It also became the destroyer of the nation's slums, an activity which at first had been a social operation but in 1949 also became a tool of the private building enterprise.

By 1963, Federal Housing Administration insurance had soared to $88 billion. From 1938 to 1963, the Federal National Mortgage Association had spent $12.5 billion to buy 1.2 million mortgages, while a host of new federal agencies had sprung up to busy themselves with innumerable private ventures drawing upon the federal largess or credit. Simultaneously, federal credit and insurance of their deposits made the savings and loan associations the nation's largest mortgage lenders on homes and one of the most influential lobbies in Washington.

The government assistance to building was not without its benefits for the five million families who in 1963 owned FHA-aided homes; the millions of war veterans who became home owners; the 940,000 families in aided multifamily projects; the more than 27 million home owners who were helped to repair their dwellings; the 540,000 families in low-rent public housing; and the countless others who borrowed from the burgeoning savings and loan associations. Many little folk who bought homes with thin equities saw their values rise to twice or three times their original cost, and many joined the middle class, thanks to their going into debt at the right time.

Once the federal government had admitted the private operator into the fraternity of enterprises enjoying federal gratuities, it found itself continuously revising the formula for the aided undertakings. Either the private entrepreneur felt he was not getting enough profit or the federal agencies thought they were being too liberal. A golden mean had to be found under which the amount of gold assigned to the entrepreneur would not be too mean. Thanks to federal credit, the former small-time operator was soon able to build large apartment houses as well as hundreds of suburban houses in a single operation.

By 1949, however, federal housing ventures had grown so discrepant that Congress thought all the housing programs should be harnessed to a goal. The goals of a government are the ends toward which the public purpose is directed. Goals express aspirations, but, like campaign oratory, they are too often promissory notes with no fixed amount and no due date. The goal in the 1949 act was put as follows:

The general welfare and security of the Nation and the health and living standards of its people require housing production and related community development sufficient to remedy the serious housing shortage, the elimination of substandard and other inadequate housing through the clearance of slums and blighted areas, and the realization as soon as feasible of the goal of a decent home and a suitable living environment for every American family thus contributing to the development and redevelopment of communities and to the advancement of the growth, wealth, and security of the Nation.

This was no mean national dedication. But it was in the subsequent portions of the act that the clue to how the goal was to be met was revealed. The law said:

1. Private enterprise was to be encouraged to serve as large a part of the need as possible.

2. Government aid was to spur private enterprise to serve more of the total need.

3. Local public bodies were to be stimulated into sponsoring programs for better neighborhoods as well as providing homes at lower costs but again only through the medium of the entrepreneur-builder.

4. Slums and blighted areas were to be cleared and low-income families rehoused by public agencies but only where private enterprise was not functioning.

The 1949 legislation was called an "omnibus" housing act. It presumably included something for everybody. It was clear, too, that the time was not yet ripe for scuttling the public housing program in cities where it had been going on fitfully since it had been ventured as an experiment fifteen years before. But despite the Congressional curtsy to the problems of urban low-income families and to the "advancement of communities" the general aim was becoming patent. Under the terms of the act, Congress was no longer to view the federal function as a direct operation (as in federal slum clearance and public housing, the Tennessee Valley Authority, or road building). Instead, housing programs and community improvement were to be carried out to respect the private enterprise process. The entrepreneur was to be the main artery through which federal slum clearance money and credit were thereafter to be channeled. General welfare in housing was to be served by entrepreneurial welfare. This applied both to FHA programs as well as to the new urban renewal program which the 1949 act authorized.

The Residual Welfare

If public welfare and private welfare were to find common cause in a common effort, it could be justified politically only if it also brought some dividends to the common man, i.e., the "people" at the base of the social and economic pyramid whose "health and living standards" required the government intervention essential to assure "the growth, wealth and security of the nation."

The people, under the new formula, however, were now to be mostly the remainder-men, the residual legatees after the direct beneficiaries had had theirs. It was presumed and, it is fair to say, hoped, that the residuum would not be insubstantial. The full credits to the builder and the federal insurance of mortgages would provide the builder with more, longer, and higher credits and speed his production of homes. Since FHA-insured mortgages would be larger, the home buyer, by borrowing more, would be putting in less. He would also be given a good lifetime within which to liquidate his debt. With all these attractions, it was anticipated that the portion of the rank and file who could afford to buy dwellings would expand. Indeed it did expand—mainly on the open land outside the cities. With improved conditions and easier terms, the proportion of home ownership soared from a low of 43 per cent of all occupied units in the 1940s to 63 per cent in 1963.

While federal aid to FHA and the savings and loan associations boomed the suburbs and the newer cities of the West, it somehow fell short in the older urban centers. Of the 58.3 million units constituting the national housing stock in 1960, about 20 per cent were classified as unsound (8.4 million required repairs to make them livable, 3 million were dilapidated, of which some 2.3 million were inhabited.)[1] Of the occupied units, 6.2 million lacked private toilets, baths, or running water. Within the metropolitan areas, most of these deficiencies were found in the central cities which had experienced their fitful and distorted growth during the first ascent of industrialization and the first influx of cheap labor from the world's hinterlands.

The urban renewal formula launched by the 1949 act was thought to take care of both the slum-bound cities and their slums. If the slums could be razed and the sites rebuilt, the cities could be restored as rightful competitors for the good life and the good taxpayer. Though the federal government itself had cleared slums and built public housing from 1934 to 1937 and in 1937 had transferred the operational responsibility to the cities, the 1949 urban renewal formula turned over house production on slum-cleared sites to private entrepreneurs.

[1] The total number of units reported dilapidated in the 1960 census is undoubtedly an understatement of the units in this condition. Considerable evidence to substantiate this resulted from a post-enumeration census. A figure of 4 million for the number of dilapidated units is more accurate (U.S. Census of Housing, *Components of Inventory Change*, 1960, Part 1A).

The cities would buy the land or condemn it for them. The cities would clear the sites of tenants and write down the land costs to make the price attractive to the entrepreneurs. The entrepreneurs, not the public, would own the product, and for all practical purposes, they could pocket whatever profits the projects would net. Projects built for those who could pay the going price of the new dwellings would have higher assessed values and yield the cities more taxes. Mortgage insurance or direct federal loans would sweeten the entrepreneur's profit and inspire him to bid for the cheap land. The loss resulting from the sale of the land would be shared two-thirds by the federal government and one-third by the cities.[2] Given such federal impetus and municipal cooperation, new buildings would supplant the slums, new revenues at least five times more than the old sites yielded would pour into the slack city treasuries, slums would disappear, the cities would begin to convalesce, and the general welfare would be served all around.

Urban Renewal in History

Renewal of cities is no more novel in history than building new cities. Kings and parliaments over the centuries have widened streets, built parks, created new districts, and made room for new rows of houses. Baron Haussmann's dramatic performance in Paris during the reign of Napoleon III was a major renewal scheme and sparked other European cities to follow suit. Dublin experienced such improvements during the reign of Charles II (1660–1685) and again during the reign of Queen Anne and George I when the Irish Parliament set up the Wide Street Commissioners who swept through Dublin's old alleys and slums like a mammoth tank, carving out the broad carriage-ways that make it possible to cross the city today.[3]

A wave of renewal schemes reminiscent of the current American variety and aimed at clearing slums with the aid of private enterprise surged through British cities in the second half of the nineteenth

[2] Now one-fourth for the smaller cities.

[3] Charles Abrams, *Urban Renewal Project in Ireland (Dublin)*. United Nations Department of Economic and Social Affairs, April 25, 1961.

century. In 1866, for example, Glasgow renewed a tract of eighty-eight acres representing the whole of the ancient town. Parliament authorized purchase of the property and demolition of one of the densest slums of Europe (as many as 1,000 persons to the acre). After clearance, streets were laid out, and the property was sold for rebuilding.[4] Relocation of tenants was part of the Glasgow scheme, and tenants were not evicted until alternative houses could be found for them.[5] In addition to private housing built for them, the city put up seven model tenements at a cost of £90,000 which were thereafter sold to private owners "because being erected at the expense of the city, they were considered as public charities and were consequently unpopular."[6] Renewal and expropriation were also undertaken in Swansea, Wolverhampton, Derby, Nottingham and Newcastle-upon-Tyne.

Even today, renewal programs, partly spurred by the movement in the United States, have been undertaken in such countries as Great Britain, France, Israel, Ireland, and Denmark;[7] the renewal movement has traveled to Asia where Singapore, in 1963, requested a UN mission to advise it on the clearing of its central area slums, and a program that proved a fiasco was launched even in Lagos, Nigeria.

The American Concept of Urban Renewal

While renewing cities was long accepted as a national prerogative in the Old World, the assumption of national responsibility in America was a revolutionary concept, for under the doctrine of state sover-

[4] Renewal was financed by a special tax of sixpence to the pound for five years (reduced to fourpence after the first year) and twopence for ten years thereafter. The tax yielded £350,000 and supplied sufficient capital for all improvements. The net cost including suits lost, upkeep cost of land lying idle, and all expenses of management was estimated at about £180,000. Negotiations were carried on by a private agent, and no major improvement was made until all the land affected by the scheme had been bought (M. T. Reynolds, *The Housing of the Poor in American Cities*, quoted at length in *Encyclopedia of Social Reform*, Funk & Wagnalls, 1896, p. 1326.

[5] The knowledge that they were to be dispossessed caused builders to erect housing for them on the outskirts of the town where land was available.

[6] Reynolds, p. 1327.

[7] Leo Grebler, *Urban Renewal in European Countries*, Graduate School of Business Administration, University of California, 1963.

eignty, the condition of the nation's cities was not a federal concern. This concept held fast even after the nation had become 70 per cent urbanized. That the state was never *concerned* about renewing its cities did not unbind the constitutional straitjacket.

It was apparent from the nature of the legislation that the main motivation that prompted the new national involvement was not the creation of the city beautiful, the city efficient, or the city solvent. It simply sought to expand slum clearance—already a national purpose—but it would now become another vehicle for private investment supported by new forms of federal assistance.

There was at least one questionable aspect of the new formula. The "serious housing shortage" which Congress's goal had promised to remedy was most serious for those city folk who occupied the slums marked for destruction. These slums may have been eyesores to the city officials, but they were shelters for the families who could afford nothing better. And so they occupied the several million homes that were ramshackle or dilapidated, and the millions of houses lacking toilets, baths, and running water or needing major repairs to make them livable.

It was indeed hard to see how removing the urban slum dwellers' houses, bad as they might be, could either cure the serious housing shortage to which the 1949 act dedicated itself or provide these people with homes they could afford. Congress's answer, however, seemed simple: (1) Some public housing moneys would continue to be earmarked for the cities under the original slum clearance formula to rehouse the families displaced, and (2) the evicted families could be moved into other quarters in the existing urban stock. The act authorized payment of the families' moving expenses to speed their departure.

There was another complication. As the economy expanded and as FHA aid and savings and loan mortgages were speeding the move of white families to the suburbs, millions of Negroes, Puerto Ricans, and Mexicans poured into the cities. These people moved into the slums vacated by many of those who were now buying suburban homes under the easier terms. Of the minority families moving into the cities, the Negroes were the most numerous. The faster the Negro family filled the vacancies in the cities, the faster was the white exodus from the sections he entered. Urban renewal's steam shovel functioned mainly in the areas where the minorities had secured their footholds. About 70 per cent of those scheduled for urban renewal evictions were nonwhite, and a substantial number of the rest were poorer folk, including elderly families. Since the Negro's income was only about half that of the whites, FHA-aided homes and those financed by the savings and loan associations were beyond his means; even if he could afford them, the new white suburbs would not allow him to come in.

The most home-hungry portion of the population now scurried about from one slum to another in search of more enduring footholds. Although the Housing Act of 1949 had authorized 135,000 public housing units annually, Congress after 1954 cut the authorization to 35,000–45,000 annually. The frittered public housing program became more a pretext than a refuge, for the program was hardly big enough to accommodate its own displacees, much less those displaced by road programs, code enforcement, and urban renewal as well. Surprisingly, not many of the displaced were either eligible, able, or anxious to move into the public housing projects. This was particularly true of the white displacees, many of whom looked upon them as institutionalized havens for the impoverished.

Despite its subventions, the renewal program for some reason could not get off the ground from 1949 to 1954. One reason was that it was new and untried. Regulations had to be framed, sites selected, land assembled and appraised, and builders found who were willing to invest in drawing plans and making estimates in the hope they would land the jobs. In areas with housing shortages, tenant resistance to eviction slowed the city's hand. Elsewhere private redevelopers seemed not too keen to bid for projects that would not bring the high rents required to pay the going charges. It seemed simpler to build in the suburbs than to brave the tedious routines. Besides, the federal financing terms for mortgages were not as lush as they were in the city's outskirts where the "Section 608" formula, which will be discussed later, was providing bonanza opportunities.

Urban Renewal and the Housing Problem

By 1954, it appeared clear that urban renewal needed modification to make it work. But one of the troubles was that some of the senators who had laboriously shaped and launched it, and who were now being asked to extend it, had unfaltering memories. They had offered urban renewal as a housing measure. Its catchwords (housing shortage, slums, and a suitable living environment for every American family) had tethered it firmly to housing reform. The act had defined an eligible area as one "which is predominantly residential in character" before acquisition, or which after acquisition is to be redeveloped "for predominantly residential purposes."

The slums to be torn down were what was meant by "residential in character." What was to be built on the site was to be better, if more expensive, housing. Through slum clearance and better housing would come better environments. Simultaneously, through public housing, the evicted slum dwellers would get better shelter at costs they could afford. It had all seemed simple and logical to the Senate sponsors.

Senator Robert Taft, who had been the measure's most forceful advocate, would not allow himself to be distracted by those who had pressed for an enlargement of purpose beyond housing, for the good senator was a Christian at heart to whom "no room at the inn" was a gnawing deficiency in a great and progressive society.

"I do not believe that public housing is socialism," Senator Taft told me in an interview, "if it is confined to the furnishing of decent housing only to that group unable to provide housing by its own means. We have long recognized the duty of the state to give relief and free medical care for those unable to pay for it, and I think shelter is just as important as relief and medical care."[8]

"Perhaps we do not care about them [the slum dwellers] so much," he said on another occasion, "but most of them have families and we do have an interest, I think, in providing equal opportunity for all the children of the families who are brought into being in the United

[8] *New York Post*, January 28, 1948.

States . . . particularly food, clothing, shelter, medical care and education. . . . All of us acknowledge the duty of the community to take care of those who are unable to take care of themselves."[9]

It was Taft's underlying liberalism which made him a champion of the less privileged and his circumspect conservatism that impelled him to keep the federal power from going "beyond housing and beyond the elimination of slums." The plight of the cities or the need for better cities was not to be confused with the need for housing. In holding to the "predominantly residential requirement," the Taft subcommittee had said it "is not convinced that the federal government should embark upon a general program of aid to cities looking to their rebuilding in more attractive and economical patterns."

Under the Taft formula, the principal devices were to be destruction and construction—destruction of slums, construction of housing for "every American family." Higher-priced housing would accommodate those who could pay the redeveloper's market rents. (Under other programs FHA would take care of part of the middle-income group also.) Some "relocation" was seen as inevitable, but relocation was to be no substitute for public housing, which together with slum clearance and private rebuilding was an indispensable part of the Taft triad.

Perversion of the Urban Renewal Formula

It was not long, however, before the renewal–public housing program (under which urban renewal displaced the public housing rehoused) lost contact with its public housing partner. Public housing, like the Moor in *Othello,* had done its reverence in justifying urban renewal and could now go. The unexpected development was disclosed five years later in the following colloquy between federal officials and Senator Paul Douglas (who with Taft had been a primary sponsor of the renewal formula):[10]

[9] *New York Post,* April 27, 1949.
[10] *Hearings on Housing Act of 1954,* S. 2889, S. 2938, and S. 2949, Senate Committee on Banking and Currency, 83rd Cong., 2nd Sess., 1954, Part I, pp. 91 ff.

MR. FOLLIN (*Commissioner of Urban Renewal*): Fifty percent of those displaced are found to be eligible for public housing.

SENATOR DOUGLAS: How many have actually been rehoused?

MR. FOLLIN: I doubt if there is enough experience, Senator, to give you a figure which would stand up over the long run.

SENATOR DOUGLAS: This is a very crucial question. What is happening is you are clearing areas and this creates a public obligation which we recognized in the Housing Act of 1949 to see that these people are offered an opportunity, if their incomes were not sufficient or if they were forced, because of race, to be adequately accommodated in public housing. If that is not being done, slum clearance while removing an esthetic blot upon the community—some health blights, and so forth—is working an injustice upon the most helpless groups of all.

MR. FOLLIN: If you will permit, we would be glad to file a statement and give the information to date.

SENATOR DOUGLAS: I would like to pursue the question further: Have any of the slum clearance or urban redevelopment sites been made available for public housing?

MR. FOLLIN: In a few instances.

SENATOR DOUGLAS: How many instances?

MR. FOLLIN: Probably 3 or 4.

SENATOR DOUGLAS: Out of how many?

MR. FOLLIN: How many out of how many projects?

SENATOR DOUGLAS: Yes.

MR. FOLLIN: There are 52 projects that are under contract.

SENATOR DOUGLAS: Almost all the projects have been cleared and they have been used either for business or for residences for upper income groups, but the people who were displaced from these areas are not rehoused in the areas themselves?

MR. FOLLIN: Only to some extent.

SENATOR DOUGLAS: To a very slight extent.

MR. FOLLIN: Yes, sir.

After the Administration submitted a memorandum stating that "public housing will be built in 10 of the 85 urban renewal projects," the questioning was resumed.

SENATOR DOUGLAS: All I am saying is, if out of 52 sites which have been cleared, there are only 3 instances in which you have erected public housing to take care of the people displaced from those sites, it is obvious that the new uses which you are now developing for these areas [are] not to house low-income groups, but to house those in upper-income groups, or higher-income groups, and for business purposes. The public housing, therefore, of necessity, must be located elsewhere. I would like to ask why you have come to that decision.

MR. COLE (*Administrator, Housing and Home Finance Agency*): We have not come to that decision.

SENATOR DOUGLAS: That is what has happened. . . . certainly when we got the original bill through Congress, it was the intent that a considerable proportion of those displaced were to be rehoused in the areas which were cleared and the debate, itself, was very clear on that point. I can remember Senator Cain, of Washington, taking me to task on the matter. I got a written statement from the then Administrator that these areas were to be used and it was on that promise in large part that we got the bill through.

MR. COLE: I would agree with you heartily, sir, that much of the discussion with respect to slum clearance was tied in with the need for public housing, and a great deal of the acceptance of public housing was based upon the need of those people who were displaced by reason of slum clearance in urban redevelopment.

Housing Administrator Cole then added that "the problem of displaced persons and the relocation of these displaced persons is one of the most complex, difficult, and, may I say, sometimes almost insoluble problems."[11]

Thus the legislation which Congress had enacted to help solve the slum problem was evicting many more slum dwellers than it was rehousing. It was only one of the many examples of how legislation passed with the best of intentions is ultimately perverted during the administrative process. In the long run, the profit motive somehow operates as the undesignated but effective legislator while the public obligation is pushed under the rug.

The perversion was not entirely the fault of the officials. The formula had been faulty from the beginning. It was not devised to pull cities out of their troubles. There had been no independent investigation into the financial aspects of slum developments, the ramified nature of the housing problem, or the predicaments of central cities and the temptations they would enforce. It could have been foreseen that the slum dwellers would not be rehoused on the cleared

[11] *Ibid.,* p. 94.

sites and that little if any public housing would be built for them on vacant sites.[12] The economic motivation had been the dominant ingredient in federal housing recipes from the inception and the stated ideal of better housing for everybody had simply supplied the sweetening, the coloring, and some of the political palatability. Since the welfare of the building industry had won equal place with the people's welfare in the 1949 act, it seemed inevitable that sooner or later the interests of the lower-income families would be forgotten. When the entrepreneurial and the general welfare are bracketed in the same legislation, it should not be surprising that the social purpose will be subordinated. It was.

[12] For an exchange of views on this matter between Senator Douglas and the writer, see Charles Abrams, *Forbidden Neighbors*, Harper & Row, 1955, pp. 250, 251.

Chapter

6

Urban Renewal Is Renewed

UP TO 1954, urban renewal lay in the dumps. Some 211 localities were interested, but only 60 had reached the land acquisition stage. The best its administrators could say for it was that the program had "gained momentum."[1] Of the $500 million available for grants, only $74 million had been committed. "Committed," like "allotted," "allocated," and "earmarked," is officialese for money put aside but not yet used. The Renewal Commissioner told the Senate in 1954 "there is plenty of grant money left, and plenty of loan money."[2] What he needed was more applications.

The passage of five years with almost nothing to show for all the fanfare was hardly progress. But the renewal administration was hopeful—"there is a real ground swell of interest," it told the Senate committee.

The word "renewal" means to restore to freshness, perfection, or vigor, and it became clear by 1954 that the urban renewal program had not made the cities fresh, perfect, or vigorous. But restoration of freshness, perfection, and vigor to cities had only been the name not the aim of the formula. It had been devised primarily as a slum

[1] *Hearings on Housing Act of 1954*, S. 2889, S. 2938, and S. 2949, Senate Committee on Banking and Currency, 83rd Cong., 2nd Sess., Part I, 1954, p. 235.

[2] *Ibid.*, p. 216.

clearance and housing program, and it was assumed that urban renewal might be the by-product. By 1954, however, not only had the cities not been renewed—the slums were not being renewed either. A new approach was needed. The program itself had to be "renewed" and the Eisenhower Administration rose to the occasion.

The Administration proposed a new formula under which each community would now have to present a "workable program," dealing both with the causes and the consequences of slum formation and urban decay. To qualify, a site no longer needed to be a slum but could be blighted. In addition to public housing for displacees, rehabilitation was made possible (Sections 220 and 221). The new workable program would require the affected community to be consulted, and the city was to be stimulated into better enforcement of building codes and conservation of economically sound neighborhoods. Once the city presented its workable program, all of the federal aids, new and old, would become available. The private builders would, as before, be the main functionaries in the urban renewal performance, and they could have either cleared sites turned over to them for new building or they might have FHA-insured financing for rehabilitation of old ones. The new Section 221 would also provide mortgage insurance to help rehouse the displaced families.

Another addition to the Housing Act of 1954 was the extension of the powers of the Federal National Mortgage Association. FNMA could now commit itself to buy mortgages on housing in urban renewal areas as well as act as a secondary market facility to provide liquidity for home mortgages. FNMA later became an important factor in the financing of mortgages on urban renewal projects.

The 608 Windfall and the Move Toward Conservatism

After the House had passed the Administration bill, but while the Senate's housing committee was still weighing it, another Senate committee had been hearing some sensational charges on how the government was being milked by builders under the FHA program.

One of the aids that had been devised to help the builders put up houses with little capital was Section 608 of the Housing Act of 1942. It was originally devised for war housing and was revived in 1946 to stimulate postwar rental projects through 90 per cent FHA insurance.

For twelve years, the 608 arrangement sanctioned by Congress went on without investigation. Emboldened FHA officials had openly told builders they need have "no risk capital or permanent capital investment" and that they could get back whatever money they invested "before one spade of earth is turned."[3] FHA officials also told builders they could inflate their cost estimates, their land prices, their architectural and other fees. Builders did not hesitate to oblige. A whole web of deceptions was spun which made it possible for the knowledgeable to build projects with costs running into the millions without investing a dime. Some made dummy leases between themselves and wholly-owned subsidiary corporations at a spurious rent for ninety-nine years. FHA would then insure a mortgage on the leasehold and upon default would have to pay the fictitious rent for the duration of the lease. The mortgages insured by FHA so far exceeded investment that builders withdrew millions above what the projects cost.

The builders' costs were in many cases 30 per cent less than FHA estimates,[4] while land values as filed with FHA were as much as five and six times the actual cost.[5] The huge bailouts, the fantastically inflated land prices and building costs, and the lease-backs at fictitious rentals were long an open secret. In some cases, FHA even allowed builders who had already "mortgaged out" (gotten all their money back from the insured mortgage) to increase their mortgages and draw out more than they had done already. Some rental projects were designed not as housing but as commercial hotels, but they benefited from the huge FHA mortgage insurance anyway.

In 80 per cent of the 543 projects examined, the mortgages were higher than the costs. In the 437 projects scrutinized in 1954 by inquisitive Senator Homer Capehart and his committee, mortgage proceeds exceeded total costs by more than $75 million. The pro-

[3] *FHA Investigation,* Report of the Senate Committee on Banking and Currency, 83rd Cong., 2nd Sess., 1954, p. 40.

[4] *Ibid.,* p. 30

[5] *Ibid.,* p. 41.

moters appropriated the excess although the law provided that mortgages were not to exceed 90 per cent of estimated cost.

Three speculators put up only $6,000 for a $12,500,000 project
in Virginia. They each went on the payroll for $20,000 a year; each
got his $6,000 back in a few weeks, and when the building was
completed, there was $2,250,000 left over from the mortgage, which
they promptly pocketed. As if this was not enough, they then distributed the $2,250,000 among themselves as "capital gains," paying
only 25 per cent of the profits to the government.[6] In Glen Oaks,
Long Island, $4,500,000 of the mortgage proceeds remained to be
milked from the sponsoring corporations after completion of the
project.[7]

All this was or at least should have been no surprise to any but
the unknowing public and a few incurious senators.[8] What was surprising, however, about the Senate investigation was the sensation
which the "disclosures" made and the rude awakening it brought.
When builders told Senator Capehart's committee that the country
would not get rental housing unless builders could bail out without
any investment, Senator Capehart called it "a great disappointment
to a committee whose members believe so completely in private enterprise." But as dissenting Senators Fulbright, Robertson, Sparkman,
Frear, Douglas, and Lehman had to concede, "it was going too far"

[6] *FHA Investigation*, Hearings before the Senate Committee on Banking and
Currency, 83rd Cong., 2nd Sess., 1954, Part 4, p. 3468.

[7] *Ibid.*, p. 3469.

[8] See, for example, Charles Abrams, *Revolution in Land,* Harper & Row,
1939, pp. 258–261, for a discussion of bailouts fourteen years before the investigation. "If it [FHA] had considered at all the speculative and disorganized
state of the building industry, it would have realized that the only projects of
this nature that would be undertaken subject to such rules would be precisely
those which it sought to bar—operations that were monuments to legal ingenuity
and financial legerdemain. The builder would get his profit anyway, but only
through the inflation of land cost, cubage, construction cost and fees, and
through similar devices intended to facilitate the immediate withdrawal of
all or most of the equity capital from the operation. . . . If FHA wished its
large-scale program to expand, it necessarily would have had to permit loans
on a per-room basis that equalled or exceeded the actual cost. . . ." See also
Charles Abrams, *The Future of Housing,* Harper & Row, 1946, pp. 234–236,
where I again pointed out the cost inflations, wash sales of land, and the
bailouts.

to assert that "all who overestimated costs and received excessive mortgage money were guilty of legal 'fraud.' "[9] The good senators were implying that the government itself had sanctioned the bailouts, that both political parties had voted the law making them possible, and that it was poor sportsmanship for one coventurer to wrap itself in the cloak of virtue and blacken its associate. The government policeman had also been implicated in the deal and to turn about and become the accuser was not exactly cricket.

Though a few officials and builders were indicted for corruption and corrupting, the "608" disclosures have quietly passed into history. But they left their mark on federal officialdom in the years following 1954. Congress, with a first-hand view of how the government was being bilked, considered overhauling the formula. But it then passed the 1954 legislation with few modifications; for, as the House's managers of the legislation put it:

. . . Throughout the conference there was complete agreement that while there was necessity for strengthening the housing laws to prevent the reoccurrence of past abuses, it was also imperative that the changes made not be of such a nature as to make our Federal housing laws unworkable or as seriously to impair the assistance which they should properly give to the encouragement and continuation of a high volume of housing production and housing improvements for our people.[10]

FHA officials, however, who had openly encouraged builders to come and get it thereafter moderated their sales talks and became more circumspect in appraising property subject to 90 per cent mortgages. But not long after the 608 scandal had been forgotten, it again became plain that if rental housing and urban renewal programs were to go on, too tight a leash on profits would act as a drag on incentive. Urban renewal applications continued at a snail's pace.

Neither Section 220 nor 221 assistance produced much volume either. Although a builder of a 220 project could have a mortgage at 90 per cent of replacement cost, Section 220 failed to entice many builders. Nor did Section 221 produce the volume anticipated, even

[9] *FHA Investigation*, Report, p. 7.
[10] *Housing Act of 1954*, House Report 2271, 83rd Cong., 2nd Sess., July 17, 1954, pp. 63, 64.

with its 90–100 per cent insurance. An HHFA evaluation of Section 221 housing in December 1959 showed progress as "spotty and uneven."[11] Only nineteen communities at the end of September 1959 had more than 50 per cent of their quotas under construction or had obtained approval for mortgage insurance. At the end of 1961, although terms had been twice liberalized and applications had increased, less than 36,000 units of Section 221 housing had been insured by FHA in the whole country. The program was lagging far behind the certified need. In general the houses built under the program were drab, reflecting the eagerness to bail out. Some of the rental projects were worse than the owner-occupied slums they replaced. However much one might dislike the "608" device, it had, in contrast, produced 464,000 dwelling units. There now had to be a sort of give and take, with just enough give and just enough take. Section 207, an early device for rental housing construction which allowed insurance up to 90 per cent of estimated value with a mortgage up to $20 million and an interest rate of about 5¼ per cent (plus insurance premium), was continued as a builder's tool, and appraisals were made more generous. When Section 207 still failed to produce as much housing as 608, it was successively liberalized. Not long thereafter 90 per cent mortgages on private nonprofit projects under Section 221 were elevated to 100 per cent, whereupon entrepreneurs showed somewhat more interest.

In the early years of the decade that followed 1954, the renewal administrators tried to walk the tightrope between conservatism and liberalism. But this becomes particularly hazardous when the tightrope is only a thin thread of equity representing the renewer's investment (if any). If the federally aided financing is on the conservative side, there will be no investors. If it is too generous, there is bound to be a default and perhaps another investigation. As the years wore on and bidders remained indifferent, the renewal administration continuously liberalized appraisals and financing. Though only 26 renewal projects were completed by January 18, 1960, 699 projects

[11] Albert Thompson, *An Evaluation of the Section 221 Relocation Housing Program*. A Report to the Housing Administrator, December 1959.

were approved for federal assistance. Though the prospects were
getting better, they were still not good enough to generate a flood of
bidders.

The Nature of the Renewers

With the steady liberalization of financing, however, more renewers
appeared on the scene. They, like some of the earlier bidders, were
mainly novices ready to venture on the long shots, the pioneers who
higgled, compromised, and yielded to hard bargains; they worked out
the tax gimmicks and contract terms before they had become standardized. When, in the brief period of administrative caution, these venturers tossed their hats into the ring, they took the chance of losing
their shirts as well. But if they were lucky to emerge with a commitment through the federal and local routines, they might sometimes
wind up with a deal. Or they might find themselves wedded to a local
partner who had the lubricating oil which made the local political
machine turn. It was still no easy job in those days.

Among the audacious first to try his hand was James H. Scheuer
of New York. Scheuer had a social as well as a financial turn of mind
and had been associated with housing and civic organizations in New
York City as well as with groups opposing race discrimination. His
social viewpoint appealed to some of the local agencies.

Scheuer was awarded one of the urban renewal sites in Washington,
D.C., another in Cleveland. Later he won the bids in Sacramento,
St. Louis, and Marin County (California). In Washington and Sacramento, Scheuer associated himself with Roger Stevens, an investor in
theatrical operations as well as real estate. (Stevens had also taken on
the well-publicized New Haven project on his own.) In Washington
and San Juan, Scheuer teamed up with the HRH Construction Company of New York City. He later also signed up the Brookline,
Massachusetts, deal after an amateur developer got into trouble.

As official manuals were simplified and dozens of liberalizing
amendments were made to the regulations and statutes, other bidders

steadily entered the competition. Some were well known, some were complete strangers to building operations. Jerome Rappaport, a Massachusetts lawyer, took on Boston's West End redevelopment site. Marvin S. Gilman, a young, liberal-minded Long Island lawyer, tackled the Baltimore project. Among the more seasoned builders were the late Herbert Greenwald of Chicago, who was awarded the Detroit and Newark projects; the Minskoffs, New York builders, won the Red Rock Hill site in San Francisco; and the well-capitalized Kern County Land Company was awarded a Santa Monica project. Venturesome William Zeckendorf, some of whose real estate transactions and financial embarrassments have made front-page sensations, took on one of the projects in Washington, adjoining Scheuer's. Boston's Louis Perini successfully bid for San Francisco's Golden Gate project against keen competition; Eichler Homes, Inc., headed by Joseph L. Eichler, a forward-looking builder of small homes, took over two San Francisco sites. Ferd Kramer and Arthur Rubloff were among the investors for some of the twenty-six Chicago schemes. Zeckendorf by this time also won a Chicago bid and until he got into trouble, was eagerly sought after by mayors looking for a "live wire" to spark their moribund projects.

With rare exceptions, however, the bidders were neither the big capital pools, the tycoons of industry, nor even the Levitts of home construction. They were more likely to be small-fry parlayers of profits, petty newcomers or speculators looking for a chisel wherever it could carve out a fast buck. Local pride being what it is, local builders were often given preference, even when they were under-capitalized; and they might join hands with an outsider who was more experienced or better-heeled. In a few places, local merchants sponsored or organized syndicates in the hope of salvaging their downtown investments, and an educational institution might see a chance of improving its surroundings by having the land acquired and redeveloped.

The same general pattern of labored activity continued into the 1960s, with few in big business or among the big capital pools show-

ing interest in urban renewal. A few more recent exceptions were
Reynolds Aluminum Corporation in Philadelphia and Cincinnati;
General Electric Company was reputed to be backing the builders of a
project in Kansas City and Hartford; and the Aluminum Corporation
of America (Alcoa). But their appetite for more of the same seemed
slender. They were experimenting and seemed far from ready to
make full commitments to renewal investments.

The experience of Alcoa best exemplifies the experiences of big
business and may forecast the prospects of its future interest in renewal operations. Alcoa's interest in real estate was sparked in 1960
when it thought more use of its building products would enhance its
general operations. After being drawn into two major real estate
ventures in New York City and Los Angeles by William Zeckendorf,
Alcoa also bought substantial interests in eight renewal projects, six
of which had FHA-insured mortgages: Three were in New York City,
one was in Pittsburgh, one in Philadelphia, and one in San Francisco.
Its interests in the projects ranged from 25 per cent in the Golden
Gateway in San Francisco (jointly with Perini) to 90 per cent in
Society Hill, Philadelphia, and in Kips Bay Plaza, New York. When
Zeckendorf ran into financial trouble, Alcoa took over operations.

It had first been drawn into the renewal business as a seed money
angel, but it has "seen enough to know that we have had it." It has
no plans to buy into any further renewal developments. Whether it
ventures further will depend on how its existing investments fare. It
likes the depreciation write-offs urban renewal permits. The urban
renewal game is not one for "half-way measures and weakly-sponsored
programs." Proximity to slums, FHA delays, and frustrations at the
local level are among the headaches; rent ceilings are another. The
developer must have "more leeway to make his own mistakes." City
taxes are too high. "We're learning the hard way. We have the con-
viction that urban renewal is essential if our cities are to survive and
that Alcoa can play a constructive role in that battle and bring home
to its shareholders a reasonable return on their investment." But it
finds that traditional private financing is much simpler to deal with
than a government mortgagee, and that urban renewal can succeed

only through a "team effort of public and private agencies willing to enlist for a long, hard fight."[12]

Stuyvesant Town

The most prominent absentees from urban renewal investment were the life insurance companies. These capital pools are among the largest in the nation, and in 1963, 1,500 of these companies had more than $140 billion, mostly represented by policy reserves. These reserves had grown by more than 70 per cent in ten years.

Life insurance companies are not new to the real estate game; they have always invested a substantial portion of their assets in mortgages, and they are capable of financing a host of projects without going to their vaults or calling upon FHA assistance. They have built great office buildings and even some housing projects like Metropolitan's Parkchester. These companies would have been expected to be among the main bidders for renewal investments. But they have continuously remained aloof. That they did stems partly from the experience in 1943 of the largest among them—the Metropolitan Life Insurance Company.

Six years before the 1949 act, Metropolitan had been induced by Parks Commissioner Robert Moses to try its hand at redeveloping eighteen square blocks of old buildings in the Stuyvesant Town area, on New York City's Lower East Side.

Metropolitan's venture differed from the current urban renewal formula in that it called for neither federal assistance nor a write-down of land cost. Metropolitan was also willing to limit its cash profit to 6 per cent. Exemption of the new buildings from the real estate tax and limited dividends, it was thought, would produce low rents and a safe investment.

Metropolitan wanted as little regulation as possible, particularly as to the kind of tenants it could take in. It had always viewed federal

[12] Leon E. Hickman, Executive Vice-president, Alcoa, "Alcoa's Renewal Role Explained," *Journal of Housing* (National Association of Housing and Redevelopment Officials), May 1964, pp. 190–195.

intervention into mortgage insurance as a prelude to regulation of insurance companies and to federal intervention in other forms of insurance—including possible competition with life insurance itself. So repugnant was the thought of federal expansion that it had bought no FHA-insured mortgages for its massive mortgage portfolio, looked upon public housing with disdain, and shunned even prime local housing authority bonds. As city slums brought more social protest and as the threat of a growing socialization of low-rent housing by the city's housing authority loomed larger, the insurance company decided it would demonstrate in its Stuyvesant Town project how private enterprise could clear slums with its own mortgage money and provide moderate-priced housing at a reasonable profit. The first urban redevelopment project and the forerunner of the present formula was the result.

A new state urban redevelopment law was specially tailored to accommodate Metropolitan's effort. As arranged by Moses, the city would take the land by eminent domain, oust the existing occupants, and resell the cleared site to Metropolitan at cost. The city would allow a 25-year tax exemption on the new buildings and Metropolitan, besides limiting its return, would agree to rent the dwellings at no more than $14.60 monthly per room. This could be graduated upward with the city's approval if the 6 per cent investment rate was ever impaired. Metropolitan simultaneously built Riverton Houses, a Negro project in Harlem composed of 1,232 units under the same formula as Stuyvesant Town. This, it thought, was in line with the "separate but equal" theory then widely accepted as the way to tackle the racial question.

Although the housing provided in Stuyvesant Town and Riverton was low-rent and tax-exempt, tenants did not have to be low-income. When Metropolitan insisted on renting to whom it pleased, tenants earning as much as $50,000 a year became beneficiaries of the huge annual tax-exemption subsidy. The cost of the land was about $17 million; the buildings cost about $100 million. At a 4 per cent tax rate on the buildings, the city's subsidy was thus about $4 million a year. The city would have done better had the land been presented to the company at no cost, for the city would then have recovered its contribution from the new stepped-up tax revenues in less than five years. By granting a subsidy which benefited tenants who needed no subsidy, the city was virtually making a gift mostly to high-income tenants of $4 million annually, equivalent to a subsidy of $2 per year paid by every New York family. Had there been no tax subsidy but only the land gift, Metropolitan would also have been free of regulation of its rents. It would have been a more sensible deal all around. Cooper Village, Metropolitan's unregulated and unsubsidized investment adjoining Stuyvesant Town, supports this reasoning.

For a company that despised regulation of any kind, the regulation of its rents was bound to prove an unhappy arrangement. When Metropolitan's board chairman Frederick H. Ecker told a reporter that Negroes would not be accepted into Stuyvesant Town, there was a storm of protest followed by a lawsuit charging that Metropolitan, in accepting tax subsidies, could not discriminate against Negroes. Though Metropolitan won by a 4–3 decision,[13] it lost public esteem. A local law shortly thereafter outlawed discriminatory practices in tax-exempt projects and some Negroes moved in.

Regulation against discrimination was not Metropolitan's only setback. To make up for rising building and operating costs, the company sought to increase rents by $3 a room per month. The tenants protested to the city's Board of Estimate, which had to pass on every increase. Although the board approved the increase, the company did not relish the publicity; and while the deal has proven profitable, it has not enhanced the company's public image, which is a vital asset in selling life insurance. Metropolitan undertook no similar projects thereafter.

Stuyvesant Town, nevertheless, demonstrated many things: that the presence of qualified Negroes in a project does not drive out the white tenants or endanger the company's investment; that urban renewal schemes are sound in sound cities and can be rentable and profitable investments for the big capital pools when the city assembles the land and clears the site. It also suggested that the proper formula for

[13] *Dorsey v. Stuyvesant Town,* 299 N.Y. 512 (July 19, 1949).

renewal was not tax exemption for high-income families but assemblage of the land coupled with a write-down in land cost. In this respect, it laid the groundwork for the new formula of 1949.[14]

While it demonstrated these things and the potentials for renewal investment, however, Stuyvesant Town chilled renewal interest by life insurance companies. Nor did the ensuing bureaucracy in the program's operation rekindle that interest. In their public relations bulletins, the life insurance companies vaunt their urban renewal projects as "pioneer" contributions to the nation but the companies have continued to prefer putting their cash mainly into effortless investments like stocks, bonds, and mortgages. That their interest is vital to the program's success is certain. That it can be reinstated is less certain. It depends on whether a few brave companies can again be induced to venture in the right cities, whether they venture successfully, and whether the red tape that circulates in federal and municipal officialdom can be cut.

Renewal's Successes and Failures

Up to 1965, bidding on renewal projects remained selective and unspirited, except in cities where prime land was at a premium. In the 1960s, when New York had been experiencing a building boom, renewal contributed to it infinitesimally; and, in fact, it contributed very little to the construction activity in the nation's cities as a whole—less than 1.5 per cent of building in larger cities was on renewal sites.

[14] Metropolitan was not the only big insurance company to venture into slum areas. The University of Chicago launched a plan for improving the Hyde Park–Kenwood area surrounding it and the New York Life Insurance Company was persuaded to build a high-rise project on the 101-acre slum site. The project, built in a predominantly Negro area, has been predominantly Negro-occupied. A luxury unit has been opened nearby with monthly rentals of $53 a room, mostly for whites. It has not rented too well at that figure, although the insurance company expressed "great satisfaction with its investment." New York Life, however, has shown no interest in any renewal investments under the federal program (*Architectural Forum,* May 1962, p. 122). Equitable Life has built an office building complex in Pittsburgh, but it too has not ventured into renewal operations. Prudential has built an office building complex in Boston under a limited dividend scheme which enabled it to secure a reduced tax rate, but it has not undertaken any operations under the renewal statute.

There were successful projects in some cities but most were slow in coming off the drawing boards. Urban renewal was not drawing big capital into the cities or moving with the speed of suburban developments.

According to a progress report submitted to the Subcommittee on Housing of the Senate Committee on Banking and Currency in 1962, "Federal assistance in 81 urban renewal projects had been completed, 548 more were in various stages of project execution, and 384 were in the planning stage."[15] When federal assistance is "completed," it does not mean that all the projects have been finished—they may not even have been started and may even lack a sponsor. It means simply that the land has been disposed of and a financial settlement made by the federal government for its acquisition. Nor does being in "various stages of project execution" mean that buildings are going up. It means only that the plan and the loan contract have been approved. After considerable slum clearance, there was still little to show in new dwellings—a portion of the 81 at best.

Meanwhile Congress increased urban renewal appropriations from $2 billion to $4 billion. But there was no better assurance that these dollars would all be turned into brick and mortar. On the contrary, considerable brick and mortar may have been reduced to rubble with no prospect of new brick and mortar going up in its place. Applications for federal assistance were still coming in, particularly from the larger cities, but from one-quarter to one-third of the projects applied for by cities had been canceled at one time or another.

If there was a lag in project progress, there was no lag in the number of press releases. Projects throughout the country were announced in glowing copy accompanied by pictures showing how the new sections would look. But this only encouraged existing owners to stop making repairs and speeded the removal of tenants anticipating eviction. Some sites were eventually cleared by bulldozers, some were eroded by the elements. New Brunswick, New Jersey, which had filed its plans for a shopping center, hotel, and office building in the early

---

[15] *Progress Report on Federal Housing Programs, Subcommittee on Housing,* Senate Committee on Banking and Currency, 87th Cong., 2nd Sess., 1962, p. 77.

stages of the program, cleared a ten-acre site, but for years it vainly sought a developer to build on it. Cambridge leveled a slum site for an office building but found no bidders until at long last the Massachusetts Institute of Technology helped obtain a friendly sponsor. It soon became clear that an earmarking of funds for renewal was no guarantee that projects would be built. It might nevertheless mean that the site might go into decay or that the tenants would be ousted.

As amplified later, urban renewal has contributed some important improvements, but with all the favorable financing and the excellent depreciation factor, why has the program been so slow in breaking through?

A basic obstacle has been the poor general condition of the older cities. When the city is in trouble, all its problems—slums, racial questions, and population losses—beset the projects as they do the city itself. Where urban renewal advances, it is because the city is sound and because economic conditions justify investment. In these cases, urban renewal supplies the builder with an assembled plot of cheap land and with good financing. But where the city has no market of upper-income tenants, urban renewal projects will find no market either. If there is a market for one or two high-rental projects, one or two renewal projects will succeed and the rest will falter or fail. If, while the renewal negotiations are taking their tedious course, a private builder decides to put up buildings for a similar group, he will absorb the potential renters on whom the renewer counted for his profits.

This situation should surprise no one. Larger cities are losing population or, what is more serious, losing masses of higher-income people and gaining those of lower income. They are gaining a minority group whose ascent to higher income is far more sluggish. Some demand for multiple dwellings may be expected from a thin market of renters, from elderly people returning to the city, from those partial to the city, from single people, couples, and others who want to be closer to their work, shops, or friends. But in a waning city, this is a limited market at best.

The City as Joint Venturer

Red tape is, of course, indigenous to the urban renewal fabric. But compounding the trouble are the mixed motives of the cities. Most would like to see fine buildings cover their slum sites. They would like them tenanted by good taxpayers (mostly white and high income) on as little land coverage as possible—but with as much brick as possible to yield the maximum tax revenues. The more brick, however, the more apartments will be thrown on the market and, if the market is thin, so will be the renewer's prospects.

Selling the land at too low a cost will burden the city with a proportionately higher contribution toward the land subsidy. Some cities, therefore, jack up the asking price for the land. Too often cities also seek the highest and best use for the land, i.e., "that use which may reasonably be expected to produce the maximum net return to the land over a given period of time." These requirements force the builder to pierce the vertical frontier and flood the market with unrentable units. Social objectives and the real needs of communities are too often pushed into the background. Nor are the sites chosen always the kind that guarantee the high rentals projected. One reason is that minorities—Negroes, Puerto Ricans, and Mexicans—have often moved into the slum site at or near the city centers. When ousted they tend to move toward the edge of the renewal sites. The schools then fill up with the children of the minorities. Condemning these areas as well as the initial site may again produce a project too big for the rental market to absorb. The outlying area with its all-white school offers the builder less of a problem. Why, says the builder, should I buy into the central city's headaches? Some of these headaches are the following:

Interdepartmental squabbles and local pressures and politics often make negotiations difficult. Local taxes may take as much as 20 per cent of a project's gross rent and often more. To sweeten a deal, a builder may be promised a low assessment, a zone change, or a relaxed building code provision, only to have a succeeding mayor renege on the promise. Boston, whose tax rate has soared to 10 per cent of assessed value, agreed to fix the tax on renewal projects at 20 per cent of rent for the forty-year life of the first mortgage, but the legality of the arrangement is by no means assured. Another problem is relocation. The housing authority may be unwilling to give priorities to the displaced tenants, or the hard-core tenants may hang on, while the builder's money is tied up and his overhead goes on. The long span between the award and the completion of negotiations with the Urban Renewal Administration and with FHA and FNMA, as well as the delays of site clearance, may arouse unexpected pressures from local citizen groups, adjoining owners, displacees, and others. It takes at least two years to get a project into the preparatory stage for execution, another three before it is put up for bid. Clearance may take another two years. Meanwhile, problems of clearance, increased building costs, a sagging market, a strike by one of the building trades, and a host of other frustrations may crop up.

A device adopted by some cities has been the design contest in which redevelopers are required to compete on the basis of the "best plan" if not the best land price as well. As much as $20,000 can be spent for designing a moderate size project and $75,000 for a large one. The spirited competition for San Francisco's Golden Gate project cost some of the losers a ransom. Bidding was active because the sites were prime, the city sound for investment, and the prospect of gain substantial. But similar contests on less important projects are not worth the trouble, and there is no assurance that even San Francisco would again enjoy a rush of entries for another design contest. One renewer says, "An urban renewal design contest winner is the one architectural possibility which will not be built." In other words, the winning sponsor will thereafter try to redesign the project to more economical specifications. The city may or may not agree. If it agrees, it is being unfair to the other competitors; if it disagrees, the sponsor may drop his deposit.

Another discouragement is that in a nation better known for third-ward politics than for good taste, a truly meritorious design will be rejected in favor of a routine plan submitted by a developer with better than routine political connections. This happened in Denver, where the renewal agency rejected by a margin of one vote a brilliant design prepared by Eugene D. Sternberg. The rejected drawings were promptly sought by the University of Colorado's School of Architecture for exhibition.

Sometimes renewers have spent time and money because they thought the best design would win, only to discover that the renewal agency was primarily concerned with getting the highest price for the land. In Santa Monica, California, the renewal authority let it be known that project design would be the main criterion. But instead of acting when sealed bids were submitted, the authority asked the four top bidders to bid again against each other. One developer who had spent $50,000 on a plan said he would never enter a design contest again.

Spending money to prepare a bid is not unusual in ordinary public works operations. A bidder figures he will land about one job in four and charges the expense of estimating to general overhead. When he wins a public works bid, he knows he has the job. This is not always the case in urban renewal. Winning the bid may be only the first round in a renegotiation skirmish.

Where there are no design contests, sites may be sold to the highest bidder by sealed or open bid with or without a minimum or the sale may be negotiated. In other cases, the local renewal agency will fix the land price as well as prescribe the design criteria. This is good for the city if there are bidders. But in the long run, the critical questions for the bidders are how little cash will be in the deal and whether the project will rent at a profit. If the specifications are too onerous, the cost and cash investment will be too high and the prospective tenants scarce.

Nor does winning the bid always mean the project will be built. As little as 1 per cent of project cost has been sufficient to bind the city, while the bidder can often stall for months before he is called upon to excavate. Meanwhile he seeks his best mortgage, peddles his contract for a profit, or looks for a backer. If all this fails, he defaults with only a nominal loss. Only the dummy corporation that signed the contract can be sued.

The bureaucratic routines that discourage responsible sponsors are not always the fault of the city. Federal officialdom is dispersed into a number of agencies, each with a stake and each with its own ideas on value, rent levels, design, and location. There are also separate opinions on whether the program is "workable" and whether relocation requirements have been complied with. (Federal interest in relocation too often rises and falls with the pressures and protests of local citizen groups.) Federal and local estimates of a project's value are apt to differ. And when the builder has little or no cash investment above the insured mortgage, the appraisal process is little more than the transposition of psychic equities into vested illusions. Rent projections may be valid when made but unrealistic by the time all the approvals have been secured, the negotiations completed, and the project built. Yet the federal officials who assume the responsibility cannot be blamed entirely; they must face the criticism of Congress if a project fails. Always looming in the background is the General Accounting Office, ready to criticize after the fact, and since criticism is easier when the responsibility for decision has been elsewhere, the GAO has been fearless and unsparing.

Problem Projects

Each city has had special problems, just as each project has special characteristics. In a city like New York, where 80 per cent of the people are tenants, moderate- and even high-rental housing may be a fair risk—provided there is no overbuilding. New York City also gives partial tax exemption as well as low interest loans to limited dividend projects in urban renewal areas. In these instances, the owner can offer apartments well below the market rents. Unlike New York City, most other cities are unwilling to give tax concessions or float bonds to make some of their renewal financing attractive. Nor is every city as good a hunting ground for profit as are New York, Chicago, or San Francisco.

If the renewer succeeds in getting a cleared site in a choice area in a choice city for which new tenants will clamor, and if he can get the site at a bargain price as well as with a full mortgage, he will reap a bonanza for his efforts. But there are flops as well as bonanzas. Here are a few examples of the flops:

Five highly touted Cleveland projects were among the first to get FHA insurance commitments under Section 220. Despite civic backing and the ardent hopes that prompted them, all the projects got into trouble. Four years passed before one of the projects was set to go. Thereafter, two years were consumed in clearance and nearly another two years before financing procedures were completed. The city's representation that "a vast and able-to-pay reservoir of prospective tenants already exists" was never fulfilled, and the FHA market survey that supported this proved overoptimistic from the beginning. When the new buildings were completed, moreover, prospective renters were discouraged by the surrounding slums. With continuing vacancies and tenant turnover plaguing the projects, some of the owners ran out of money. Repairs stopped. Whites would not move into the projects when they saw most of the first units rented to Negroes, while Negroes went on a rent strike and picketed one of the projects because it was not "integrated." High taxes took 20 per cent of gross rentals compared to less than 13 per cent in the outlying areas, impairing the competitive aspects of in-city investment.

In Cincinnati, Reynolds Aluminum Company built 322 moderately priced units in an old Negro slum area for cooperative occupancy. Required downpayments were as low as $500 and monthly maintenance costs $88. But selling the co-ops was as hard as selling long dresses in a short-dress season. After prolonged advertising and hawking, only 50 per cent were sold. The reasons given were that the project still had a slum stigma as well as a school problem; Cincinnati's vacancy ratio was high; even Negro customers wanted neighborhoods with higher prestige value than the Reynolds' job offered. Reynolds' executives blamed the high land prices,[16] but the main snag

---

[16] David P. Reynolds, Executive Vice President of the company, was quoted in 1961 as saying: "The task of rebuilding and revitalizing decayed urban areas is large enough to absorb the managerial and productive energies of a large

was that the site was too near a slum and that the market for the product did not exist.

A Detroit project designed by Mies Van der Rohe failed to attract buyers for its houses, and they had to be rented to help pay carrying costs. When even renters balked, the project defaulted. Scheuer's rental project in Sacramento remained only 50 per cent rented more than a year after completion, and Marvin Gilman's Baltimore project experienced similar troubles. In Philadelphia, Reynolds met slow renting, and some of the other Philadelphia projects were meeting a similar fate.

In November 1963, FHA analyzed 89 projects on urban renewal sites which had reported all of their units ready for occupancy by December 31, 1961. Of these projects, there were 86 rental projects financed by FHA (Section 220) mortgage insurance and three projects financed under Section 221.[17] Thirty per cent of the Section 220 projects containing a third of the insured rental units experienced such poor occupancy as to require mortgage modification or foreclosure.

Three projects were in default, though vacancies were less than 7 per cent, indicating that rent levels were too low to support carrying charges. One project under Section 221 which had all of its 286 units ready for occupancy by April 1959 had 31 per cent in vacancies; another, with 154 units, had 57 per cent in vacancies.

Among the reasons given by HHFA officials for the poor occupancy record were that commitments were made without proper market analyses and that there was competition with private FHA (Section 207) projects—one arm of the government was competing with another in the same areas.

The reasons for defaults most frequently cited by the local insuring offices were "rents too high" and "poor surroundings." But among

---

segment of American business. . . . These are the reasons behind Reynolds participating in urban renewal. Our success in this program over the past two years indicates that we will continue and expand our urban renewal operations" (*Federal Bar Journal*, Summer 1961). Whether this will be true remains to be seen.

[17] Section 220 has been liberalized by Congress so that it could become a more practical tool for urban renewal. It provides the builder with an insured mortgage amounting to 90 per cent of replacement cost.

other reasons given by HHFA officials were that the marketability studies were undertaken by the local agencies, who were inclined to overestimate prospects. FHA verification of the rent projections and of rentability too often came after the land had been cleared and sold. It should, of course, not be expected, when all public commitments have been made, tenants ousted, and the land cleared, that FHA will be inclined to say: "We made a mistake; let's not go ahead." An empty tract in the center of a city can be a burial ground for political prospects. Federal mortgage insurance based on premature studies or to fulfill enforced commitments is hardly sound business.

The biggest reason for the large quota of duds was conceded by Neal J. Hardy, formerly FHA administrator: "You cannot keep doing urban renewal at $60 a room. . . . There is simply too thin a market in most cities for it."[18] In some cities, the market may be thin with rentals half that. With the rental vacancy rate in central cities averaging more than 6 per cent in the 1960s, and with many of these vacancies in the higher rental ranges, any new project at high rentals is a wildcat speculation.

Another reason for the failure of some projects is the poor location of the sites. Most of those relocated enter nearby housing. If they are Negroes, as most are, the neighborhood and the school are viewed by white renters as "low-class." A good school with good teachers may make the difference between success and failure, but cities are often too poor to pay the price. The renter who takes a five-room apartment in the central city may have to add to his cost the tuition fee he pays a private school. In a suburb he is more apt to find a good free school.

Still another reason for defaults is the top-heavy financing, which enforces top-heavy rents and leaves little room for error or mishap. Moreover, the tax assessor is too often influenced by FHA's appraisal and is loath to assess the property at less than the 90 per cent mortgage. Rental projects built ten years ago at lower costs are more attractively priced and may offer better accommodations.

The percentage of home ownership has been going up since the

[18] *Architectural Forum*, July 1962, p. 103.

1940s, and easier FHA terms have not always made the multiple dwelling competitive. Within a twenty-minute ride from the city center, a home buyer can often acquire his own ranch house or split-level with a 10 per cent downpayment. Large apartments and town houses in renewal projects that might offer competition to suburban homes are costly and have generally experienced renting trouble. The main market in cities is for the cheaper compact unit for the small family, and even this market is most often thin.

Most cities and some developers think a low land cost guarantees a sound investment. But too frequently, the city after writing the land cost down, restricts the amount of land that may be built on and the benefits of the lower land cost is then lost to the developer.

To keep prices down, investment minimal, and carrying charges low, some developers have omitted essential nondwelling facilities or services which could make projects more attractive. Rooms are not always soundproof, ceilings are too low, closets few, and standards minimal. While better building might assure solvency in the long run, the developer with a nominal investment is not looking to prospects ten years ahead. The project must pay right away. Too many operators, moreover, are capital-short and cannot carry the property during the tough renting period.

It is not intended by this somber summary to write off the renewal program as a fiasco but rather to point up that sick cities infect their real estate and that urban renewal possesses no special immunity when it exposes itself to the cities' sores. Nor can a few renewal projects built over a city's slum areas be the magic potion for restoring the city to health. A 90 to 100 per cent mortgage may induce a renewer to stake his pittance; and, despite the city's predicament, he might win the gamble. But while it will renew the builder's fortunes, it will not renew the city's vitality.

In short, the large number of misadventures in renewal only emphasizes the large number of ailing cities. The harsh levies cities impose reflect their anxiety to garner more revenues for their sinking treasuries. The delays and impositions by federal officials reflect their fear of criticism and their efforts to keep the program going while trying to avoid defaults in situations where defaults may be inevitable. The large number of vacancies in projects reflect not the lack of a market for dwellings in cities but the lack of a program that will make the units available to the waiting market of moderate and lower income families whose needs are being ignored. Until renewal is directed toward providing housing at realistic rents and renewing cities instead of renewing a few slum or blighted areas, it will continue to show an abnormal quota of failures and a continuing indifference of responsible investors to its offerings.

The Rosier Side
of Renewal Investment

IF THERE HAVE BEEN STRIKE-OUTS in renewal, there have also been hits. Urban renewal is a gamble for small stakes with a fortune if the cards fall right and a small loss if they fall wrong. With government financing, the stake is generally only about 3 per cent for the risk taker (about the same percentage as the house gets on a Reno crap table). For the shrewd builder the money staked may be nothing at all.

According to *Architectural Forum*, it works as follows:

... the builder buys an urban renewal site for, say $1 million, and plans a $10 million apartment project. He gets a Section 220, FHA-insured mortgage for something around $10.8 million (90 percent of replacement value of land and buildings, plus a 10 percent builder's profit). This leaves him with only $200,000 of his own capital in the project. And the potential for gains on this small equity investment is tremendous: After deducting interest (say $567,000 at 5¼ percent) and mortgage amortization (at, say 1½ percent annually, or about $162,000) from an estimated net income before depreciation of 10 percent, or $1.1 million, the builder-sponsor is left with pretax income of $371,000. After corporate income tax, the net income is about $178,000—a yield of almost 90 percent on his cash investment. To top it all off, the builder can, and generally does, claim depreciation at an accelerated rate on the value of the building and thus can "shelter" his taxable income to the point where, in the early years of the project at least, his tax is almost nothing.[1]

[1] July 1962, p. 103.

If the deal works out this way, the renewer should never be poor again. And if deals were presented to FHA or FNMA with these lush profits, the rumble of scandal would be heard again on Capitol Hill. But there is never any certainty that the rent roll will materialize as expected or that operating costs will be precisely as hoped. The charges that can be estimated accurately are interest, amortization, and FHA fees. Those that can be approximated within reason are building costs, taxes (particularly when agreed to), payrolls, and other operating expenses. The big "maybe" is the rent and vacancy schedule. A projection must be made to the federal agency, and the renewer will present it roughly as shown in Table 3.

On paper, the projected net return of $15,300 is small. But the figures as presented to the federal officials are not the figures the builder puts down on his confidential pad. Behind both sets of figures lie a host of intangibles which will tell whether the renewer's fingers have the golden touch or will be burned.

The projected building cost will normally be more than actual cost. All or most of the builder's and sponsor's building profit of 10 per

TABLE 3

ESTIMATE OF PROJECT COSTS

Land improvements	$ 40,000
Construction cost	3,500,000
Fees: Builders' general overhead (1.74%)	62,500
Architect's fee at 4.5%	160,000
	$3,762,500
Carrying charges and financing	
Two years at 5¼%	
Interest, plus taxes, insurance, FHA insurance, FHA examination fee, FHA inspection fee, financing expense, title and recording	390,000
	$4,152,500
Legal and organizational	100,000
Builder's and sponsor's profit at 10%	425,250
Total estimated development cost excluding cost of land	$4,677,750
Land purchase price	200,000
Total	$4,877,750

TABLE 3—*Continued*

Less mortgage	4,388,975
Equity required	$ 488,775
Working capital	88,000
Total estimated settlement requirements	$ 576,775

ESTIMATE OF ANNUAL OPERATING EXPENSE

Administrative and management	$ 15,000
Operating expenses (i.e., lighting and power, elevator maintenance, fuel, janitor supplies, lighting and miscellaneous, water, gas garbage removal, payroll)	$ 70,000
Total	85,000
Replacement reserve	14,000
Total operating expense	$ 99,000
(Total operating expense per room)	105
Projected income	$510,000
Less vacancies 7%	35,700
Gross income expected	$474,300
Operating expense $105 per room	$ 99,000
Taxes	64,000
Total operating expense and taxes	$163,000
Cash available for debt service ($474,300 less $163,000)	311,300
Annual fixed charges:	
Interest at 5¼%	230,000
Amortization 1%	44,000
Mortgage insurance	22,000
Total annual fixed charge	$296,000
Cash available for income taxes, corporate taxes, dividends, or surplus ($311,300 less $296,000)	$ 15,300

cent (or $425,250) will be pocketed. This leaves the renewer with a cash investment of only about $151,525 (i.e., $576,775 for total settlement requirement less $425,250). To this the renewer adds some extra outlays for actual building costs (probably 3 per cent at best), the FNMA discount fee, working capital, and a few other extras. On the other hand he will make savings on architect's fees (some renewers do their own architecture and some renewers are their own subcontractors), and perhaps on some other items. If he is a shrewd builder and holds costs to a minimum, he should have an investment of $150,000 or less, which is a tiny pivot around which to twirl a $5 million investment and a $474,300 rent roll.

The projected net return, which determines whether he has a good or a bad investment, is also on the conservative side. In addition to the builder's and sponsor's fee and the saving on the architect's fee, the items which are overestimated and which could offer the renewer three times the $15,300 estimated as his net profit are the following:

1. *Vacancies.* If the project is sound, the vacancies should be no more than 2 to 3 per cent. This would mean an additional net profit of $20,400–$25,500 a year. (Of course, if the project rents badly, the vacancies may be 7 per cent or more.)

2. *Operating expenses.* The $105 per room is an outside figure. A saving of $5000–$7000 ($5–$6 a room) should be expected.

3. *Replacement reserves* are excessive for a new building. Repairs included in maintenance should cover most of the essential replacements, particularly in the first ten years of operation. (The reserves, however, will be held in escrow.)

4. *Administration and management.* A saving can be made here, particularly with self-management.

5. *Taxes.* These are usually overestimated to hold down the net profit shown. The builder will usually try to get a firm commitment from the city for a smaller tax than he projects to FHA. Whether he is successful depends on the official disposition and the competition.

Adding the $15,300 listed as profit to the savings, the net return in a sound and rentable project should be closer to $50,000. A normal transaction showing $50,000 a year should be worth at least $500,000. The real profit in the deal lies in two additional items, i.e., the possibility of a higher rent schedule and the depreciation item. The depreciation item is a highly advantageous factor, as is shown later. It can make the deal worthwhile even if it shows an annual loss.

Even if the property pays expenses but no profit throughout the life of the loan, the developer can create a latifundium worth $5–$10 million as the mortgage is paid off. As one renewer put it, "I'm build-ing an estate. Land does not depreciate and the buildings may appre-ciate as well as depreciate."

Lastly, if the rent schedule warrants a rent roll of $565,000 instead of $510,000, the deal is worth at least an additional $500,000. The total value above the mortgage would then be well over $1 million. At the proper time and when the mortgage has been reduced by the amortization, the renewer is set to refinance the deal with a conven-tional mortgage and free himself from FHA restrictions.

If the project is rentable, there may be other pleasant potentials:

A few cities have given tax concessions in one form or another to sweeten the deal and meet the rental market. Examples are Boston, St. Louis, and New York (for moderate-income housing). Statutory tax concessions are also possible in Michigan, Minnesota, and Wis-consin, among others, in the form of assessment freezes or tax relief.

One of the recent inducements permitted (by Paragraph 9, added to Section 220 of the Housing Act of 1959) is the allowance to the developer of "non-dwelling facilities" or stores. This can prove highly advantageous if the project is well located. Stores may be local retail shops catering only to the project's captive tenants (a grocery store, drugstore, etc.), or they may consist of a substantial one-story develop-ment with a whole series of shops drawing the custom of the entire neighborhood. If the site is in a good downtown area, ten stores with a net rent of $30,000 may add a value of $300,000 to the project's net worth. The builder moreover can build the stores at considerably less per square foot than the apartments.

A redeveloper who builds small units and common service rooms for the aging may also see the opportunity of converting the property into a hotel. While hotel-building is taboo for FHA assistance, FHA can-not veto the conversion after the loan is refinanced.

An adroit developer may build a single section of a project, and if it rents build the balance. If the renting is dubious, he may sell or abandon the other sections of the project. Sacramento, Boston, and New York all have projects that were buildable in sections. Sometimes FHA insists on such sectional building.

Finally, if the rental market is soft and the renewer feels that he can attain his stabilized income only by renting below the market, he can apply for financing under Section 221(d)(3) or 221(d)(4). Here he may have to sacrifice some of his prospects of speculative gain but, without much rentability risk, he can realize an adequate builder's profit and perhaps something more.[2]

A word should be added on projects that go wrong. In conventional mortgaging, a default spells foreclosure, but a government mortgagee will be lenient, will put off principal payments, and may indulge the default for years. This gives the renewer a chance to make a comeback without investing another dollar.

The Quest for Stabilized Income

Whether the renewer has made a hit or a miss hinges on what is known as "stabilized income." This is the settled income after the project has been sufficiently exposed to the rental market.

A hit is assured if the right cities can be induced to select the right sites. The sites which will capture the renewer's interest will not be in the deep slum areas but in the better central sections. They may be the city's gray areas, i.e., the well-located sections that are a bit frayed but still strategic, or they may have a cluster of poor minority residents whose presence is viewed as a challenge to the section's status and whose removal might elevate it. In real estate parlance good sites are called "merchandise." When a contiguous parcel of land in a sound area can be put together into a single parcel and acquired at low cost, the renewer has a piece of merchandise. If it is a commercial site and he can get a well-rated department store as his main tenant, he will have little difficulty getting other tenants. He then has a "packaged deal." He can sell all or a share in it at a handsome profit before he has laid a brick.

Here is where the city's mixed motives in urban renewal are brought face to face with the market's hard realities. The city would like to see its slum cleared, but there must also be a bidder ready to build

[2] For an exposition of 221(d)(3) and 221(d)(4), see Appendix A, p. 127, below.

or the city will have a humiliating lot on its hands. The city therefore becomes as much involved in the real estate business as the
renewer. It must come up with a paying transaction for the builder
if it is to be paying for the city.

This seeking after the good, sound, stabilized income has more
recently made the socially informed urban renewal program into
something more like a run-of-the-mill commercial transaction. If the
slum (that festering cancer responsible for crime, disease, delinquency,
etc.) is well located, it is good real estate. It will bring bidders and
gain federal or private mortgage funds. If the site is poorly located
or in a city with a weak market, it will be ignored by renewers.

The drive toward the better central sections and gray areas has
been a perversion of the urban renewal purpose, and as more and more
renewal projects fail, the better, not the worse, sites will be sought.
Since a slum or blighted area is any section which the renewal agency
designates as such, the site might be a slimy slum, a slim slum, or no
slum at all. The existence of the slum is no longer the true reason for
eminent domain, for displacement, for federal loans at low interest or
for land subsidies. The main question is whether the section is good
enough for a high-rental project. Public purpose is now too often
private purpose. Similarly, the federal government has steadily become more interested in producing a sound real estate operation than
clearing a slum or improving the housing conditions of the poor. With
a whole inventory of unsold land in cities, the new drive—if urban
renewal is to go on—is and will be for the good lands, not the bad
lands.

The Blight That's Right

The blessings of good site location are best illustrated by examples
in three cities with good real estate markets.

Kips Bay, on Second Avenue and Twenty-ninth Street, New York
City, awarded to William Zeckendorf, was no more a slum than any
other patch of real estate in the mixed metropolitan belt that is
central Manhattan. New Yorkers are cosmopolitan—they do not mind

living in a section with old buildings, provided the location they live in is central. A sprinkling of slum miscellany in fact often counts as charm, and a nearby ghetto, if interesting and south of Negro Harlem, can be a magnet for the upper crust, not a repellent. Above Fourteenth Street up to the East Fifties, for example, is an extension of the Bowery, with decrepit rooming houses and cheap saloons catering to bums and panhandlers as well as to some decent poor and upper- and middle-class folk. But when the Third Avenue elevated went down, apartment houses rented briskly at $70 monthly per room and up, and land brought $50 a square foot or more.

The prime area for residences and stores in Manhattan lies along a short stretch of land from East Ninety-fifth Street to the business section in the East Fifties, then skips down to Chelsea and Greenwich Village, which are also prime rental markets. These areas hold some of the city's best real estate—they are accessible to subways and attract walk-to-work enthusiasts. The tribute for living here ranges from $65 monthly per room to as high as a $150,000 cash payment for a cooperative apartment on which the running costs may be $500 monthly thereafter.

Second Avenue and Twenty-ninth Street, the site of Kips Bay, lies within the boundaries of one of the sought-after sections in this general area. It is a blend of old tenements and stores—but only a ten-minute walk to the United Nations and another five minutes to the Grand Central office complex. Far from being a slum, the Kips Bay renewal site sold to Zeckendorf at a subsidized bargain was one which any developer would have bought without a write-down, and he would have put down hard cash on the line to boot. Far from having to depend on FHA for aid in financing, the developer could have gotten a liberal mortgage at low interest from almost any institution. Tenants could have been expected to bid for the new units as they might for apartments in the city's swankier sections. An investor would have had to pay $30 a square foot for a few initial sleepers and $80 to $100 a square foot for the holdouts—if they were willing to sell at all.

Urban renewal's biggest blessing, however, is its power to assemble

land at market prices. An assembled plot is worth far more than the
sum of the individual plot values. Another blessing is the ability
to oust tenants. Some tenants in Kips Bay had long leases; some had
built up commercial good will worth more than the land and buildings.
But for renewal's condemnation power, landlords might hold out for
too high a price. Or they might refuse to sell at any price. (One reason
might be that a forced profit activates a 25 per cent federal tax on
the unwillingly realized capital gain.) Urban renewal in these cases
is the official juggernaut that overrides these personal problems. It
substitutes the public decision for the private and assigns the private
property to another against the will of the first. And so Zeckendorf
got the Kips Bay site not only all cleared and all assembled but at a
mark-down price to boot.

New York's Washington Square South was always a strategically
located area and no slum at all in the real estate sense. The old
buildings that abutted on Washington Square North and West had been
inhabited by the city's Brahmins, writers, businessmen, and professionals who could afford rentals of $150 to $600 a month. (President
Franklin D. Roosevelt, for example, had leased an apartment a
stone's throw from the "slum" at 37 Washington Square West for
occupation upon his retirement.) A social worker would be hard put
to find a single symptom of slum life or an abnormal ratio of disease
or infant mortality. He would have been more apt to find a score of
real estate operators trying to buy into the area, and a long waiting
list of other social workers looking for one- and two-room studio
apartments at $70 a room per month. Nevertheless, a sixteen-story
fireproof apartment house, some good loft buildings, and a new six-
story elevator building were all condemned as slums and were wrecked
to make way for an urban renewal complex composed of a seventeen-
story private development and an extension for New York University.
After acquiring the sixteen-story apartment house, the university first
sought to reoccupy it as it stood but was restrained from doing so by
the Rent Administration. NYU got the site it wanted at about a fifth
of its market value.[3] In back of the NYU portion of the site, two new

[3] No one else could bid on it because the condition of purchase was that it be
used for "educational purposes."

sixteen-story units were erected by an operator on the remainder of the site. Rents run upward of $65 monthly per room.

Villagers question whether the change has been for the better, and most say it was for the worse. Old buildings, whether lofts or residences, have always supplied the Village with the convertible inventory that provides it with its coffee houses, restaurants, off-Broadway theaters, artist studios, and its general diversity. The lofts also supplied many jobs. The new buildings will be unchanging and have added little to the neighborhood's value. Instead of completing the third unit of the plot, the developer sold its still undeveloped land to NYU for dormitories and faculty residences. In 1963 the developer also sold the two completed sixteen-story buildings to the university for $4 million above a mortgage of $20 million. The NYU dorms will rise thirty stories into the spaces Villagers always wanted to reserve for their morning squints.

One of the aspects of the transaction which Villagers still gripe about is that the project had hardly been approved when the Planning Commission zoned down the whole nearby area to preserve the modest four- to six-story heights of existing buildings. In short, the city made private owners keep their buildings low—but it subsidized the urban renewer's ascent to forbidden altitudes. As if this were not enough, the city sold part of University Place to the renewer, so that he could build his tall buildings over the street on a superblock. Thus a main artery was forever closed to the public. When the street disappeared, heavy traffic was diverted to Lower Fifth Avenue, one block west, feeding into crowded Washington Square Park. Robert Moses and the Planning Commission then proposed cutting a wide road through the park. But by this time the outraged Villagers were shocked by the shenanigans and blocked the move.

There were other renewal sites in New York City that were neither slum-dreary nor blight-gray but which were nevertheless consigned to the wreckers for urban renewal. Penn Station South, Cadman Plaza in Brooklyn Heights (ten minutes from Wall Street), and Chelsea (adjoining Greenwich Village) are examples. A site in one of the city's costliest sections, i.e., the downtown Wall Street area has also been branded a slum. It will be resold to accommodate the New York Stock Exchange and other enterprises.

New York City's Coliseum site of 6.32 acres was hardly a slum within the recognized definition of the word. It was located in Columbus Circle, one of the city's most valuable areas. The former chief architect of the city's Housing Authority testified that only 10 per cent of the tenements in the area were substandard or insanitary, and that only 2 per cent of the total area was a slum. Most of the tenements in the section had sanitary toilet facilities, running water, heating, ventilation, safety devices against fire, and facilities generally suitable for pleasant living; there were minor building violations on some; and four-fifths of the site's value was represented by parking lots and nonresidential structures, including a 22-story bank building assessed at $1,500,000. Yet the area was condemned as a slum and the prevailing court opinion ratified it though conceding that "none of the buildings are as noisome or dilapidated as those described in Dickens' novels or Thomas Burke's Limehouse stories of the London slums."[4] There was nothing it could do about it, said the court "unless every act and decision of other departments of government is subject to revision by the courts." Nothing short of "corruption or fraud" could stay the city's hand, the court continued. A trial of the slum issue was refused. The dissenting opinion, commenting on the majority view, said: "It does very well to cite Dickens' novels or Thomas Burke's 'Limehouse' stories of the London slums of other days, but these have nothing to do with condemning the Manufacturer's Trust Building in this slum area assessed at $1,500,000 in order to make way for a Coliseum—a laudable object, to be sure, but not one whose connection with slum clearance is so clear as to be taken for granted without a trial."[5]

Los Angeles shows a similar leaning toward sound and buildable plots which eminent domain can assemble for the site-hungry renewer, with higher taxes as an important by-product. Los Angeles hums with activity and teems with builders calling for land. Bunker Hill, Los

---

[4] *Kaskel* v. *Impellitteri*, 306 N.Y. 73 (October 23, 1953).
[5] *Ibid.*, p. 83.

Angeles' main renewal site, adjoins its office and hotel section, which is also the site of many public buildings. The Bunker Hill site is ripe for private developments, but rises sharply from the busy section nearby to a clifflike neighborhood above, reached by a quaint funicular. The bluff is inhabited largely by a Spanish-speaking minority and by elderly folk in modest, well-located houses. These people have proudly adorned the bluff with landscaping, giving it the welcome appearance of a stabilized neighborhood amid a convulsive, automobile-dominated city. Los Angeles boasts few such anchored settlements. The only argument that can be made for acquiring the site is that the existing use is not the best use. It is, in other words, just another good piece of real estate which urban renewal will more intensively develop. It will also yield the city much more in taxes and make more room for a developer and his tenants.

Diamond Heights in San Francisco, composed of 325 acres, was only 15 per cent occupied, mostly with small houses set on a hill that commanded one of the most beautiful views in the city. Nevertheless the claim was sustained that it was "blighted."

If any decision bridged the gap between the real slum and what urban renewal called a slum, the Diamond Heights decision[6] did so. The area was a strategic and a valuable piece of real estate. It was ripe for residential, institutional, and commercial use, was located only twelve minutes from the center of town, and would probably have been redeveloped or rehabilitated in time through the normal processes of the market. San Francisco's Redevelopment Agency left little doubt as to one of the motives for the acquisition. Diamond Heights and its two other projects, it said, were expected in a "tax sense" to make

. . . redevelopment good municipal "business." The three projects under way promise an annual tax increase conservatively estimated at $5,000,000 above preredevelopment levels. This is an increase of nine times the present tax return, computed at current rates. It should be clear that notwithstanding total net costs of approximately $23,000,000 (two-thirds

[6] *Redevelopment Company of San Francisco* v. *Hayes,* 122 Cal. App. 777 (January 26, 1954).

absorbed by the federal government and one-third defrayed mostly through the financing of public works by the city and county), it will not take San Francisco long to enjoy a rich "profit" from the redevelopment process.[7]

For its frankness in disclosing the city's real motivations in urban renewal, the redevelopment agency deserves a trophy.

The Golden Gate and Western Addition projects in San Francisco's old market area are also in the city's hub. Golden Gate is in the downtown office section and though blighted is a prime real estate site for any redeveloper. This is also true of the Western Addition. The same impulse toward prime real estate is also noticeable in Chicago, Louisville, Philadelphia, Sacramento, New Haven, and booming San Juan.

The courts have sanctioned these takings of private property with the deference with which William Jennings Bryan once defended Scripture. If the official word is that the whale swallowed Jonah, it is so, and if the official word is that a section is a slum or blighted, that is so, too.

The situation points up one of the dilemmas of the renewal program. Concededly bad sites will not rent; good sites will rent better but do not require clearance and redevelopment as much as do the slums. Should the condemnation power be used to assemble only the better sites while the slum sites are left to fester? This was hardly the intent of Congress when it enacted the program. But the dilemma is implicit in the present renewal formula. It cannot be claimed that the selection of better sites is unjustified in every instance, since there are cases where a section should be put to a more appropriate use and where the larger interests of the citizenry justify it (the numerous projects abutting on a downtown area, for example). But in these cases the public purpose should be frankly stated as being replanning, not slum clearance, and where land is taken for replanning as distinguished from the traditional public purposes, the whole compensation formula must be revised to accord better compensation to owners and lessees and better treatment to those who are evicted.

As for inducing builders to invest real cash in slum sections, they

[7] *Annual Report,* San Francisco Redevelopment Agency, 1960, p. 7.

will not and cannot be expected to do so unless the new project will pay, and this calls for a subsidy formula for the slum families that will make it possible for them to pay the rents the renewer requires. These proposals and the justification for them will be elaborated in the chapter that follows.

Appreciating Depreciation

The development of the United States has been nudged and shaped by a variety of drives. "Forty acres and a mule" described the foray into the frontier. "To plant more cotton to buy more land to plant more cotton" spurred the development of the South and Southwest. From the days of President Harding through the 1950s, "front money and a contact" became the cry of the new crop of budding or busted entrepreneurs in quest of the jackpot. Though the slogan has not yet been coined, the entrepreneurial drive in our day is being conditioned by tax avoidance. Freedom from taxation is emerging as a fifth freedom for American enterprise.

The term "20 per cent tax free," "capital gains deal," "depletion allowance," "deductibles," "high depreciation factor" and "tax shelter" dominate the language of business and shape its incentives. The amount of the takeout now counts for the small fry as it does for the Leviathan.

With a tax system that lops off 52 per cent of corporate profit and up to 91 per cent of a tycoon's annual intake,[8] entrepreneurs have focused on areas yielding the highest return that can actually be pocketed. Big deductions are more sought after than big salaries. "Net after taxes" has replaced "gross earnings" as the mark of the sound venture. The right choice of the depreciation rate, i.e., "straight line," "accelerated" ("double declining balance"), or "sum of the digits" may make the difference between big gains, little gains, or no gains at all.

The tax bracket and the tax shelter have affected the real estate investor as they have the financier, stock speculator, and oil driller.

---

[8] Reduced for 1965 to 48 per cent for corporations and a maximum of 70 per cent for individuals.

A real estate deal that shows a continuing deficit might still be worth a fortune. This is true of an urban renewal deal as it is of other real estate.

Depreciation and Urban Renewal

Like any commodity with a limited life, buildings depreciate, yield to the elements, or grow obsolescent. A building's allotted duration varies with the type of structure and equipment (about 2 per cent for the building and 4 per cent for equipment). The depreciation on building and equipment will average, say, 3 per cent. The owner may deduct such depreciation each year as an expense on his income tax form. The building may, of course, depreciate fully in less than thirty-three years or it may appreciate (if replacement value rises), but the 3 per cent approximation is a deduction the tax collector will generally allow.[9]

The more costly the building, the greater the deductible depreciation; and the larger the mortgage, the smaller the actual investment. This is where FHA rental and urban renewal operations work to the investor's advantage. The 90 per cent mortgage enables him to buy into a building with a big depreciation factor while committing very little cash. If the annual rate of allowable depreciation is greater than the annual cash profit, the owner can pocket the profit while taking a loss for income tax purposes. He will not only pay no tax on the cash profit earned, but he may charge his book loss against any other profits he may have made.[10]

To improve these prospects, the income tax law allows the builder

[9] When a building is fully depreciated, the owner may no longer deduct depreciation; if he sells the property, he usually pays a 25 per cent tax on what he gets above his capital cost, with the accumulated depreciation deducted from his cost. Depreciation affects the building owner as it does the owner of machinery, though machinery is accorded a shorter life and therefore a higher depreciation rate.

[10] Amortization of the mortgage, however, is not allowable as an expense. For the owner to have a higher annual cash profit, the amortization should be as low as possible. The FHA and FNMA long-term mortgage has helped considerably. Thus while the amortization rate may be 1–1½ per cent, the depreciation rate can be 3 per cent and sometimes more, leaving a good margin for depreciation over and above the annual repayments on the mortgage.

a choice of depreciation rates. He can deduct the depreciation on the building on a "straight line basis," i.e., a fixed rate of 3 per cent, or on a "double declining balance basis," i.e., taking a larger depreciation in the earlier years and a lower rate in the later years. Such an accelerated depreciation may be 5 per cent annually in the earlier years of a property having a forty-year life. Since FHA- and FNMA-assisted ventures involve heavy investments in depreciable buildings with small cash outlays over the mortgages, the accelerated depreciation allowance can run into hundreds of thousands annually. During the construction period and before depreciation starts running on the building, the redeveloper will also be able to deduct accruing interest on the mortgage advances, taxes, and other items.[11]

If handled deftly, for example, an investment of $487,000 for a taxpayer who was in the 75 per cent bracket would actually net a profit of 10 per cent annually while the book loss would range annually from $60,000 to $250,000. The investor should have recouped his whole investment through the tax shelter in the first three years and thereafter, as shown, have additional deductions until the end of the depreciation period.[12]

These are figures for an investor to conjure with. They have sparked intense interest in the urban renewal operation by those in high tax brackets. They have also encouraged entry into the urban renewal transaction of a new party, i.e., the renewer's financier or backer. The financier will arrange to buy the property during the period when the property shows a book loss. If he is in the 50 per cent tax bracket, the tax he avoids paying should, in a proper transaction, more than equal his cash investment in the first few years even if there is no cash profit.[13]

[11] These can also be capitalized and added to the depreciable cost if the developer so chooses. For the calculations in an actual case see Appendix B, p. 130, below.

[12] For the details of the transaction see Appendix C, p. 131, below. After 1964 the maximum tax rate was cut to 70 per cent for individuals, but the calculation would not be materially altered.

[13] The backer can make various arrangements with his builder-partner, such as buying 100 per cent of the deal at a stipulated profit (and thereby taking advantage of the whole depreciation) or buying the property and giving the redeveloper an option to repurchase a half-interest after the backer has taken advantage of his tax deductions.

In the earlier urban renewal deals, the renewer could not apply excess depreciation loss against taxable profits in other transactions, e.g., the corporate owner could only deduct depreciation from the profits of the specific transaction. But to induce more developers to venture, FHA thereafter made it possible to utilize these excess losses by allowing the property to be held in trust for individual beneficiaries. The "losses" then assumed real value for the high-income taxpayer in an urban renewal transaction.[14]

If the deal promises to be good (i.e., in an area where the rental market is good), the redeveloper has a bonanza and can get all the backing he needs. If it is a border-line deal, he must find someone with a steady taxable income who is willing to take a "flyer" with little to lose. If the deal has an outside chance of succeeding, investors can still be found to share the gamble with the renewer on the theory that if the investment is lost, the tax deductions will more than compensate for the lost cash investment. Even if the project is foreclosed after five years, the taxes saved in that period may equal the cash investment staked and lost.

It is wrong, however, to single out urban renewal investment as the only or even the main form of tax dodge. Its tax benefits exist in all big building operations and are a pittance compared to oil-well depletion allowances, tax-exempt bonds, and other escapes. Depreciation, moreover, is taken by all business enterprise. If it did not exist, the returns expected on FHA and urban renewal investment would have to be much greater to attract investors and builders.

In short, urban renewal, like other real estate deals, can be profitable or unprofitable. It may be unprofitable on paper and still be profitable to investors to whom the depreciation element is an asset. If it yields a cash profit and has a book loss as well (as almost all profitable deals do) it becomes "top merchandise."

[14] In New York transactions under the state's Mitchell-Lama law, a trust arrangement for individual beneficiaries was not yet (1965) permissible. But even here it is possible for the investor to take advantage of excess depreciation by creating a subsidiary corporation to erect the building. The "losses" of the subsidiary can be offset against the profits of the parent corporation in a joint return.

Renewal has therefore become a selective quest for good sites where there is both net profit and depreciation. "Slums" and "blight" are the brands that are stamped on good as well as bad real estate to produce the necessary inventory. The federal government supplies the financing to implement the transaction and permits the depreciation allowance which makes the game exciting—and sometimes worthwhile.

Appendix A
Section 221 (d)(3) and (d)(4)

In 1961, two additional lettered subdivisions, 221(d)(3) and 221(d)(4), were added to Section 221. They were prompted by the plight of the displacees from urban renewal sites and the growing criticism against evictions. Section 221(d)(4) authorized 90 per cent FHA-insured loans (based on replacement costs) to private developers at 5¼ per cent interest. Maximum loans were fixed at $12,500,000, and FHA premiums could be waived. The projects were actually of little use to displacees, and few could afford them. But the terms were useful to developers. All they had to do was "offer" the displacees a priority for sixty days after which they were free to rent to whom they chose. (Needless to say, few builders exerted themselves to secure displacees, even if the displacees could afford the accommodations.) The interest rates were attractive to the developer, and the waiver of the insurance fee was a benefit, too. FHA allowed the builder a building fee of 10 per cent of project cost which, with other perquisites, could give him a fair profit for his effort, particularly if the project cost ran into the millions.

The new Section 221(d)(3) was a more significant innovation. It offered a new type of program for multifamily units and was intended to stimulate "nonprofit corporations" into building for "the many families whose incomes are sufficiently high so that they are not eligible for public housing."[1] Slum clearance was not only not a requirement, but the law expressly made local housing authorities ineligible. The section aimed to provide cheaper rental housing made possible by a below-market interest rate—3⅛ to 3⅞ per cent (fluctuating with the government bond rate) with no FHA premium. Mortgages could be up to 100 per cent of estimated replacement cost for "nonprofit mortgagors" and up to 90 per cent for limited dividend corporations. Maximum mortgage amounts were $12.5 million per project. Since no lender would make a mortgage at 3⅛

[1] *Report on H.R. 6028*, 87th Cong., 1st Sess., 1961, p. 11.

to 3⅞ per cent, FNMA would buy the mortgages and FHA would insure
them.

The fact that the sponsor under 221(d)(3) was to be a nonprofit
builder (church, citizens' organization, etc.) dissipated Congressional fears
that 100 per cent loans might mean a reversion to bailouts. But it could
also qualify private builders operating through a limited profit corporation or those who would undertake "nonprofit" operations at a building
profit but not an operating profit.

Since the private entrepreneur was the most enterprising, it was not
long before he became the main force in sponsoring 221(d)(3) operations
for limited profit and also at no operating profit.[2]

TABLE A-1

PROFIT PROJECTION ON LIMITED DIVIDEND CONSTRUCTION

| Example: | Cost of Land | $ 100,000 |
| | Cost of Building | $1,000,000 |

Allowable building fee (10 per cent of building cost)	$100,000
Actual building fee	30,000
Net profit on building operation	$ 70,000
10 per cent investment required on building and land	110,000
Less profit reinvested	70,000
Actual cash investment	$ 40,000
Allowable return at 6 per cent per annum on $110,000 investment	$ 6,600

Q.E.D.: Profit equals $6,600 on $40,000 or 16+ per cent.

The principal virtue of 221(d)(3) nonprofit ventures is that there is
almost no gamble in renting. With a 3⅛ to 3⅞ per cent mortgage, the
builder or investor is fairly sure of keeping the project full and has an
edge over the builders who pay 5¼ to 6 per cent for their mortgage
money. They are, in other words, offering a good commodity about 20

[2] Under the limited profit arrangement, a limited dividend corporation had
to have a 10 per cent equity above a 90 per cent insured mortgage. If the
corporation was owned by a builder, FHA allowed him a building fee of 10
per cent—just about equal to his equity. Thus he would have little or nothing
in the deal but his actual building fee, which would be about 3 per cent of
cost. The difference of 7 per cent would be a cash profit. Since the builder
would be allowed 6 per cent profit calculated on a 10 per cent investment, his
actual return would be 16 to 20 per cent (See Table A-1).

per cent cheaper than a comparable rental project under other 90 per cent insured financing.

If the builder organizes a 221(d)(3) job on a "nonprofit" basis, he is entitled to a fee determined by "local scales." FHA in 1963 set a guide for local scales at 4½ to 6 per cent, but the profit is more than the minimum in practice. To land a nonprofit job, the entrepreneur has two alternatives:

He can sponsor a cooperative under Section 221(d)(3), taking advantage of the favorable interest rate and the 100 per cent mortgage. By organizing the cooperative venture, he would reap the building fee as well as other incidental profits. He should find more enthusiasm from prospective cooperators because of the low interest and small down-payments as well as the benefits of the deductions from income tax for interest and real estate taxes which the government permits.

The builder could also induce a genuine nonprofit organization to build. While a main hope of 221(d)(3) was that true nonprofit organizations like churches and unions would rush to take advantage of the liberal terms—and some have—the builders often spur that interest to gain a profit. Thus the three devices, i.e., limited profit, cooperatives, and nonprofit operations, all become inducements for private builders. Where the rents under traditional or 90 per cent insured financing are too high for the market, financing under 221(d)(3) will be sought.

As of June 30, 1964, there were 308 projects with 44,000 units built or being processed. They charged a median monthly rent of about $87 per unit for three- and four-person families. Maximum income limits ranged from $4,500 (in Hearn, Texas) to $9,000 (in Chicago) and $11,700 (in Alaska). Because Congress might frown on the high rentals which would have to be charged in large cities with higher building costs, projects have won approval mostly in areas of low-cost construction.

Although most applicants were private entrepreneurs willing to build "without profit" or for a limited profit, there were also a few genuine cooperatives and nonprofit corporations among the sponsors. The administration says the potential number of applications will be "almost unlimited." The lower rents (about 20 per cent below market) which the lower interest makes possible should indeed tap a market that is "almost unlimited." For here at last the entrepreneur can be assured of a "stabilized gross income" and a market of stable renters looking for a break.

Appendix B

Total Depreciable Cost[a]	$3,135,000

1. Building at 75% of total (50-year depreciation) — 2,351,250

2. Equipment at 25% (20-year depreciation) — 783,750

    A. Straight-line basis
        (1) $2,351,250 at 2% — 47,025
        (2) $783,750 at 5% — 39,187

        Total first year straightline depreciation — $ 86,212

    B. Accelerated double declining balance basis
        (1) $2,351,250 at 4% — 94,050
        (2) $783,750 at 10% — 78,375

        Total first year at accelerated depreciation — $ 172,425

If the taxable income is — 54,057
And the depreciation under A is — 86,212

The excess tax *loss* will be — $ 32,155

If the taxable income is — 54,057
And the accelerated depreciation under B is — 172,425

The excess tax *loss* will be — $ 118,368

[a] In this example, the owner finds it better to take two separate depreciations for building and equipment. He may do this instead of averaging both into a round 3 per cent. He is allowed a higher rate on more perishable equipment than on a building.

Appendix C

CASH FLOW AND TAX BENEFITS TO TAXPAYER IN THE 75 PER CENT BRACKET WITH 100 PER CENT INTEREST IN TRUST

	Cash Flow to Investor[a]	Gross Tax Deductions	Tax Shelter In Excess of Cash Yield (Col. 2 minus Col. 1)	Cash Value of Excess Tax Shelter to 75% Taxpayer	Cash Flow Plus Tax Savings (Col. 1 plus Col. 4)	Rate of Return on $487,000 Investment Per Annum	Cumulative
	(1)	(2)	(3)	(4)	(5)	(6)	(7)
1962[b]		$ 90,000	$ 90,000	$ 67,000	$ 67,000	27.5%	27.5%
1963		250,000	250,000	187,000	187,000	38.4	33.0
1964		320,000	320,000	240,000	240,000	49.3	38.4
1965		130,000	130,000	97,000	97,000	19.9	33.8
1966		120,000	120,000	90,000	90,000	18.5	30.7
1967	$49,000	110,000	61,000	46,000	95,000	19.5	28.9
1968	49,000	100,000	51,000	38,000	87,000	17.9	27.3
1969	49,000	90,000	41,000	31,000	80,000	16.4	25.9
1970	49,000	80,000	31,000	23,000	72,000	14.8	24.7
1971	49,000	70,000	21,000	16,000	65,000	13.3	23.6
1972	49,000	60,000	11,000	8,000	57,000	11.7	22.5

[a] Assuming 10 per cent return beginning in 1967.
[b] Six months.

Chapter

8

Dislocation and Relocation

BEFORE 1934, security of possession was a contractual arrangement between landlord and tenant or mortgagee and owner. Since government had limited functions, there were few evictions to make way for public improvements. The ouster of 8,000 families from a single site, as in New York's West Side renewal area, would have been unthinkable. Thirty years later, the expansion of public power at all three levels of government made it thinkable.

After 1934, major land operations covering 10 to 30 acres per project arrived with public housing and expanded thereafter with highway programs and urban renewal. As these programs advanced, mass evictions became more frequent. While the urban renewal program was still grounded, public housing was the main slum executioner, and it had removed 206,000 slum units by June 30, 1954.[1]

Though only a fraction of those displaced were accommodated, evictions for the public housing program went unchallenged because it not only cleared slums but built new dwellings for some of those it dislodged. As evictions for freeways, parks, and other operations soared in number, they, too, were tolerated as the inevitable conse-

[1] In 1938, when continued demolition threatened rising rents and hardship, I urged postponing demolition in favor of building on vacant sites. See *Shelter* (1939) reprinted in M. B. Schnapper, *Public Housing in America*, H. W. Wilson, 1939, p. 88. I learned, however, that once slum clearance had acquired popular appeal, a change of policy to favor vacant sites was all but impossible.

132]

quences of a growing society's growing needs. But evictions by urban renewal were met less hospitably. The program was both a newcomer and a hybrid in the genus of public operations. It ousted the poor to make way for the more affluent, and the more it accelerated, the more it exposed its ethical ambiguities. Soon after President Kennedy took office, it became the most controversial program in the administration. Its evictions brought civic groups to the defense of the victims, and the program was more often denounced than it was defended. Relocation was called a "dirty word" and dislocation the "Achilles heel" of the program.

Increase in Urban Renewal Displacements

As of June 30, 1963, more than 157,000 families had been displaced by urban renewal.[2] The official estimate is that 530,000 households will be displaced in the eight years following 1965[3] while unofficial estimates put it closer to 2 million. As of December 1961, 112,721 families were "relocated."[4] To be relocated presumes that good housing was found for the dislocated at rents they could afford.

Urban renewal has not been the only program that destroys peoples' homes. The total annual displacement from dwelling units through all federally assisted programs was about 71,000 a year, representing 97 per cent of all direct federal and federally assisted displacements; urban renewal accounted for 47 per cent of this total.

Code enforcement, which has become part of urban renewal's "workable program," has also begun to take an increasing toll of poor peoples' dwellings and increased the number of evictions. In California, for example, the schedule of families to be displaced in

[2] Statement of Urban Renewal Commissioner William L. Slayton before the Subcommittee on Housing, House Committee on Banking and Currency, November 21, 1963.

[3] *Real Property Acquisition in Federal Programs,* Committee on *Public Works* (Print No. 31), 88th Cong., 2nd Sess., December 22, 1964, pp. 19, 20.

[4] Included among those claimed to be relocated were 7,895 who concededly moved to substandard housing, while the "unknown" numbered 15,842. Less than 19,000 went into public housing (*Progress Report on Federal Housing Programs,* Hearings before a Subcommittee of the Senate Committee on Banking and Currency, 87th Cong., 2nd Sess., August 29, 1962, p. 44).

two years from July 1962 shows an increasing number of evictions both for code enforcement and urban renewal (Table 4).

TABLE 4

	Programs Certified		Programs Awaiting Certification	
	Number of Families	Per Cent	Number of Families	Per Cent
Urban renewal	3,166	44	5,922	31
Highway	318	4	2,570	14
Code enforcement	2,734	38	9,193	48
Other	1,002	14	1,283	7
	7,220	100	18,968	100

SOURCE: Robert B. Bradford, Director of Public Works, California, letter to Marshall Kaplan, Report Coordinator, Governor's Advisory Commission on Housing Problems, July 12, 1962.

The most serious aspect of urban renewal is not that it is the only housewrecker but that, when added to the rising number of other displacements, it is compounding an already serious housing problem for the poor. It displaces a group for whom private operations have not provided homes; a group that cannot pay the rents in urban renewal projects; a group that is the most difficult to rehouse. Public housing is not providing the alternative shelter for most of those people. Unless some better way is found for housing the growing number of dispossessed, urban renewal may sooner or later find itself unrenewable. If this happens, a program with some marked benefits for cities and one which could have far more benefits if it were reinforced by adequate housing legislation, would be lost irretrievably.

Relocation Requirements

Before a federal loan or grant is made for urban renewal, the local renewal agency must come up with a "feasible plan to relocate the families on the renewal site." It must, under the law, demonstrate that "there are or are being provided, in the urban renewal area or in other areas not generally less desirable . . . and at rents or prices within the financial means of the families displaced from the urban renewal area, decent, safe, and sanitary dwellings equal in number to the number of and available to such displaced families and reasonably accessible to their places of employment."

It is in their effort to fulfill this requirement and in their unnecessary insistence that it is being scrupulously fulfilled that renewal administrators have had to resort to misstatements of fact rare in the annals of official reporting. And it is this as much as the dislocations themselves that has drawn the fire of critics.

In extenuation it should be said that this provision of the Housing Act of 1949 is itself a glaring self-contradiction and an impossible obligation to fulfill. If there are ample and well-located "decent, safe and sanitary dwellings" in the urban renewal area which slum dwellers can afford, presumably there is no housing problem. If there is no housing problem, there is no need for the public housing the law authorizes. All the statutory pronouncements on the existence of a housing problem would be so much double talk.

The Urban Renewal Administration has compounded the statutory deception by defining what is considers the "basic elements of the standards outlined in the law."[5] It requires that the displaced families be relocated in houses with these minima:

1. Safe, weatherproof structures in good repair

2. Bathroom facilities with hot and cold running water and an inside flush toilet all in good working order

3. Good kitchen facilities with hot and cold running water

4. Good sewage disposal with a functioning plumbing system

5. Heating facilities either central or with flue-connected space heaters

6. A good safe wiring system with electrical services

7. A window for every room

8. Space standards adequate for the family's size and composition so as to avoid overcrowding

[5] *Urban Renewal Administration, Technical Guide 9—Determining Local Relocation Standards,* August 1961.

9. Two separate means of egress with all equipment in sound condition free of rats or debris

10. Conformance of the dwellings with all local codes and ordinances.

The relocation housing with these standards, says the federal agency (and the statute), must also be within the means of the family to be displaced.

These excellent specifications assume there are plenty of vacancies to choose from; that the vacancies are in good standard houses; that the rents are reasonable; that they are well located; that shrinking the poor man's housing supply by clearances will not affect the price or availability of what remains; that the average low-income family does not know that such better opportunities exist; that public officials can do better than the tenants themselves in finding good units even when the officials have to find them for hundreds of families simultaneously. They also assume there is no shortage at all in the cities where the houses are to be demolished, no housing problem and no slum problem except in the slum targeted for removal.

The trouble is that the ability to meet these specifications is denied by the Housing Act itself which concedes a "serious housing shortage." The shortage is made worse for those who cannot afford better and who are evicted from what they have. If they are not white—and about 70 per cent of those evicted are in this category—they are denied the "one commodity in the American market that is not freely available on equal terms to everyone who can afford to pay."[6] In sum, relocation not only assumes that the serious housing shortage cited in the law does not exist for low-income families but it also assumes that reducing the housing supply for those who need housing most settles the housing problem for them. It implies that the evicted families may even be better off after they are ousted than before.

It is these discrepancies between law and fact that have made the renewal administrators the perplexed executors of a statutory absurdity and turned them into jugglers of statistics. It ignores the fact that when poor families are put out of their homes, they are compelled

[6] *Report of U.S. Commission on Civil Rights,* 1959, p. 534.

to leave neighborhoods, friends, and surroundings of their choice; they are forced to take their children out of schools, sometimes twice or three times in a few years; they leave their churches and sometimes the city itself. If they do get better accommodations, as some doubtless do, they are compelled to pay higher rents and usually more than they can afford.

The exceptions are those cities with so many vacancies in slum and nonslum areas that pushing people around does not matter much. These are usually the troubled cities, some of whose real estate has been emptied by the trek to suburbia. The difficulty is that where such vacancies are ample, the market for new high-rental dwellings created by urban renewal is not good, and the renewal agency is hard put to find a bidder for its projects. There may be some cities that have ample vacancies in slums, while simultaneously enjoying a shortage of high-rental dwellings. But these are few. The attractive projects tend to be in cities where there is a sharp demand for dwellings by all income groups, and, in these cities, displacement too often brings hardship and relocation plays a game of musical chairs with people's homes.

How Relocation Has Relocated

One of the main reasons for the cavil heaped upon the federal renewal agency has been that in the selection of sites, the law requires it to respect the principles of local autonomy and decentralization. This means that the local agency does the displacing and the relocating with the federal agency standing in the background. The Urban Renewal Administration will generally not disapprove a site chosen locally, simply because it is chock-full of home-hungry Negroes at the dawn of a new day or elderly poor in the evening of their lives. Though he could do so, the federal administrator does not usually superimpose his judgment on that of the local renewal agency. As the federal reports on urban renewal relocations put it in 1963, "The data summarized in this publication necessarily are limited to the monthly LPA

[Local Public Agency] reports."[7] If the federal agency stood by this qualification, it could be charged only with an act of omission. But when putting its case for further appropriations before Congress, the federal commissioner justified both past and present local performances without reservations. "On the whole, as the statistics show, the relocation aspects of urban renewal are being done well. . . . The success of relocation is particularly noteworthy. . . ."[8]

The requirement for a feasible plan of relocation has been similarly left largely to local initiative. In this way, not only has responsibility for eviction been delegated, but the culpability has sought to be delegated as well. It is then given absolution. Federal renewal administrators are, of course, no different from most other administrators. They have a timetable and must show records of performance and speed. They would hardly be prepared to cancel a project because a local certification that ample quarters existed for the evicted was untrue when certified or is no longer true.

To prove its relocation plan feasible and show that standard housing is on hand for the displaced families, local agencies may assign a staff member to record his opinion of what is standard housing and how much of it is available. The report is then forwarded to the federal people. At year-end, the local findings are tabulated, made part of the federal report, and for all practical purposes, thereby given federal authentication.

Until 1961, when Dr. Robert C. Weaver was appointed to head the Housing and Home Finance Agency, there were only two people in Washington assigned to deal with the whole nationwide program of relocating the evicted. Thereafter, on November 21, 1963, the Urban Renewal Administration reported to Congress that of the 157,412 families "relocated" by June 30 of that year, about 21,000 were either unknown, moved out of the city when they were evicted, or were otherwise unaccounted for ("miscellaneous"). Of those who were either relocated or the condition of whose housing was known,

[7] Statement of Urban Renewal Commissioner William L. Slayton, *Relocation from Urban Renewal Project Areas,* HHFA, Urban Renewal Administration, 1962, p. 7.

[8] Slayton, House Subcommittee on Housing, p. 414.

7.8 per cent (or more than 10,600 families) moved into substandard housing; 45.9 per cent (or about 63,000 families) were said to have moved into standard private rental housing; 21.2 per cent bought standard housing; and 25.1 per cent moved into public housing.[9]

If the statistics as presented by the local authorities with which the urban renewal administration "was particularly pleased" are correct, the performance passes muster. But by the commissioner's own admission, about 29 per cent of the families in 68 renewal project areas studied had incomes of less than $200 a month. In 1961 about 57 per cent of the displaced families were eligible for public housing, in which the median income for acceptance was $3,200 a year. Yet at least three-quarters of those displaced did not go into public housing—presumably because the families were too large, their incomes too low, they preferred not to, or for other reasons. (An HHFA 1965 survey showed only 13 per cent of the displaced going into public housing.) Nor was there a single reference in the commissioner's testimony to Congress as to the rents which the relocated families were paying or had to pay in their new quarters. If his testimony was correct, it is a fair presumption that either good standard housing is available in the nation's cities for our poor families and that it is available within their means, or that displaced families are being forced into standard housing they cannot afford or that they are being crowded into smaller quarters. An assertion that slum families earning $200 to $250 a month can be found decent housing fulfilling the law's specifications and within their means runs counter to every previous finding of Congress and to the known facts of slum life in the nation's central cities. It implies that for the poor there is no housing problem and that the solution for their housing problem is to put them out.

The definition of what is good housing, "standard" housing, or better housing than that from which the family has been evicted is, of course, largely subjective.[10] The old house may have fewer rooms than what the renewal agency offered but be in a better neighborhood

[9] *Ibid.*, p. 412.
[10] Referring to the problems of the Census, the former Assistant Chief to the Census Housing Division said: ". . . the subjective elements entailed in this

or be near a good park and playground. It may have had a bath in the kitchen but was near a good school or good neighbors. It may have been substandard but been a short walk to work. But it is a fair assumption that what the family chose for its accommodation before it got the eviction notice was, all things considered, the best it could get at the price.

The local renewal agency's "statistics" ignore all aspects of the relocation housing except their physical standards. In almost all cases, the local agencies neglect or lightly pass over the fact that the evicted families paid higher rents after relocation. In Boston's West End project, 86 per cent paid higher rents, with more than half the households paying at least $30 a month more and two-fifths paying at least $40 more. Before relocation, only 20 per cent paid a fifth or more of their income for rent, but 43 per cent paid this much after relocation. In Philadelphia, 72 per cent of the tenants relocated paid increased rents, with the median rent $33 before and $46 after relocation.[11] Paying more rent than a family can afford can do it far more harm than living in a slum, for a family surviving on a subsistence level must then buy less food and clothing. Statistics showing improved housing for the evicted, even if true, are not the whole truth.

It would be too much to expect that the findings of the "standard" housing into which the evicted families moved or were moved should always be free of bias or wishful thinking. A local redevelopment agency which had chosen a site, obtained municipal approval, grappled with the requirements of the Urban Renewal Administration, finally found a sponsor, and gone through the many other laborious steps the law required, would be sorely embarrassed if one of its employees reported a few years later that standard housing was in fact not available at rentals "within their means"; or that a third of the families

---

classification [the condition of housing] rendered it one of the weakest among all the housing statistics collected" (Frank Kristoff, "The Increased Utility of the 1960 Housing Census for Planning," *Journal of the American Institute of Planners,* February 1963, pp. 40–47).

[11] Chester Hartman, "The Housing of Relocated Families," *Journal of the American Institute of Planners,* November 1964.

displaced went back to the slums; or that the slum residuum to which they were relegated was less desirable than what the slum dwellers had occupied before. Such a report might well defeat a renewal agency's plans if not its mayor as well.

Washington, D.C., has been trying to clear and redevelop its Southwest slum for twelve years. It had to find a site, get site approval, fight a lawsuit, draw numerous plans, obtain a myriad of federal approvals, and overcome local opposition. Finally the project was ready to move. But 4,657 families had to be relocated, and after almost a dozen years, some tenants were still stubbornly hanging on. Seventy-six per cent of those occupying the Southwest area were Negroes, and more Negroes have moved into Washington since. About a third of those displaced were given units in public housing—a high proportion compared to other cities. But concededly about one-fourth "slipped back into bad housing," according to the local director of the program, and most of those chose the slum next to their old slum. "Admittedly, Southwest Washington was cleared only at the price of creating the need for additional clearance in parts of Northwest Washington and a spread of blight in a segment of the Northeast."[12] Those relocated, the local director admits, had to pay 15 to 25 per cent more rent than before. It has been a long ordeal for the director during those twelve years. Manifestly his agency could not have stopped along the way to confess that all could not be satisfactorily rehoused, that many were forced to pay higher rents than they could afford, and that it was virtually impossible to find standard quarters for large families after the agency had certified that there were good houses for all. Nor, after the Urban Renewal Administration had put out thousands of families could the local administrator or the federal government say it was all a mistake.

Another View of Relocation

Relocation problems, of course, vary among cities. In some, the exodus to the suburbs has been so rapid or the city has lost so much population, that a long trail of houses has been left behind which

[12] Robert C. Weaver, *The Urban Complex,* Doubleday, 1964, p. 54.

evicted families can occupy. In others, new sections, formerly white, have been opened up to Negroes by professional block-busters capitalizing on white fears or by mass exodus caused by Negro infiltration, loss of industries, or other causes. In still others, the desperate local renewal agency is the city's own block-buster—this has been called "integration." But it is notable that even in a city like Philadelphia with a 5 to 6 per cent vacancy rate and a 27 per cent Negro population, relocation has been a serious headache which long obstructed its renewal progress.

Strangely, almost all local renewal agencies claim they have had little trouble in complying with the federal requirements; people ousted from their homes are said to be better off than they were before. Some, indeed, may be. There are the families whom the writ got out of the rut; there are some who lacked the money to move and did move when they got it from the renewal agency; there are others who never knew there were such bargains around as those the agency found for them. And there are still others who should have paid more for their shelter and now do so. In some cities a valiant relocation official may have braved the exclusion belt and got his Negro families into a section previously reserved for whites. There is also the viewpoint put forth by the director of Washington, D.C.'s redevelopment agency, who told the writer, "People have to be disturbed," by which he presumes that eviction is for their own good.

Yet in most cases the presumption is reasonable that a family does not like to be disturbed; that it prefers its own choice of neighborhood and house; that it is the best judge of what it can afford, how much it should spend for rent and how much it should spend on the children. One could add that if enforced relocation is the blessing it is said to be, it should be undertaken even in the absence of an urban renewal program. A social program to push poor people from their present quarters should in fact prove even a better answer to the housing problem than subsidized public housing. The way to solve the housing problem of the poor is to get them out and make them pay more rent whether they want to or not.

Although the Urban Renewal Administration reported that from the commencement of the program to June 1960, 7 out of 10 nonwhites and 8 out of 10 whites had been rehoused in standard housing,[13] it is not surprising that studies by more circumspect sources cast some doubt upon the validity of the official statistics.

A careful comparison of the Boston renewal agency's findings with those made by the Center for Community Studies on the West End relocation in Boston showed that, while the local agency found that less than 2 per cent of the West End families moved into structurally substandard housing, the number according to the independent study was 25 per cent. Cleveland's local renewal agency showed 71 per cent of the buildings in its Erieview project as substandard, but an inspection by the U.S. Comptroller General showed only 20 per cent as substandard.[14] Other studies show that local data recording was poor, self-serving, and inaccurate, that social and physical features of the relocation housing were ignored, and that the standards set by the law were compromised in about half the cases.[15]

In a study of 41 cities with relocation programs, made over a four-year period extending from 1955 to 1958,[16] it was found that 26 cities did little more than take an eviction census, advise the families of possible deadlines, and thereafter leave them to their own wits and resources to find shelter elsewhere.[17] In 14 of the cities, families

[13] *Relocation from Urban Renewal Project Areas,* pp. 6–11.

[14] *Premature Approval of Large Scale Demolition for Erieview Project I, Cleveland,* Comptroller General of the United States, Report to Congress, June 1963.

[15] See other studies cited by Hartman (note 11, above), including Gordon N. Gottsche, *Relocation: Goals, Implementation and Evaluation of the Process* (West End project, Boston), Philadelphia Housing Association, November 1958. Hartman concludes that local reports stress "achievements" and either minimize or ignore negative consequences. He advocates that relocation responsibility be taken away from the local renewal agency.

[16] This period is embraced in the record of the urban renewal program's accomplishments as portrayed by the Commissioner to Congress on November 21, 1963.

[17] Harry W. Reynolds, Jr., "The Human Element in Urban Renewal," *Public Welfare,* April 1961.

received no official information about their displacement other than a handbill announcing the demolition date.[18]

Some 70 per cent of those relocated in the 26 cities studied chose to enter nearby housing that was substandard, overcrowded, and unsafe, lacked central heating and hot water, and had shared toilets—a far cry from the relocation standards of the Urban Renewal Administration. About 80 per cent of the relocated families paid higher rent after moving. Only one-third of the 41 communities gave relocation counsel on a family-by-family basis. In almost every area, there was a chronic shortage of good housing to which the displaced could be referred.[19] Only 11 of the 41 cities reported a sufficient number of acceptable two-bedroom dwellings and in only 5 cities were there enough three- and four-bedroom units.

Code enforcement was often ignored or suspended because it might slow the relocation process. Only 10 per cent of the cities as much as collected information about satisfactory vacancies.

Within four cities of more than 1 million, only 25.9 per cent of all displaced families accepted dwellings offered by the relocation authority.[20] About 90 per cent of those who relocated themselves went into substandard dwellings. In Philadelphia it was found that 70 per cent of the families dislocated by all programs were living in shelter that violated the housing code.[21] In Cincinnati about half of those displaced found their way into substandard shelter.[22]

Studies by one federal agency of another's operations are more apt to whitewash than to darken a sister agency's performance. Yet a 1963 study by the U.S. Department of Health, Education, and Welfare says:

[18] Of 5,722 families from four sites in three of the larger municipalities studied, 34 per cent had lived in the areas selected for renewal for 30 years or longer and 22 per cent had lived there 20 to 30 years. Work had been near home for 46 per cent of the principal wage earners. About 93 per cent of these families were nonwhite.

[19] Harry W. Reynolds, Jr., "What Do We Know About Our Experiences with Relocation?" *Journal of Intergroup Relations*, Autumn 1961, p. 346.

[20] *Ibid.*, p. 350.

[21] *Relocation—The Human Side of Urban Renewal*, Philadelphia Housing Association, November 1958.

[22] "A Strategy for Improving Housing in Greater Cincinnati," New York, Action, Inc., 1960, mimeo., a study for the Citizens Development Committee, Cincinnati.

"assurances about relocation have often rested on superficial surveys . . . a degree of skepticism about local reporting is in order . . . it can hardly be said that the general picture of relocation has provided reason for applause . . ."[23]

Once families move or have moved, the record of what happens to them is lost in oblivion. In a number of the suburban areas of St. Louis, Negro pockets were uprooted for urban renewal or highways and the occupants forced into the city proper. Negroes in Arlington County, Virginia, and Montgomery County, Maryland, are being pushed into the nation's now dominantly Negro capital under the aegis of urban renewal. In some cities, displacees are treated simply as welfare clients and given rent supplementation from welfare funds to compensate them for leaving the sites. In other cases, housing authorities refuse to accept displacees, feeling that they are not obliged to pull renewal's chestnuts from the fire. In a settlement of one-story houses in Stockton, California, where thirty-two Negro churches were torn down in a single area, the Negro families were left to their own resources. I saw them dispersed into the poorer sections outside the city where there are virtually no building laws and where a dismal shack could be erected without interference.

Relocation and Housing Shortage

Vacancy ratios vary among cities as do the physical conditions of the dwellings and the rents demanded for them. The 7.5 per cent rental vacancy rate which was average for the country in 1963 may still mean a housing shortage for poorer families. In New York City, vacancies in 1963 were ample at $60 a room, but there was a housing famine in lower-rental units.

Los Angeles renewal officials boast that few families have been hurt by dislocation. Yet California statistics show that from 17 to 24 per cent of its renter families (most of them having incomes of less than $4,000 annually) pay 35 per cent or more of their incomes for rent

[23] Alvin L. Schorr, *Slums and Social Insecurity*, Social Security Administration, 1963, pp. 62, 65.

(Table 5). A renewal project in Sacramento had rented less than 50 per cent of its units more than a year after its completion, but nearly 20 per cent of the families in that city were paying more than 35 per cent of their income for housing. Housing conditions in a city are not fully disclosed by the small number of slums or the large number of vacancies.

TABLE 5

RENTER HOUSEHOLDS PAYING 35 PER CENT OR MORE
OF INCOME FOR HOUSING, 1960

	Number	Per Cent of Total
Bakersfield	5,781	16.7
Fresno	6,939	18.1
Los Angeles-Long Beach	219,566	22.6
San Diego	29,385	23.5
San Bernardino-Riverside-Ontario	15,937	19.6
San Francisco-Oakland	86,399	20.6
San Jose	13,295	23.0
Santa Barbara	4,907	21.4
Stockton	4,971	18.3

SOURCE: Donald L. Foley, Wallace F. Smith, and Catherine Bauer Wurster, *Housing Trends and Related Problems,* Table 23, C19. Original source was 1960 Census.

About 20 per cent of the nation's renter families pay 35 per cent or more of their gross income for rent (Table 6). The lash of eviction falls most heavily on those who have the lowest incomes and the least to say about their housing. The Negro, for example, earns about 47 per cent less than the white and must face discrimination even when there are vacancies at prices he can afford. The next most numerous victims of displacement are elderly people to whom eviction may spell tragedy. They lack both mobility and money. The increased emphasis on demolition by urban renewal and other programs has made life for many an unending trek from one slum or furnished room to another. Children are uprooted from schools, and building a stable life within a context of rootless living becomes virtually impossible.

TABLE 6

RENTER HOUSEHOLDS PAYING 35 PER CENT OR MORE
OF INCOME FOR HOUSING, 1960

Metropolitan Area	Number	Per Cent of Total
New York	422,337	18.5
Chicago	194,510	20.8
Los Angeles	219,566	22.6
Philadelphia	80,626	21.3
Detroit	77,098	24.7
Baltimore	42,107	24.1
Houston	28,654	22.2
Cleveland	42,113	20.4
Washington	55,601	18.5
St. Louis	50,352	21.3
Total 212 metropolitan areas	2,812,850	20.3

SOURCE: U.S. Census of Housing, 1960, Metropolitan Housing HC(2), Table A-3, except U.S. total SMSAs from Table B-3.

Eventually, as displacement for urban renewal, highways, code enforcement, etc., continues, dislocation must come to a halt. In the absence of a massive housing program for low-income families, urban renewal must remain a limited program, limited not only by the small number of rentable units it can produce but by the number of people it can evict.

In New York City, where there was virtually no vacancy rate for low-income dwellings in the 1960s, a huge displacement program was nevertheless being pursued. On April 23, 1963, it was announced that 86,000 persons (about 1 per cent of the city's population) would face orders to move in two years. In addition, 2,000 commercial tenants were scheduled for ouster from various sites in the same period. The main reason for the evictions is urban renewal. Only about 15 per cent of those evicted go into public housing. About 70 per cent of those notified are left to find their own shelter; they get $300 to $500 for their moving expenses and trouble. The remaining 15 per cent are relocated under a "finder's fee" program. In this case, the city gives a landlord from $150 to $300 as a bonus for taking a tenant.

(The payment of such a bonus by a tenant himself would violate the city's rent control law, but the city which operates the law exempts itself from its operation.) Families in New York City scurry from one slum to another before the bulldozer, often being relocated three or four times[24] in a few years. A survey of 709 tenants of a site required for public housing showed that 49 per cent moved into sections mapped for future development.[25]

New York City in 1965 was the only large city in the nation with rent control and its rent control law quavers with language reciting the plight of its famine-struck tenantry.[26] The findings which preceded the law's enactment said that it was not uncommon to find tenants living under substandard conditions, who were paying more than 50 per cent of their incomes for rent. Between 1950 and 1960, 18 per cent of households protected by rent control were paying more than 35 per cent of their incomes for rent. They were mostly low-income families.[27] As much as $180 a month for a single furnished room had to be paid by the relief agency to house some of its welfare families.[28]

It is nevertheless claimed in New York City as elsewhere that tenants get better dwellings than they had before they were ousted. The illusion exists because in New York, as in every large city, there is an annual turnover in dwellings. The vacancy ratio may be nil, but apartments come into the market due to death, movement from one apartment to another, removal from the city, and other causes. This turnover is about 8 per cent annually, and it is this turnover that the relocation agency tries to pre-empt. The shortage is thus held constant or made worse and continuance of rent controls is made a certainty. Vacancies are so intensively sought that an obituary notice is apt to bring more applicants for the apartment than mourners to the wake.

[24] "City Hopes to End Relocation Woes," *New York Times,* August 13, 1962.
[25] *Tenant Relocation Report*, New York City Planning Commission, January 23, 1954.
[26] *Administrative Code,* New York City, Chapter 41, Section 41–1.0.
[27] *People, Housing and Rent Control in New York City,* City Rent and Rehabilitation Administration, December 1963, p. 11.
[28] J. Anthony Panuch, *Building a Better New York,* Final Report to Mayor Robert F. Wagner, 1960, p. 75.

Like other cities, New York has been demolishing buildings for urban renewal and thus reducing the vacancy rate in dwellings for low-income people. Such demolitions by urban renewal, public housing, and private building eliminated 135,000 dwellings between 1950–1960, mostly in the low-income market. By pre-empting the few vacant apartments resulting from turnover, a small percentage of the evicted families might be rehoused. But no one seems to care about the conditions of the 70 per cent of the city's displacees who had to scurry about for their own shelter in a tight market.

The problems of evicted commercial tenants are often worse. In the 481 renewal projects around the country in 1961, a total of 26,900 nonresidential establishments were scheduled to be ousted. The maximum paid to these establishments was $2,500, the average payment for moving expenses was less than $900, and payments for property losses averaged $1,630.[29] These payments (including moving costs) averaged about $1,400 in 1963.[30]

Little is known of the plight of these small businessmen, and as the urban renewal commissioner conceded in 1963, "satisfactory data on the success of business relocation are difficult to develop." As he also concedes, a number of these are "marginal enterprises." Among the 2,000 commercial tenants faced with eviction in New York City alone, for example, are those to whom a small store in the slums means livelihood—and its loss may mean loss of livelihood. Over the years, the butcher, grocer, or druggist has developed a trade. Moving to another location means losing that trade, dismantling or sacrificing his stock, and starting all over again. He rarely gets part of the compensation in the condemnation proceedings even if he has a valuable long-term lease, for most standard leases contain a waiver of the award or its assignment to the landlord. Nor does it often do a storekeeper much good to be given a first call on a store in the new project. Since years elapse between his ouster and the completion of the

[29] *Relocation from Urban Renewal Project Areas*, p. 22.

[30] Slayton, House Subcommittee on Housing, p. 414. Recent legislation authorized payment up to $25,000, but a payment of this size would be made only in an atypical case, such as a printing plant.

project, the storekeeper must open up elsewhere, take a job, or join
the army of the impoverished.

The destruction of 2,000 stores in a single city like New York, or
of 27,000 in the nation, inevitably destroys much of the life of the
city and much of the values that made the neighborhoods pulsate. If
2,000 small enterprises in a single city were wiped out by a disaster,
Congress would go into action. Yet not an eyelash is blinked when
the disaster is planned under the name of public programs.

One of the deficiencies of the renewal program is that sites may
be cleared and people evicted with no prospect that the sites will ever
be built upon. As of December 1963, 16,550 units were under construction but renewal had built far fewer units (54,400) than it had
destroyed (260,000), and where a project is still-born, the ousters
were unnecessary. But officials take a different view. Urban Renewal
Administrator James Lister said of the ailing Cleveland development,
"Even if we don't find ready builders for St. Vincent housing, just
clearing the land to get rid of those slums justifies what we are doing."[31]
In short, desolation is a blessing.

Often the mere designation of a site is enough to frighten the
residents into moving. In many cases, no bidder may ever be found;
one-fourth to one-third of the projects are dropped by cities after
slum designation. The sole accomplishments then become mass dis-
lodgement of people and destruction of their little enterprises.

The Problems of Policy Revision

The dislocation and relocation practices have been the program's most
shameful aspect. But it is only fair to say that the renewal administration of 1965 should not be blamed for the misfeasances of predecessors.
It should be said also that the hardships of the evicted families have
awakened a new interest by social agencies and civic leaders in the
problems of discrimination, poverty, and ignorance, which had thereto-
fore been swept under the rug. The 1964 legislation which authorized
a rent subsidy for not more than a year to a displaced family was also

---

[31] *House and Home,* May 1962.

a step in the right direction, though a small one. Urban renewal, moreover, is responsible for less than half the families displaced by public action.

With the displacements of families threatening the renewal program, Mr. Weaver acknowledged that the "quality of relocation had to be improved."[32] He accepted the past criticism as "justified" and as "reflecting a disregard for human values." Though he did not disaffirm his own renewal administrator's ratification of the local statistics before Congress, he conceded that "abuses, failures, and maladministration" require "significant reforms," and he promised to strengthen the administrative machinery, upgrade the quality of the statistics, and require higher minimum standards, more frequent field inspections, and more stringent reviews of relocation plans.[33] This gave hope of a better performance for the future.

Shortly after he had tightened up on the local relocation practices, Mr. Weaver asked the Bureau of the Census to interview 2,842 families who had been relocated from renewal areas from June to August of 1964 in 132 cities.[34] Only 2,300 families could be interviewed, of whom 1,090 were white and 1,210 nonwhite. The rest either moved out of the area, could not be found or interviewed— a significant commentary in itself. Nearly two of every five relocated families who were found and interviewed had incomes below $3,000, and nearly the same proportion earned between $3,000 and $6,000. The incomes of half of the nonwhite families and one-quarter of the white families were below the $3,000 level. The report suggests a marked improvement in relocation practices during the three-month period. Ninety-four per cent of those interviewed were found to be living in "standard" dwellings. The "standard" dwelling, however, includes deteriorating dwellings if they have sanitary plumbing and running water; 6 per cent moved to substandard units (dilapidated dwellings and those lacking plumbing). About two-thirds found

[32] Weaver, p. 104.
[33] *Ibid.*, pp. 102–112.
[34] *The Housing of Relocated Families,* Housing and Home Finance Agency, March 1965. See also news release of Housing and Home Finance Agency, March 18, 1965.

shopping the same or better than before, and 71 per cent found the transportation as good or better, although 45 per cent reported that their churches were further away. Only 10 per cent of those with a fixed place of employment changed jobs in the period following the move. Seventy per cent of the families found their own accommodations.

Although Mr. Weaver's new policies should be credited with achieving some improvement in relocation practices, the report reveals that the median gross rents of the relocated families rose from $66 per month to $74, and the median proportion of income spent for rent from 25 per cent to 28 per cent. This was interpreted as a moderate increase, but the report shows also that before relocation, 36 per cent of the families relocated had already been paying 20 to 34 per cent of their income for rent, but after relocation, the percentage of families paying such rents rose to 44 per cent. Worse still, 24 per cent of the whites and 36 per cent of the nonwhites before relocation had been paying 35 per cent or more of their income for rent. After relocation, the number of families paying such burdensome rents rose to 26 per cent for the whites, while 36 per cent of the nonwhites were still paying 35 per cent or more of their income for their shelter.

The report discloses no information about the new neighborhoods, the availability of schools and playgrounds, and implies that as long as standard housing is found, the rent that a family is forced to pay is irrelevant even if it exceeds 35 per cent of the family's income. "Poverty was common among the families covered by the survey,"[35] the report concedes. It also shows that despite their poverty, only 13 per cent of the displaced families moved into public housing; a quarter of these or only about 3 per cent were whites.

However well intentioned an administrator may be, he is no miracle man. He can halt a local program or two and send more federal officials to check on local practices, but the primary responsibility for the weakness in the program and its abuses is at the door of Congress; the injustices will continue until Congress provides a major program to rehouse not only the families displaced but those who are

[35] Ibid., p. 2.

bleeding themselves to pay their rent. Recent programs, including 221(d)(3) and rehabilitation, may help a little but they are neither enough nor good enough.

With the increase in public programs requiring re-use of land, families throughout the nation are being subjected to hardships that are not of their own making. The swelling number of evictions are due not only to renewal operations or to the vastly increased spending for traditional public purposes but also to the recent expansion of the condemnation power for many other purposes under the broader concept of public benefit. Singling out the renewal program for cavil is indicting only one of the culprits, for urban renewal at least has an obligation to rehouse—whether it does so well or badly. Other displacement programs, such as highways and code enforcement, have no such obligation. The renewal program has therefore highlighted one of the hidden injustices of all clearance operations.

In all programs that evict families, there should be a requirement that the families be subsidized to the extent of the difference between what they can afford and what they are compelled to pay for decent housing in decent neighborhoods. This is particularly important for families in the lowest income group. In some European countries, the obligation is accepted for a period of five years, while factories are built simultaneously for the evicted businesses. For the family earning only $3,000, the least the world's richest nation can do is provide it with the rent supplements that make life livable. The failure of the Administration's proposals of 1965 to provide rent supplements for these families was their most glaring deficiency.

If our older cities are to be substantially renewed, more sites will have to be found in the years to come and, unfortunately, many more people will have to be displaced—for new and better dwellings, for more parks, schools, and open spaces, for code enforcement, for cultural improvements, and for education. For a real renewal of our cities, in fact, the eminent domain power will have to be expanded far beyond the limits of slum clearance. But it will not be enough simply to oust poorer families from their footholds. Without providing them with a decent alternative, and without offering them housing within their means—in suburbs as well as the cities—our cities cannot be improved, and without the needed improvements, these cities will be unable to meet the exigencies of an urban society, much less of a "Great Society." This is the problem confronting not only the renewal program but numerous other programs that will be required for the city's betterment. The federal administrator can try to straddle the issue and the local agencies can give him the "facts" on the basis of which he can tell Congress that its impossible requirements are being complied with. But, in the long run, it is only Congress that can provide the essential subsidy formula to meet the issue realistically and honestly.

Chapter

9

Some Blessings of Urban Renewal

THE MASS DISPLACEMENTS of the renewal program have led to an increasing barrage of criticism that could be satisfied by nothing short of the program's repeal. These critics are as naive as those who unconditionally defend the program in its every aspect.[1] A program which siphons federal money into our languishing cities would be a legislative curiosity if it did no good at all. If it did no more than incite some eight hundred cities (not to mention the thousands of other communities receiving planning grants) to take a constructive look at their environments and replan them, it could not be rated a total loss.

The renewal law has virtues as well as vices, and the vices exist largely because the measure is actually a half-measure. What the program needs is amplification, not abolition, a complementary housing program to make it workable, and an enlargement of its basic concept to do what its name implies. In a nation whose affection for its cities is inconspicuous, it makes no sense to scuttle any program, however imperfect, that aims to help them. In politics, it is always

[1]See, for example, Martin Anderson, *The Federal Bulldozer*, M.I.T. Press, 1964, in which the author makes some good criticisms of the program, makes no mention of its virtues, and then bluntly asks for its repeal. If the same technique were applied to foreign aid, relief, old age assistance, Medicare, public housing, or, for that matter, any federal program, no federal program would deserve continuance.

easier to amend than to win something new, and harder to regain what has been lost than to supplement what exists. In criticizing the deficiencies of the performance, moreover, the critic is obliged not only to assess the past experience but also to envisage the program's potentials under an administration that has learned from its mistakes. With this in view, some of the accomplishments of the program are summarized in the following sections.

Rationalization of Disparate Plots and Traffic Problems

American cities were built mostly in spurts and grew in metastasis. While grace may show itself in a period piece here or there, or in a surviving "money no object" opus by a Stanford White or lesser genius, the general imprint has been that of the jackpot, not the temple. Careful planning of a city or a subdivision was the exception, for the spur was land speculation and turnover, not long-term utility. The spark given to city planning by the building of the nation's capital was extinguished in the subsequent rush for gain. The development of the railroad, machine, and industry smothered whatever interest existed in the better city environment. The gridiron plan of the East moved on to the West. Laid out by land companies, a site could be sold without the buyer or seller ever seeing it. Cities grew thereafter in fitful response to the needs of the incoming poor, and no city was ever built well during a mass migration of poor people.

The New England town and its common survived in places. But American cities mostly reflect the odds and ends of slapdash—the minimum flat or bandbox erected on small lots quickly to house immigrants—and when a town was planned, it was often of the sordid company town variety.

Happily our engineering knowledge was limited in the nineteenth century; much of what was built facing the streets was dispensable without excessive loss. Unhappily, what we are putting up today will be lasting and much of it will not be much better. We are more competent engineers, but design is still shaped by the quick buck.

Urban renewal has the potentials for correcting past errors. Its most important asset is the power of land assemblage, the proper use of which can rectify obsolete street patterns and help create more wholesome environments planned as workable units. New Haven is a good example, Boston's old waterfront promises another. Neither would have been possible without the right to assemble plots and rebuild according to plan.

The power of land assemblage makes possible the establishment of contiguity between plots and the bringing into use of land with unmarketable titles that have held up development of whole sections; it facilitates the synchronization of public and private improvements as well as the planning of cohesive shopping centers. It allows room for more squares and parking spaces and is a useful tool for a long overdue rebuilding of cities enslaved to the 20- to 25-foot lot, the traffic-laden street, and the gridiron pattern. It provides the opportunity for enlarging the street system surrounding the new projects, the closing of streets where necessary, the diversion of traffic, the addition of streets or widening of intersections. It makes possible the creation of footways separating pedestrian traffic from the automobile, and two-level or double-decked streets which have been talked about ever since Leonardo da Vinci put forth his plan for a model city. It facilitates running the new highways into the central city's shopping centers and the creation of off-street parking and enclosed parking spaces. In short, the renewal project supplies a multipurpose opportunity in place of the piecemeal efforts to correct traffic problems, provide playgrounds and open spaces, provide neighborhood amenities, and new housing, public and private.

Encouragement to Aesthetics

The exercise of public power to enforce aesthetics as well as safety, comfort, health, morale, and welfare had long been restricted by the courts.[2] Now, since the Supreme Court's decision in *Berman* v. *Parker* (1954), official agencies no longer need show that a slum is a slum

[2] *Haller Sign Works* v. *Physical Culture Training School,* 249 Ill. 436 (1911): "The courts of this country have with great unanimity held that the police power cannot interfere with private property rights for purely aesthetic purposes."

with all the abominations ascribed to it by criminologists and slum-sisters. In this respect, it may ultimately induce fewer projects that displace the poor. Like patriotism, however, which George Jean Nathan once described as the arbitrary veneration of real estate over principles, the aesthetics of some renewal operations venerate profit above honor.[3] Under a system in which every investment dollar over the 90 per cent mortgage is held to a minimum, a renewer may see beauty as costing too much and yielding too little. So too, some officials with the new power over beauty may in beauty's name condemn a Negro settlement for a park or a project.

Yet not all officialdom is devoid of moral and aesthetic sensibilities, and some have given their architects and planners the latitude to design something seemly. Others have become concerned about losing their old architectural landmarks and have called upon urban renewal to preserve them. With more than 1,500 projects approved for more than 740 communities and only 118 completed by 1964, an over-all appraisal is premature. But if there are projects that are not much better than the run-of-the-mill speculation, there are also those with merit. When profit is the motive, the influence of better design may be subordinated, for it is not easy to effect a good compromise between design and dollars. But since William Slayton took over the Urban Renewal Administration, a serious effort has at last been made to make design a major factor.

One now sees plazas and pedestrian malls, underground parking, and a better relationship between buildings. The manufacturers who were to build plants in New Haven had always relied on stock plans pulled out of a file by an industrial engineer—today they have been induced to employ architects. Elsewhere builders have been shown preliminary models of new designs which had never been within their contemplations and they have begun to accept them. The combination

[3] Alexis de Tocqueville reflected that the people of a democratic nation "will habitually prefer the useful to the beautiful, and they will require that the beautiful be useful" (*Democracy in America*, Century, 1898, II, 56). After de Tocqueville, however, America became more interested in what was salable or rentable, rather than beautiful. The architect who can produce something that is profitable as well as beautiful is the still-undiscovered genius.

of rehabilitation and new building as part of a single project now makes for a project unity which could never have been achieved before. The use of landscaping interspersed in a project (as in Hartford Plaza), more spacing between buildings, and the placing of schools as part of the project (as in New Haven), are other gains.

Thus there are bright spots in the total picture as well as dismal ones, but without the pressure for something better, all or most would have been the routine speculation or stock plan. Washington, D.C.'s Southwest project, New Haven's contributions, Philadelphia's Society Hill, San Francisco's Western Addition, and Detroit's Lafayette Square are among the program's better contributions. There will doubtless be others and one of the most hopeful signs is that the more prominent architects have been brought into the picture—I. M. Pei in Pittsburgh, New York, Boston, and Philadelphia; Mies van der Rohe in Detroit and Baltimore; Paul Rudolph in Boston and New Haven; William W. Wurster in San Francisco; Minoru Yamasaki in Honolulu—while others are being given the chance for the first time to add design to profit criteria. "By slow degrees, we are learning a new technique," says the architectural critic, Douglas Haskell, and urban renewal is supplying the occasion. How much of the product will be better in the end will depend not only on the architects but on a more enlightened federal policy, on whether the market in a city justifies the additional investment, and on whether more cities will subordinate their yearning for higher tax receipts to better architecture and planning.

Spur to Civic Interest

If the patterns of cities are chaotic, the interest of citizens has been inert. If the slumberers have been occasionally aroused to protest, it has usually been because of the threatened destruction of a landmark they were accustomed to pass but never look at. Rarely has civic exertion been expressed in a passion for the creative.

Recently, however, the central city's loss of population and the departure of chain stores has brought out a kind of last ditch, never-say-die gallantry among the good-citizen residuum. They have been

joined by the real estate men and department store owners as well as
by leaders of the threatened institutions. The Charles Street Center in
Baltimore was initiated and planned largely by a group of downtown
businessmen who saw both the handwriting on the wall and the figures
on their balance sheets. In Washington, D.C., and Providence,
Rhode Island, similar groups helped with the new plans for the downtown area. In Boston, the Chamber of Commerce put up the initial
planning funds for studying the city's waterfront area, and businessmen
have also sparked interest in New Haven, Hartford, Philadelphia,
Cincinnati, Norfolk, St. Louis, Denver, Pittsburgh, and Cleveland.
The renewal program has aroused a keener interest in urban disorders.
Outside specialists have often been called in to take a look and
prescribe. The interest of David Rockefeller in the redevelopment of
New York City's downtown is one of the hopeful examples.

In 1948, when I was a housing columnist for the *New York Post*
and tried to plug city planning, the city editor would tell me to get
back to the subject of rats biting babies.[4] City planning now makes the
front page if for no other reason than that the suburban threat to
the department store has alerted the paper's business department to the
link between downtown sales and newspaper profits. The *Washington
Post* or the *Louisville Courier* will publicize, serialize, and editorialize
anything on urban renewal, and the *New York Times* will give a tome
on city or regional planning more attention than the fight over Fanny
Hill.

Impetus to Civic and Cultural Improvements

Cities are perennially in need of new courthouses, parks, schools,
administrative buildings, and other improvements which growing
financial embarrassments have forced them to shelve. Urban renewal
is far from being the wand that waves such improvements in, but it
has sometimes been the persuader that goads officials into taking a
second look at some of the fading blueprints in their pigeonholes.

[4] This wasn't such a good idea either for an evening paper. The editor soon
discovered that people stopped buying it because it spoiled their appetites for
supper.

One of the most important contributions has been the large number of public schools that have been generated by the credits the renewal program allows against the city's contribution to the write-down of land cost. While it is hard to determine precisely how many of these schools would have been built without the renewal inducement, there is little question that the program has been responsible for a good proportion.

Good civic and cultural centers (if there were a federal program that helped finance them) would be a gain for cities. Our own centers are far from rivaling the Forum and the Acropolis, nor do they compare with the examples of Venice and Stockholm, but some have won the plaudits of architectural critics.[5] Norfolk's $15 million Civic Center will have a thirteen-story municipal building and four other structures as part of an extensive downtown development. Boston has started a government center with an estimated cost of $185 million. If more centers were properly located and if they included some skillful focuses of interest to which people would be drawn, civic spirit would get a sizable lift.

So with cultural improvements. Culture in the United States has depended largely on private support, and less than 4 per cent of all corporate contributions go to the arts. In contrast to Europe, even public museums depend on hard-won gifts and on membership dues for survival, and the city's penchant has therefore been for the stadium, paying coliseum, and big auditorium. Less than a third of the cultural centers being built or on the drawing boards can accommodate more than one of the performing arts and many are little more than sports arenas or convention halls. A small town will build a costly swimming pool and do without a library. The promotion of the "progress of science and useful arts" encompassed in the federal constitution was only to protect copyrights, and not until the 1960s did the President designate a special consultant on the arts. His role, however, seemed to have been confined to making public statements, one of which was: "The American people have been slow to recog-

[5] Lewis Mumford, "Civic Art," *Encyclopedia of the Social Sciences,* Macmillan, 1942, II, 493.

nize that artistic and cultural expression is closely related to the vitality of institutions."[6] Federal interest in culture, meanwhile, has been confined mostly to agriculture.

The most dramatic cultural example is Lincoln Center in New York City. The project originated when Carnegie Hall was scheduled for demolition and the Metropolitan Opera decided to move. A site was available under the urban renewal program which "answered the real estate riddle of an adequate site at a reasonable price in the heart of skyscraper-crowded Manhattan."[7] Lincoln Center of the Performing Arts was born. "For me," said John D. Rockefeller, "new horizons began to open. Since the war my work had been concentrated in the international area. I had begun to think more seriously of my responsibilities as a citizen of New York."[8] His assumption of responsibility led to an investment by him and other sources of $170 million for the housing of the performing arts and a seating capacity for 12,000 patrons in six new buildings.

While urban renewal spurred both this citizen activity in New York and its new cultural center, the site for Lincoln Center was acquired not because culture was a public use authorizing the taking of $7.5 million in private land, but because the site was called a slum. To comply with the statute, high-rent housing had to be built on the site though it had no logical place in a cultural scheme. The statute also led to the building of a single center when a few smaller centers strategically placed in several sections of Manhattan—on the East Side, West Side, and lower Manhattan—would have reinforced existing entertainment clusters.

Lincoln Centers or at least their smaller cultural equivalents are needed in many cities. They should be authorized by state laws, and the power of eminent domain should be granted. Their fulfillment should depend neither on the provision of housing on the site nor on the selection of a slum area as a prerequisite. They are more within the range of public use than slum razing for high-rental project build-

[6] August Heckscher, *New York Times Magazine*, September 23, 1962, p. 39.
[7] *New York Times,* Supplement, September 23, 1962.
[8] *Ibid.,* p. 14.

ing. That urban renewal has spurred civic and cultural improvements that might have been stillborn is a big plus for the program.

Buttressing Interest of Religious Institutions

The multiplication of religious institutions and associations has been one of the most striking features of America's religious and social life. The church's influence, said James Bryce, was stronger and deeper in America than in European communities.

Bryce's observation was not unfounded. During the immigration period churches not only ministered to the poor but built homes for the aged, parochial and industrial schools, settlement houses, YMCAs, and immigrant aid societies. Social conscience combined with religious gospel to become a main force in the drive for municipal reform; it helped give urban issues an ethical focus. The recent shifts to suburbia, however, have effected a break with the city. They are confronting church (and synagogue) with some difficult choices.

The church could elect to remain—"Upon this rock I will build my church and the gates of Hell shall not prevail against it." And if it does, it might try to draw its constituency from a greater distance or resolve to win the new neighbors into its fold. It might also elect to retain the old seat while branching out to the suburb as well. It might resolve to do none of these and become a mobile church, laying a claim upon American engineering genius to build it a demountable chapel and spire so that it could follow the mobile trend and fulfill its mission on wheels.

The advent of urban renewal, public housing, public works, and federal aid to suburban growth has added not only new problems but new dimensions for the church. Thus far, too many churches have been destroyed and their people forced out of the neighborhoods in which these institutions had been a binding force. (The destruction by Stockton, California, of more than thirty Negro churches is an example of what should not be done.) But a number of churches have assumed leadership. They have spurred a greater social responsibility for the less privileged and influenced officialdom to revise their eviction and relocation policies. The 300-unit development under Section 221(d)(3) of the St. John Missionary Baptist Church in South Dallas and the 520-unit development of the Wheat Street Baptist Church in Atlanta are examples of constructive cooperation. The Presbyterian Synod in St. Louis not only chose to remain in the Mill Creek area but expanded its church and integrated it, so that it will play a more creative role in a new and extended neighborhood, part of which had been in an all-Negro renewal area. A few churches are building housing for their elderly and for their displaced poor [under Sections 202 and 221(d)(3) of the housing acts] and more are becoming interested. This could become a major force in redevelopment, particularly if a national organization emerges—interdenominational if possible—that could guide the local churches in their operations or undertake the projects directly where necessary.

Spur to Institutional Expansion

The site locations of American universities and colleges have varied with the judgments of their founders. Oxford and Cambridge were built in isolated communities far from the turmoil of London, while universities in Paris, Cologne, Milan, Lima, Caracas, and Mexico City were built in the cities. So, too, in the United States, some universities chose urban locations and some the rustic hinterlands. New York University and Columbia located their buildings in New York City, the University of Pennsylvania in Philadelphia, the University of Chicago in Chicago, the University of California was sited at Berkeley, and Stanford at Palo Alto, while a host of institutions chose the backlands.

The desires of the founders, however, were not always respected as the surge of industry and people enlarged the urban orbit. Only a small bridge now separates Harvard and the Massachusetts Institute of Technology from Boston, while the city of Cambridge itself has burgeoned into a busy industrial center that has engulfed both institutions. Berkeley is now within the shadow of San Francisco.

Meanwhile institutional needs for space have swelled. Enrollments in the last three decades have tripled and are expected to accelerate in the three decades ahead. Some $15 billion is the estimated expenditure for new buildings to meet the needs of expansion and enrollments in the decade ending in 1970.

But as the need for expansion has grown, the university's ability to expand has become more restricted. Unlike a church housed on two or three lots, the university cannot move with its extensive chattels and classrooms to some secluded site in a suburb shielded from the pressures of the city.

Urban renewal not only sparked the university's interest in general planning, citizen education, and urban problems, but gave it the impetus for assuming responsibility in the replanning of its adjoining areas.[9] Write-downs of land cost provided cheap sites while below-market federal loans under the college housing program have helped them build student dormitories—by 1964 about $2.1 billion in low-interest loans had been approved by the Community Facilities Administration for such purposes.

Urban renewal's main benefit for the university was that it lent the power of eminent domain for acquisition of land. In 1962, sixty-four universities were proposing acquisition of 970 acres from local renewal agencies at an estimated cost of $28 million.[10]

The university, after all, is still part of the city's lifeblood, the seat of culture and enlightenment, the source of essential skills and professions, the fountainhead of research. A city suffers less from losing a major industry than from losing a university.

What may be said of universities may be said also of hospitals which are growing institutions vital to any city. Like the universities, they lacked the eminent domain power, and the advent of urban renewal has helped some of them acquire land at low cost for their expansion programs. Philadelphia and Chicago are outstanding ex-

[9] Special provisions of the law have helped materially. Section 310 permits waiver of the predominantly residential requirement and permits a credit to the city for expenditures made by the university for acquiring and clearing the property in or around an urban renewal project.

[10] "Universities, Their Role in Urban Renewal," Address by William L. Slayton at the University of Pennsylvania, September 20, 1962.

amples of university interest and Boston, Chicago, New York, and Norfolk of hospital interest in renewal operations.

The "Town and Gown" problem, however, with its undercurrent of citizen suspicion, is aggravated when the tax-exempt institution becomes involved with the displacement of people. Though better public relations and greater interest in the community would help, the university has all too often isolated itself from the neighborhood's problems. New York University's support of a road through Washington Square Park is an example of how to make the town distrust the gown. (Recently NYU has shown a little more respect for the townsmen.) When MIT helped the beleaguered Cambridge renewal agency dispose of its vacant site by drawing industry into a research center, and when the University of Pennsylvania actively participated in Philadelphia's replanning, they set good examples of university cooperation.

Inducement to Industry

One of the most pressing problems of cities is that of holding their industries or making room for new industries. The exodus of an industry not only brings unemployment but loss of purchasing power, foreclosures, emigration of people, and lower tax revenues. Inability to expand or to find suitable land is one of the reasons for exodus. High taxes and the inducements offered by other communities in the form of free land, low taxes, and easy financing are other reasons.

Urban renewal is one of the devices being employed by hardpressed cities to induce industries to stay where they are. When the Cornell-Dubiler Electric Company contemplated leaving Providence for the South, Providence made land available to it in an industrial park. New Britain, Connecticut, was able to hang on to the American Hardware Company by offering to buy its land and buildings as part of an urban renewal project, demolishing the buildings, and reselling the cleared land to the company. When Sargent and Company threatened to move its lock manufacturing plant to Kentucky, New Haven induced the company to stay by buying a twenty-six acre industrial site on which the company will build a $4 million plant. A large food terminal will also be located on the site. An attractive site made possible by urban renewal may draw other industry to the city. Thus New Haven brought back the hardware firm of H. B. Ives Company which had already moved to suburban Hamden by offering it a square-block site in its Wurster Square renewal project. A number of other cities have been able to attract industries only by assembling the land on which factories could be built.

Rebuilding Downtown

Though urban renewal started as a measure to clear the city's slum towns, its emphasis has steadily veered toward rebuilding the city's downtowns. The growing need to salvage the city's threatened business centers coupled with the private redeveloper's enthusiasm for the still solvent downtown residential sites gradually brought pressure on Congress to broaden its purpose. "Over the years . . . it became clear that the construction of good neighborhoods was intimately tied to the economic health of the community. The revitalization of industrial, commercial, and downtown areas so as to attract job-creating private investment, was realized as a necessary goal to which urban renewal could make a substantial contribution."[11]

A 10 per cent exception to the "predominantly residential" requirement of the law was put into the Housing Act of 1954; this was increased to 20 per cent in 1959 and raised to 30 per cent in 1961. While 70 per cent of the federal funds still had to be used for writing down land cost for slum clearance or residential building, the rest could be used for other types of developments. "The economic, institutional and cultural bases of community life are increasingly recognized as necessary to the creation and continuing existence of good homes in sound urban neighborhoods," said a Congressional committee.[12]

---

[11] *Housing Act of 1961* (H.R.6028), House Committee on Banking and Currency, 87th Cong., 1st Sess., June 1, 1961, pp. 25, 26.
[12] *Ibid.*, p. 26.

In addition to the funds available directly for downtown renewal, cities also increased their selection of the slum, pseudoslum or "non-slum but called slum" areas near downtowns, so that a majority of renewal sites have tended to be either in or near the business centers.

Where the designated downtown area was occupied by poorer families, they were detached from their well-located anchorages. In other cases, businesses were moved to make way for the better-paying enterprises that would brighten up trade and bring more people to the waning city centers. There have been some dramatic examples of downtown rebuilding spurred by urban renewal.

Providence proposes to transform its downtown into five cohesive precincts. The present New Haven Railroad terminal and tracks will be relocated, a new civic center will house a new state office building, a new city hall, and other civic improvements. Provision will be made for parking and for a new station; and there will be a new convention hall, garages, a bus terminal, and an arena, while a new office center and a pedestrian mall will serve as a thoroughfare between the large stores and the new Weybosset residential community.

In addition to its downtown Golden Gateway project, San Francisco's plans call for a billion-dollar rapid transit system, including a subway under Market Street and the abolition of all vehicular traffic (except some buses) to make way for a twenty-block-long pedestrian mall with intersecting malls and plazas.

Cleveland's Erieview project will link the waterfront and the retail office section, once separated by a group of old buildings, into a project which will ultimately entail $125 million of new investment. It is anticipated that new housing and offices around the commercial area will help support the new retail facilities. Other important downtown rebuilding is taking place in Pittsburgh, Sacramento, Philadelphia, Minneapolis, New Haven, Norfolk, and Boston.

Some major chain stores, whose presence pegs a new retail section, are often reluctant to make commitments in the declining areas. They have already established branches in nearby suburbia, find them profitable, and see no reason for supporting competition with investments they have already made. But urban renewal has challenged their continued outward drift. It has offered the big stores more space, parking, and a cohesive shopping center. As a result companies are taking a second look at the city and a growing number are electing to stay. Macy's will move into three renewal sites and calls its action a "new trend."

An official of the Sears, Roebuck Company told me that the downtown sites have advantages for the company, not the least of which is the built-in market of central city buyers who can walk to the stores. The main problems, he says, are getting the highway to feed into the downtown and providing ample parking for the suburban customers. New Haven, among other cities, exemplifies how cooperation between highway planning and urban renewal can salvage a city's downtown. The distance of suburbia from the store is less important than the number of traffic lights. But what often discourages the chains, the Sears official says, are the long delays in getting the program underway and the opposition of some local merchants fearing the competition.

However imperfect the effort, the move by cities to revitalize their main streets is at least an acknowledgment that something more than new housing and slum clearance are needed to restore the city's health and since regenerating a city's downtown is a vital part of its medication, this phase of the renewal program is one of its more important contributions.

Provider of High-rental Housing

Cities inhabited only by the poor are poor cities. A city is the crossway of the great unwashed and of those who have cleaned up; of the many both below mediocrity and above it. Homogeneity when voluntarily created in a single section of a city may be good and even colorful, but homogeneity in a whole city can be a bore, whether it be homogeneity of income, class, race, or age.

The suburban revolution has effected too sharp a class shakeout, leaving the poor in the central cities and too many of the upper-income families in the power-mower belt.

The result has been a loss of purchasing power for many establishments like art, craft, and antique shops, and the theaters, restaurants, and good hotels that add to a city's spirit. A city with nothing but chain groceries and a few five-and-dime stores hardly inspires tourists to circulate their money. A city with higher purchasing power helps the less privileged in employment and in opportunities. It may also bring more investment into the city from some of the better-heeled residents.

There should be no objection to building a string of multiple dwellings at $60 monthly per room, if there are customers for the product; and, if the market existed, some would be built even without urban renewal aid. But there is little question that many would not be built because the land could not be assembled and because the land cost would be too high. Nor would they be built where they serve the city's best interests. A well-planned project attracts high-income tenants who might otherwise shift to suburbia.

The main trouble with building for higher-income families has been the pushing around of the poor. If the low-income families could be adequately housed—and this does not mean confining their choices to public housing projects, other slums, or paying rents they cannot afford—the inconveniences inflicted upon them might at least be atoned for. But there is not yet an adequate program allowing use of renewal sites for the displaced families or for financing enough good housing elsewhere, particularly in suburbia.

Prop for Lower-priced Housing

The flaws in one piece of legislation often lead to the shoring up of another. The renewal program has stimulated support for public housing appropriations that might otherwise have been defeated. It made no moral sense, even to opponents of public housing, to authorize ousting of low-income families without providing at least a compensatory alternative. The program has buttressed the public housing agencies in the 2,200 localities that have them; in the four years preceding 1965, the number of participating localities has increased by 700, mostly in smaller communities. A good number of these have organized as a result of existing or contemplated urban renewal programs.

So too, when it appeared that only a fraction of those evicted moved into public housing, $10 million was appropriated to finance experiments under a "Low-income Housing Demonstration Program"; in June 1963, there were twenty-three such demonstrations. On a very small scale, some of these experiments provide direct subsidies to families, others are experiments in design techniques or rehabilitation. Pilot schemes, when successful, sometimes serve as potent arguments before Congressional committees—public housing, for example, started as an experimental program. If the schemes affirm the validity of family subsidies and Congress can be persuaded to supplement the present public housing formula with a family rent subsidy for the lowest-income group, one of the most constructive devices for solving the slum problem might materialize.

The Section 221(d)(3) formula, with its 100 per cent loans at below-market rates (3⅛–3⅞ per cent), is another device spawned out of the renewal program and one of the most promising in its prospects. It enabled a reduction in normal market rents by 20 per cent, which has been a help to some moderate (not low-income) families. It has also stimulated some rehabilitation and generated a widening interest by churches and civic organizations in building housing under a nonprofit arrangement.

The significance of the program is that it is the first step toward direct federal loans for low-income families. The second step—still to be taken—is to cut the interest rate to a level which would make it possible for families earning $3,000 a year to buy or rent homes built by private and nonprofit builders. The big question—and the big potential—for FHA, FNMA, and the entrepreneur under this profit-nonprofit formula is whether a realistic mean can be found which will afford the private builder a reasonable building fee and hold down his penchant for the windfall. The answer is: It is possible, if not yet probable.[13]

If a formula evolves under which a responsible building industry will sponsor enterprises for a reasonable fee without having to stake any investment, federal housing policy could well take a turn toward private sponsorship of moderate- and low-rent housing operations. The know-how of private enterprise and the diversity of ownerships would be gains for these families. But to reach the lower-income families, particularly in the big cities, either the interest rate would have to be considerably lower or tenants would have to be subsidized directly.

If the arrangement works, 221(d)(3) may mark the evolution of a novel contractual arrangement between government and the responsible private entrepreneur under which the entrepreneur, for a limited fee, produces dwellings in line with improved government standards. If the process is to succeed, however, double bookkeeping must be removed from the operation; a realistic fee should be allowed the developer to spur his interest; a reasonable charge should be allowed for management; there should be no fictitious building fees and charges winked at by federal officials. Projects would have to be built at actual cost plus a fixed fee representing profit, and the profit should be made known to all parties and adequately certified.

Much will also depend on whether some of the larger corporations in American enterprise can be induced to enter the field under such an arrangement. At one time, company housing played a prominent part in home-building operations. The motives were not always pure,

[13] A ray of hope is shed in the experience of New York's Mitchell-Lama law in which the state and city make loans to builders at low interest rates and also grant tax exemption up to 50 per cent of the normal real estate tax. The apartments rent at about $30 a room per month, which is well below market. The builder's incentive is a 7 per cent contracting fee on cooperatives and 10 per cent for limited dividend operations. Since the actual building fees may amount to 3 per cent or less, the difference is pocketed as profit. If the builder chooses the limited dividend formula, it should net him 12 per cent or more on his cash investment, plus the depreciation advantage for income tax purposes. Builders of cooperatives under the law look to the 7 per cent building fee for their profit. A $10 million project thus gives them a fee of $700,000 for their trouble.

but the ethics of big business, while not yet to be confused with Christianity, have improved—there are generous hands as well as itching palms. The question is whether big industry will rise to the occasion. A real effort by the President after a White House conference of businessmen and insurance companies might induce more of them to take the giant step.

Section 221(d)(3) is not the only program authorizing liberal loans to private enterprise at below market rates. Congress also passed Section 202 of the Housing Act, authorizing the Community Facilities Administration to make fifty-year loans for almost the total development cost at interest rates of a quarter of one per cent above the government rate so as to encourage rental projects for the elderly. The sponsors were to be nonprofit agencies, and FNMA was to buy the mortgages which, under later legislation, could cover the entire cost.[14]

The nonprofit programs were no sooner launched than private entrepreneurs began to sidle into the areas reserved for nonprofit organizations. As the FHA administrator put it: "Because of well-intentioned but inexperienced and unsophisticated applicants, and private entrepreneurs posing as nonprofit sponsors, there has been need to move with caution." Yet it is hard to see how the profit element can be kept out of the nonprofit program; and when 100 per cent loans were authorized, housing applications soared.

The big question in these operations is whether the entrepreneur will be satisfied with a good fee for his profit or will look for the bonanza. But the potential in the programs for a new kind of liaison between government and responsible entrepreneurs is there, and it is primarily the renewal program that exposed it.

[14] Section 231 of the Housing Act of 1959 authorized FHA to insure mortgages on rental accommodations for elderly people built by "nonprofit-motivated" agencies. Where the sponsor was a public agency or a "nonprofit-motivated" entrepreneur, the mortgage could be for as much as 100 per cent of replacement cost. The mortgage on profit-motivated projects could not exceed 90 per cent with a maximum interest of 5½ per cent. The 5½ per cent rate dictated higher rents than most of the elderly could pay. The public housing program had already allocated a portion of its low-rent units for the aged, and some specially designed projects were built.

Until recently cooperatives were hard put to get started. Federal and state laws offered them little assistance except in New York. Single homes were often better buys than those built under cooperative legislation. Until the condominium arrangement was made feasible,[15] a cooperative usually depended upon the continued ability of all its members to meet fixed charges. If a few defaulted, the rest had to pick up the tab to keep the mortgage on the property from going into default.

Another handicap was the lack of a central cooperative that not only understood the complicated problems of organizing, financing, building and managing, but could guide and build for its "daughter" co-ops as HSB (Hyresgästernas Sparkasse-och Byggnadsförening) is doing in Sweden. In the absence of know-how and leadership, the cooperator's advantages in cooperating were never impressive.[16] What was gained by the elimination of profit and other advantages was lost in conflicts, inexperience, and noncooperation by cooperators.

Greater interest was generated when FHA insured forty-year mortgages on cooperatives at 5¼ per cent interest plus one-half per cent for insurance. The loans could equal 97 per cent of the replacement cost. Cooperatives were also authorized under Section 221(d)(3) for displacees and other families in the moderate-income group.[17]

[15] One of the deterrents to cooperative investment had been the blanketing of the mortgages over all the units in a project. Under the condominium arrangement, each cooperator has title to his own unit, and default of others does not affect him. Loans on the individual units became possible when FHA was empowered to insure mortgages on them.

[16] Some central leadership has now been supplied by the Foundation for Cooperative Housing and its subsidiary, the FCH Company. The FCH Company has a national office at 322 Main Street, Stamford, Connecticut. Two other cooperative organizations function; they are the United Housing Foundation and the Association for Middle Income Housing, Inc. Except for a Virgin Islands project sponsored by the latter, both organizations operate primarily in New York City.

[17] The forty-year financing at the original 3⅛ per cent interest for debt service was $3.65 per $1,000. Thus on a $12,000 loan the monthly debt service would be about $44, or about 20 per cent below the total monthly charges under the 213 program. (See David L. Krooth, "How Cooperative Housing Can Help Urban Renewal," *Federal Bar Journal*, Summer 1961, p. 340.)

Cooperatives might also provide housing for the elderly with loans for the full development cost. Write-down of land cost in an urban renewal project and FNMA mortgage aid also helped.

With the 97–100 per cent loans, the small downpayments required, and the favorable income tax deductions permitted to cooperative owners, cooperators showed more interest, and so did some labor unions. The ability of urban renewal agencies to supply the land to them at low cost has already spurred the International Longshoremen's and Warehousemen's Union in San Francisco to build a cooperative on cleared land; a project of 752 units on a renewal site in Paterson, New Jersey, has been built; and New York City has made a number of urban renewal sites available for cooperative development. While cooperatives still do not benefit the low-income families, legislation may some day permit subsidized cooperatives for their benefit. New York City's offer of cheap financing and substantial tax exemption for moderate-income projects may also spur other cities to follow suit.

If, through the stimulus of urban renewal, cooperatives emerge as important producers of nonprofit housing and perhaps even of subsidized housing for low-income groups, it would be a major advance.

Increased Tax Revenues

Successful redevelopment of a site creates a substantial tax-paying asset which should compensate the city for its subsidy in five to eleven years. Thereafter the city enjoys a clear gain (see Appendix A, p. 181, below, for the calculations). As the calculations in Appendix A show, through a contribution of $2 million for the land cost, the city could gain an extra $600,000 in annual revenue and thereby recoup its investment in a few years. When a city creates a new $600,000 annual income, the capitalized value of that gain is at least $10 million. This should far more than compensate for any losses during the development period when the buildings do not produce revenues. Urban Renewal Commissioner Slayton has estimated that the increase in assessed valuations on projects started or completed will be from $575 million to more than $3 billion, or a 427 per cent increase. The San Francisco Redevelopment agency confirms (see Appendix A (2) (3), below) that urban renewal can be "good business" for a city. Whether it is "good business," of course, depends on whether the project gets a sponsor, and a number of cities have been disappointed in their expectations. But despite one opinion to the contrary, the projects that are completed should prove profitable to the cities, even if it takes ten years to complete them.[18]

The cities have made no bones about the profitability of their renewal operations. They have publicized the new-found treasure in handsome brochures for citizen consumption and made it a leading argument for pushing more and bigger programs.[19] California renewal agencies have, in fact, been able to borrow the cost of their cities' contribution to the land subsidy by pledging future revenues.

There is nothing wrong about a city making money as a dividend of its public operations (like profiting on marriage license fees), but the issue gets down to a finer logic:

The main purpose of a city is to act for the health and welfare

[18] The statement by Martin Anderson (*The Federal Bulldozer*, MIT Press, 1964, p. 172) to the effect that tax increases in cities with renewal programs are a "myth" and that "it is doubtful if the program will significantly increase tax revenues to any specific city" is not substantiated by the facts in a number of "specific" cities with completed programs. See Appendix A (2) (3), below.

[19] Typical quotations from urban renewal brochures are the following: "The Downtown Project in East Orange will cost an estimated $3,500,000. The return for the sale of the land should reduce this cost to about $2,900,000 of which $966,000 will be contributed by the City in public improvements. The increased tax revenue should be nearly $200,000 more annually than is presently being returned. Within 5–6 years the City will have amortized its investment. Public funds will have been spent to give private funds the opportunity to work. In the long run this partnership will keep our economy healthy as well as help to stabilize the tax rate which is choking most of our large cities." (*East Orange, New Jersey, Urban Renewal Program*, Progress Report and Development Guide 1960–1961, Citizens Advisory Committee and Housing Authority, n.d., p. 14).

"In 1953 the property tax revenue from Southwest was $553,409.77 ($592,-016.00 at current tax rates). It is estimated that the yearly tax revenue after completion of redevelopment will be $4,846,221.00. . . . Redevelopment offers one of the best methods for enhancing the value of the taxable property in the city. The increased property tax revenue from the redeveloped Southwest will repay the District's share of redevelopment in less than six years" (*Rebuilding Southwest Washington*, District of Columbia Redevelopment Land Agency, Annual Report, 1961, p. 13).

of its people—which is the governmental function. The city also has proprietary functions, involved with the properties it owns for governmental purposes (sidewalks, asphalt plants, piers, etc.). The proprietary activities may not be extended into the real estate business; "municipal trading" as practiced in foreign countries has rarely been countenanced here. Although the city may profit as an incident of its authorized operations, private gain or speculation as a main aim are not within the contemplation of its charter. The traditional rule is that a city is organized not to make money but to spend it.

Urban renewal offered the opportunity to cash in on some of the builder's profits, and the cities reached for the money. In the absence of adequate state and federal aid to help meet their soaring commitments, they sought whatever revenues they could lay their hands on. The trouble is that when a city gets mixed up in its motives, it is apt to subordinate its social obligations to its financial prospects. This is what has happened in many renewal operations that have been called "successful." It became less important to clean up a slum than to clean up in tax collections. There are instances when both the public good and the public treasury have been enhanced, and in these a gain can be chalked up against the deficits of urban renewal. But it is a sad commentary that cities should have to look for profitable ventures to pay their costs of governing. It highlights the desperate plight of cities and the need for an overhaul of the federal-state-city tax system looking toward a more equitable distribution of revenues and aid.

Assessing Urban Renewal

In assessing public programs, gains and losses cannot be quantified as in private operations to arrive at a precise profit or loss figure. Financial benefits cannot be offset against social costs nor an increase in revenues juxtaposed against the misery of people evicted from their homes. There are cities that can boast new downtowns and apartment houses, fresh revenues and other gains from the program; and if its faults and virtues could be put on the scales, what would tip the balance against it in a number of cities would be the uprooting of families, their increased rent burdens, and the numerous other hardships inflicted upon them. Yet the same objection could be made against demolition for streets, roads, traffic, bridges, and airports— why make some people flee to enable others to fly? Why should the people without cars be inconvenienced for the sake of those who can afford them?

By 1965, of 27,000 acres bought by cities since 1949, 10,439 had been resold; of the remainder, 7,400 acres were still uncleared, another 3,308 were cleared but lacked a sponsor. About 5,879 cleared acres were close to sale. Viewed from its inception in 1949, the record is not impressive, but viewed from its more recent acceleration, the progress is promising.

It takes time and effort to get projects underway, and while some may never see mortar, it would be rash to predict the program's failure. The renewal law confronted the cities with a task for which they were unprepared and which their officials had to learn the hard way. They had to win public support for a new program, master the involutions of the real estate enterprise, try to achieve good design while making it profitable for the renewers, replan whole sections, move people *en masse* while dealing with the racial issue, and do all these things while the federal officials were also groping with the program and changing the rules in the middle of the game. Moreover, the planning profession which was to supply these officials with the expert personnel is itself in embryo and the two-year graduate courses given at a few good universities have hardly equipped the candidates for the job. Yet all in all, considering the program's novelty and the obstacles, it is a miracle that so much was accomplished. It is a credit to the Weaver-Slayton administration that after years of stagnation, the program has begun to show more and better results.

Doubtless, the program has done many cities good and some more harm than good. However, the issue is not whether it has done more harm than good but whether its faults can be rectified so that it can do better.

From its inception, the program's shortcomings were acknowledged, and efforts were made to correct them. The 1950 act made forty revisions while the 1954 legislation gave it a major overhaul. New FHA aids, FNMA, Sections 220 and 221, (a), (b), (c), (d), (d)(1), (d)(2), (d)(3), and (d)(4) were rushed to its rescue. Thereafter, comprehensive planning and rehabilitation were emphasized and other programs brought in to supplement it. The widespread interest in planning which the program has generated is an important accomplishment. But Congress has been unwilling to face the real issues, and despite all these changes, the program's basic defects remain:

1. It overemphasizes slum clearance and lacks an adequate housing program for those it evicts and for those who live in the slums it proposes tearing down. It makes no provision for rehousing these people except in the cities.

2. It relies almost exclusively on the speculative profit motive for the clearance of these slums and the rebuilding of slum neighborhoods. Some of the projects cannot show a profit and should be developed for other purposes—more parks, playgrounds, etc.

3. It deals primarily with only one aspect of the city's predicament, i.e., housing and slums, while it ignores its others—poverty, social unrest, school problems, racial frictions, physical obsolescence, spatial restrictions, decline of its economic base, and the lack of financial resources to cope with its major difficulties. The poverty program is only a feeble start toward grappling with a few of these problems.

If the program continued its demolitions until every slum had been leveled, the housing problem would become incomparably worse and the housing conditions of low-income people would be aggravated with each demolition. The answer to a city's blight is not its destruction (without providing alternative shelter), but the removal of the causes and the improvement of the city so that it will become part of the better society.

The fundamental weakness of the renewal program is that it assumes that cities are sound for investment; that slum clearance and rebuilding in cities can make them sound if they are not; that the operations can even be profitable, if only the land cost is written down and the mortgage money is offered to the builders. Urban renewal puts the cart before the horse. If cities could have better schools, recreation, and environments, if they could cut their tax levies and provide their needed improvements from their revenues, and if they could be made pleasanter, safer, more interesting, and more convenient places in which to live and work, the demand for city living and housing would appear automatically in many areas. Mortgage money without FHA or FNMA assistance would become more plentiful, and private builders and merchants would scramble for the profit opportunities available. Urban renewal could then become a more constructive tool for assembling land, replanning obsolete layouts, and providing recreation, schools, housing, and other amenities to new, well-planned neighborhoods.

In sum, the urban renewal program is an important tool for cities and deserves continuance and expansion. But if it is to be a more useful component of a formula to regenerate cities, it must also do far more than it has done to date. It must be further implemented, be more selective in its authorizations, and sufficiently free of pressures to reject applications that are profit-motivated but not socially useful. It must show qualitative and not merely quantitative results. It must aim to improve cities, not simply speculative prospects.

America's vitality in the past was reinforced partly by its plurality of cultures and the contributions these cultures made to the American environment. These cultures are disappearing with the emergence of newer generations, and with their passing is also going the plurality of the environments which these varied cultures created. Diversity is giving way to a stagnant uniformity and a spiritual fatigue. Television in the parlor, automation and its routines, the monolithic additions to cities, the endless rows of duplicate suburbias and road programs are leading inevitably to an environmental homogenesis in the nation, the consequence of which will be a nationwide monotony. The urbanization and suburbanization of American life is becoming a treadmill when it should be a frontier. This is the real challenge that urban renewal should be confronting. This goes for the housing program as well.

A young country is seeing its cities go to seed before they have borne their fruit. Its cities, not yet old enough to boast antiquity, are showing all the symptoms of senescence. They are losing population at a time when the nation is racing into urbanization. They are poor and becoming poorer, and the more they tax to meet their needs, the heavier become their burdens.

If urban renewal has accomplished nothing else, it has stimulated a new interest in cities and highlighted the need for doing something about them before it is too late. If its impositions upon individuals have been oppressive and if some of the cleared sites may never see brick and mortar rise over them, something hopeful may yet be discovered in the rubble. If Congress can be aroused to keep looking and searching for the real causes and cures of urban erosion, urban renewal and its concomitant programs will be a gain.

If the housing and urban renewal administrators were more forthright in confessing the incompleteness of what Congress has given them, were more willing to admit the hardships the programs have caused, and proposed the proper means for easing them, they would be less subject to criticism. If, instead of asking for statutory pittances and telling Congress that these will furnish the answers, they would proffer the remedies they know can be constructive, they might win wider public support. But they cannot be expected to carry the ball without the support of the President. In the long run, it is the prestige of his office and the leadership he gives to the issue that will determine the destiny of our cities and the contributions an urban renewal program can make to their progress.

Appendix A (1)

Acquisition cost of site	$10,000,000
Resale price to redeveloper	4,000,000
Land subsidy required	6,000,000
Contribution by federal government	4,000,000
Required cash contribution by city	$ 2,000,000
Assessed value of private improvement and land	30,000,000
Annual tax rate at 3 per cent of value	900,000
Less taxes previously received from slum	300,000
Tax increment to city from new improvement	$ 600,000

Appendix A (2)

Redevelopment and Taxes: 800 Units of High-rise Apartments in San Francisco [Two Residential blocks (bounded by Jackson, Davis, Washington, and Battery streets) in the Golden Gateway]

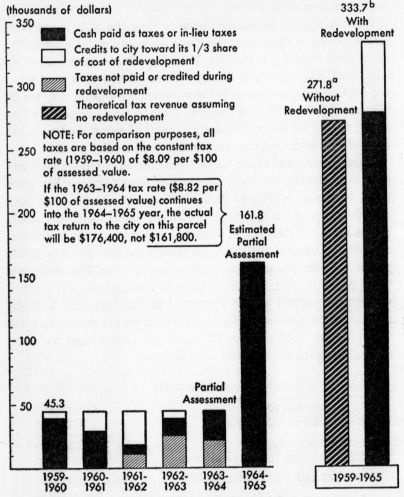

(thousands of dollars)

Cash paid as taxes or in-lieu taxes

Credits to city toward its 1/3 share of cost of redevelopment

Taxes not paid or credited during redevelopment

Theoretical tax revenue assuming no redevelopment

NOTE: For comparison purposes, all taxes are based on the constant tax rate (1959–1960) of $8.09 per $100 of assessed value.

If the 1963–1964 tax rate ($8.82 per $100 of assessed value) continues into the 1964–1965 year, the actual tax return to the city on this parcel will be $176,400, not $161,800.

333.7 [b] With Redevelopment

271.8 [a] Without Redevelopment

161.8 Estimated Partial Assessment

Partial Assessment

45.3

1959-1960 1960-1961 1961-1962 1962-1963 1963-1964 1964-1965

1959-1965

Source: San Francisco Redevelopment Agency, December 16, 1963.

[a] Total taxes 1959–1960 through 1964–1965 at original 1959–1960 assessment value, assuming no redevelopment and a flat tax rate.

[b] Total taxes 1959–1960 through 1964–1965 actually paid (1964–1965 estimated partial assessment) or credited to the city, assuming a flat tax rate.

Appendix A (3)

Estimates of Assessed Values in San Francisco's Redevelopment Areas

(millions of dollars)

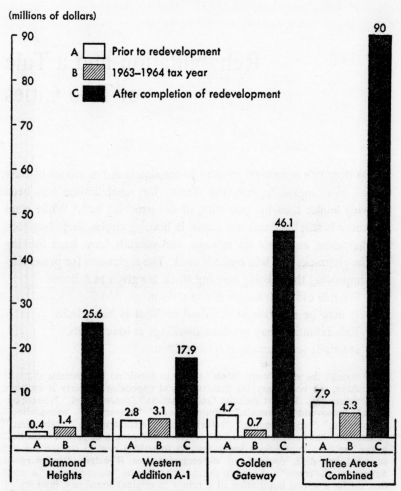

A ☐ Prior to redevelopment
B ▨ 1963–1964 tax year
C ■ After completion of redevelopment

Source: San Francisco Redevelopment Agency, December 16, 1963.

Chapter

10

Rehabilitation and a Tale
of Two Cities

FROM DUBLIN'S GEORGIAN FRONTS to the stately old mansions of New York's Washington Square, the clamor for rehabilitation has been growing louder than the pounding of the wrecking ball.[1] While slum clearance is still the dominant theme in housing circles, there has been an increasing emphasis on salvage, and officials have been looking for the gimmicks that will make it work. The arguments for preserving and improving the existing housing stock are given as follows:

- What is old is no longer per se a slum.
- It may be superior in standard to what is being built.
- Rehabilitation may produce dwellings at lower rents.
- It entails fewer tenant displacements.

[1] Although the single word "slum" seems to brook no compromise short of destruction, the vocabulary for preserving and improving property is multiple and confounding. The list includes "rehabilitation," "conservation," "redevelopment," "renovation," "repair," "improvement," "conversion," "remodeling," "restoration," "reconditioning," "refurbishing," "reconstruction," "rebuilding," "alteration," and "modernization," all of which still seem to be part of "renewal" whose inclusive implications imply making something new to replace the old or what has died, decayed, or disintegrated (see *Webster's Dictionary of Synonyms,* cf. "renew"). Added to the medley might be "redintegration," a word that carries a strong implication of a return to original soundness, integrity or perfection, i.e., the opposite of disintegration.

184]

• It does not uproot existing neighborhoods and facilities but maintains them with their diversity.

• It can be done more quickly.

• It is less of a rental gamble than is a new multistory apartment house in an untested renewal area.

These imputed virtues have led Congress to complement the renewal process with various rehabilitation aids, and a growing number of cities have boldly embarked on programs to preserve and refresh tired sections once rated as ripe for demolition.

The blessing of official approval was given to the effort on March 9, 1961, by President Kennedy:

As we broaden the scope of renewal programs looking toward newer and brighter urban areas, we must move with new vigor to conserve and rehabilitate residential districts. Our investment in nonfarm residential real estate is estimated at about $500 billion—the largest single component in our national wealth. These assets must be used responsibly, conserved, and supplemented, and not neglected or wasted in our emphasis on the new.[2]

The President's statement was quickly followed by the Urban Renewal Administration's announcement of plans to retain 128,500 of 235,000 targeted dwelling units in 135 localities.[3] Congress authorized a new improvement loan program in urban renewal areas and then created a similar program outside such areas.

Instead of basing mortgages on estimated replacement cost, the Federal Housing Administration was permitted to base them on the property's value before the rehabilitation plus the estimated cost of the rehabilitation. FNMA was empowered to buy such loans. Federal savings and loan associations and national banks were authorized to make improvement loans insured by FHA. The 1964 act went further —it barred federal assistance for demolition of any site which could be rehabilitated, and twenty-year loans at no more than 3 per cent interest were authorized for rehabilitation in renewal areas.[4]

[2] 107 *Congressional Record* 3410, daily ed., March 9, 1961.
[3] *Urban Renewal Notes,* Urban Renewal Administration, March–April, 1961.
[4] The loans could equal the cost of rehabilitation but not in excess of $10,000 per dwelling unit, or $50,000 for a business property. A $50 million revolving fund was authorized for the program.

After almost thirty years of dedication to destruction, Congress's action was a welcome sign of belated good judgment. Three per cent money will help, but unfortunately there is no sign that the new effort will at last bring an answer to the housing problem. For federally sponsored rehabilitation, the infant in the ever-growing family of housing programs, portends to mature into a homunculus despite its fresh inoculations of Congressional hormones. The fault lies primarily in the complexities of America's housing inventory, the neighborhoods to which it is moored, and the motivations that lure capital into real estate investment.

The frailties and potentials of rehabilitation are hidden in the 58.3 million units of America's housing, of which some 10.6 million units in 1960 were rated as substandard, including 8.1 million which were deteriorating and 4.2 million which were sound but lacking in some or all plumbing facilities.

One of the troubles with rehabilitating these structures is that the housing inventory is heterogeneous, varying across the nation's 3,500-mile breadth in age, physical condition, obsolescence, design, location, materials, occupancy, rental range, financing, house and room sizes, coverage, and flexibility. There is no standardized blueprint that can apply to all buildings. Their repair, rehabilitation, or alteration for other uses also depend on building codes, land values, tax rates and assessments, rental markets, mortgage availability, knowledgeable entrepreneurs and the lucubrations of federal housing officials as they try to write general rules for a multitude of diversiform cases.

If substantial rehabilitation of our slum areas is to be spurred, subsidies will be needed to enable the slum tenants to pay the rent required by the added expenditure, and in each instance, a determination will have to be made as to whether the buildings are worth saving. Unless continuing subsidies are part of a city's rehabilitation program, the mass displacements of poorer families caused by extensive alterations may aggravate rather than alleviate their housing conditions.

Pilot rehabilitation projects sponsored by public agencies (a project

in Harlem, New York City, undertaken in 1965, is the most publicized example) are of little consequence unless they demonstrate
their feasibility on a large scale. If a pilot project depends on extensive
foundation support, on subsidy arrangements that will not be extended to others, or that make no sense to other owners as investments, it will remain an isolated venture in the same old sea of slums.

Whether buildings will be altered or not is also hinged to the behavior of the millions of owners, some of whom have money and
some of whom have money troubles. Rehabilitation in their case depends also on their sentimental attachment to properties, on the age
and mobility of the owner or his wife, and on whether the owner
must move out while the job is being done.

Since no two buildings and no two cities are of a piece, each building and each section require separate study to see if rehabilitation
pays; and that it pays does not always mean that the owner will go
ahead. A section like San Francisco's Bay Area may sparkle into life
and generate a whole series of epidemic investments, while another
will continue victimized by the elements until it crumbles.

Three forces that can generate fixups are a general increase in income, a housing shortage that spurs an effective demand, or a return
to the city of people who want to live there and can pay the price.

Rehabilitation should be part of any federal housing program, but
it will never be the main or exclusive answer to the slum or the housing problem. If there is to be large-scale rehabilitation, a city must
also be a sound and attractive place in which to live. If it is made so,
rehabilitation will be speeded.

There are numerous sections in a city where rehabilitation can be
spurred by a happy chain of circumstances. A block of well-located
old buildings may have remained seedy for years. A brave investor
buys several and rents them profitably to personable tenants, restoring
status to the neighborhood. The whole row may then witness uplift,
as has happened in Philadelphia.

A section of a city with an elevated railway may have turned into
the ambulatorium for derelicts and the haven of cheap saloons. In

New York City, the removal of the tracks and pillars along Third
Avenue near the Murray Hill district signaled a boom in high-class
apartment houses, office buildings, and some reconditioning.

Spread over a deserted pier may be old factories and warehouses.
For decades, the area has been an industrial slum, dark, deserted,
and dangerous at night. A few of the smaller old warehouses are
altered by a venturesome investor who provides a floor for each
tenant to subdivide as he sees fit. He opens the view to the water,
rents one or two buildings, and spruces up a few more with similar
success. In Boston, such a section on the waterfront took on attraction as a building site not only for spot rehabilitation but for urban
renewal.

In San Juan, Puerto Rico, an old monastery was remodeled into an
attractive hotel. Some fine old Spanish mansions that had seen their
day were given a lift by a few brave investors. Others became interested in similar adventures. With the city's aid in healing or concealing some eyesores, the whole section began to reveal its hidden
charm and rehabilitation activity was stepped up.

A fine section of costly homes tapers off into a stabilized Negro-
occupied section of sound, well-sited, but deteriorating houses. Prices
in the fine section go up with a growing demand for homes. The
number of purchasable parcels is limited but a few people buy homes
in the direction of the Negro-occupied section. Others follow and
the deteriorating section gradually grows into an extension of the
finer one. This happened in Washington, D.C.'s Foggy Bottom and in
Cambridge, Massachusetts.

The Brooklyn Heights section of New York City slowly deteriorated and gave way to cheap furnished rooms. The pressure of
housing shortage, however, forced a few families to buy homes.
Flower boxes and a few trees appeared, inspiring others to follow
suit. The section again became fashionable and drew substantial investment in rehabilitation.

A well-located section of a city becomes the habitat of artists and
intellectuals in search of cheap apartments or studios. A few art galleries spring up. The section acquires atmosphere and becomes the

oasis of the curious with a thirst for adventure. A few good restaurants and sidewalk cafes make the oasis flow with better cheer. Soon rents go up, inspiring landlords to remodel to meet the surging demand. This happened in San Francisco.

General Rules for Rehabilitation

The mysterious forces that operate favorably on one section or city and not on another are difficult to identify. Investors looking for the answer in real estate texts and federal officials scampering to Baltimore and elsewhere in search of prototypes will face disillusionment. There is no book of rules that gives all the answers. There are, however, a few suggestions that may be drawn from some successful ventures:

• Rehabilitation deserves a try only when the projected net income compensates for the projected trouble and risk. Costs are a guess when one breaks plaster. Fixed estimates are hard to obtain, and when the job is finished, the contract price will usually be swelled by extras. On completion, the rent levels will depend on the market and on the section, not exclusively on the cost. Outlays that ignore the rental market and the section may go down the drain.

• The attractive shell of a building is one of the great investment seducers, but represents only a fraction of total development cost. (In Reynolds Aluminum's venture in Baltimore, purchase price per building was $5,000; alteration cost many times that.)

• The smaller gamble is the house in which interior walls can remain and in which additional amenities can be installed without substantial structural changes. Here estimates are less of a guess. In these cases, it may pay to do a block at a time—provided, of course, total investment is validated by net income.

• Scottish baronials boasting the rugged virtues of Caledonia and alcazars with overgenerous hallways and heraldry-ridden porticoes are a headache for the architect and a money trap for his client. Wrecking the structure is preferable to wrecking the investor.

• City taxes are an unknown quantity, accounting for up to 25 per cent of gross rental income. Taxes and tax valuations almost always go up, rarely down. A city with an appetite for taxes may eat up the profit. A mansion with an already high assessed valuation is the fixed starting point for a tax hike after alterations.

• The cost of alterations sometimes exceeds the cost of a new house.[5] The latter can be estimated more accurately and may be a better investment. Conversely the larger lot coverage permitted for structures put up under older building codes dictates retention of the old wall structure even if it means gutting the inside. (Some owners tear out everything inside the building, rehabilitate it, then knock down the walls and replace them with new walls. They do this to take advantage of the lot coverage permitted by the old code or zoning law.)

• A venture in rehabilitation means gambling on the neighborhood more often than the structure. If as a result of alterations, a section shifts from a low-rent to a high-rent class, the venture may prove a bonanza. But the section may be so bad that no face lifting will enhance its economic complexion.

• City regulations may spell the difference between success and failure. Obsolete or complex building codes that no one can interpret, finicky inspections, rent controls, overrigid zoning and occupancy restrictions as often reflect dominant group pressures as they do civic and business wisdom. An unaltered building may stand for decades without bringing in the building inspector. A conversion invites a complete going over, often for the first time in a generation, and may yield a fatal list of unanticipated violations. (This and rent controls were two causes for owners' hesitancy to remodel in New York City. Simultaneously, ability to free buildings from controls by demolition and rebuilding encouraged the leveling of many fine residences.)

• Just as regulation can prove a chore, city cooperation can prove a boon. Subventions for repair may take form in tax abatement or

[5] As Colley Cibber, England's eighteenth-century poet laureate wrote:
     Old houses mended
     Cost little less than new before they're ended.

remission. New York City grants a tax remission which may equal 70 per cent of rehabilitation cost over a ten-year period. Other inducements are rent increases allowed by its rent administrator for rewiring, heat installation,[6] and other improvements.

• Existing amenities in the old structures may be invaluable as magnets. Some well-designed old buildings are museums of built-in antiques. High ceilings, large rooms, eighteenth century town house styles, fireplaces, French windows, storage basements, woman-size kitchens and man-size toilets, backyards, gardens, bay windows, or skylights may draw customers from the new minimum-standard multiples and set off the spark that makes the remodeler's prospects glow. Old masonry walls leak fewer sound decibels than the skimpy partitions of new houses. (In one New York City apartment house, a tenant's unsuccessful effort to regulate his neighbor's snores had to be resolved in a criminal court. In another case, a push-button station changer is said to have controlled a neighbor's television set.) Parking space and proximity to garages, trees, and window boxes are assets; knocking down fences to create a large court has also proved an attraction.

• Rear buildings and alleys, once classed as obsolete by reformers, may satisfy the yearning for privacy in the current era of high-speed traffic, trucking, and tumult.

• A low purchase price is deceptive—it costs about the same to alter a house in a high-rental as in a low-rental section, but the profit differential may more than justify paying more for the shell in the better area.

• Alteration for sale may pay where rental may not. Tax advantages to the home buyer and the emotional magnetism of ownership are important factors in determining design. Alteration for a two-family house may have tax deduction advantages for purchasers occupying one of the units. (Half the cost of repairs and of depreciation may be deducted as expenses.) Architects of structures cannot be

---

[6] When I was State Rent Administrator and allowed landlords a $4 monthly rent increase per radiater installed, landlords not only happily installed heat in their tenements but a few put radiators into closets as well.

expected to be architects of the balance sheet. The owner must tell them the kind of alteration he wants. A specialist in alterations can often save an owner thousands; a novice can ruin him.

• Income taxes play many roles in the rehabilitator's tax position. The investment in the improvement, for example, can be written off in a short term against income. In some cases part of the outlay can be deducted from taxable income as a repair.[7] In an owner-occupied two- or three-family house, the owner can also deduct half to two-thirds of the upkeep and depreciation from his rent income as well as local taxes and interest.

• Good mortgage conditions are a prime factor not only in spurring rehabilitation but in increasing the net return on the cash investment. A 9 per cent return on an unmortgaged property may go to 12 per cent on the net cash investment after the property is mortgaged. Reliance on high-rate second mortgages for financing may absorb all the net profit. In this respect, liberal FHA financing may speed alterations. The size of the mortgage, however, may bring a high assessed valuation and taxes—city valuers too often fix valuation in relation to the amount of the mortgage loan.

• The character of a neighborhood and its amenities are vital elements. Remodeling for families entails consideration of such factors as good schools, play spaces, child friends, and safety. But this counts less for conversions into small efficiency units for childless occupants. Proximity to work location and downtown as well as to interesting people are important in all cases. So is closeness to theaters, good restaurants, institutions, and shopping.

• Conversion for residences is not an absolute. Some buildings may be more suitable for offices, stores, or for institutional or mixed uses. The investor's sharp instinct as to the highest and best use will determine whether he has big or small profits or none at all.

• The presence of minorities in the area, contrary to most realty

[7] The general rule is that ordinary repairs not adding to the property's value or increasing its useful life can be deducted as an annual expense. Repairs which appreciably prolong the building's life are considered as capital additions; they are not deductible as expenses but can be added to the tax base and depreciated annually against the depreciation reserve.

texts, is not an inevitable invitation to financial disaster.[8] When a Chinese could live almost anywhere in New York City, he could not do so in San Francisco. Colorful ethnic formations may add spirit and value to adjoining sections but the hypercritical might flee them. While occupancy by Negroes is sometimes more challenging than that of other minorities because of white prejudice or the social or economic status of a particular Negro group, Negro occupancy may not disturb a community if the neighborhood is stabilized and if troublemakers are not on hand to spur fears. Remodeling for Negro occupancy may even bring higher rents in some places, since the rise or fall of values often depends upon the ability of a minority to bid up prices.

A Tale of Two Cities: Louisville and New York (Greenwich Village)

These generalizations do not apply at all times and in all cases. The experiences in Louisville and New York City will highlight some of the intangibles and potentials.

Louisville

While its 390,000 people never felt they were living in a boom town, Louisville has always enjoyed a relatively unruffled stability. Its department stores have paid dividends regularly, and its people have shown continuing pride in their institutions. For a Southern-oriented city, Louisville is on the liberal side; segregation in public places is disappearing. The city-sponsored University of Louisville, the central library, orchestra, art gallery, children's theater, auditoriums, and annual fund-raising campaigns show that the city is closer to the enlightened main than to the Southern backland. When four of Louisville's denizens bend over a piano and a bourbon to exalt "My Old Kentucky Home," the vision is of a fireside, not a slum. Though a U.S. expressway has made a deep gash in its heart and though parking lots for horseless carriages now mar its core, the sound of the

---

[8] See Charles Abrams, *Forbidden Neighbors,* Harper & Row, 1954, p. 285.

hoof continues to call up the presence of pure inbred speed and courage on the bluegrass not far away.

But more recently, as families have been finding better bargains on the outskirts only a half hour's ride from downtown, the grass outside Louisville has been more often sundered by steam shovels than hooves. For a small downpayment, one can get a split-level overlooking the Ohio River, give running room to the kids, and provide them with a good school. The result has been that the new Kentucky home has been steadily competing with the old one in the city.

This development has given Louisville's proud citizens no little concern. For years, civic forces supported by the university have tried to make a stand against the drift outward and the blight inward. They have seen the downtown churches and institutions follow the outward trend. The city's department stores fear the competition of peripheral shopping centers already on the drawing boards—this could loosen the city's most vital economic peg.

The section on which civic concern has centered is a two-mile corridor leading from the commercial hub to the university. This corridor still houses many of Louisville's institutions near the commercial core and runs into a group of old residences stretching to the university campus. Many of these houses were erected around 1880 when abridgement of space or upholstery was disdained as inelegant. The prestige of a family was judged among other things by the amount and quality of the crystal in the chandeliers. Though they stand firm on their ample lots, and though most show the effects of the elements, the old structures have survived like hardy, courageous widows who seem due for the long stubborn life. Face lifting and toning up internally would go far toward making some of them more attractive as well as useful, and this has become one of the persistent aims of Louisville's better citizens. But, constructed originally as one-family units, the buildings suffer from an internal spatial sprawl that would require an excessive amount of housekeeping. Though tolerable in the age of livery and servants, this has proved a costly chore in the era of efficiency units.

Already the section in which these sad homesteads stand has been marred by a funeral parlor, a gas station, and other inconsistencies of trade bawling out their wares in a jumble of signboards. The widowed houses themselves, austere in structure, contribute to the discord by lamenting their situation in the form of "For Rent" signs, "Bedroom," "Adults Only," "Sleeping Room," "Men Only," "Ladies Only," "Children Accepted," and similar displays. The houses are tenanted by the aging, transients, bachelors, couples of modest means, and a few students. In 1961 three of every four houses had vacancies available to boarders who rented by the bed ($6 per four-poster) or by the room ($12 for two berths) with breakfast thrown in at 50 cents. The competition for roomers is brisk, the turnover is continuous (especially on the upper floors), and the vacancies frequent. Though most of the houses were well kept, the furnishings were timeworn. The landladies were not yet ready to yield their properties to the Negroes not too far away, nor were the Negroes ready to bid for the breach.

Since the structures were sound, well spaced, and well sited, the temptation to alter them for better uses in 1961 was great. Indeed, unless something dramatic was done about the whole corridor area, the section was destined to go further downgrade and hedge the university with creeping blight. Some selective acquisition and improvement of buildings, it was thought, would spur other improvements by owners and reverse the dismal trend.

The university's proposal was to buy some of the houses (by condemnation if necessary) and convert them into soundproofed, air-conditioned, neatly furnished apartments, each to accommodate a dozen or more students. Faculty and other families would be lured from the suburbs by the attractive accommodations and rents. A "Town and Gown Club" would occupy one of the larger structures and help wed the interests of the university and the neighbors to the regenerated section.

The main problems lay in the limitations of the existing house patterns, the costs of altering them, and the sparseness of the potential revenues. Asking prices for the houses in 1961 ranged from as little as $16,400 for a house on a lot 33 by 100 to as high as $85,000 on a lot 100 by 100. The average price of houses was $33,450 each.

The university projected the annual income of some ninety-two completed dwelling units in twelve structures (planned as a starter) at $64,000 and the expenses at the same figure.[9] The cost of altering each house was estimated at $100,000, making an initial outlay of $1.2 million—a tidy sum for tidying up only twelve buildings. But this could not be helped, for the houses were lusty in space and would devour plaster and paint without pity.

On analysis, the alteration was held to be too risky a proposition—not only financially but from the standpoint of what it would accomplish. Rehabilitating a few buildings would not guarantee reinforcement of the area nor spark the private rehabilitation needed to give the whole section the desired shot in the arm. Liberal federal financing might help, but a substantial subsidy would help even more. Even with this, the fate of the area as a whole would remain uncertain. Much more than a rehabilitation of a dozen houses and a "Town and Gown Club" was needed to pull the section out of the doldrums.

Houses and Neighborhoods

What makes a neighborhood like Louisville's corridor survive or decompose remains one of the unresolved mysteries of the American scene. Essentially, a neighborhood is a fortuitous product of many individual decisions, each of which acts upon the others and ultimately on the neighborhood itself, ending up either in a sad row of streets or in what the sociologists call the "sound community." The neighborhood ails or thrives because of a variety of elements—social status, proximity to work, types of neighbors and kids, rent levels, grades of architecture, clean or dirty streets, arboriculture, obsolescence, school conditions, environmental pegs or nuisances, nostalgias, social and institutional anchorages, and a host of miscellaneous intangibles running the gamut from political to nuptial expediencies. The members of the neighborhood are usually less interested in spiritual agglutination than in being left alone to their separate cares. Their consciousness of neighborhood becomes aroused when something threatens it, at which time they may suddenly identify its values and rise to their defense. But there must be something to defend and something to fight for or against.

[9] See Appendix A, p. 207, below, for breakdown of figures.

A neighborhood is often as sensitive to rumors as a bank, but sometimes it establishes a granite solvency for the oddest of reasons. Mrs. Grundy's sudden sale of her manor house when a Negro doctor moves into the block may scar one neighborhood, while the appearance of a dozen painters, poets, and pseudo-intellectuals (not too disreputable) in a few new coffeehouses (disinfected, heated, and illuminated with a maximum of candle power) may spur the teen-agers into ecstatic pride and even head their parents for a second look at the neighborhood's new "uniqueness." "Neighborhood stability" is just one of those catchwords of the planning and real estate trades— we know it exists but can't tell why. The numerous zoning proposals and the billions invested in public housing have not produced the passkey to the secret of the healthy neighborhood. Nor is the homogeneous suburb or urban renewal's conservation program the new link to Utopia.

If a neighborhood is to become attractive again, one answer (though not the only one) is that it must draw or hold the type of families who make for the suburbs. But this is easier said than done. An exemplary elementary school, a neighborhood center, a great church and related institutions, however, can sometimes supply the vital impulse. They may bring to an ailing neighborhood what the realtor calls a boom and the local pastor a blessing. In Louisville, the upper-income wives told me in 1961 that a top-flight school for their children would be a more alluring magnet for them than the refurbishing of the buildings. But each neighborhood has its own problems and may require its own special solutions. FHA financing may help, but it is not always determinative. Improvement of nearby houses is good, too, but it is more often the consequence than the cause of neighborhood revival. Louisville's problem accents this though Congress and federal officialdom still lean toward brick, mortar, and mortgage insurance as the true and only stimulants.

Greenwich Village, U.S.A.

No section has stirred more helpful controversy and excited more planning interest than Greenwich Village, an odd-shaped lobe of New

York City running south from West Fourteenth Street to Broome
Street and east from the North River to Broadway. One hears planning
theories spun in the Village that would have banished a student from
the Harvard planning school in the Gropius era. But in the Village
as elsewhere around the world, people are taking a second look at their
old sections and trying to rediscover their values. What is old is no
longer old-fashioned and what is antique not always antiquated. Even
the word slum, the most pugnacious in the planning glossary, no longer
churns up the same demolition instinct. Quite the contrary. In Greenwich Village, where the word has become a slander, its mere whisper
will send Villagers to their venerable bastions. A country with less than
two centuries of tradition behind it was finally induced to look at what
has survived, and Greenwich Village was where the first great pitched
battle for the right not to be renewed was fought and won.

   Greenwich Village is an annoying contradiction in that it violates all
the rules in the planning books, but functions. Old lofts, factories, bars,
and shops stand side by side with costly remodeled houses. The presence of cheap tenements does not agitate neighborhood equanimity.
Proximity of a poodle barber, a basement borscht bistro, and an old
Jewish cemetery have not stopped the surge of real estate values between Fifth and Sixth avenues. Alleys built for horses are stable real
estate, bringing the highest rentals. Crooked streets which planning
and highway officials thought a monstrous relic of a planless past are
viewed as part of the section's charm. In Greenwich Village anything
new is suspect. There will be frenzied opposition when the latest style
apartment house threatens to replace some flaking brownstones, or
when a city official thinks a park should be updated or a crooked street
pattern straightened. Greenwich Villagers want no planning officials
to encumber them with their help and trust neither their taste nor
their judgments. They recall only that whenever the city offered them
a public improvement it gave them something worse than what they
had before. In place of its busy old Jefferson Market, officials built
a grim jail for fallen women and maladroit shoplifters. Their precious
Italian section was almost cleared as a slum, its colorful espresso shops
threatened by a public housing project. Robert Moses offered to bisect

their little park with a roadway and gave them a private renewal project that took away two of their streets. It was no wonder, therefore, that when James Felt, his successor, proposed a renewal plan for the West Village, Villagers saw a Trojan horse behind Felt and drove the pair off.

Despite its stubborn unorthodoxies, Greenwich Village has been one of the few areas of the country in which rehabilitation has paid without a cent of federal help. The old-law tenement which was the reformer's target for a century has been turned into neat studio apartments; lofts have been converted into ateliers; basements that were good only for coal cellars became thriving night clubs while stables have been turned into off-Broadway theaters. How and why this has happened in the Village and not elsewhere remains one of the mysteries of the urban stage.

Though the narratives of ex-Village poets, Hollywood apostates, and artists leave the implication that it was they who made the Village what it is, they were only one of many factors responsible for this functioning hybrid. What makes a section thrive or wane is often rooted in its history, and to understand why the Village thrives despite all the planning rules it violates, one has to understand four events that have contributed to its physical environment.

The first was yellow fever, which from 1819 to 1823 sent panic-stricken people into the Village's then wooded areas. They put up shacks and stores in as little as twenty-four hours which were so skimpy they were dispensable and were ultimately replaced by better brick structures. But if few of the shacks survived, many street patterns fixed by the first foundations did. A crooked street is hardly what planners would approve, but like a squatters' village, something human emerges out of the jagged shapes and fortuitous forms and these remain to plague taxi drivers and delight the residents today. When the checkerboard pattern was laid out for the rest of the city in 1833, the Village was ignored, and the old cowpaths and crooked streets remained. As the city grew wider and higher, the Village pattern stood fast as it was.

A second event that helped make the Village what it is was the Brahmin invasion between 1820 and 1850. The city's paupers were disinterred from their Potter's Field on Washington Square and the Rhinelanders, Griswolds, Boormans, and Johnstones built their mansions facing the new Washington Square Park. They poured swank into the section east of Sixth Avenue (now known as Avenue of the Americas to everyone but Villagers). The commoners who served the gentry lived in the slums of Sixth Avenue or on West Eighth Street. The fine buildings of the gentry have survived to give the section some of its grace.

A third event was the wave of immigration that overtook the Village a few decades later. Viewed as a disaster, it turned out a boon. Up to about 1875, no other section of the city had held so small a proportion of foreigners and so large a proportion of Negroes—servants, footmen, stewards, etc. But by 1910, half the population in the blocks south of the Square was of foreign parentage or birth, most of them Italian. With the growing servant problem, the rising cost of maintaining a butler and his retinue, and with the breath of Europe's new off-scourings drawing closer to the mansions, the Brahmins deserted Washington Square for Park Avenue and the Upper East Side, leaving their structural legacies behind them. The Negroes dispersed into other belts, ultimately centralizing in Harlem.

The fourth event was the remodeling craze that swept the Village in the 1920s. By this time, the old isolation of the Village had been pierced by a widened Seventh Avenue and its subway while Sixth Avenue, which had led to a dead end, had also been cut through to become part of the vehicular main. Greenwich Village with its tenements close to its mansions, with its factories and its foreign born, with the outpouring of its gentler blood and the inpouring of plain-bloods and social deviates, seemed hardly destined for a happy future.

But if real estate transactions lagged, life went on and drama went along with it—the drama of people seeking privacy inside, and activity outside, as well as the drama of Eugene O'Neill and other upstarts struggling for recognition on McDougal Street or in the little theaters near Sheridan Square.

After 1921, however, some real estate activity manifested itself amid all the controversies. And it was this activity, one of the oddest developments in real estate history, that ultimately salvaged the Village's special configuration for posterity. A group of odd-ball investors who knew no better chose to marry their untutored creativity to their speculative urges. Only the Village could have spawned the brood. The investors were frustrated writers turned speculators, some with lucky lucre, some with nothing but faith and a backer. They included widows with a yen to build skylights and wives of sculptors enchanted with the potentials of paint and plaster. Some did well for a time, others went for broke and made it. Still others borrowed at usurious rates on second, third, and fourth mortgages to complete the last word in subsoil duplexes or rooftop arboretums.

Somehow customers appeared for the units—stenographers, sharing the room rent; long heads, eccentrics, landscapists, and escapists; paintslingers and inkslingers with legacies; sculptors in search of high ceilings and low rents, lowly people with lofty hopes, patrons of the salon, and just plain folk who liked fireplaces or walking to work. A few brave uptown builders ventured to build a new apartment house or two, but most still laughed at the idea. Soon, however, the demand for remodeled units exceeded the supply. Among those who competed for them were the paying ordinaries, the promising geniuses, and a few uptowners who did not mind the company. In the odd combine, a spirit became faintly evident, the spirit of escape and retreat, of calm within earshot of the big city's fury. The Village was changing. Its old-law tenements became neat studio units, store fronts bulged with odd trinkets, antique furniture, or books, and trees and flower pots appeared in the small remodeled houses of the dirty, noisy section west of Seventh Avenue. The hybrid of 1910 had become the mongrel of the 1930s. But it was an interesting mongrel imbued with the strains of some wealth on Lower Fifth Avenue and poverty on Bleecker Street; of bearded beatniks brushing with bigwigs, browsers, and bookkeepers; of tearooms, speakeasies, steak houses, burger merchants, and hangouts for those in search of a noisy drink or a quiet reverie.

The odd-ball remodeling boom pegged the Village to its physical past. When the depression arrived, however, most of the remodelers lost their shirts. It was a sad end for these pioneers. But enough remodeling had been done in the 1920s to make it too costly to assemble contiguous plots for new buildings. When conditions looked up in the 1940s and 1950s and when uptown builders sensed there was good real estate below Fourteenth Street after all, they were hard put to find 10,000 feet in a single unremodeled parcel which they could assemble at low cost for an apartment house.

As Village real estate boomed and the search for plottage intensified, the continental Brevoort Hotel and the Lafayette went down to make way for more apartment houses. Wanamaker's department store closed its doors. Educational and other institutions expanded; and new generations of investors, builders, and speculators were now ready to buy wherever they could. New multiple dwellings went up on the few cheaper sites that could still be assembled, and with rent controls on old buildings but not on new, more of the old mansions like the Rhinelander houses on Washington Square and a Mark Twain house on Fifth Avenue went down to make way for the control-free apartment houses. These were filled by middle- and upper-class folk who now saw the area as an interesting stockade in the New York wilderness. But despite an incipient building boom and an expansion by hospitals, schools, and institutions, there were enough well-paying remodeled dwellings to frustrate mass assemblage and mass destruction. Greenwich Village was punctuated by the monolith but not yet dominated by it. Despite new rows of apartment houses, it had somehow continued to maintain a precarious balance.

Urban Renewal Comes to Greenwich Village

The Greenwich Village of the postwar era emerged a partly ruined monument of the nostalgic past, but it somehow retained its vitality. It could not be stanched by the influx of a new crop of kindly suburban widows and couples into the Fifth Avenue hotels and apartment houses, the chain-store fronts, and the growing number of Bronx-style restaurants for visiting beefeaters. It took in stride the uptown rogues looking for an easy test of their virility, the homosexuals and Lesbians at their specialized bars. It turned a deaf ear to the shrieks and shouts from the Woman's Penitentiary to their visiting friends below, and to the occasional marijuana raids loudly reported by the tabloids. But its essential attractiveness as a neighborhood somehow survived. Bookshops teemed with browsers looking for the right paperback and coffeehouses were patronized by teen-agers who seemed safely ensconced behind a flickering candle. The Italian settlement, resented a half century before, continued giving the Village a touch of Milan behind its dangling cheeses. As espresso steamed out of the great metallic mammillas, the customers somehow found they had something to talk of besides the weather. And out of the air thick with bad poetry and good pizza had come more of the off-Broadway theater to demonstrate that what failed on Forty-fifth Street could run for years below Sheridan Square.

The Greenwich Village of the 1960s was part of the brave new world still living mostly in the old one. The builders who had bought in from the 1940s to the 1960s were doing exceedingly well with monthly rents now $80 a room and up. The Village had become a prime section for real estate investment. Everyone, it seemed, wanted to live there. But now came the storm.

In 1961 the New York City Planning Commission announced a $300,000 preliminary planning grant in anticipation of a renewal project for the West Village, which like the rest of the Village was a composite of rehabilitated houses, factories, shops, and the general bouillabaisse it had always been. The record of past municipal action was not one to spark the confidence of Villagers. The $300,000 study grant forecast a vast renewal scheme, uptown style. Jane Jacobs, Villager, mother, and an editor of the *Architectural Forum,* organized the local forces for resistance. She had just written *The Death and Life of Great American Cities,* the main theme of which was that large cities are a long way from the demise predicted for them by Patrick Geddes, Le Corbusier, and their followers; that the mixed uses which planning officials forbid by pat zoning laws are not always bad; that the self-contained new towns cherished by Clarence Stein, the Geddes-Mumford school, and their British and American disciples are not the last word in sound living; that the public housing project is not the poor man's Utopia; that there is life and hope in cities if only we look for the elements that stir them—the lights, the people, the shops, the miscellany that are the lifeblood of the bustling metropolises.

The Jacobs viewpoint was an antithesis to the Geddes-Mumford thesis and, as such, put in timely issue the contention that all great cities were doomed. Her book came like a breath of fresh air into a stuffy room. No one but an addicted Village dweller could have written it. Yet what was missing in both the thesis and the antithesis was the vital synthesis. Put simply, it is that there is no single simple answer to the complex needs and demands of human beings with their eccentricities and the diverse requirements called forth by the alternations in human yearnings and in life's cycles. The big city is one answer but only one; the new town is another, but only another. The real answer lies in expanding the options available to the individual with his mysterious urges and his unswerving search for something new, different, better—or worse but cheaper. Variety of cities and sections, new towns, existence of movement and movability from one scene to another are among the essential ingredients for the transient, unpredictable, and dissimilar Americans.

The real answer requires not only identifying the citizen's preferences, but also enlarging the range of his elections. These are never static, and they cannot be satisfied for a whole lifetime by suburbia alone or public housing, mobile living, cooperative projects and condominiums, or by new towns or old cities. Each of these may find a place at some time in life. Each has to be improved and its values rediscovered. Meanwhile, new neighborhoods must be built better and be more accessible. Greenwich Village with all its diversity is not true diversity standing alone, but a diversity in isolation. There are those to whom it would be unamusing and dull. True diversity exists only where there is a diversity of diversities.

The Planning Commission's sally into Greenwich Village was ill-fated. It drew no support within the Village, none in the city, and not even Mayor Wagner had a good word for it. After challenge, the commission filed a report promising no drastic changes but only a blending of improvements into the existing character of the area. It was an unacknowledged and a belated tribute to Mrs. Jacobs' crusade.

The Need for Escape Hatches

Greenwich Village has problems as well as charm, and its problems have spawned local citizen groups and paper organizations that have made it perhaps the most overorganized neighborhood in the nation. But it highlights in its inner conflicts New York City's defaults— defaults common to many other big cities. Though Census data are silent on the point, America's bored are growing faster than its population. So are the number of curiosity seekers, teen-agers in search of thrills, songs, or verse, and of the many others descending on Washington Square Park on week ends for a look at life or something more sensual.

A main trouble with our cities is their failure to recognize the need for escape hatches. The more the city fails to supply the needed diversions, the greater the pressures on the few outlets like the Village —for the city folk as well as the suburbanite.

In the 1920s, New York City could boast a quota of exciting places, most of them created and sustained by the interaction of people and enterprise. Yet Luna Park has given way to a housing project; Harlem, once sprouting as a tourist, jazz, and dance center, became "unsafe" and was declared out of bounds; Central Park, which might have become an evening stroller's paradise with a little official imagination, was virtually closed to people after dark; the Aquarium, with the view of boats, water, Miss Liberty, and the Wall Street skyscrapers was ruthlessly demolished; so was the nearby Washington Market with its bear meat, partridge, and venison, composing an epicure's museum without counterpart. Also scheduled to go are the still thriving market gardens, radio shops, and magnetic miscellany; and in their place, the Port Authority will build the nation's two biggest skyscrapers for the state's bureaucrats, the needs of the port, and the cash paying tenants who can make up the operation's deficit.

Times Square remained, but had gone honky-tonk because there was nothing else in the city for the honky-tonkers. New York City's waterfront, which could have supplied imaginative recreational novelties, was walled up with housing projects. Stuyvesant Town, Washington Square Village, and some of the forthcoming urban renewal projects are or will be enclaves with "no trespassing" signs. Lincoln Center is for the music lovers but not the lovers.

New York still retains some of its old treasures—the impressive skyscraper area (but dead after nightfall), the East Side night clubs (for those who can afford them), Chinatown (once listed for slum clearance), the theaters and the restaurants that make the "Steak, New York cut" famous, the Lower East Side (now calling itself the "East Village"), the department store windows and their fabulous sales. But something has gone out of New York that has not been replaced. Too many concessions have been made to the automobile and too little to the stroller, the city child, and the spirit-weary. More interesting streets to walk and see other people walking, more alternatives like a Tivoli on Welfare Island, a cultural center for Harlem to make it part of the main instead of thirty-story public housing projects, could go a long way toward taking some of the pressures off Greenwich Village. The Village is a stage and to many it is an illusion; but because it is one of the few escapes from tedium that remain, it is getting the pressure. It is bearing up well, but it cannot do the job alone of making the city interesting and vital for the surging throngs in search of something that is just not more of the same.

The function of the city threatened by the suburb, automobile, and television set is essentially to challenge sameness and ennui. It must find new ways of making itself more interesting as well as preserving what is worth keeping. Among these are the varieties of little enterprises which keep changing and going in and out of business until they ultimately provide what the people want. The diversity which Greenwich Village expresses in its miscellany of shops and people and living habits is perhaps in a planning sense what John Stuart Mill defined as freedom: "pursuing our own good in our own way, so long as we do not attempt to deprive others of theirs or impede others in their efforts to obtain it."

Urban renewal and city planning officials would better earn their keep if they were trained in something more than demolition, zoning, density control, and their other stock in trade. They require a keen knowledge of the secrets of human interest, activity, and recreation, of the needs and troubles of the human spirit, of the forces that make one city beat and another languish. These are the real frontiers of planning and renewal, but few officials have as yet embraced the heresies.

Appendix A

Projected Income
    92 units at $58.50–$65 per month with a
       10 per cent vacancy allowance (12
       rent-free faculty units not included in
       income) $64,584

Projected Expenses

Heat, coal, light, sewer, water	$13,200	
Paint, paper, roof, etc., maintenance fund	12,000	
Cleaning, grass cutting, etc.	5,000	
Maid service for unmarried students (2 × $1,700)	3,400	
Taxes	9,720	
Insurance on real estate	1,014	
Insurance on furniture	178	
Furniture repairs and replacements	13,800	
Other repairs estimated at $500 per house	6,000	
Total yearly expense		$64,312

THE LARGER

PERSPECTIVES

Part

III

THE LARGER

PERSPECTIVES

Chapter

11

Implications of the New Federal System

The first step is to break old patterns—
to begin to think, work and plan for the
development of entire metropolitan areas.
—President Johnson, State of the Union Message, January 4, 1965

IF THE NATIONAL EFFORT to rebuild our cities limps along aimlessly and fruitlessly, an important reason is that the national power to deal with its urban problems is checked by antiquated theories of states rights, home rule, and local autonomy that no longer make sense in an era in which 70 per cent of the American people are concentrated in cities and their sprawling metropolitan formations. Though the primary responsibility for the general welfare has been conceded to the federal government since 1937,[1] and though general welfare and urban welfare are interwoven and interdependent, the state continues to check its exercise in all matters in which the welfare of urban people are involved.

Under the cloak of home rule and local autonomy, the state has passed down much of its own sovereign responsibilities to a myriad of local (mostly suburban) governments, each of which is concerned with its own welfare to the exclusion of its neighbor's. With the federal welfare power held in check by the states and the states' welfare

[1] *Steward Machine Company* v. *Davis*, 301 U.S. 548 (1937).

power held in check by rural and suburban local governments, what is known as the general welfare has ceased being general.

The federal incapacity to deal directly with the urban problem has produced a system that can find no classification in political theory and no justification except as a vestige of an era that has passed. Its consequences are a national impotence to deal with the problems of poverty and substandard education, with the misery of the environment in which poor people live, and with the financial burdens and growing social costs the cities can no longer bear alone.

The system has virtually exempted from governmental control a host of metropolitan regions composed of thousands of minor jurisdictions with common problems and with problems interlinked with those of the central city.

It has created a bizarre federalism under which the expanded general welfare state is emerging into a business welfare state.

It has ushered in a system of local financing that guarantees immunity from levy of the large aggregations of personal and corporate wealth while simultaneously socializing a growing number of enterprises formerly in the private sector.

Because the nation enjoys prosperity, we have accepted all the shortcomings of the system in the belief that those shortcomings are part of what makes it work. But the system works despite the impediments, not because of them. In a period of national prosperity, it is an anomaly that slums and poverty continue, that cities are insolvent in an age of cities, that they are ugly, unlivable, and unable politically to cope with their growing predicaments.

National Welfare and National Sterility

The states rights shadow that still hovers over federal-city relationships was first drawn in a dispute at the time of the nation's founding as to precisely the kind of political creature the fledgling United States was to be.[2] Since that time, the bucolic America envisioned by Jeffer-

[2] See Appendix A, p. 238, below, for the background of the dispute and for a restatement of the constitutional issues in light of the present situation.

son has shrunk to a small residuum, and an urban America has supplanted it. The forces released by the age of machines and corporate enterprise could no longer be coped with by the segmented group of state sovereignties Jefferson envisioned. As the twentieth century drew on, economic and social well-being became inextricably involved with the destinies, aspirations, and survival of an urban people. At the turn of the century, almost 63 per cent of the aggregate tax revenues were levied by state and local governments. Today, nearly 70 per cent is levied by the federal government. Once the federal government had acquired the paramount levying power on incomes and the spending power that went with it, federal hegemony over the other levels of government seemed inevitable.

But although the central city has become the center of the very social problems—poverty, slums, crime, and delinquency—which should invoke the federal welfare power and bring to the cities the federal aid it authorizes, the federal government, except for some relatively inconsequential aid in the form of public housing, urban renewal, and some recent token help like the poverty program, has remained isolated from the central city's problems and its needs. Its isolation is secured at one end by Congressional unwillingness to face up to the real responsibilities of an urban society and at the other end by the states' inadequacies or indifference.

The guardians of the archaic formula and the most eloquent voices in opposition to direct federal aid to cities are the small local governments mushrooming around the cities, the private beneficiaries of the formula, and the states themselves. Their sentiments and their concerted power were demonstrated when President Kennedy in 1961 proposed the creation of a Department of Urban Affairs.

The Executive Director of the National Association of County Officials told Congress:

Many of our officials from counties, townships, and other smaller units of government in urban areas have been apprehensive that a new Urban Department would favor the large central city at the expense of the other units of government located in the typical urban area. Most of the large cities are actually declining very sharply in population. The urban growth has been in smaller incorporations and urban county areas outside the

central city. There is fear that if the central city can deal directly with
the Federal Government there will be less desire to work cooperatively
with the other units of government of the area.[3]

This argument, paraphrased, is that since the central cities are
ailing, they should be allowed to die. As long as they are weak, their
subordination to their satellites is assured, but if they are made sound,
they might assert the claims of the millions who live in them. The
federal government should, therefore, give them no voice in the national councils and no help.[4]

The National Association of Home Builders, whose members make
their profits primarily in suburbs, urged the measure's defeat not only
in behalf of the suburbs but also in defense of the tillers of the soil.
President Kennedy's proposal, said the home builders, "will give
Washington clear direction over metropolitan areas and widen the
breach between them and our smaller cities and our rural and semi-
rural areas."[5]

The executive committees of the Governors' Conference and the
Council of State Governments put the powerful influence of the states
behind the opposition. They told Congress:

Creation of such a department would focus upon the Congress considerably greater pressure for new programs of Federal aid. . . . Clearly, a
national-urban power complex does not give hope for balanced Federal-
State-local cooperation. There is grave risk that the proposed bills could

[3] *Establish a Department of Urban Affairs and Housing,* Hearings on S. Res.
288, Senate Committee on Government Operations, 87th Cong., 2nd Sess.,
February 14, 15, and 16, 1962, p. 158.

[4] The fact that Robert C. Weaver, Administrator of the Housing and Home
Finance Agency, was a Negro and seemed the natural choice for the new
cabinet office did not lessen the fear that, with a cabinet member representing
cities, the federal government might try to ease the plight of the urban Negro
and possibly accelerate his migration to the Northern suburbs.

[5] *Establish a Department of Urban Affairs and Housing,* p. 251. Its 1965
policy statement modified its prior position and approved establishment of the
cabinet post for urban affairs, provided that "primary recognition is given to
the role of privately financed housing" and proper safeguards are set up to insure "a high level of operations" for FHA and FNMA (*Department of Housing
and Urban Development,* Hearings on H. R. 6654, H. R. 6927, H. R. 7052,
H. R. 7108, H. R. 7176, House Subcommittee of the Committee on Government
Operations, 89th Cong., 1st Sess., April 5 and 6, 1965).

weaken both State and local government eventually and would add power and authority only at the center.[6]

The drum-beating for states rights brought the South to the side of the anticity trinity and sealed the fate of the Kennedy proposal. The measure went down to defeat. Nor will establishment of such a department give any more assurance that federal aid to cities will be substantial. If established, its concern with urban affairs will add little more than what is authorized by existing housing legislation.

President Johnson's program to relieve poverty in the cities met a similar assertion of state sovereignty over cities. In the original legislation, the war against poverty was to be waged mainly through a federal-local alliance. But the issue of states rights asserted itself in committee hearings and on the floor, and the bill could not pass until the House had written into it a veto power by governors for the two key sections—the provision for community action programs and for youth corps training centers.

Ever since 1934, there has been a move to enlarge the federal power to embrace some city problems—in slum clearance and housing, in urban renewal, in regional planning, in racial equality, and in problems of poverty. From 1934 to 1937, the first important breakthrough came with the direct imposition of the federal power over urban housing and the building of new cities.[7] But as the years have passed, there has been a relapse in the federal authority—and with every effort to reassert it, the power of the states and of the peripheral jurisdictions has succeeded in setting it back. As the federal function expands, state sovereignty is not only tightening its hold on the cities but asserting sovereignty over federal spending as well.

The Regional Maze

The federal failure to assume its general welfare function has also given each little suburban government surrounding the city the power to veto any move toward regional rationalization. In 1962 there were

[6] *Ibid.*, pp. 130, 131.
[7] For the circumstances leading up to the assertion of federal sovereignty and to its later subordination to state prerogatives, see Appendix A, p. 238, below.

91,185 local agencies composed of municipalities, townships, school and special districts, and counties. Some 212 standard metropolitan areas[8] today embrace man-made formations, many of which cut across the illusory boundaries of the states. They encompass some 18,000 local units of government that contain the nation's productive apparatus. Yet these 18,000 units of government function independently of each other with no central governing authority and without the semblance even of loose regional confederations. They lack a corporate existence, a leadership, a sense of being, a capital, and a common judicial agency from which they can seek redress for another's misdoings. Though they have common problems in water, transportation, sanitation, schools, parks, air pollution, and hospitals, they depend for action on the unanimous consent of all the governments concerned in any special problem—a tiny hamlet can frustrate the needs of a metropolis. The taxing powers of these freewheeling governments are divided among hundreds of jurisdictions within each region so that a rational allocation of their common resources is impossible. They compete with each other for industries, exclude each other's people from homes by zoning and other devices, and nullify any hope of areawide planning for the common good of the region's people.

In 1961, President Kennedy told Congress:

The city and its suburbs are interdependent parts of a single community, bound together by the web of transportation and other public facilities and by common economic interests. Bold programs in individual jurisdictions are no longer enough. Increasingly, community development must be a cooperative venture toward the common goals of the metropolitan region as a whole . . .

Pointing out that land is the nation's most precious resource and that the haphazard suburban development was contributing to "a tragic waste in the use of a vital resource now being consumed at an alarming rate," he directed the Housing and Home Finance Agency and the Secretary of the Interior "to develop a long-range program and policy for dealing with open space and orderly development of urban land." But though he made "an effective and compre-

---

[8] There are 400 such areas if smaller formations are included.

hensive plan for metropolitan or regional development" a prerequisite
for federal aid, the same frustrations by state and smaller local
bodies continue as before.

Many problems of an intercity or regional nature might be resolved if the state assumed the planning function. But state planning
laws today are mostly dead letters—promising in preamble, but
palsied in power and poor in purse. Fifteen states in 1961 had no
planning laws at all, and most of the others depended on the voluntary action of the localities. Like the federal government, they may
sometimes persuade, plead, and press, but they will never compel.
When exhorted to act for regional cooperation, state governors are
still ready to preach the gospel of *inter*state cooperation—the achievement of which is difficult and therefore politically palatable—while
ignoring almost completely the job of *intra*state cooperation which
is legally enforceable and therefore politically embarrassing. As the
states have become dominated by suburban and rural interests, they
continue to rest on the home rule and local autonomy principles
as their reasons for not interfering in the interrelated problems of
the region. Local autonomy and home rule have thus been woven
into a screen for justifying state withdrawal from responsibilty for
the growing intercommunity concerns.

That the time may come when the present state and local
frustrations will enforce federal action was suggested in a recent
report by a Congressional commission.

. . . Wholesale assumption of metropolitan area functions by the
Federal Government is now recommended by few, if any, thoughtful
people; but it will surely come to pass if the only alternative is chaos,
disintegration, and bickering at the local level. To those who question the
justification for the degree of increased Federal responsibility recommended in this report, the Commission would point out that moderate
Federal action now, designed to stimulate more effective State and local
action, is much to be preferred to a more unitary approach at a later date.[9]

"Moderate Federal action" was taken thereafter in the form of
federal aids to regional planning, but no better prospect of coopera-

[9] *Government Structure, Organization, and Planning in Metropolitan Areas,*
A Report by the Advisory Commission on Intergovernmental Relations, U.S.
Government Printing Office, 1961.

tion has appeared, and more and more "thoughtful people" are con-
cluding that the only alternative to "chaos, disintegration, and bickering" is precisely a more positive assertion of federal power.

The regional planning that is needed today is not simply some
financial aid to regional transportation, water development, air pollution, or similar problems of common concern. What is needed is a
regional renewal program for the nation's metropolitan areas and
the regional agencies to carry it out. And such a regional renewal
implies the creation of workable units out of the complex webs of
conflicting jurisdictions so that they can function more efficiently in
their own and in the national interest. Regional renewal calls for
the same imaginative enterprise that spawned the Tennessee Valley
Authority, and in some areas it may even require a similar assumption of federal financial responsibility and leadership, including
federal land acquisition, land planning, and land development if
necessary. It calls for a recasting of federal aid programs so that
they will meet not only the needs of cities but also of the regions as a
whole. It means taking a look at the educational systems of the central city and its peripheral units, their health requirements, their
physical, financial, and social needs, and making them function
rationally for the good of the whole region and its people. It means
also the chartering of regional agencies by the state where possible
or by federal charter when necessary.

The Legal and Constitutional Basis for Federal Intervention

The legal and constitutional basis for more direct federal intervention already exists. So does the logic. Intervention is no longer dependent on the presence of an emergency—though the emergency
is already upon us. The link of interstate commerce to transportation is clear. The right of the federal government to spend for a particular purpose carries with it the right to employ either regulation
or eminent domain for the same purpose. If, therefore, the federal
government is authorized to regulate in the general welfare, to spend
for the renewal of cities, or to provide decent homes for the poor,
it may employ not only the spending power but any power best cal-

culated to achieve the purpose. It may employ cities as its agents to perform that purpose, or it may move directly. No law or logic any longer stand in its way—only a Congress beset by pressure groups or with its eyes turned to the rural past.

Development of land use classifications by areas, retirement of poor lands, and federal aid to rural zoning programs have been long accepted.[10] The logic for similar controls in an urban age is no longer questionable. The commerce power has been upheld for river valley programs[11] and single states are no better posed to deal with population flows that intensify the housing problem than they are with river flows. Nor do the crime and disease attributed to slums respect state lines any more than floods do. Fifty-three of the nation's metropolitan areas either border on or cross state lines, and there should be little question that federal jurisdiction to plan (or build if necessary) is justified in these areas. The pivotal place of the building industry in the national economy is also accepted as affected with a federal concern, and any program to widen its operations within or outside the cities would also fall within the federal power.

Moreover, with the explosion of the 57-megaton bomb, which could level the whole New York or Chicago metropolitan regions, there is no longer any constitutional question about the federal government's legal power to plan and replan regions. Nor is there any doubt about federal power to defend the United States through the expansion of a defense housing program, either during or in advance of emergency, or to influence population redistribution and the impressment of land for any purpose essential to national security or national welfare. In fact, the megaton bomb has made the United States one single region in which the old state and city lines have become meaningless.

[10] See *Certain Aspects of Land Problems and Government Land Policies*, U.S. National Resources Board–Land Planning Committee, 1935, pp. 104–118, 129.

[11] *U.S.* v. *Appalachian Power Co.*, 311 U.S. 377 (December 16, 1940). ". . . Floods pay no respect to state lines. Their effective control in the Mississippi Valley has become increasingly a subject of national concern, in recognition of the fact that single states are impotent to deal with them effectively" [*Oklahoma* v. *Atkinson Co.*, 313 U.S. 508 (1941)].

If the states are unable to do their share or refuse to do so, it is the duty of a federal government dedicated to the general welfare to assert its own prerogative—not solely through a program for the demolition of a few slums or through a token public housing, renewal, or transportation program, but to the fullest measure of its responsibility and through the most practical uses of its authority. To refuse to deal directly with cities on matters concerning the general welfare until the state consents or, worse still, to submit to the wills of little governments before it can assume jurisdiction over what is conceded to be of national urgency is for it to deny its sovereignty and to abdicate its function in an urban society.

The Business Welfare State

A consequence of the states rights doctrine has been the emergence of what can be identified as the beginnings of a business welfare state. Its main features are (1) escape from federal taxation and (2) the removal of stake and risk from business enterprise. Since the states were the "original sovereigns," the federal government they created in 1789 was held to be inhibited from taxing them or their "instrumentalities." These instrumentalities were not only their subordinate governments, big and small, but the bonds issued by any of them.

Local governments, hard pressed for cash and for employment opportunities, have extended their operations in areas that were formerly in the entrepreneurial domain. Court decisions upholding public housing and other operations had abandoned the "use by the public" theory and speeded the "public benefit" test, i.e., that public money may be spent and private property acquired not only when the property was to be used by the public (a park, for example) but whenever it benefited the public. Public benefit was most often what public officials thought was a public benefit, and it was not long before private enterprise was not only made an eligible beneficiary[12] but also became the main beneficiary.

[12] *Dorsey* v. *Stuyvesant Town Corporation*, 299 N.Y. 512 (July 19, 1949). Cert. denied 339 U.S. 981 (June 5, 1950).

A whole new set of uses has now been authorized, such as parking lots, garages, factory buildings, and industrial estates. Since these were now for public benefit, tax-exempt bonds could be issued by cities and states and land compulsorily acquired for the purposes.

The bonds which state and local governments issued for these new purposes as well as the interest paid on them are immune from federal levy. The hard-pressed central cities and the smaller suburban governments issued these bonds by the billions. As more and more state and local operations formerly private are added to the tax-exempt inventory and as more tax-exempt bonds continued to be issued for the broadening purposes, the sources of federal levy shrink. Simultaneously, the federal capacity to borrow for its own programs in the competitive money market also declines.

Impact of Tax Exemption

To understand the attractiveness of tax-exempt bonds, one must know the impact of taxation on profit. The investor with $3 million who invests it to make a speculative 12 per cent return—say, in a second mortgage transaction—normally risks the loss of his capital. In 1963, such taxable income of $360,000 a year would have netted a married investor only about $82,000 after federal taxes. The investor is thus left with a net profit of about 2¾ per cent on the $3 million invested. Instead of risking his money in a 12 per cent investment, a knowledgeable investor with substantial capital will buy tax-exempt bonds of states, municipalities, and their public agencies yielding tax-free returns of 3½ per cent. He will then make $105,000 with almost no risk—and with no tax to pay.[13]

This escape from levy through purchase of tax-exempt bonds has in recent years begun to play an influential role in the financing not only of public housing and urban renewal but of numerous transac-

[13] Under the reduced 1965 schedule, the $360,000 income in a 12 per cent investment would net the investor $137,000. In 1964, it would have been $119,000.

tions (essentially private) which are financed by public agencies out of the tax-exempt bond issues.

By April 1962, for example, twenty-two renewal agencies or cities in the California region elected to sell exempt tax allocation bonds to finance the local share of their net project renewal costs. A total of 56 projects were involved, and the federal grants for 45 of the approved projects totaled an estimated $200 million.[14] The federally tax-exempt bonds for California alone will total $64,415,000. The tax-exempt interest rates run in one case to 6 per cent—a normal thirty-year municipal bond should pay not more than about 3½ per cent. A 6 per cent bond to a corporation in the 50 per cent tax bracket is equivalent to a 12 per cent return on a taxable investment. The number of renewal bonds, however, is minuscule compared to tax-free bonds for other purposes.

That the uses for which tax-exempt bonds are issued may be profit-making does not impair the tax-exemption feature, if the private portion of the operation is "incidental." Thus a city may, as in Pennsylvania, issue bonds to build a paying garage which it leases to a department store (a garage is viewed as part of the city's traffic responsibility). The Port of New York Authority was allowed tax exemption on its bonds which were issued for the building of an eleven-story office building, most of which it rented at a profit;[15] and it will do so again in a massive adventure involving the issuance of $350 million in exempt bonds for the construction of two 110-story buildings in downtown New York rented largely to commercial tenants. The rents collected from the private tenants will be more than sufficient to pay off the bond issue.

Industry Moves into the Tax-exemption Preserve

As cities small and large compete for industries inside and outside the 212 metropolitan regions, they are offering to build factories for them as an inducement and are issuing tax-exempt paper

[14] For a list of the cities, see *Report on Housing in California,* Governor's Advisory Commission on Housing Problems, January 1963, p. 63.
[15] *Bus Terminal* v. *City of New York,* 273 N.Y.S. 331 (June 20, 1934).

to finance the land and buildings. More recently, the industries that have been taking advantage of the tax-exemption sanctuary include the blue chip companies, some of whose officials are the most eloquent in their opposition to anything smacking of "socialism."

Tax-exempt industrial development bonds have financed the operations of such corporations as Armour, Allied Paper, Olin Mathieson Chemical, American Machine and Foundry, Borg-Warner, Georgia Pacific, and United States Rubber. Much of the investment and risk which these and similar companies once took under the old private enterprise system is now assumed by the public which finances the purchase of both their land and buildings. The first bonds for such purposes were issued in 1959 for $5 million; but from 1959 to 1963, there were sixteen additional issues; and in the four years up to 1963, more than three times the amount of industrial bonds were issued as in the preceding twenty years. The practice is only in its initial stage, but a widespread use of the device is now inevitable.[16]

While the quest for industry goes on in the troubled older cities, smaller municipalities without industries are also employing the tax-exemption privilege to draw them from these older cities. The municipalities may be one-horse towns, but the privilege of issuing tax-exempt bonds applies to them as it does to New York or Chicago.

Louisport, Kentucky, with all of 610 people and with a total property valuation of $330,000 and an annual budget of $2,300, has been able to land a 785,000-square-foot aluminum rolling mill by marketing a $48.5 million tax-exempt bond issue. With the proceeds, the town will buy the fully equipped plant upon its completion. It will then lease it to the Harvey Aluminum Company. Harvey Aluminum will not only get a plant without an investment, but will save about $250,000 a year in property taxes on the mill.

---

[16] States as well as ailing cities have also issued tax-exempt bonds to draw industries. Pennsylvania, Rhode Island, and New York State now make loan funds available for factory building and issue tax-exempt bonds when necessary for the purpose. Scranton even builds plants and rents them to industrial firms, while Philadelphia set aside 1,000 acres of city land for sale to companies needing plant sites. Chicago is moving to hold its industries in similar ways. Tax-exempt bonds for industrial purposes rose from $18 million in 1959 to $193 million in 1964 for an elevenfold increase.

Cherokee, Alabama, with all of 300 residents, sold $25 million in bonds to build a chemical plant. Annapolis, Missouri, with a population of 334, approved a $5 million bond issue in 1963 to help finance a roofing materials plant. A 3,400 acre plot outside St. Louis in a township containing only eight registered voters incorporated as Champ, Missouri, voted a $3,250,000 bond issue to finance a can company's operations. Eufaula, Alabama (population 8,357), thought a 60-unit Holiday Inn would produce 27 new jobs, so it marketed a $600,000 issue to build it. Union County, Arkansas, sold tax-exempt bonds so that it could lend the money to a private company. On the more risky ventures, interest rates often run higher than on nonexempt commercial loans made by banks.

In the four years preceding 1965, more than $400 million in industrial development bonds have been sold. In 1950 there were only three states that permitted their municipalities to sell such bonds—in 1963, there were 27.[17]

The Special District—Tax-exemption Opportunities Move into Real Estate

The state sovereignty doctrine, the failure of the federal government to take a firm hand in local needs and financing, and the enlargement of power at the local levels have combined to inspire creation of even more ingenious devices, one of which is the "special district." A special district is technically a creature of the state, set up for a single purpose, such as building a school, a sewer, or a water system. Often the device is a city's or county's only way of financing its much-needed public improvements. Some are set up to avoid tax limitations imposed by state constitutions, but the main motivation has been the ability to float bonds at the lower interest rates made possible through the grace of federal tax exemption of the bond interest.

It was not long before the device was adopted by a new breed of real estate operator nosing into the freewheeling Shangri-la of tax exemption. Protected by the doctrine of states rights and "reciprocal

[17] *Wall Street Journal*, November 22, 1963.

immunity," it is emerging into a practice that is little more than a racket. In a number of states, any real estate speculator may set up a special district, float tax-exempt bonds, and use the proceeds to pay for his utilities or other expenses which normally would have had to come out of his own pocket. The organization of the special district varies between states, but a few examples will demonstrate how it has been operating.

On the Sacramento River in California, an owner of a 170-acre farm needed $550,000 to develop a resort subdivision. No bank would lend it to him on his dubious security. He got five relatives and employees to petition the county to call a vote on setting up a special district. Since the owner and his signatories were the only voters, the district was approved 6–0. They elected their directors and floated bonds for his utilities, a marina, and streets. Soon after the money was borrowed, the district defaulted on its interest payments.[18]

In Texas, a water district covering only three-tenths of a square mile and having only four voters elected to enjoy the tax-exempt prerogatives of a full-fledged city. A few miles outside of San Francisco, a real estate development firm bought a tract of vacant land for $12.9 million, on which it placed a mortgage of $9 million. It then organized a special district, with authority to issue $55.5 million in tax-exempt bonds to build streets and utilities for a new Foster City housing 9,000 families. These tax-exempt bonds, offered to the public to yield 5.6 per cent annually, were secured by the district's anticipated tax levies. (The sales literature, issued by a Seattle bond house, said that the 1962–1963 valuation of the land was $23,206,000, though the county figured the land was worth $3,805,000; it was assessed at only $761,350.) Since the developer owned almost all the land, it was able to elect its own three-man governing board to issue the bonds to enable clearing and developing the land for resale to builders.

The Embarcadero Municipal Improvement District near Santa Barbara, organized by two speculative developers of 1,320 acres, was authorized to issue $8,874,000 of general obligation bonds; but the plan struck a snag when a Los Angeles mortgage firm that had lent

[18] *Wall Street Journal,* January 14, 1965.

money to the developers went broke. After some of the operations of the special district came to light, an indictment charging misuse of public funds and conspiracy was filed against the developers.

Another developer with 100,000 acres in the Mojave District got nine friendly residents to petition for an election to form a special district for a new city with a projected population of 100,000. The proposal, of course, passed unanimously, and the district sold $3.2 million in tax-free bonds to build a swimming pool, streets, and utilities. Four years after the project was launched, the new city was still short of its population estimate by 99,000 people.

A speculative subdivision called Country Club Park in California that floated $680,686 in tax-free bonds went broke; and, to the surprise of the bond buyers, there were mortgages on the land with a prior claim. The court described the district as "a melange of greased palms, sticky fingers, side deals and secret profits, misfeasance, non-feasance and malfeasance, diversion of funds . . ."

Despite some ugly experiences, the use of the special district as a speculative financing device has spread far and fast. There were 14,424 special districts of all kinds in 1957, and by 1962 they had grown to 18,323. California alone had 1,962. "More often than not," according to the *Wall Street Journal,* "the districts are formed by residents of small unincorporated areas who don't wish to shoulder the tax burden of full-scale municipal government."[19]

After years of tolerance, the misventures and sharp practices of some of the districts have stirred the concern of California, Texas, and Nevada, as well of the Securities and Exchange Commission. But the concern is involved with the malpractices rather than with the use of the device by speculators as a tax escape. It is legal as long as the entrepreneurs are free of deceit. Legality was recently affirmed by a California court for an issue of $178 million of tax-exempt bonds to finance a reclamation of 4,382 acres of land by a special improvement district in Redwood City. The bonds had been unanimously approved on June 16, 1964, by two voters, both officials of the landowner. There were no other eligible voters because no one lived on the acreage. The

[19] *Wall Street Journal,* January 14, 1965.

city will now issue the bonds to fill in the land and provide the utilities, and the landowner will hopefully pay the bonds issued through future taxes. Seventy million dollars in bonds for reclamation are secured by land in the district, assessed for tax purposes at only $354,450.[20]

Tax-free financing by special districts is being used also by small towns like West Palm Springs, California, to build cableways for skiers and sightseers; the San Jacinto District is building restaurants with part of the proceeds of a $7.7 million tax-exempt bond issue; and a growing number of other petty jurisdictions are moving in on the tax-exempt privilege to launch a host of new enterprises formerly in the private domain. They often lease the property at a profit to an entrepreneur.

A brochure recently offered the public a tax-exempt bond which could be converted into the stock of a private company that wanted to build a factory in a small locality. The bond buyer was given two licks at possible profit—a tax-exempt security issued by the locality or, at his future option, the speculative shares of the company.

Private special districts are not the only venturers into the frontier of tax exemption. A "city" may hardly be distinguishable from a speculative real estate subdivision located on a distant prairie. In one California city, the streets are privately owned. Some cities are nothing more than industrial enclaves, whose main aim is to avoid taxes and public responsibility. Others lack so much as a personnel staff.[21] But all may issue tax-free bonds through an authority or special district and often without legal limit on the amount.

In sum, speculative real estate is also getting under the tax-exemption umbrella. The cities, counties, townships, and hamlets are cooperating in private operations or engaging in them directly because they can borrow the money cheaper by offering the tax exemption inducement. White House memorandums have been issued suggesting federal guarantees of municipal obligations where tax exemption is

---

[20] *Wall Street Journal,* January 11, 1965.
[21] Stanley Scott, in *Metropolitan California,* Governor's Commission on Metropolitan Area Problems, 1961, p. 107.

waived,[22] but few of the localities will accept the offer. Nor are the chief executive and his agencies interfering with present processes even where posed to do so, i.e., through placing conditions on grants or putting pressure on the municipalities under threat to withhold federal aid.

The City's Plight and the Socialization from the Right

The older cities are borrowing and taxing because their budgets have soared while their sources for tax levy have shrunk. They are taking advantage of the tax freedom because the federal government is not helping them cope with their expanding needs. The suburban governments and hamlets are simultaneously borrowing for their requirements and taking advantage of the same tax immunities. Not to be left out of the picture, industry and the speculative operator have joined the roster of tax-free beneficiaries.

As tax collectors, local governments have their limitations. They depend primarily on the property tax for their revenues. While such revenues may go up in suburbia with its development and expansion, most older cities have virtually reached the limits in tapping real estate for their surging costs. Resort to sales taxes is difficult (it sends buyers to the suburbs for their purchases), and it is particularly difficult where states have pre-empted the tax. Income and payroll taxes only increase the flight from the city.

As for the states, while they more than doubled their assistance to local governments in the ten years to June 30, 1960, the proportion of state aid to local governments has just about stabilized.

Meanwhile, taxes of local governments have increased sharply—from $38 per capita in 1946 to $126 in 1964.[23] Limited in their ability to tax, they are issuing tax-free bonds and the number of these have been spiraling upward.

Gross local debt has risen from $13.6 billion in 1946 to $68.4

---

[22] *Report of the Committee on Federal Credit Programs to the President of the United States,* U.S. Government Printing Office, 1963.

[23] See Appendix B, p. 250, below.

billion in 1964, while state debt grew from $2.4 billion to $25 billion. In the same period, federal debt increased from $269 billion to only $312 billion.[24] On a per capita basis, local debt in that period rose from $97 to $357, while federal debt per capita actually declined from $1,924 to $1,629.[25]

Almost a third of the $10.3 billion of state and local bonds sold in 1963 were to finance educational facilities, 13 per cent were for water and sewer facilities, 8 per cent for highways and bridges, and 13 per cent for refunding of previous bonds; the rest was for other purposes. About $32 billion of these bonds, or about a third of the total state and local bonds outstanding, were bought by individuals and trusts; commercial banks owned $28 billion, insurance companies $15 billion.[26]

One of the best potentials for issuing more bonds is through the issuance of revenue obligations, i.e., bonds secured not by the local government's general revenues but by the revenues of a specific project. While general obligation local long-term debt increased 128.4 per cent between 1950–1961, revenue bonds and other limited obligations increased 692.3 per cent.[27]

To enable issuance of more revenue bonds, the local government must find new projects which will pay enough to retire the bonds with interest; and the temptation is to go into more enterprises which are either in the private domain or which were taxpaying private risks and which the local governments now assume for the company through the issuance of bonds (e.g., building a factory for an industry and paying the bonds through the leasehold rent or building an industrial park for a number of industries). It is the tax-free revenue bond which is being used to launch the dubious real estate ventures of speculators.

The pressure for socialization of operations had generally come

[24] See Appendix C, p. 251, below.
[25] See Appendix D, p. 252, below.
[26] In 1964, municipal bond sales made a record of $10.6 billion (Statistical Bulletin of Investment Bankers Association, February 1964 and February 1965).
[27] *Debt Obligations,* Monograph No. 1, Municipal Service Department, Dun and Bradstreet, Inc., October 10, 1963, p. 4 and Exhibit 1.

from liberal and radical sources, and the opposition had always come from Wall Street and business sources. Today the pressures are also coming from the industries getting free plants as well as from Wall Street. To sell more tax-exempt bonds, more private and quasi-private operations must be socialized. A hungry market of investors waits upon each new issue of tax-exempt bonds, and the investment houses are not missing their opportunity.

I was first struck by the implications of these pressures in 1936 when, as a New York City official, I was asked by one of the largest Wall Street bond houses whether I could induce the city to acquire the Consolidated Edison Company, a tax-paying public utility. A sale of tax-exempt bonds by the investment house would provide the capital. Everyone, said the bond house executive, would "benefit"— the city would be paying less than Consolidated for the money it had to borrow to acquire the company. Since it could borrow tax-free money at a lower rate than the company could, and since it would pay no income tax on operational profits, utility rates could be lowered for the consumer.

Everyone would doubtless have been better off—except the federal taxpayer. Nor only would the tax on profits disappear, but the sale of the tax-exempt bonds would have immunized the investors against federal levy for a generation.

The justification for the tax-exempt bonds issued by states and their creatures, e.g., that the state was the original sovereignty and that since "the power to tax is the power to destroy," taxation of the state would give the federal sovereignty the power to do death to the states, can bear rethinking a century and three-quarters after the country's founding. There are thirty-seven states out of the fifty from which the federal government did not derive its limited powers— and if one talks of who created whom, the parenthood in most cases is probably the other way. Nor is the federal government any longer a limited sovereignty, obliged to let the states and their creatures give tax immunity for entrenched wealth while those who venture their capital legitimately must pay the going rate. Finally, whatever may be the logic behind exemption from levy for the traditional purposes (and there is a better case for public housing than for many purposes less public in nature), it makes less sense in the case of the swelling functions of a quasi-private and proprietary nature. If the law cannot be changed, the federal influence should certainly be strong enough to induce the issuance of tax-paying obligations. This will simultaneously call for an assumption of those responsibilities which the cities can no longer bear. The real test of whether the federal government will assume some of these obligations will come with the reduction of federal expenditures for defense and the way in which revenues will then be allocated.

Socialization of Risk in Housing

The move toward the business welfare state originated in the home-building industry during the New Deal era as an emergency measure. Until then, a fairly clear line could be drawn between the private and public domains in housing and other enterprises. President Hoover, the most ardent spokesman for a free private enterprise, had argued that under the system, the United States had become prosperous and efficient while government operation was bureaucratic and lacking in the incentives and inventiveness of the entrepreneur.[28] The *laissez faire* theory which he espoused was not much different from Adam Smith's, viz., that government should leave to the entrepreneur everything except public institutions and works in which "the profit could never repay the expense to the individual."[29]

With the advent of the Roosevelt Administration and in its effort to prop up the home-building and mortgage-lending enterprises, the federal government, through the Federal Housing Administration, moved into the mortgage insurance business, which was once a private undertaking. This was done in the name of "encouraging private enterprise." A similar formula was later fashioned for home loans to war veterans. The government's contingent liability on government-

[28] Herbert C. Hoover, "Government Ownership," Address delivered in Washington, D.C., September 29, 1924.

[29] Adam Smith, *Wealth of Nations,* Edinburgh, Adam and Charles Black and Longman's, Brown, Green and Longman's, 1750, Book V, p. 325.

insured and loan guarantee programs in 1962 totaled more than $60 billion.[30]

Although the two basic elements of private enterprise—stake and risk—are taken from the shoulders of the entrepreneur and lender and placed on the government's, a premium of one-half of 1 per cent was presumed to pay operating costs and provide reserves for losses. The operation has not been a losing proposition since building costs, house values, and incomes have gone up almost continuously since 1934.

There is, however, a vast difference between subsidizing an industry as part of a depression emergency and continuing it as a permanent part of the system. There is also a substantive difference between traditional insurance of risk and socialization of risk. The elements of an actuarial formula in an insurable risk require: (1) a statistical measurement of the probability of a risk happening on the basis of known experience; (2) a hazard that belongs to a class large enough to conform to the theory of probability; (3) the possibility, however remote, that the hazard will cause personal and direct loss to the insured; (4) that the premiums paid for the risk come from a sufficient number of exposed individuals so that there will be money enough to make good the loss caused on any one transaction.

A mortgage 90 to 100 per cent of value is no more an insurable risk than a zero to 10 per cent margin account in Wall Street, and value of real estate is just about as fluctuating. Nor is risk improved with time, for on a mortgage with a constant payment of interest and amortization, depreciation virtually keeps pace with amortization for a decade or more. Thus during the period of greatest hazard, there is no actual reduction of the risk.

The home owner does invest more than the downpayment when he furnishes his home and moves into it. Despite the fluctuations of value, he will also tend to hold on for emotional reasons. But from an actuarial standpoint, the risk is hardly one which is insurable. A rental project is even less insurable. An example is a project with 114 units, the insured mortgage on which is somewhat under $1,600,000, leaving

[30] *Report of the Committee on Federal Credit Programs,* p. 29.

a cash investment of about 10 per cent. With rebates and builder's fees, the investment should be no more than 3 to 5 per cent. The projected net profit is listed as only $5,909 (see Appendix E, page 253, below). A 25 per cent increase in taxes, a rise of 3 per cent in the vacancies or rent losses, a drop of 3 per cent in the expected rental, or an increase of 10 per cent in operating cost would wipe out the thin margin of return (operating cost generally goes up with the years and rarely down). A fractional increase in each of these items (which is by no means unlikely) would bring the same result. A $5,909 profit (before taxes) on a rental of almost $200,000 is so marginal that no sane mortgagee would consider buying such a mortgage without a government guarantee.

The federal mortgage insurance scheme fails to conform with most if not all of the actuarial criteria for insurance risks. Default would cause no serious personal loss to the operator, for he stakes only a nominal amount of his cash on a gamble. The risk of loss to the government is not calculable by the theory of probabilities, for there is no known experience proving that real estate values go up and not down. Nor is the one-half of 1 per cent premium sufficient to justify the government's risk, which is particularly hazardous during the early stage when the mortgage is at its maximum and the first big test of rentability arrives.

The fluctuations of the rent and building cycles continued on the whole to operate favorably for FHA and the insured builders from 1935 to 1958 and in this period, FHA built up premium reserves of close to $650 million. Thereafter, however, the mechanisms faltered. Acquisitions of homes by FHA exceeded the increase in defaults, rising fifteenfold from a minimum of 1,054 properties in the last half of 1957 to 15,940 in early 1962. The cost of taking over a house is about $1,500 and sometimes more. According to Neal Hardy, then FHA administrator, "both the nation and FHA have been fortunate in the postwar period that no recession between 1937 and 1960 was of such magnitude as to result in major increases in foreclosures, although increases in defaults have consistently occurred in recession periods." In short, said the FHA administrator, as long as property

values were rising, there was less danger of foreclosures. But with the
first downturn of economic activity national or local (which was the
first real test of FHA's actuarial formula), the cracks in the structure
appeared.[31]

Because of the relative novelty of the insurance and guarantee devices in housing, the theories underlying their use have hardly received
attention. The report of the Committee on Federal Credit, composed
of the Secretary of the Treasury, the Budget Director, the chairman of
the Council of Economic Advisers and the chairman of the board
of the Federal Reserve System, sanctions their use "when credit needs
arise from risks or uncertainties which, in the opinion of private lenders, are too great or too unpredictable to encourage investment of
private funds, but are not excessive when spread over many loans."[32]
This argument hardly makes sense for FHA rental operations, the
loans on which are not only highly excessive but are also highly
hazardous.

The report also says that since FHA-insured mortgages involve
longer terms and therefore "such a high proportion of total investment
that private institutions cannot legally lend without the protection of
federal insurance," FHA insurance is held to fall within the authorized
category. Were this argument correct, there would be no need to insure the entire mortgage for builders. The government's underwritings
could be on second mortgages, not first mortgages. Since the first-
mortgage market operates well in most parts of the United States when
mortgages amount to 66–70 per cent of value, it is unnecessary for
FHA to insure the entire mortgage. By insuring the junior interest
in an 80 to 90 per cent mortgage, private enterprise would be substantially restored to the first-mortgage market without the need for
federal insurance. The fact that savings and loan societies are functioning as uninsured mortgagees on small homes throughout the country
and have steadily pushed FHA out of the competitive market renders
the committee's defense of FHA operations baseless.

[31] *Progress Report on Federal Housing Programs,* Hearings before a Senate
Committee on Banking and Currency, 87th Cong., 2nd Sess., August 29, 1962,
p. 7.
[32] *Report of Committee on Federal Credit Programs,* p. 17.

It is not contended that FHA has no role to play in mortgage financing. Its insurance might be justified during emergency periods when the mortgage market has slackened and building activity has sagged so that it imperils the economy. It might operate also in places where no mortgage market exists, e.g., where there are isolated defense installations in which private mortgagees might hesitate to invest without government insurance. It is also justified where a public as distinguished from a private or purely speculative purpose is involved. As an insurer of second mortgages, it might play an important role if savings and loan associations could be induced to make more conservative first-mortgage loans on homes and FHA insured the secondary financing. It could also play a useful role as an insurer of home ownership security by offering an owner insurance against foreclosure due to unemployment, illness, or death—this would perform a public as distinguished from a private purpose. Where private lenders demur, FHA insurance might also be justified in other areas of social purpose, such as insuring mortgages for low-income families who are being subsidized by the government. In short, FHA insurance can be justified in particular cases, but it has little justification as a tool for giving government guarantees at high interest rates on speculative operations and on market operations that should be financed privately.

Federal Guarantees of Liquidity

As federal operations expanded in housing and building, the federal government soon became not only the insurer but also the direct financier, subsidizer, and joint venturer under a widening variety of mechanisms.[33] They embraced trailer lot development, college dormitories, private nursing homes, and almost every other kind of rental housing project.

One of the more recent government innovations with far-reaching implications is the Federal National Mortgage Association, rechartered

[33] A list of the operations would cover at least pages. For an abridged list of these vast involvements, see my summary appended to *Report on Housing in California* (note 14, above), pp. 74 ff.; and *Progress Report on Federal Housing Programs*, pp. 91–132.

in 1954 to perform the function of mortgage merchandising for the private mortgage market. FNMA buys FHA and Veterans Administration mortgages from private lending institutions and sells mortgages to them when they want it. They may be long- or short-term loans and include speculative ventures as well as cooperative projects and those under 221(d)(3). It also buys defaulted government-guaranteed mortgages. In 1964, it held about $4.8 billion in its mortgage portfolio. It obtains its necessary capital from the Treasury and by floating its debentures on the open market.

In practice, the mortgage lender not only has FHA insurance of its risk, but it can have its money any time it asks for it. Thus, although mortgages are bought at yields geared to long-term interest rates, the instrument is actually short term.[34] Under this arrangement, an interest rate not much higher than the government rate would seem to be warranted. But interest rates on such prime investments are little less than the going rate on uninsured mortgages.[35]

In short, the government now not only makes it possible for builders to embark on risky ventures with little or no cash but it underwrites risks in the mortgage business and provides liquidity to the lending institutions when they no longer want the paper. The thin thread of equity (if any) provides the dubious margin that "justifies" the adventures. Social purpose, the rationale for most subsidized operations, has become the palliative for the removal of the gamble from private building speculations and mortgage investments and for passing it onto the government.

Unless these mechanisms are reshaped to benefit low-income groups or fulfill similar social purposes, the emerging trend of the system

[34] For a criticism of FNMA practice, see *Report of the Committee on Federal Credit Programs*, p. 23.

[35] FNMA is not the only agency guaranteeing liquidity to lenders. The Farmers Home Administration's insurance of farm real estate loans, Commodity Credit Corporation crop-support loan guarantees, defense production loan guarantees, and Small Business Administration deferred participations all permit the private lender to turn over the guaranteed portion of his loans for cash at any time. Government insurance is now also issued for housing loans to foreign governments.

would seem to be toward a "socialism for the rich and private enterprise for the poor."[36]

Revising the Mechanisms

By 1965, the perversions of the general welfare purpose in housing and real estate operations were by no means final or complete. Though the socialization and subsidization processes (for the richer taxpayer) have embraced the bulk of housing operations (and may be only at their beginnings), a slight shade of social purpose slowly trickled into federal housing policy through below-market loans for the elderly under Section 202 and projects under Section 221(d)(3). The patent irrationality of urban renewal displacements had been making itself felt, and since public housing was no longer supplying the bulk of the accommodations for the evicted, some formula had to be devised to appease the federal conscience.

These low-interest programs represented the first federal acknowledgment that reduced interest rates are the key to meeting the social purpose in housing—whether the agent be private or public. If the rate could be further cut or its costs reduced by an annual interest subsidy or a subsidy to the family, a logical and a socially informed program might then move into focus. Such formulas could also prove the key to a workable rehabilitation program for existing housing.[37]

In 1965, however, under pressure of the Budget Bureau, the Johnson administration recommended to Congress that it "phase out" the direct lending program under 221(d)(3) and for the housing of the low-income elderly. FHA insurance of mortgages at about 5½ per cent interest coupled with subsidies to families for those above the

[36] I have used this phrase in previous writings and am grateful to Michael Harrington for popularizing it.

[37] The bonds need not all have been issued by the federal government, but some might have been issued by local governments in the form of non-tax-exempt bonds which the federal government would guarantee while it simultaneously subsidized the family or the interest rate.

lowest-income group was proposed as the alternative. It is probable that the pinch of competitive tax-exempt bonds may have also played a part in the administrative decision, for to the bond-buying market, a sound tax-exempt bond is a more lucrative investment than a federal obligation on which taxes must be paid.

Without direct federal loans, more government guarantees of speculative mortgage loans for higher-income families and more secondary market operations will go on, while those who need housing most would be left to their own devices.

The overriding issue is whether we are aiming to feather the nests of entrepreneurs or to build homes for the forgotten families, 9 million of whom have yearly incomes below $3,000 a year, 5 million of whom have incomes below $2,000 a year, and the 5 million single people with incomes below $1,500. As the situation stood in 1965, nest-feathering was in the ascendant, while social purpose was being moved into the background.

Appendix A

The present housing and urban renewal formulae under which the federal government bows to state sovereignty in the exercise of the welfare power and under which it carries out housing programs through local housing authorities and local renewal agencies instead of through the federal government are, in a sense, a historical accident. The same accident deters the federal government from building new towns as it did in 1936, and is responsible for the continued issuance of tax exempt bonds not only for housing and urban renewal, but for the expanding number of dubious local operations under the loose "public benefit theory." Because I was counsel in two of the pivotal cases which effected the shift in policy, I am able to provide some of the background information.

One of the main issues after the Constitutional Convention had been whether the general welfare clause of the Constitution was intended to be an independent clause which authorized the new federal government to act in the national good or whether it was merely a qualifying clause authorizing the spending of money exclusively under the enumerated powers that preceded it (interstate commerce, war, post roads, etc.). On the side of the strong and independent federal welfare power had stood Hamilton and Monroe. They were reinforced in their view by Judge Story's conception of what had happened at the convention. Supporting the more constricted position were Madison and Jefferson, abetted in the years that followed by Presidents Polk, Pierce, and Buchanan.

Whatever may have been in the minds of the founders, all were convinced that the states would remain the dominant power in the centuries that lay ahead. Jefferson left the Convention content in the thought that the new federal government was little more than an American department of foreign affairs, while Hamilton dolefully conceded that the peoples' affections toward their own states would soon make them indifferent toward the infant nation.[1]

The feeling that the state was supreme persisted even during the century that followed. "Many people in France," wrote de Tocqueville, "imagine that a change of opinion is going on in the United States, which is favorable to a centralisation of power in the hands of the President and the Congress. I hold that a contrary tendency may distinctly be observed."[2]

Even after the state secession thesis had been shattered at Appomattox, Lord Bryce, while acknowledging a well-defined division of responsibility between the two great levels of government, thought Jefferson not unrealistic in comparing the federal government to a foreign affairs department. An American, he wrote, "may, through a long life, never be reminded of the federal government, except when he votes at presidential and congressional elections."[3] Yet if de Tocqueville and Bryce were to return for a look at America's political system today, it would appear as strange to them as Rip Van Winkel's Catskill Village looked to him after his twenty-year slumber, for the bucolic America envisioned by Jefferson has shrunk to a small remnant of its original design.

But if the old dispute over the meaning of general welfare should have been resolved by events, it remained unresolved until the New Deal, and it was not until Franklin D. Roosevelt took office that an effort was made to remove the ambiguity for all time.

The New Deal Challenge to the Constricted Welfare Concept

Neither the states nor the cities in 1933 were in a mood to reject any federal largess on legalistic grounds, while for the federal government to

---

[1] "Upon the same principle," wrote Hamilton, "that a man is more attached to his family than to his neighborhood, to his neighborhood than to the community at large, the people of each state would be apt to feel a stronger bias toward their local governments than towards the government of the union" (*Federalist Papers*, No. 17).

[2] "So far is the federal government, as it grows old, from acquiring strength, and from threatening the sovereignty of the states, that I maintain it to be growing weaker, and that the sovereignty of the union alone is in danger" (Alexis de Tocqueville, *Democracy in America*, Century, 1898, I, 535).

[3] *The American Commonwealth*, Macmillan, 1895, p. 425.

close its purse on the 13 million unemployed would have been a catastrophic default. It was at this juncture that low-rent housing and other federal assistance to cities were struck upon as devices for priming an economic recovery. Harold L. Ickes, as head of the Federal Public Works Administration, was placed in charge of the federal public housing program and proceeded to buy sites for the purpose within the states' land preserves; he drew plans for his projects, built houses, and, where private land owners refused to sell their land, he boldly acquired it under a presumptive and politically (if not yet constitutionally) acceptable power of eminent domain.

Mr. Ickes was not alone in crossing the Rubicon of state police power over city affairs and over national welfare generally. The United States had simultaneously proceeded to replan the Tennessee Valley and had set up a federal Authority to prevent floods and stream pollution, provide cheap power, control the soil, and improve navigation, irrigation, and recreation.

Rexford Tugwell's dream during these trying days was the most far-reaching of all as a challenge to state power. As federal Resettlement Administrator, he had conceived a vast federal program for the building of new towns similar to Britain's Welwyn Gardens. He aimed to achieve (in Ebenezer Howard's words) "a union of city and country life in which every foot of land was planned to eliminate waste and to provide its inhabitants with pleasant and spacious living."[4] Tugwell saw a vision of such greenbelt towns around every metropolis with a

> . . . chain of similar suburban communities around its borders. They would offer an opportunity for orderly efficient expansion. The greenbelts, linked together, would form continuous permanent open spaces around the city, protecting it and each suburb from overcrowding and sprawling, haphazard suburban development and encroaching industries.[5]

Tugwell studied a hundred cities and selected for his first ventures three tracts in Wisconsin, Ohio, and Maryland, all on the peripheries of busy cities. When President Roosevelt drove to Greenbelt outside Washington, D.C., he called it "an experiment that ought to be copied by every community in the United States."[6] The stage was set, it seemed, not only for a regeneration of the older cities but for a new-town move-

---

[4] Quoted in *Greenbelt Towns,* Resettlement Administration, September 1936.
[5] *Ibid.*
[6] *Prince Georgian* (a newspaper), Mount Ranier, Maryland, December 25, 1936.

ment in the areas around them. It was a direct federal assertion of national sovereignty in matters involving the nation's physical environment.

When Roosevelt visited Greenbelt, Maryland, and asked about the attitude of the local bodies, he was told that "splendid cooperation had been given by the county commission, the county and state school authorities, State Road Commission, Chamber of Commerce, Washington Suburban Sanitary Commission, county newspapers and the nearby towns. Cooperation was 'complete.' "[7]

The situation was no different in the case of Mr. Ickes' public housing projects. States which would have been expected to put up the "No Trespass" sign against federal intrusion unhesitatingly passed enabling laws authorizing cities to cooperate. Even more, when attacks were made upon Mr. Ickes' authority to invade their constitutionally protected dominions, cities and states filed briefs to support Mr. Ickes' position. Southern senators who in another day might have passionately defended the sanctity of state prerogatives became the stoutest defenders of federally initiated housing. When legal questions were raised that people occupying federal property might be under the exclusive jurisdiction of the federal government, might not be entitled to vote, sue in the state courts, or send their children to state schools, Congress quickly cooperated by enacting two laws preserving such rights.

A tradition of 150 years which had made the power over environment the preserve of the states and the forbidden territory of the federal government was thus broken. The first onslaught on the formula of state sovereignty since the Civil War was met not by the states calling out their militias, but by welcoming the invader with open arms. The states rights monolith fell quietly under the impact of emergency.

If there were some who feared the consequences of the federal intrusion, the fears subsided with the promise of local participation. When the Tennessee Valley Authority assured grass roots administration to the governments in the region, it was not long before TVA was not only welcomed but also actively supported by the states wherever cooperation was needed.

Similarly, the opposition to the federal power in housing and new-town building disappeared with the promise by Messrs. Ickes and Tugwell that the federal government would, after acquiring the land and after building the projects, dispose of them to the local communities.

"Government will withdraw," said Mr. Tugwell, "except for insisting on competent management to protect its investment and interests.

[7] *Ibid.*

Public housing authorities and other public bodies will hold and manage the properties. In drawing the original charters, care will be taken that the towns will be permanently administered as planned communities. Land and buildings will bear their full share of state and local taxation, and from these tax revenues, schools and other public services will be supported in the normal way. The government will be that which is appropriate to the size of the town under the laws of the state."[8]

Thus, up to 1936, a formula had been carved out of the necessities of the era under which the federal government had assumed the initiative and responsibility for rebuilding urban and suburban America.[9] It claimed that its authority to plan cities and grapple with the slum and housing problems was inherent in the welfare power. The government could go into cities or suburbs, build towns as England had been doing, clear slums and replan neighborhoods as it pleased. By 1937, the Public Works Administration had undertaken 51 projects in 36 cities (as well as Puerto Rico and the Virgin Islands) and had provided approximately 21,770 dwelling units for some 87,000 persons.

Had the two programs gone on unchallenged, the building of housing and new towns as well as federal influence over regional development might today have been viewed as being as laudable a federal purpose as building TVA's or Boulder Dams. Urban conservation might have taken its place of honor with soil conservation, and federal open space programs would have won the esteem held for federal parks. As Congress broadened the scope of urban aid and housing in the years that followed, it is even conceivable that the "ridiculously fragmented" region that is "more complicated than any other that mankind has yet contrived or allowed to happen,"[10] might have been set aright by the corrective federal power.

This, however, did not happen. The formula of direct federal building faded from view. The old pattern of hundreds of little autonomous districts was restored. Housing and city and regional development were returned to state and local controls. The idea of building new towns was forgotten. The federal government became the paymaster and underwriter of private risks under a string of assorted programs without theme or aim. Urban renewal was subsequently added to the amorphous string.

Federal withdrawal from direct responsibility for building and re-

---

[8] *Greenbelt Towns.*

[9] While the federal government had built housing on a previous occasion during World War I through the Emergency Fleet Corporation and the United States Housing Corporation, it had been done as an exercise of the war power, not the disputed general welfare power.

[10] Robert C. Wood, *1400 Governments,* Harvard University Press, 1961.

building occurred not because local operation was seen as a more efficient or more democratic formula. It was an almost fortuitous by-product of the New Deal drama during which President Roosevelt and the Supreme Court had differed on the meaning of "general welfare." At President Roosevelt's urging, Congress had enacted a succession of dramatic laws implementing his New Deal. But the conservative court of the 1930s had been paying homage to Jefferson and Madison, not Hamilton or Franklin D. Roosevelt, and in sixteen months, the old court had invalidated eight New Deal laws while sustaining only two. It was during this period that cases challenging the federal power over housing, new towns, and TVA were working their way for argument to the Supreme Court and it was in the framework of the anti-New Deal rulings of the then constituted Supreme Court that the lower courts also were rendering their anti-New Deal decisions limiting federal powers.

The Challenge to Federal Jurisdiction over Cities

One of the first constitutional challenges to the New Deal advance into urban problems and state jurisdiction over them was by a stubborn Louisville citizen whose land Mr. Ickes had sought for a housing project. The general welfare power, the owner contended, was not an independent power after all, as Hamilton, Monroe, Jackson, and Story had claimed, but an *ultra vires* intrusion upon the states in contempt of Jefferson and Madison.

Yet whatever may have been in the minds of the founding fathers in their day, the fact was that since the Civil War and the industrial revolution, the federal government had exercised many more powers than the limited ones delegated to it in 1789. In fact, had it not done so, it could never have coped with the exigencies of the emerging society. It had freely embarked on such extraconstitutional deviations as appropriating money for Indian depredations in Florida and Minnesota, fires in New York City and San Francisco, tornadoes and cyclones in the South, yellow fever epidemics, grasshopper scourges, floods and droughts in many places, as well as earthquakes in Venezuela and wars or famines in Ireland, Cuba, India, or Russia. In these circumstances there would seem to have been sufficient precedent for the federal government to relieve the distress of its unemployed or its slum dwellers as well as build cities and good housing for those who needed it.

But the precedents in fact were not yet precedents in law. They had been acquiesced in during the period of limited federal sovereignty but had never been legalized. Out of necessity, but also out of an unwillingness to pass on the thorny dispute over the general welfare clause, the Supreme Court over the previous years had etched out for the "limited federal

sovereignty" a devious device which had permitted the federal government
to go on spending for any purpose it chose by never giving a taxpayer his
day in court. The federal government, the court had held, derived its
funds not only from taxes but also from the sale of its lands, and a taxpayer's action was therefore considered too "remote," "minute," "indeter-
minate," and not "justiciable."[11] As long as the federal government could
go on spending money, however illegal the purpose, the issue could never
come to a test. But the issue could be raised if the federal government
tried to affect an owner's property rights by acquiring his land. The owner's
interest would then no longer be "remote" and the constitutional issue
would be "justiciable."

Federal officials had therefore always scrupulously avoided putting a
determinable issue before the courts. The federal government had long
spent money—legally or illegally—but had carefully abstained from condemning land where its spending powers could be tested.

It was during the period in which the Supreme Court was leveling New
Deal legislation piece by piece that the Louisville challenge to Mr. Ickes
was working its way through the lower courts, soon to be laid before the
still unchastened tribunal of last resort. The lower federal courts were un-
kind to Mr. Ickes. He had been enjoined from condemning the Louisville
owner's land for public housing, and the Circuit Court of Appeals had
upheld the injunction. Mr. Tugwell, meanwhile, had fared no better in
the lower courts and was prevented from proceeding with one of his
towns in New Jersey.[12]

Mr. Ickes, nevertheless, resolved to take the issue before the conservative Supreme Court and confidently filed his brief contending that the
federal government had the right to clear slums, buy land for housing, or
condemn it. The general welfare clause of the Constitution, he contended,
gave the federal government the right to condemn land for the purpose or

[11] Respondent's brief in Supreme Court in *U.S.* v. *Certain Lands in Louisville,
Kentucky,* 78 Fed. 2nd 684 (July 15, 1935); Appeal dismissed, 297 U.S. 726
(March 30, 1936).

[12] In this case, a taxpayer's suit was upheld and the incapacity of the
ordinary taxpayer's right to question federal spending was distinguished as
follows: "In those cases [i.e., *Frothingham* v. *Mellon* and *Magnano Co.* v.
Hamilton] the individual was a taxpayer in the same position as millions of
other citizens paying federal taxes. In the case at bar the plaintiffs are taxpayers
in a municipality having a population of only 6,500 (many of whom are not
taxpayers) the chief portion of the revenues of which is derived from real
estate." The taxpayer was therefore held to "suffer such a direct and immediate injury from the detachment of a large portion of the taxable property of
the township and the resulting increase in taxation, as will give them a standing . . ." (*Township of Franklin* v. *Tugwell,* 85 F 2nd 208, May 18, 1936).

for any purpose related to the health and well-being of the American people.

The case, however, was never heard by the Supreme Court, for on the eve of the argument, White House officials became fearful that an unfavorable ruling by the then existing court on the general welfare clause might strike down the whole New Deal spending program. For if the federal government had no right to spend for housing under a general welfare power, what other constitutional power sanctioned its right to spend for unemployment, etc.? How the anti-New Deal Supreme Court would in fact have ruled remains in the realm of conjecture. The lower-court decisions denying the federal government's right to embark upon housing and new towns became the established law, at least for the time being.

The Muller Case—A Way Out Is Found

Meanwhile, two events worked toward salvaging the bones of Mr. Ickes' housing program. The New York City Housing Authority had proposed a project of its own on the Lower East Side, entailing the remodeling of some tenements, financed with the help of relief labor and materials. When Andrew Muller, the owner of two of the tenements, refused to sell, the local housing authority filed eminent domain proceedings and speeded the case to the state's highest court. The court sustained the local authority's right to acquire the land as a proper exercise of the state's police power.[13]

With Mr. Ickes facing a still hostile Supreme Court, it now seemed that a formula could be framed for continuing the housing program without gambling on whether the federal government could acquire land and build housing directly. Under the Muller decision, a local housing authority would now acquire land for public housing and the federal government would advance the money. Since no taxpayer could question the right of the federal government to spend money and since no owner could challenge the right of a local authority (a state instrumentality) to condemn land, a traversable, if circuitous, path would be paved for circumventing any legal barriers raised by a taxpayer or an owner. With the Muller case as a precedent, local authorities in other states prepared for similar tests in their own state courts. A quick succession of favorable state decisions citing the Muller case as authority followed. This was the first step toward the new relationship under which the federal government was to retreat to the role of lender and spender while the local govern-

[13] *New York City Housing Authority* v. *Muller*, 270 N.Y. 333 (March 1936).

ment would be the initiator and operator. The course had been marked
out from necessity, not choice.

The new arrangement might have continued as a temporary expedient
except that Mr. Ickes was proving a hard man for the local authorities to
get along with. He had been a crusader before he had become an administrator; having exposed corruption in Chicago, he was terror-ridden lest
its specter turn up in his own yard. The surest guarantee against corruption, he felt, was Mr. Ickes himself. So he proposed to do the whole job,
with each local authority simply acting as his scrupulously supervised *alter
ego,* condemning the land needed and then turning it over to him to do as
he wished. He might ultimately turn the projects over to the authorities
though he would not reveal the terms of the arrangement and the controls
he would exercise.

The local housing authorities were faced with the choice of accepting
surrender or finding a substitute for Mr. Ickes. Now armed with the legal
sanction to do the job directly, they pressed for a new law which would
set up a separate U.S. Housing Authority that would give them federal
funds to acquire the land and build housing locally.

Such a federal law was passed by Congress in 1937. The program was
decentralized with the federal government now posited as the financier and
subsidizer and the local housing authorities as the acquirers of land and
the actual builders and managers of all future projects. This remains the
formula today.

The Belated Sanction of Federal Power

By the time the new decentralized procedure had ripened, a second
event—Mr. Roosevelt's re-education of the Supreme Court—was gradually becoming fact. Between March and June 1937 the Court, partly
reconstituted and partly reconciled, began to ratify the New Deal program in one decision after another. It upheld a State Minimum Wage
Law, the Farm Mortgage Act, the amended Railway Labor Act and, in
a ruling on the social security program, it held that the general welfare
clause of the Constitution was an independent and a substantive power
rather than the constricted one of the more conservative founding fathers.

> It is too late today for the argument to be heard with tolerance that
> in a crisis so extreme, the use of the moneys of the nation to relieve
> the unemployed and their dependents is a use for any purpose nar-
> rower than the promotion of the general welfare.[14]

[14] *Steward Machine Co.* v. *Davis,* 301 U.S. 548 (1937), *Helvering* v. *Davis,*
301 U.S. 619 (May 24, 1937).

In vain did Justice McReynolds expatiate his dissent with citations from Jefferson and Madison. The judicial die was cast and the federal government was pushed ahead toward becoming a full-fledged government empowered to function wherever the national welfare demanded it. Had Mr. Ickes been permitted to take his case to the highest court, it is barely possible that he would have won. Had he been able to wait, he would certainly have won.

In any event, the stage was now set for legalizing federally built housing, slum clearance, new towns, and federal aid to cities generally. The only question that remained was whether the power applied only during emergency periods or generally. The test came in Ohio in 1945, where an Ickes project was challenged as not being within the power of the federal government and hence subject to state taxation.[15] Housing, which had been ruled by the lower courts to be outside the federal power in the depression period, was in the period following the recovery considered to be a federal purpose and lawful forever after. Irrespective of emergency, the federal government was now vested with the full right to act in the general welfare in housing and in the building of new towns. Had Mr. Ickes been a more judicious administrator, the federal government might conceivably have remained (as it did in TVA) an active and effective participant in the building of a better environment for the nation's people.

By this time, however, the decentralized pattern had become firmly rooted. The federal government was now simply setting the general rules, approving the contracts, and turning over the subsidies to the local authorities. Though at last possessing the power to build housing, it fitted itself into the established groove and continued to let the local governments do the job. It adopted the same formula for urban renewal in 1949. It simultaneously helped insure mortgages for privately developed housing, which was being built mostly in the suburbs. As for the new-town program, it had already been forgotten and there was by this time no pressure for its restoration.

It is not argued that if the federal government had continued clearing

[15] *Federal Public Housing Authority* v. *Guckenberger,* 323 U.S. 329 (1945). In that case the Circuit Court had held that though the evils of bad housing are local in their origin, their effect may become so widespread as to create a menace to the national welfare and that Congress therefore had the right to deal with them. The Supreme Court dismissed the attack on the constitutionality with these blunt words: "Little need be said concerning the merits. Section 1 of the Housing Act declares a policy to promote the general welfare of the nation by employing its funds and credit to assist the states and their political subdivisions to relieve unemployment and safeguard health, safety and morals of the nation's citizens by improving housing conditions. . . . Challenge of the power of Congress to enact the Housing Act must fail."

slums and building public housing in cities, it would have been more efficient than the local authorities. Nor is it argued that it should have resumed building government towns without using private builders or providing home ownership. But it is contended that it would have had more comprehensive jurisdiction over the nation's regions and would have been free of the petty jurisdictional limitations they prescribed. It would have made or influenced better plans for the millions of acres now sprawling throughout suburbia. By offering each jurisdiction the right to build or not to build but asserting the right to do so itself if the jurisdiction refused, it would have retained concurrent authority over the national environment and been better posed to foster its proper development, either through public or private mechanisms. It would have been able to fill the gaps where housing and new cities were needed and where it did so, dispose of it to the states or local governments. The possession of the power would, in fact, have brought better cooperation and made its exercise essential only in few cases.

The Reversion to State Hegemony and Local Confusion

Though the federal government now had the power to plan and build new cities or rebuild old ones or to deal with cities directly without the state's veto, Congress soon elected to renounce that power by its own act. It was not merely that the procedures evolved to circumvent the constitutional uncertainties had become well seeded, but that new and more powerful forces had come into being between 1936 and 1949. Suburban power by this time had marshaled its forces and become more articulate. It saw the central cities as a threat and direct federal treatment with the cities as a forerunner of regional controls. By insisting upon a reversion to states rights, suburban power could better influence the course of federal policy and the flow of federal funds. In Congress, it could see to it that its peripheral smaller governments would get a greater share of the federal largess. The beneficiaries of that largess, i.e., the suburban home builders, organized to resist aid to the larger cities for public housing, community facilities, or other assistance. The states and the suburban real estate interests aligned themselves on the side of their influential suburbias.

Meanwhile, the decisions of the more liberal Supreme Court against racial restrictive covenants and school segregation, followed by the Executive Order against housing discrimination and the more recent ban on discrimination in public accommodations and the voting booth, soon brought Southern power to the side of the states rights, suburban, and real estate interests. It, too, now insisted that any federal assistance to cities shall be implemented only through the state or with the state's consent. Thus the formula that had been set for public housing in 1935 to circumvent the decisions of an irreconcilable Supreme Court and two years later to circumvent an irreconcilable federal works administrator had become in the 1950s a device for restraining constructive federal action in what were clearly welfare purposes.

The States Rights Enigma in the New Urban Society

In the nation of farms envisioned by Jefferson, it would have mattered little whether state boundaries were drawn by straight lines, angles, or curves. And since economies were localized and travel arduous, the states served vital and practical functions as decentralized governmental units. While no one will contend that these boundaries conform to any economic realities today, political logic and political reality do not always go together. Sensible or not, the states do exist as deeply rooted traditional actualities, and it would be impossible to reshape them without revising the whole rationale of Senate representation and geographical boundaries and without drastically revolutionizing the political system upon which the governmental process now rests.

Nor is it contended that the existence of state power is devoid of all merit. The diversity of laws and the opportunity for experimentation hold real values in that they permit the citizen to exercise choices which might not exist under a strong central government. The diversity of divorce laws between states is an example, and if Congress, under the political pressure of one influential group, were given power to enact a law as rigid as New York State's or North Carolina's, life for many might be intolerable. But this is a far cry from asserting that, in an urban society whose industrial products and people can be conveyed from one coast to another in six hours and whose problems are national in scope, a central government must subordinate its authority on nationwide and welfare problems to fifty separate jurisdictions and to thousands of smaller jurisdictions to whom the state delegates authority. The continued failure of the states and local governments to meet their responsibilities must, in fact, lead to the greater growth of the federal power, if not ultimately to the disappearance of the states as forces in American life. The values of state power can still be salvaged by a realistic reapportionment of federal and state authority over the welfare imperatives.

Appendix B

FEDERAL, STATE, AND LOCAL TAX RECEIPTS,
SELECTED FISCAL YEARS, 1902–1964

| | Per Capita | | | | Percentage Distribution | | |
Year	Total	Federal	State	Local	Total	Federal	State	Local
1902	$ 18	$ 7	$ 2	$ 9	100.0	37.4	11.4	51.7
1913	24	7	3	14	100.0	29.2	13.3	57.6
1922	68	31	9	28	100.0	45.7	12.8	41.6
1927	81	28	14	38	100.0	35.6	17.0	47.4
1932	64	15	15	34	100.0	22.7	23.7	53.6
1934	70	23	16	31	100.0	33.2	22.4	44.4
1936	83	30	21	32	100.0	36.6	24.9	38.5
1938	110	45	30	35	100.0	41.4	27.0	31.6
1940	108	42	32	34	100.0	39.2	29.2	31.6
1942	172	100	37	35	100.0	58.1	21.7	20.2
1944	389	313	40	35	100.0	80.6	10.4	9.0
1946	357	276	44	38	100.0	77.3	12.2	10.5
1948	377	277	54	46	100.0	73.6	14.3	12.1
1950	364	251	59	53	100.0	69.1	16.3	14.6
1952	546	412	73	61	100.0	75.5	13.3	11.2
1953	569	428	76	66	100.0	75.2	13.3	11.5
1954	566	421	77	68	100.0	74.3	13.6	12.1
1955	537	387	78	73	100.0	72.0	14.5	13.5
1956	600	434	88	78	100.0	72.3	14.7	13.0
1957	634	456	94	84	100.0	71.8	14.9	13.3
1958	628	444	95	89	100.0	70.6	15.1	14.2
1959	627	433	100	94	100.0	69.1	15.9	15.0
1960	709	495	113	101	100.0	69.8	15.9	14.3
1961	720	497	118	105	100.0	69.1	16.3	14.6
1962	756	516	126	114	100.0	68.3	16.6	15.1
1963	795	543	134	118	100.0	68.3	16.9	14.8
1964	832	563	142	126	100.0	67.2	17.4	15.4

SOURCE: Computed by Tax Foundation. Population, excludes armed forces overseas; figures are as of middle of the fiscal year.

Appendix C

GROSS DEBT OF FEDERAL, STATE, AND LOCAL GOVERNMENTS,
END OF SELECTED FISCAL YEARS, 1902–1964
(millions)

Year	Total[a]	Federal[b]	State[c]	Local[c]
1902	$ 3,285	$ 1,178	$ 230	$ 1,877
1913	5,607	1,193	379	4,035
1922	33,072	22,963	1,131	8,978
1927	33,393	18,512	1,971	12,910
1932	38,692	19,487	2,832	16,373
1934	45,982	27,053	3,248	15,681
1936	53,253	33,779	3,413	16,061
1938	56,601	37,165	3,343	16,093
1940	63,251	42,968	3,590	16,693
1942	92,128	72,422	3,257	16,449
1944	218,482	201,003	2,776	14,703
1946	285,339	269,422	2,353	13,564
1948	270,948	252,292	3,676	14,980
1950	281,472	257,357	5,285	18,830
1952	289,205	259,105	6,874	23,226
1953	299,852	266,071	7,824	25,957
1954	310,190	271,260	9,600	29,331
1955	318,641	274,374	11,198	33,069
1956	321,619	272,751	12,890	35,978
1957	323,566	270,527	13,738	39,301
1958	334,530	276,343	15,394	42,793
1959	348,816	284,706	16,930	47,180
1960	356,286	286,331	18,543	51,412
1961	363,994	288,971	19,993	55,030
1962	379,003	298,201	22,023	58,779
1963	392,303	305,860	23,176	63,267
1964	405,113	311,713	25,000	68,400

SOURCE: Department of Commerce, Bureau of the Census, and Treasury Department.

[a] Public debt of the United States Government.
[b] Short- and long-term debt outstanding.
[c] State and local debt for 1964 estimated by Tax Foundation.

Appendix D

GROSS DEBT OF FEDERAL, STATE, AND LOCAL GOVERNMENTS: PER CAPITA AND PERCENTAGE DISTRIBUTION, SELECTED FISCAL YEARS, 1902–1964

Year	Per Capita				Percentage Distribution			
	Total	Federal	State	Local	Total	Federal	State	Local
1902	$ 41	$ 15	$ 3	$ 24	100.0	35.9	7.0	57.1
1913	58	12	4	42	100.0	21.3	6.8	72.0
1922	301	209	10	82	100.0	69.4	3.4	27.1
1927	281	156	17	108	100.0	55.4	5.9	38.7
1932	310	156	23	131	100.0	50.4	7.3	42.3
1934	364	214	26	124	100.0	58.8	7.1	34.1
1936	416	264	27	125	100.0	63.4	6.4	30.2
1938	436	286	26	124	100.0	65.7	5.9	28.4
1940	479	326	27	127	100.0	67.9	5.7	26.4
1942	688	541	24	123	100.0	78.6	3.5	17.9
1944	1,644	1,513	21	111	100.0	92.0	1.3	6.7
1946	2,037	1,924	17	97	100.0	94.4	.8	4.8
1948	1,855	1,727	25	103	100.0	93.1	1.4	5.5
1950	1,861	1,702	35	125	100.0	91.4	1.9	6.7
1952	1,858	1,664	44	149	100.0	89.6	2.4	8.0
1953	1,895	1,682	49	164	100.0	88.7	2.6	8.7
1954	1,925	1,683	60	182	100.0	87.4	3.1	9.5
1955	1,939	1,670	68	201	100.0	86.1	3.5	10.4
1956	1,922	1,630	77	215	100.0	84.8	4.0	11.2
1957	1,899	1,588	81	231	100.0	83.6	4.2	12.1
1958	1,930	1,594	89	247	100.0	82.6	4.6	12.8
1959	1,976	1,613	96	267	100.0	81.6	4.9	13.5
1960	1,979	1,591	103	286	100.0	80.4	5.2	14.4
1961	1,988	1,579	109	301	100.0	79.4	5.5	15.1
1962	2,041	1,604	118	319	100.0	78.6	5.8	15.6
1963	2,085	1,622	123	341	100.0	77.8	5.9	16.3
1964	2,117	1,629	131	357	100.0	76.9	6.2	16.9

Appendix E

The estimate of receipts and expenses is as follows:

Income

Dwelling rent	$191,357	
Parking	7,812	
Total gross income	$199,169	
Less vacancies 7 per cent	13,395	
Less vacancies 7 per cent on		
other income	547	
Total vacancy deduction	$ 13,942	
Gross income expectancy	$185,227	$185,227

Expense

Total operating expense	46,801	
Estimated real estate taxes	20,250	
Total operating expense	$ 67,051	67,051
Cash available for debt service		$118,176

The mortgage on this property is $1,592,460. Therefore:

Interest, first year, @ 5¼ per cent is	$ 83,603	
Amortization @ 1.3 per cent	20,702	
Insurance premium @ 0.5 per cent	7,962	
	$112,267	
Cash available for income taxes,		
corporate taxes, dividends, or		
surplus	$ 5,909	

The Housing Problem: The Need for Objectives

FROM PRESIDENT HOOVER to President Johnson, federal objectives in housing have stemmed primarily from an interest in home ownership or in the building industry rather than from a concern for cities. As President Hoover said to a conference of housing experts in 1931:

To possess one's own home is the hope and ambition of almost every individual in our country, whether he lives in hotel, apartment, or tenement. . . . Those immortal ballads, *Home, Sweet Home, My Old Kentucky Home,* and *The Little Gray Home in the West,* were not written about tenements or apartments . . . they never sing songs about a pile of rent receipts.[1]

It was to stir the "home ownership aspiration" as well as "to revitalize the building of homes as a factor of economic recovery" that President Hoover conceived the Home Loan Bank System.

Implied in the policy was a new "vine and fig tree" concept that the tenements and rented dwellings of the old cities stood for a defunct past and that in the suburbs lay the exuberant future. The way to

[1] Address of President Hoover delivered at Constitution Hall, Washington, D.C., December 2, 1931. Fully quoted in *Housing Objectives and Programs,* ed. John Gries and James Ford, National Capital Press, 1932, pp. 1 ff.

254]

solve the housing problem (as well as inspire economic uplift) was by underwriting the mortgage investments of the frozen savings and loan associations and thereby building the new home-owning America—mostly in suburbia, where the associations would mainly operate. Under the Hoover concept of private enterprise, this could be the permissible exception for government intervention—while *laissez-faire* would function as usual in the tenement-ridden cities.

In the post-Hoover years, when the welfare of the building industry became more pressing a motivation than the "home, sweet home" of our immortal ballads, federal programs were enlarged to embrace rental housing as well; and by 1949, the long catalogue of housing agencies and housing programs involving billions had brought the government into the housing picture with both feet. The declaration in the 1949 act gave all these efforts a nimbus—a decent home in a decent environment for every American family. Here at last was the semblance of a goal. But fifteen years later, the nation was almost as far from having attained it as ever.

The many federal housing programs launched since 1934 did achieve gains—when billions are lent and spent, some money is bound to turn into houses. But the fruit of each effort always left a blemish. Thanks to the Federal Housing Administration and the Veterans Administration, home buyers have acquired title with smaller downpayments and with a single mortgage—but they also contracted debts for life. Slums were torn down under the public housing program but Congressionally imposed financial restrictions produced too many projects that were monuments to architectural mediocrity. We built some rental housing for the middle class—but as building costs went up, we liberalized the room count and lowered the standards so that many houses are smaller per cube and less desirable than those built in the freewheeling twenties. We improved some planning techniques and increased the number of cul-de-sacs, but compared with the phenomenal gains made in technology, housing and planning techniques have advanced hardly at all. We increased the proportion of home ownership—but have lengthened the mileage to work and made home ownership as precarious an obligation as ever. The nation now has more rigid zoning and higher building standards, but the new codes have only zoomed building costs and excluded the poor. Our suburbs provide more open space, but in encouraging their expansion, we created a division of American neighborhoods into islands of the elite and of the unwanted, and we threatened the solvency of our central cities in the process.

With all the formulas for building and subsidizing housing, we have not yet struck upon a good device for clearing slums and rehousing the slum dwellers, improving the shelter of large families, migrants, skidrowers, the poor, and the elderly. We have failed in the very areas where the need and justification for government aid is greatest.

Since the nation has prospered, people on the whole are better off than in the 1930s when the housing program began. There have been more repairs, more automobiles, more homes bought, and more money to buy and repair them; there are also more refrigerators and washing machines and more money and roads to escape the congestion and frictions of city life. But the housing programs themselves and the billions they cost had less to do with whatever improvement there was in housing than what federal administrators claim (except perhaps in the sense that government spending whether for roofs or rockets spurs employment and steps up the purse's capacity to buy or improve one's homestead).

Our housing programs also benefited from a few unanticipated breaks. The urban renewal program, which the 1949 act said would help rid us of the housing shortage, could never have got off the ground if not for the flight to suburbia, which made it less difficult in some cities to relocate slum dwellers. The USSR's megaton bomb also spurred bigger defense expenditures, thereby booming home buying; and inflation made an unanticipated gift to home owners by cutting the real value of mortgages in half. Inflation also vindicated FHA and VA guarantees and validated the claim that home ownership is sound —and could even be profitable.

Yet considering that in 1925, before any federal aid was thought of and when our capacity to produce was only a fraction of what it is today, the small disorganized housing industry built as many as

937,000 homes, it is not improbable that the industry forty years later might have increased its building capacity by another 50 per cent without most of the federal aids.

Our biggest boast—that housing in cities has improved physically— also highlights our biggest default, e.g., that the environment in cities has simultaneously deteriorated. While census figures indicate that housing conditions have improved since 1940, crime, according to the FBI, has doubled in the same period (after 1958, the crime rate was said to have increased five times as fast as the population). No matter what the census figures show, housing conditions cannot be rendered decent unless the environment is made decent also (the Harlems of New York and elsewhere have many fine houses and are among the worst of environments). Nor, as the cities sag under the weight of their new social and financial burdens, can the environments of the cities be improved and their social problems be dealt with unless they are made financially able to deal with them.

Defining Objectives

If the enormous credits and subsidies under the federal housing program are to meet the objective of a decent home in a decent environment for every American family, the federal government must be prepared to meet five indispensable requirements:

1. It must acknowledge that sound housing, whether in old or new cities, cannot be secured without making the cities sound. If the city is in trouble, the new investments are bound to be in trouble, too. As long as the city continues to be in trouble, it will not be poised to improve the environment of which housing is only one part.

2. It must be prepared to move toward its objective with all the necessary resources and all the relevant powers, without conditioning their use upon the consent of the states or their political creatures. It must be prepared to deal directly with cities or act in the regions of which they are a part when necessary.

3. It must be prepared to forego the condition implied in the 1949 act that speculative private enterprise shall be the preferred agent to

fulfill the objective. It need not exclude private enterprise and it may employ it on terms that are practical, but to insist that speculative enterprise *must* be the agent even where it cannot or will not function makes the objective meaningless.

4. It must not only be prepared to proffer a total program addressed to all groups needing housing but provide them with the opportunities to obtain what they need among a variety of choices suited to their changing needs, wants, and desires.

5. It must acknowledge that the key to meeting the housing problem lies in the low-interest financing for low-income groups and in a program of subsidies for all who require it.

Unless these prerequisites are met, the objective stated in the 1949 act will carry no real commitment. If it is to carry a commitment, the general objective—now little more than rhetoric—must be broken down into a series of specific objectives. The objectives for better housing must include at least the following:

1. Home Ownership for Low-income Families at Costs They Can Afford[2]

In 1962 the median family income in the United States was $5,956. A family with this income could properly spend $99 a month for its house cost. This was more than what half the nation's families could afford. For 39 per cent the ceiling was $83, for 29 per cent it was $67, and for 20 per cent the limit was $50—or less. No one needs to be a real estate expert to understand that good housing at these figures is virtually unobtainable.

In 1964 the average cost of houses bought with FHA insurance was $14,881 for existing houses and $16,561 for new houses. But even if house cost was down to $13,500 with a 5½ per cent thirty-year mortgage for the full purchase price, the monthly house cost would be about $127 and require an income of $7,600 a year. This would be beyond the capacity of more than 69 per cent of our families. Even with a forty-year mortgage at 2 per cent, it would be beyond

[2] For an amplification of this proposal, see Charles Abrams and Morton S. Schussheim in *Study of Mortgage Credit,* Subcommittee on Housing, Senate Committee on Banking and Currency, 85th Cong., 2nd Sess., December 22, 1958, pp. 81–86.

the reach of about 45 per cent of our families. The federal government has done almost nothing for the families priced out of the market.

Impact of financing on ability to buy homes. Interest and amortization are the main items in the cost of ownership. An interest reduction of 1 per cent on a 25-year $14,000 mortgage would reduce mortgage charges by about $100 annually. An extension of the mortgage from 25 to 35 years would mean a reduction of about $140. Elimination of the one-half per cent FHA premium charge would reduce it about another $50. Add it all up and the annual saving would be $290. Building cost would have to be reduced by $4,000 to effect the same saving, and a reduction of this magnitude could be achieved only by a miracle or a major depression.

The monthly housing expense in the Northeast on a house subject to a 30-year, $14,000 mortgage at 5¾ per cent is roughly as shown in Table 7.

TABLE 7

Interest and amortization	$82
Heat	20
Insurance	5
Taxes	25
Utilities	10
Maintenance	15
Total	$157

Assuming even that 25 per cent of income can be spent for an owned home, the required gross annual income for this house would be $7,536, which is far above the median income of American families. The mortgage charges in the table constitute more than 52 per cent of the gross monthly charges. While a cut in construction costs would reduce the mortgage, the thousands of parts and the multiple skills that go into building make a reduction unlikely. Nor is there any major economy expected in building techniques—or any indication that savings made by mass on-site construction would be passed on to the consumer.

If new housing is to be made available to lower-income families, reduction in the mortgage charges has to be a primary objective. As the table in Appendix A (page 285, below) shows, it is only when interest rates get down toward 0 per cent that the low-income family is really helped. But even an interest-free loan would not reach the very lowest group, and for these, some additional subsidy would be needed.

It is often argued that low-income families should not own homes. It is this theory that underlay President Johnson's proposal in 1965 which would provide housing subsidies in private housing only to families above the income levels of those qualifying for public housing. This would help some families but not those who needed decent housing most. It is the low-income family that has the greatest yearning for ownership and needs the security most. When home ownership is brought within its means through subsidy, all the arguments against ownership by the low-income family become untenable.

The claim is also made that the poorer folk can always buy second-hand homes. Sometimes they can—in those cities, for example, where there has been a sharp deflation of values. But in such cities, deflation of values is too often accompanied by a deflation of incomes, and the gap between income and housing cost continues. If builders built surpluses of housing, prices might go down, but they rarely go down to what the poorer family can afford. Moreover, since the evolution of the constant-payment plan and long-term mortgages, the payment on new homes remains fixed even after the house is a decade old.

If the market for homes is to be widened, direct financing must be made available by direct government mortgage loans at low interest or at no interest whatever when necessary.

A government corporation similar to the Federal National Mortgage Association, the home loan banks, and the federal land banks could do the borrowing on the open market. The government would undertake to appropriate to the new corporation the annual deficit incurred by it through below-market loans. Thus on every $1.3 billion loaned, the maximum annual contribution by the government (assuming a 4 per cent annual deficit) would be $52 million; and it can be safely anticipated that it would be much less, since only a fraction of the loans would be at 0 per cent and many would be at 1, 2, and 3 per cent. On many of these loans, the low interest rate would have to be only for a temporary period.

Government financing of 100,000 homes would entail borrowing $1.3 billion annually. This is not too onerous considering that the government debt since 1946 has declined on a per capita basis. If, however, the government elected not to float direct loans, it could provide a direct interest subsidy payable to the owner, who would then pay the market rate to the institutional mortgagee.[3] This might be a preferable approach in periods of credit stringency. The direct-lending formula or the alternative interest-subsidy formula for private or FHA-insured loans would be financed by mortgagees who would pay federal taxes, whereas bonds floated by local governments and public housing agencies are tax-exempt and purchasable by those in the higher brackets of income who escape paying federal taxes. In the long and short runs, direct federal loans or subsidizing of interest would be less expensive.

Manifestly if a low interest were fixed indefinitely, the home-buying family could sell the home at a profit or its improved income might warrant a higher rate. The program should therefore provide for a fixed initial rate (say three years) with a re-examination of family income periodically thereafter. Thus interest rates would always be geared to capacity to pay, and the burden of proof would be on the owner. He should be privileged not to disclose his income, in which event his interest would rise to the market rate. When, as, and if the family could pay the market rate, the government agency would dispose of the government loan to private lenders or, under certain circumstances, to FNMA for subsequent resale. A substantial portion of the aided families should be able to pay the going rate long before the due date of the mortgage. This would have happened in the public housing projects if the families with increased income had not been evicted.

[3] In this case, the annual subsidy for each 100,000 homes built would be not more than $78 million annually—assuming maximum subsidies for all families. This is a pittance compared to the five to six billion dollars we spend annually on agricultural subsidies.

Resales of the homes would be permitted only with the consent of the government. Such resales would be allowed if the new purchasers qualified as low-income families or if the mortgage payments were assumed on economic terms. An alternative might be to allow the owner to sell without restriction if the interest subsidy is repaid.

2. A Sound Home Ownership Structure

Under present FHA practice, the mortgagee is insured while the home owner pays the insurance premium. What is needed is a program to insure the home owner against temporary hazards—this would simultaneously reduce the mortgagee's risk.

The principal hazard in home ownership is unemployment or "curtailment of income." In 1962 this was the given reason for defaults for 35 per cent of all FHA borrowers and for about 40 per cent of VA borrowers. The second reason was "death or illness in family." In each of the six metropolitan areas studied by FHA in 1962, at least 44 per cent of the FHA, VA, or conventional loan borrowers had suffered a decline in income between the time of loan origination and the day of foreclosure.[4] The VA, after studying the reasons given for defaults both by the mortgage lenders and by the owners summarizes its own list based on 2,900 cases. The accepted reasons for default are listed in Table 8.

TABLE 8

Curtailment of income	39%
Improper regard for obligations	26
Death or illness	16
Marital difficulties	9
Extensive obligations	7
All other reasons	3
	100%

SOURCE: *Report of Loan Service and Claims Study,* Veterans Administration, April 30, 1962, p. 67.

Thus curtailment of income and death or illness totaled 55 per cent

[4] *Mortgage Foreclosures in Six Metropolitan Areas,* Housing and Home Finance Agency, June 1963.

of the reasons for default. If the reasons as given by the owners were credited, a good part of the 26 per cent of defaults for "improper regard for obligations" would be added to the 55 per cent.

There are two possible ways to protect the home owner against these hazards. A fund could be created from which distressed owners could borrow, repaying the loan not later than three years after the due date of the mortgage. Although this plan would salvage many equities, it has the disadvantage of putting the owner more heavily into debt.

The other alternative is equity insurance. If, as claimed, FHA mortgage insurance is sound, equity insurance against the risks of unemployment and illness is at least as sound; it is also more sensible. Many savings and loan associations, in fact, have arranged for covering the borrower by insurance against the hazards of illness, accident, or death, but unemployment is not yet embraced in the coverage.

Under the current FHA formula, if there is default in a single payment, the insured mortgagee forecloses and then looks to the government to pay it the mortgage in full. If payments were kept up under an equity insurance plan, the government would be saved the $1,500 cost of reacquiring and repairing the house and be spared the trouble and expense of issuing its own bonds for the full mortgage principal.

Taking three years of inability to pay as a reasonable maximum liability during the life of a mortgage, the insurance policy would have to be written for about $3,000 for a $10,000 mortgage. Experience would probably show that the insurance fund would be called upon to pay only a fraction of the maximum.

Equity insurance would be a proper use of the federal insurance function and make both the ownership and mortgage structures sounder in the long run. Because of the combined benefit to FHA and the owner, the equity insurance premium covering health and unemployment might be as little as $25 a year. Additional protection against the death of the breadwinner might also be given through ordinary life insurance or through cheap savings bank insurance as in Massachusetts and New York. Homes with conventional mortgages could also be insured, subject to approval of the risk and the fixing of an appropriate premium. If the insurance were issued on mortgages given by savings and loan associations, these societies would be safer operations and the Home Loan Bank System would be spared the embarrassment of bailing out these associations when they are confronted with multiple mortgage defaults.

An owner's unemployment status could be determined by a state unemployment insurance office on the basis of existing practices. The unemployed home owner would register with the unemployment office, which would try to find him employment; and if he fails to cooperate, he would be refused the benefits of the insurance protections. If the owner is unemployed a second time, he would continue to benefit to the extent of the balance of the insurance available under the policy.

In sum, the insurance fund would benefit the government by (1) preventing a large-scale loss of homes, a deflationary movement, and a capital depreciation due to a glut in the home market; (2) dispensing in this event with the need for huge federal outlays all at once; (3) making savings and loan societies sounder operations and cutting down on federal advances by the Home Loan Bank System; (4) saving interest on federal bonds issued to the FHA-insured mortgagees upon default; (5) making owners less inclined to drop their homes when values are down; (6) saving the government major expenditures in repairs, foreclosure charges, and resale costs upon repossession.

In 1963, foreclosures reached their highest point since the depression of the 1930s. Many homes might have been saved from the auction block had the plan been in effect. But in officialdom, anything new meets doubt, hesitation, and pain. The plan is no more novel than was FHA insurance when first tried, and it involves much less in principal liability. If the depression experience is a guide, a substantial rise in foreclosures will again force the federal government to protect home owners by buying up mortgages as the Home Owners Loan Corporation did to the extent of more than $3 billion. Under the equity insurance proposal, not only will this be unnecessary, but the owner's home would be preserved for him.

When I submitted the proposal to HHFA and FHA in 1963, it

was rejected principally because their functionaries felt the administrative costs would be too high. In the experimental scheme, FHA estimated the "high cost" at $3.5 million for the first year, $2.5 million for the second year, and $1.5 million annually thereafter. It is clear that the real obstacle is not the administrative cost but FHA's traditional aversion to innovation and to the assumption of social functions.

3. Revision of Public Housing

Conceived as a demonstration, the public housing program has shown that the underprivileged will pay their rent promptly and live as decently as do other citizens; they will raise their standards if they can; they prefer freedom in neighborhoods of their choice to institutionalization. The program also proved that a municipal agency could acquire large tracts of land within a city and operate with little or no graft; that housing for the underprivileged and replanning of neighborhoods are legal public purposes; that bonds on projects rented to the poor are salable at very low interest rates; that some of our ulcerated urban terrains can be regenerated if there is workable legislation and a practical administration.

These are no mean demonstrations. But the program has tended to defeat itself because of the conditions Congress imposed. A main impediment has been the rigid income limits for admission and for continued occupancy. Though after 1961 overincome families were allowed to remain temporarily, the income limits have been kept.[5] These limitations have caused frequent turnover and given the projects an institutional aspect. Many eligible families shun the projects because of the constant income reviews. Evictions for excessive income have ousted the more stable tenants. Since Negro income is lower than that of white families, too many of the projects are predominantly Negro-occupied, which has also brought school segregation. (In 1965, 50 per cent of all tenants were nonwhite and 27 per cent were elderly.)

[5] The low-rent tenants in the projects had a median annual income of $2,535 in 1964 (the income for elderly people was $1,441; for others it was $3,017), and they paid a median rent of $45 gross monthly (the elderly paid $33). The median family incomes of those admitted in 1964 were $2,705 for the non-elderly and $1,471 for the elderly.

When a family improves its income it should not be penalized by having to pull the children out of school, give up its neighborhood associations, and move back to a slum. An unsubsidized rent should be fixed for each apartment. The tenant whose earnings go up should simply be asked to pay a higher rent. He should be privileged not to disclose his earnings, in which case he could stay and pay the unsubsidized rent.

Building cost limitations should be liberalized so that projects can become attractive additions to the urban scene. The misassumption of public housing has been that there will always be a stratified class society in the United States and that those with low earnings deserve only housing with low standards. Another misassumption has been that the buildings will be depreciated in forty-five years. They will stand for a century. They should be built not for a permanent poor but under standards that make them desirable for people whether they are poor or no longer poor. If President Johnson's exhortations for "beautifying the city" are to be meaningful, he might set the example in federally subsidized projects.

The housing authorities are being required to house not only the families they displace through their own clearance operations but also those displaced by urban renewal, code enforcement, and public works. The emphasis of the public housing program should therefore be shifted from clearing slums to increasing the housing inventory for low-income families. This would mean selecting more vacant and underdeveloped sites (requiring little or no displacement). As amplified later in this chapter, land in the suburbs will also have to be made available for the housing of low-income families. Extensive slum demolition for projects should be resumed only when slum vacancies are sufficient to give the slum dwellers an opportunity to move more freely.

Where sites are chosen in slum areas, public housing should qualify for the same land subsidies as are available for urban renewal. The authorities are virtually the only agencies venturing into the deeper slum jungles, and they deserve treatment at least equal to that given the entrepreneur. With lower land costs, they might build to less formidable heights and to more attractive designs.

All local housing authorities should be permitted to qualify for projects under Sections 202 (housing for the elderly) and 221 (d) (3). Many authorities could induce their cities to grant them tax exemption on the improvements and thereby provide units at lower rentals than entrepreneurs can offer. Exclusion of these nonprofit agencies from the benefits of the program has never made such sense. Local housing authorities should build smaller projects that blend with existing neighborhood patterns. The massive, institutional projects in many cities have debased public housing programs in the estimation of both the public and the tenants. In smaller communities, more public housing should be built as single-family units for rental with provision for resale to the tenants upon suitable terms.

Multiple dwelling projects should be disposed of by sale or lease to nonprofit corporations whenever feasible so as to reduce the monolithic aspects of large-scale public ownership. No single income group should be confined to a single choice of its landlord or the type of housing it receives. Exclusive ownership by government of all the dwellings for which low-income families can qualify is inconsonant with a free society even if it should ever become a slumless society. Disposition of public housing projects should not imply the end of public housing but its expansion. The emphasis of the program in fact should be to provide more and more cheap housing and less and less public ownership or operation.

More federal appropriations are needed, particularly if other federal programs cause additional displacements of families. But such programs should not specify public housing as the only form of shelter available to low-income families. New devices are needed that give the less privileged more to choose from—in public, private, and nonprofit enterprises and in rehabilitated as well as new buildings.

Only 13 to 22 per cent of those displaced by renewal operations move into public housing. Many were ineligible for public housing under its present restrictions, while others rejected it. If the suggested changes were made in the public housing formula, it would become more attractive to families and less vulnerable to criticism. As it is presently operated, it can never expand into a major program, if, in fact, it continues at all.

4. A Housing Inventory Offering Reasonable Freedom of Choice

If a monthly rental subsidy equal to the present subsidy for public housing were made available to eligible low-income families, private builders or nonprofit associations could provide considerable housing for them in the city or the suburbs at feasible rents. This would encourage a more sensible distribution of families. They could choose housing near their work or near better schools. It would help dissolve the racial and economic segregation in the present city-suburban dichotomy. The private building industry would be assured of a vast market for new and rehabilitated dwellings, whether conventionally financed or built under Section 221 (d) (3), 221 (d) (4), as cooperative housing, or through other federal programs.

The subsidies to families could be reduced or discontinued as family income increases. They should not be payable on slum buildings since the primary aim should be to encourage more and better construction of new houses and rehabilitation of old ones. Low-income families displaced by urban renewal would be eligible for subsidies and so should any family normally qualified for public housing. Providing subsidies only to those with higher income, as was proposed by President Johnson in 1965, makes little sense. An adequate program should enable provision of at least another 200,000 low rental units annually without entailing too large a federal commitment. Assuming an annual subsidy per family of 600 dollars (the subsidy in 1964 paid in public housing was about $350 per family), the annual cost of the subsidy to the federal government for each 200,000 units subsidized would be about $120 million, and the benefits derived from the program through added construction and purchasing power would compensate for a good part of the outlays.

More housing for special groups. The current housing program is geared to a mythical family of husband, wife, and two or three children. It lacks adequate provision for nonaverage types such as single persons, working mothers, workers at home, widowers with small children, large families, itinerant workers, and other families with special problems. It also assumes that this average family is white, well off, can drive a car, and will either live in a suburb or pay a ransom for an apartment in the city's core. Yet there are probably more nonaverage families than average ones, even if we exclude the low-income and minority families. Apartments for large families are almost nonexistent, even in public housing. There is no excuse for discriminating against families of eight or ten persons. Nor is there any good reason for ignoring the needs of the working mother when facilities for child care would save many from despair as well as save cities relief costs for mothers unable to work and care for their children at the same time.

Housing for the elderly is still in embryo. Nor are there adequate programs to help older workers secure work near their homes. Discrimination against such workers is nationwide, and only a few states give them protection. A reluctance to upset pension plans and group insurance schemes militates against them. Under Governor Averell Harriman's administration in New York, not only was discriminatory advertising against the older worker eliminated but a program banning such discrimination was coupled with an affirmative program to persuade firms to hire older workers. It gave New York State the highest employment average of older workers in the nation. Opportunity for good housing and for employment go together, and both are needed in virtually every state.

While some advances have been made in financing housing for the elderly, the gains have been offset by their evictions through urban renewal, public works, code enforcement, and private housing. Little has been done to provide the elderly with small, attractive projects of thirty to fifty units in centrally located neighborhoods. Nor have older people been given much choice of shelter and climate. While federal loans at low interest are available to nonprofit groups, the amount of such sponsorship was still nominal in 1965, and few urban renewal projects made land available for such housing or provided dwellings within the means of lower-income families.

Section 202 of the Housing Act of 1959 authorizes direct federal loans for the elderly. But the rent schedules on current projects exclude about 70 per cent of elderly families. An adequate rent subsidy program would enable more of these people to qualify.

Nonprofit associations such as church and welfare groups have sometimes emerged as primary agencies for home building. (In Hong Kong, for example, the Hong Kong Housing Society launched by social service workers housed more than 40,000 people by 1962.) Often such groups require small sums for preliminary or organizational expenses. Advance of such seed money could make the difference between project development and project stillbirth, between genuine nonprofit operations and those undertaken for profit by entrepreneurs. What these organizations need above all is guidance in sponsoring undertakings. A nationwide nonprofit agency with adequate personnel and experience set up to build or supervise the building and management of the projects by the local groups would do much to launch such a movement. Making sites available under the urban renewal program for these efforts would expand the number of undertakings. Modification of Section 221 (d) (3) is also required in the following respects: Since interest rates presently fluctuate with the government rate, a maximum interest should be fixed; the minimum rate should be low enough to accommodate lower-income families. Loans should not be confined to urban renewal areas. Existing as well as new housing should remain eligible for the low-interest loans and so should owner-occupied homes.

5. A Realistic Slum Clearance Program

Clearing American slums has developed such political savor that little thought has been devoted to determining whether slum clearance does harm or good. A city that has cleared all its slums can have a bigger headache than a city with a surplus supply, for in a city that cleared all its slums, the overcrowding and the high rents of the new housing would make the poor man's plight incomparably worse than if the slums remained.

Slum clearance is authorized in the following cases:

- When the dwellings are so dilapidated or dangerous that there is no alternative but to tear them down

- When there is an excess of slums, and clearance will not result in a rise in rents or overcrowding of the slum dweller

- When the cost of altering or improving them is excessive so that it is cheaper to build new structures

- When the site is needed for a genuine public use, or where its location bars the essential development of the city

- When, as part of a housing program for the slum dwellers, decent housing is provided for them in advance of the clearance if possible, and the new housing is what the slum dweller wants. This requires a variety of housing programs that afford evicted families reasonable alternatives within their means.

Slum clearance is not authorized during a housing shortage or solely because the houses are old or because the city can get more taxes by ousting the poor to make way for the higher-income families.

Nor should a neighborhood be cleared when it is inhabited by an ethnic, racial, or national group whose stores or other enterprises give the city variety and interest while providing a livelihood to the owners and their workers. Neighborhoods like Chinatowns or an Italian district are often an attraction for tourists and have important values, though the buildings may not be the last word in design or amenities. The neighborhood generally tends to improve over the long run through the resources of the people themselves. Similarly, one should not consign one- or two-family homes to the wreckers simply because fewer families will be displaced. If the homes are in a socially solvent community and the site is not urgently needed for a major improvement, the justification for leaving the neighborhood alone may be stronger than for clearance. If the houses, services, and landscaping are improved, such sections often provide an interesting contrast and a necessary retreat from the massive structures they adjoin. In identifying a slum for clearance, public officials should consider not only the buildings but also the values of the neighborhood to the city as a whole.

6. *Freedom of Movement*

Much has happened since I first made my study of the minority housing problem in 1947.[6] It was then not only considered proper to discriminate but unethical not to. Since the midfifties, many foundation and university studies have explored the theme. A United States Commission on Civil Rights has issued a number of reports which have highlighted the housing problem as one of the most stubborn barriers to Negro opportunity. By 1965, fourteen states had passed laws barring discrimination in private housing and twenty-seven cities had passed laws to the same effect. Discrimination has become a prime issue on the political hustings. The President's Executive Order of 1962, though far from comprehensive, has put the moral force of the federal government behind the principle of housing equality. The year 1963 witnessed the "Negro revolution," which gave rise to more effective Negro influence and leadership. Negro militancy, mobilized at last, was precipitating changes in a few months which had not been won in a century. The Negro has won more access to public places and schools, and Presidents Kennedy and Johnson were impressed into sponsoring civil rights legislation more far-reaching than any since the Civil War.

The pattern of housing segregation has nevertheless stubbornly persisted, handicapping efforts to desegregate schools and public facilities and impeding the Negro's free access to jobs. The 1964 amendment of California's constitution to bar enactment of antibias laws in housing points up that the battle against housing bias is far from won. It is tougher because the struggle between social justice and property rights involves altering the established practices of the organized building and real estate industries and touches upon the vested interests of a large and powerful middle class. Homes to these people are their prize possessions, and when they feel them threatened by Negro infiltrations, they sometimes fight back with an arsenal ranging from public power to brickbats and bombs.

[6] Charles Abrams, *Race Bias in Housing,* sponsored jointly by the American Civil Liberties Union, National Association for the Advancement of Colored People, and the American Council on Race Relations, July 1947. This was later expanded into *Forbidden Neighbors,* Harper & Row, 1955.

Even the important gains made in principle have been meeting frustration in practice. The Negro could move into public housing in the cities but could not own a home in suburbia. If he did live in suburbia, he was apt to be slum-cleared into the central city. His right to shelter might be established by state laws, but the gulf between law and enforcement remained wide. The Supreme Court has barred enforcement of written racial covenants, but it cannot enjoin unwritten exclusions. The President's Executive Order could now bind the federal government to a nondiscriminatory policy in federally aided projects, but the projects embraced by the order were only a fraction of the total housing supply.

Between 1950 and 1960, the twelve largest cities lost more than 1½ million whites, but gained nearly 2 million Negroes. The force of the Negro's numbers in the cities has given the Negro greater confidence and more political power, but whether he will ultimately win the right to move and to live where he chooses will depend primarily on his capacity to compete economically for housing in the more open areas of the metropolises. It will also depend on how successful the suburban areas will be in keeping him out when he is able to bid for its housing.

More than antibias measures will be needed to win him that freedom in the suburbs. A first step to speed integration should be a federal measure providing home ownership at interest rates the Negro and other low-income families can afford. The profit motive being what it is, some private builders might build for the Negro market. Nonprofit groups might also do so. Rent and interest subsidies to families would also help. If the federal government not only conditioned all its aids (FHA insurance and assistance to the savings and loan associations) on nondiscrimination, but also enforced its orders effectively, the suburban barrier might be breached. Effective enforcement would mean conditioning federal housing and other aids on the repeal of subtle restrictive zoning practices and similar exclusionary devices. Effective regulations and a proper enforcement of Title VI of the Civil Rights Act of 1964, which bans federal assistance to public agencies that discriminate in federally financed projects, could be an important force. Motivation rather than surface legality should be the criterion for federal intervention. If, despite its efforts, suburban exclusion persists, the federal government should build integrated housing directly.

Thus far the battle for equal opportunity in housing has been led mainly by white Christian and Jewish citizen groups, churches, intellectuals, and do-gooders. Most of these are city people. If the battle is to be won in the long run, the Negro must hold the support of these groups as well as of his own people and achieve a common strategy.

Because the Negro is only about 11 per cent of the nation's population and because more than 50 per cent of the total Negro population is still located in the South, the real threat to neighborhood solvency is exclusion itself. It is the compulsory concentration of Negroes into ghetto areas that nurtures the widespread fear among whites that the trickle-to-deluge pattern is inevitable wherever a Negro family establishes a foothold. Fear of the Negro as a neighbor did not exist before 1920 when Negroes lived in all parts of cities. Nor would it exist today if the shortage of housing for low-income families were eased. If Negroes are permitted to move where they wish and if adequate housing programs make it possible, their presence will soon hardly be noticed, and with time and patience, they will be accepted in neighborhoods on a parity with other citizens.

If the housing shortage for low income families were eased and compulsory segregation dissolved, the emerging pattern might be one of numerous smaller but voluntary ghettos at first, but without segregation in the neighborhood schools. It might be the necessary first stage to a breakdown in the present undesirable pattern of massive Negro concentrations in the cities and the almost total absence of Negro families in the suburbs, particularly in the North.

7. The Preservation and Improvement of Existing Housing

From their beginnings, housing programs paid only lip service to improving the nation's existing housing stock. The feeling has been that new buildings can be built, supervised, and financed in volume with the same trouble it takes to patch up a few old structures. It seemed easier to build new and big than to deal with the seamier side of neighborhood environments, building by building.

When more recently the renewal program experienced difficulty in its evictions and relocations, rehabilitation moved into a more central focus, and new forms of federal aid were proffered both inside and outside urban renewal areas.

What is new is not always good and what is old not always bad. The time-worn neighborhood is often the seat of the time-honored structures, of the historic and architectural examples, of the dwellings built for use, not speculation. Their mortgage debt is low and their ceilings high; their timbers may creak, but the creak of an old rafter is pleasanter than the clatter of a neighbor's television. Many houses are on spacious lots and near one's work, hospitals, buses, and services, and their occupants often include the elderly and the poor whose established friendships, churches, and familiar scenes are values that should be reinforced, not destroyed.

Rehabilitation (including repair and additions) is a large component of the home-building economy, and in 1963 its outlays ran to $11.7 billion. Though programs to spur rehabilitation and repair have often taken form in highly publicized efforts of local groups (official and unofficial), widespread rehabilitation and repair manifest themselves most often when economic conditions improve nationally or locally and when the economics of particular neighborhoods and buildings justify the owner's added investment. In short, the rules of rentability and income apply to expenditures for rehabilitation as they do for new buildings.

There are three keys necessary to open the door to large-scale rehabilitation. One is the solvency of the cities and of the particular neighborhoods within them. Better parks, schools, and community facilities can help make a neighborhood better and spur individual house improvement.

Sound financing is the second key. As shown in the calculation in Appendix B, page 286, below, the factor which makes the rehabilitation economic is lower interest and amortization. If the interest and amortization are cut, no actual increase in rents is necessary to earn the same profit. If, in addition, the city were to encourage rehabilitation by rebating taxes, the owner's profit would go up by the amount of the rebate.

No owner, however, wants to increase his debt or go to the trouble of revamping his building unless he receives a reasonable increase in rents. If owners of existing buildings can be shown how they can have better buildings as well as larger profits, considerable improvement in the physical inventory of the nation's dwellings might follow.

The third and most important key is to create an effective demand for the rehabilitated dwellings. The structures most in need of repair and rehabilitation are those inhabited by lower-income groups. The owners will not spend the money if their tenants are unable to pay the rent increase required. A family subsidy program to assist all families who cannot pay the extra costs of the reconditioned dwellings is therefore indispensable. This would upgrade dwellings in areas where they are most needed as well as guarantee a market for the dwellings. It would improve low income neighborhoods and offer an alternative in addition to public housing. In each area, the pace of rehabilitation should be speeded or slowed to avoid excessive evictions, rocketing rents, and rises in local construction costs.

Rehabilitation by renewal and public housing agencies should accompany private rehabilitation. The value of buildings should be written down by capital subsidies where necessary, and the properties sold to private or nonprofit groups on suitable terms after the buildings are improved.

Rehabilitation of the neighborhood and the reactivation of the city must go hand in hand with rehabilitation of structures. While sound financing programs can help, strengthening the city, improving the schools, and rebuilding the social aspects of neighborhood life are vital elements in inspiring investment. There are countless numbers of houses in the nation's cities that are sound but are wasting away. They are wasting away not because they are worthless as structures but because there is no demand for them. The demand is lacking because the city is languishing, because people do not want to live in it, or cannot afford to. Until officials see this and rise to the challenge realistically, rehabilitation programs will never emerge as more than token efforts.

8. A More Effective Building Industry

In the ten years 1952–1962, the building industry produced 15 million new nonfarm housing units and housed more than 46 million people. An industry producing a high-cost product in such volume plays an important role in national employment and in economic activity. In California, for example, about 6 per cent of the employed found jobs directly in construction, not counting those deriving indirect employment from the industry. The industry's influence is such that a short-run change in direct home-building employment is multiplied 2.57 times.[7]

Despite its influence, the industry functions only for part of the market and must be expanded by low-interest loans and adequate subsidies; productivity could then go up to a least 2 million units a year instead of the 1.6 million produced currently. A comprehensive program, in fact, would envision 2.5 million units annually. But there were no signs in 1965 that Congress was ready to write the legislation that could make this possible.

There are other aspects of the industry that limit its effectiveness. It is composed largely of small entrepreneurs. A third of the Pacific Coast firms, for example, employed from one to three salaried workers with only 6 per cent hiring over twenty; 85 per cent had less than nine salaried persons on their staffs or none at all. In 1959, the median or typical builder built about twenty-four units a year.

Fluctuations in annual output and in local conditions compel many firms to make overnight adjustments, and this often means closing shop. Those who allow their overhead to continue during a slack period are doomed.

A federal policy which expands the market for low-income families

[7] W. L. Hausen *et al., Markets for California Products,* California Economic Development Agency, 1961; *Report on Housing in California,* Governor's Advisory Commission on Housing Problems, 1963, p. 14; and Frank G. Mittlebach, "Home Building in the California Economy," *ibid., Appendix,* p. 502.

when demand for unsubsidized housing dries up could fulfill a social purpose while guaranteeing a more even balance of activity and avoiding local and national recessions.

There are impediments at the local level to which federal and state policy could address itself. Local codes and ordinances are more rigorous than they were in the early postwar period, and in some cases they have raised land and building costs substantially and unnecessarily. Many of these requirements are antiquated, unjustified, and need review, but ignorance of new techniques and of new materials as well as vested interests in maintaining the obsolete prevent needed changes. So, too, zoning ordinances are often designed to exclude the low-income family or to capture as much revenue as possible for the particular community with a disregard for the welfare of other people in the region. Excessive lot requirements not only preclude settlement by those of smaller income but force developers to look for less restricted and less costly land further out. This leaves gaping sections of unused land. The new home buyers spend unnecessary hours getting to and from work, while the public spends unnecessary millions to provide them with the roads to make the journey. Although zoning and building laws are judicially reviewable, the courts are hardly equipped to determine the social and economic consequences of the hundreds of restrictions imposed by localities. One reason is that each case must be decided on its own facts; and even after a decision strikes down an ordinance, the locality gets around it by a new enactment that necessitates starting litigation all over again. If the builder wins in the long run, he can expect delays in approving his plans and other frustrations. Builders want to buy land, not lawsuits.

The states should set up independent commissions empowered to review building codes and zoning ordinances on their own initiative or on a complaint either by an aggrieved individual or a neighboring community. Simultaneously, HHFA should set up a separate department dealing with codes and should condition federal aid upon enactment of realistic codes and building ordinances. Cities affected by the exclusionary laws of their neighbors should be permitted and prepared to challenge practices that prevent their lower-income families from buying homes within their means.

Though the building industry is still small, it now includes a number of builders capable of building five hundred or more houses a year. But even if they are well capitalized, they will encounter difficulty in buying sufficiently large tracts of land. If they succeed in assembling a tract, they have trouble financing the land improvements and utilities.

If land is to be developed close to work locations and if the industry is to increase its productivity, a mechanism must be devised for buying contiguous land in large parcels and helping to finance land improvements and services. The recommendation that follows can, if adopted, break the land blockade and ease the problem of land improvement financing. It would not only help expand home building and improve efficiency but should also reduce home cost.

9. Planned New Towns and Epicentric Cities

Building good housing in new neighborhoods is as important as renewing housing in old ones. With 80 per cent of the population growth on the fringes of cities, the future of the American housing inventory is as much at stake on the periphery as it is at the core.

The entire land inventory on which our urban people live accounts for only about 1 per cent of the nation's land supply. The land cost is only a fraction of the cost of the buildings and improvements that have been or will be built over it—perhaps 10 per cent. But how that land is planned will determine the patterns under which most people will be living a hundred years hence.

Only thirty-five years from today, our population is expected to grow by 160 million people, making our total number 350 million. The rate of land consumption in metropolitan areas is at least a million acres a year. Compared to the total land supply this may not be much, but it will be the land on which most of the nation's people will live and work. It is this land, clustered around the existing cities, that will ultimately influence the course of the nation's development and its environment. The United States is a new nation still building its future, and how it uses its urban and suburban land resources will fix the burden to be borne by its succeeding generations.

The new lands that hug the central cities are being developed today by thousands of small home builders who build wherever they can buy a snatch of land they can develop, mortgage, and sell. What the land-owner considers as his vested interest and what the builder looks upon as turnover is irreplaceable and of vital importance to the nation. Its waste is far more serious than the waste of agricultural lands to the prevention of which we dedicate billions. It is this peripheral land to which the larger cities become hostage. As the land is being pres-ently developed, what will remain between the new mushroom develop-ments and the central city will be thousands of stray lots, slumlands, scrub, or dumps that will mar the intelligent development of the region. An orchard that should have remained a greenbelt succumbs to the steam shovel, while a terrain that should have been built to house people lies barren. If all the land put to urban use in orchard-rich Santa Clara County, California, since 1947, had been planned as a single subdivision, it would have occupied only 26 square miles. Instead, the developments sprawl over 200 square miles.[8] It will not be long before the 500 miles that separate San Francisco from Los Angeles will be a maze of shrapnel subdivisions and skipover forma-tions. Schools, roads, streets, and utilities will have to be supplied after this remarkable terrain has been leveled and the wasteful pat-terns fixed. In booming Puerto Rico, a chaos of speculative shacks has sprung up on its suburbs without schools, stores, churches, or community facilities; they are monuments to monotony and the sordid exhibits of unregulated subdivision.[9] What is happening in California and Puerto Rico is also happening in almost every growth area in the nation—we are developing clusters of "sluburbs" around our slum cities from which disenthrallment will be impossible.

[8] Samuel E. Wood and Alfred E. Heller, *California Going, Going . . . ,* California Tomorrow, 1962.
[9] See Charles Abrams, "Report to the College of Engineers, Architects and Surveyors on Resolution P–147," San Juan, Puerto Rico, New York, 1962, mimeo. In 1962, a new chairman of the Planning Commission halted further subdivisions and imposed new "guide lines" for unitary neighborhood de-velopment.

In the cities, the power has been granted to acquire land, factories, and office buildings and evict the people who live and work there. It is the displacement of people that has caused delay and red tape in the renewal program. Yet in the new areas where no displacement or demolition is necessary, the power has not yet been granted. Here the land that represents only a small fraction of the ultimate value of what is put on it remains secure against acquisition. It is testimony to the manorial concepts and mystical barriers that keep us from building a better nation.

The states remain oblivious to the thousands of pygmy governments dominated by home owners and realtors who have put up the "No Trespass" sign in fear that their little islands might be overwhelmed by the city's poor. Posterity has no voice at all.

The logical way in which the nation's environment might be preserved for those who live after us is for the states or the federal government to acquire the land needed for the extension of existing cities and for new cities. Authorities could be set up with representatives from both sovereignties. The land would be planned, the schools provided, as well as water, drainage lines, and open spaces; the improved land would then be sold for private development. This would entail no lesser role for the private builder than he has under the existing land development procedure. Only the sequence of the public and private efforts would be altered.

By making the improved land available for private home building, contiguous land would be assembled and planned and more convenient journeys to work assured. Waste and scattered subdivisions would be avoided. Local autonomy would be subordinated at first but be restored thereafter, for upon completion of each development, the public land would be turned over to the existing city, a newly incorporated local government, or a regional agency. Land would be sold for the homes of the rich and the middle class while federal low-interest programs [221 (d) (3), 202, etc.] and family subsidies would enable homes to be built for the lower-paid workers as well. Proper enforcement of the expanded federal nondiscrimination order would guarantee against exclusion because of race or color. What would be built would fulfill the concept of a regional city—a place in which people of all walks of life work and live.[10]

Publicly sponsored acquisition for land development does not give offense to democratic concepts. Land has been acquired for new towns in connection with dams and other federal purposes. England has engaged in large-scale land acquisition operations to provide planned towns for industry, trade, and housing. Alberta, Canada, passed a New Towns Act empowering the government to declare any area of the province a "New Town," and a public corporation plans and finances it. After providing the necessary site improvements, the land is disposed of to private developers for industrial, residential, and commercial development.

The obstacle to new-town programs in the United States has been their association with the romanticized conceptions of the Utopian "city ideal." The notion that new-town building is "socialism" (derived from some foreign programs where the state continues owning the land) is absurd—it is anything but that when implicit in the plan is the withdrawal of the government from land ownership, sale of the land to private home builders and home owners, and the reservation to public ownership only of the schools, streets, and other traditional public services. It is no more socialism than is urban renewal in the cities. If anything, the program's main premise is "desocialization."

The use of public power to assemble land in sufficiently large parcels should be sustained by the courts in a proper test. There are many incidental public purposes that are fulfilled in such a program—

[10] In 1962, as chief consultant to the Governor's Advisory Commission on Housing Problems in California, I included such a proposal in the report of the commission (pp. 53, 60). The report urged the federal government to make loans to state land agencies set up expressly for the purpose of acquiring land for new towns. President Johnson offered such a proposal in his message to Congress on March 2, 1965. Whether the program will be carried out with a responsibility for rational regional development or for the benefit mainly of the entrepreneur will, of course, depend on how such a program is administered. Moreover, it still has to be adopted. In recommending such a program, however, the Johnson Administration has taken a long step toward planned development and better communities. For a summary of the California proposal, see my article in *Architectural Forum,* September 1963, p. 105.

preservation of open space, greenbelts, and scenic lands; proper planning, aesthetics, prevention of urban sprawl and traffic headaches; low-income housing, relocation needs, and recreational and public facilities. It is no less a public purpose to assemble land in open areas to prevent blight than to remove blight.[11]

In planning these new towns and regions, their location and their relation to the existing cores are of paramount importance. An airport should serve both the old and new developments. So should the reservoirs, the recreational and open spaces, and the traffic arteries and public transportation systems. What should be encompassed is a regional renewal of the new and the existing as an economic and social entity.

Such new developments could be built as part of dams or as incidents of land acquisition for federal parks.[12] Along the Hudson River from Yonkers to Peekskill, within commuting distance of New York City, for example, is a long and beautiful shore line which should be

---

[11] In *San Francisco* v. *Hayes,* 122 Cal. App. 2nd 777 (1954), the City of San Francisco was authorized to acquire 325 acres of which only 15 per cent was developed or occupied. The standards of blight set forth in the California statute were (1) an economic dislocation, deterioration, or disuse, resulting from faulty planning, (2) the subdividing and sale of lots of irregular shape and inadequate size for proper development, (3) the laying out of lots in disregard of the contours and other physical characteristics, and (4) the existence of inadequate streets, open spaces and utilities. The new buildings were erected (after assemblage by the renewal agency) by private enterprise—as would be the case in any new-town programs. The test is whether the eminent domain power is used to avoid a "real hindrance," i.e., a hindrance which cannot be eliminated without public assistance.

[12] The Department of Interior has, in fact, already developed a workable plan for acquiring park lands, some of the procedures of which could be applied to land development for extensions to epicentric cities and for new towns. An area could be declared ripe for planned development, after which no improvement could be made that does not conform to the development plan. The government would be required to file a plan within three years after the declaration. During the interim period, any owner could sell only to the government and the government could also acquire any land it needed by eminent domain. After acquiring the land it needed for fulfilling the planned development, the government would develop the streets, schools, and utilities and dispose of the land for private development according to the plan. If any owner wished to retain his land or develop it according to the plan, he would be privileged to do so, provided the land was not needed for public uses or to effect contiguity for a planned development.

taken for a national park. Within the area lies land suitable for the
development of several new towns. The park land can be acquired
and the sites suitable for new towns planned and disposed of for
development. Thus national parks and living areas could be created
side by side.[13]

In twenty-one years the New York region will have 5 to 6 million
additional people, or three-quarters as many as now live in New York
City. By 1985, as much new land will be developed in the region as
has been developed since the earliest American settlement. Between
1960 and 1985, the region's capital requirements for transportation,
communications and utilities, recreation, education, and other public
and social services will be $75 billion for housing, $12 billion for
private utilities, $40 billion for commercial and industrial structures.
The total required capital investment will be $175 billion, or $10,850
for every individual living in the region in 1960.[14]

Under current trends, most of the 5 to 6 million people coming into
the region will settle not in the present cities or older suburbs but in the
newly developing areas. It is imperative that the undeveloped land
not only be brought into proper use for these people but that it be
linked to the existing developments and that the most rational and
most economical use be made of the available land supply. Common
needs not only demand town planning but require that the town
planning be a component of the regional planning and replanning.
What is true of the New York region applies to most other metropolitan regions from coast to coast.

[13] Percival Goodman and Alexander Kouzmanoff, *Break-through to the
Hudson River: A Plan for Yonkers to Peekskill,* School of Architecture, Columbia University, 1964, sponsored by Richard L. Ottinger and Family.

[14] Harvey S. Perloff and Henry Cohen, "Urban Research and Education in
the New York Metropolitan Region," Regional Plan Association, July 31, 1963,
mimeo., p. 10.

Appendix A

ESTIMATED MONTHLY HOUSING EXPENSE AND REQUIRED ANNUAL INCOME
(HOUSE IN NORTHEAST: MORTGAGE OF $14,000)

Cost Items	FHA Loan, 30 Years, 5 ¾%	35 Years, 3% Loan	35 Years, 2% Loan	35 Years, 0% Loan	45 Years, 0% Loan
Interest and amortization	$ 82	$ 54	$ 46	$ 33	$ 26
Heat and utilities	30	30	30	30	30
Insurance	5	5	5	5	5
Taxes	25	25	25	25	25
Maintenance	15	15	15	15	15
Total	$157	$129	$121	$108	$101
Required gross annual income[a]	$7,536	$6,192	$5,808	$5,184	$4,848

[a] Assumes that as much as one-quarter of monthly income is spent on owned housing. The example is based on home cost in the more expensive areas. In areas where home costs are lower, wages will also be lower. The gap between income and house cost is nationwide, though the figures of home cost, carrying cost, and income may vary. If lower-income families are to be reached by federally aided housing programs, it is through lower mortgage charges that the most important reductions will be achievable.

Appendix B

Assume a building with a $3,600 rent roll, valued at $18,000, with a first mortgage of $10,000 bearing interest at 6 per cent plus 3 per cent amortization. The upkeep charges on the existing building would be roughly as follows:

Interest and amortization	$ 900
Taxes	600
Insurance	150
Superintendent	360
Light, water, and repairs	600
Total expenses	$2,610
Rents	$3,600
Expenses	2,610
Net profit on existing building	$ 990

Now assume an $8,000 alteration with an $18,000 mortgage[1] bearing a constant interest and amortization payment at 6 per cent. The expenses would then be as follows:

Interest and amortization (on $18,000)	$1,080
Taxes	600
Insurance	150
Superintendent	360
Light, water, and repairs	400
Total expenses	$2,590
Rents	3,600
Expenses	2,590
Net profit on re-habilitated building	$1,010

[1] The new mortgage would take up the existing one and consolidate it with the $8,000 advance for rehabilitation on a 25-year term. In both cases, the mortgage is reduced by the same fixed payments annually.

Chapter

13

Blueprints for American Cities

SINCE URBAN ENVIRONMENT in the United States is now influenced or created by government, it is clear that there should be objectives to guide official policies.[1] But except for a sweeping and undefined generalization in the 1949 Housing Act, promising a suitable living environment for every American family, there is not even the semblance of any environmental objectives for federal policy; nor, despite frequent references to community renewal programs and master plans, have any objectives been framed by states or cities.

One reason for the lack of objectives is that, if they are to be realistic, objectives, like master plans, must deal with the difficult problems of population location and distribution. In the past, public land policy was a main device for influencing population shifts. Today, there are also national housing programs carrying housing subsidies, federal policies on race discrimination, and a huge subsidy program for road expansion. But though federal policy can influence local, state, and regional policies, the attitudes of the old freewheeling business society have survived to induce a freewheeling pattern in officialdom. *Laissez faire* is operating between the federal government and the states, the states and their smaller jurisdictions, and between each

[1] For a more complete definition of objectives as distinguished from goals, programs, projects, and schemes, see Charles Abrams, *Man's Struggle for Shelter*, M.I.T. Press, 1964, pp. 214, 215.

local jurisdiction and its neighbors. To state objectives would mean
resolving jurisdictional conflicts, passing laws, and making policies to
carry them into effect—it is easier to let things happen in a universe
of purposelessness, causelessness, and aimlessness. It is easier also to
commit billions of dollars to roads and other improvements without
openly identifying their implications and impacts. It is simpler to
promise a "Great Society" or proffer a few pilot programs whose
pilots never set full sail into the wind. The result is that, while federal
programs accelerate the move to suburbia, slum clearance and urban
renewal policies for cities effect population redistribution only within
the borders of the cities themselves, e.g., from one slum to another but
not from a city slum to a suburban location.

If the population flow is to be freer, not only must the suburb
be made accessible to the poor family by proper federal aids, but the
city must be made a better and more attractive place to come to and
live in. No city, however, is complete master of its own destiny.
Human poverty is a nationwide problem; minority concentrations
and racial conflict stem from nationwide causes of long standing and
should be national as well as local concerns; lack of adequate educational and training facilities, teachers, and classrooms, and the ignorance and sense of futility which lie at the root of much of the poverty
problem can no longer be remedied by the cities out of their shrinking revenues; slums and slum life are no longer accepted as simply
the products of a landlord's greed or a city's poor building code.
Framing objectives on a local level only, while useful, will be incomplete unless set within the larger framework of federal objectives and
federal policies affecting cities.

Yet the city and its citizens should not sit idly by, lamenting the
city's fate or looking primarily to the urban renewal program for its
salvation. There are some aspects of physical environment that are
within their own power and are outside the scope of the renewal
or public housing programs. A city also grows on the ideas and contributions of its citizens and on their will to build their city into
something better. When the cities and their citizens know what they
want, they will be better poised to press for the assistance they need

from the state and federal governments. If, for example, every city
had a "Goals Commission," which would draw on the views of its
citizens for fresh ideas, there would be a better chance of winning
the more appropriate federal and state programs.

The suggestions that follow are neither complete nor relevant in
all places but aim to bring into focus some of the prospects and aspects
of urban life and development which are generally not considered in
official plans or in the routine programs now functioning in cities:

1. Set an Example of Better Design and Comfort in Publicly Assisted Improvements

The state of America's physical environment is a residuum—of what
is still left of nature's blessings, of what speculative profit has allowed
to emerge and remain, and of what the elements have not yet taken
away. America has seen its spurts of native architecture, its quests
for the city beautiful, its art movements, and its more recent landmark
nostalgia. But the nobler inspirations never attained dominance in
the American urban scene as they have in Europe's cities. Not that
Europe's planners and architects are better or more sensitive than
ours. But in Europe, the long past has always stood out as a conditioner, a past in which beauty, elegance, or style had a value to those
who imposed it and to their successors who respected it. It was not
the product of the industrial age alone but of many ages; America's
cities are a profusion of recencies—of the speculative urge, of the
procession of industrial superventions, of a subordination of natural
beauty to utility and profit, and of the assault by industry's most recent
contribution, the automobile.

Before the advent of federal housing programs, the typical urban
development, except for the undeveloped fringes, was on one to four
lots of about 20 by 100 feet each. Assembling a whole city block for
rebuilding was an almost impossible task. By 1940, however, most
cities were empowered to acquire large areas of slum properties for
low-rent housing, while FHA insurance made it possible for the small
builder to finance larger and taller operations with a nominal investment. Thereafter, urban renewal operations began to involve substan-

tial commitments to environment. Contemporaneously, engineering progress made it possible to build structures that require larger investments with more staying power. The result is that the patterns that are being presently created will condition those of the future more than ever before. Depending upon what it builds today, the city faces the prospect of future amelioration or future sterilization.

The architecture of cities falls generally into two broad classifications: (1) price-no-object architecture, which includes public building, institutional investments such as universities, museums, temples, shrines, private mansions, and prestigious office buildings; (2) balance-sheet architecture, which is the choice of the builder or investor whose design is influenced by rents, rentability, minimum investment, maximum mortgageability, easy salability, and quick net profit.

In price-no-object architecture, budgetary considerations may be subordinated to impressiveness, long-term utility, public relations value, or the quest for immortalization in marble. In speculative architecture, the builder is more concerned about frozen assets than frozen music. If he invests more than is dictated by the profit and loss account, he may wind up in the bankruptcy court. If his architect produces something good that pays off too, the architect is a genius but the profession's rare exception. The speculative city builder gives the consumer what he mainly wants—rent within his budget and good location. Rarely will the renter pay an extra 50 cents a square foot for better architecture, higher ceilings, and a more elegant facade. He might even tolerate 50 extra decibels of noise if the space is cheap enough and the location is right.

As for officialdom, its codes and regulations emphasize safety (often more than necessary), not beauty. Codes are, in fact, so drawn as to leave the architect little room for exercising originality. Simultaneously, the city's taxing authority fixes assessed values by rents or imputed rents and might even slap on a few extra digits for elegance though it does not reflect itself in entrepreneurial profit. This was the fate of the Seagram Building on Park Avenue, where the courts sustained New York City's assessor for taxing street floor land which was left open. While the city's aesthetes called the building a conspicuous masterwork, the court called it "conspicuous consumption" and sustained the assessor. Thus, while the city's planning commission exhorts good architecture, less density, and smaller coverage, the same city's tax assessor exacts a premium for each of them.

While speculative building is difficult to deal with, an increasing number of improvements are publicly initiated, financed, or subsidized. Urban renewal projects, for example, are made possible by the public purse and should be influenced by loftier motivations than those of the market place. They should be built to last and under very high standards. But the renewal formula too often binds the private renewer to pinch his pennies to earn his dollar. The 90–100 per cent mortgage leaves the renewer with little cash investment and equally little incentive for good design.

If the land cost were written down to a low enough figure, it might pay to build a varied development composed of low-rise terraced housing, some stores, institutions, recreational and open spaces, all of which might compose an interesting and useful city development. Building at different ground levels, providing a plaza or decorated promenade, might relieve monotony. But no matter how low the land cost, the renewal developer will usually try to go as high as he possibly can to work up the maximum rent roll, follow a standardized pattern in design, and garner the maximum profit with the minimum outlay. Certain heights fit the speculative formula in the larger cities—6-, 16-, 20-, or 30-story units—and these will be the types designed because they produce the minimum unit cost, the maximum gross receipts, and the maximum net return. Nor will the Federal Housing Administration intervene to insist on higher standards. Its interest rates are usually no lower than those of the private mortgage market and it is more concerned with rentability than with better design. FHA has so liberalized its permissible room count that a housewife renting a "five-room apartment" is hard put to find the missing two rooms. Nor will FNMA reduce its rates to achieve a better design. FHA and FNMA both function more or less as routine business operations. Thus ceilings will be low, room sizes small, and amenities minimal. The renter takes what he is offered primarily because of the rent, and he looks forward to moving out when a better bargain appears.

The city might be expected to demand a better-quality product, but cities are party to the renewer's motivations. They too look for the maximum rent so that they can get the maximum tax revenues. They might limit the building coverage, but if they insisted on too high a design standard, the rents would be higher than the market would pay.

So with public housing which is built entirely with public funds and bears the public imprimatur on its product. It should therefore be built to high standards. But federal law and regulation fix a maximum room cost that dictates minimum amenities, minimum room sizes, maximum building heights, and maximum economies. In this respect it runs counter to the theory behind building codes and other devices aimed at improving standards. Under codes, the law prescribes the minimum on the expectation that no builder will or can go below it— but could (and hopefully would) do better. In public housing the federal government lays down the minimum but bars the housing authority from rising above it. City officials incline toward accepting the federal restrictions with little protest.

If some of the capital cost on public housing were written off, more subsidy given, or if families were allowed to remain and pay higher rents when their incomes rose, higher design standards would be possible. But this is not what Congress intended. Public housing projects are built for the poor, and the law is written so that they will be poorly designed.

If a regeneration of areas is to be achieved, the rules of the game must be changed. The product should not only be within peoples' means but should help elevate the city's appearance. A lower land price and a low tax rate might be enough to induce a better design for renewal projects and still provide the renewer with a paying proposition. If simultaneously Congress provided rent subsidies to families, renewers could fill their projects and venture into the deeper slum jungles instead of the grey areas. Such rent subsidies would guarantee them a market and a solvent product.

The twentieth century has given us a deliberately planned architecture of discomfort that permeates both our private and public contributions. The motivations for discomfort have varied and some are understandable—like the traditional church pew with its simplicity and the need for humility in the presence of one's Maker. But less understandable are such efforts as that of a chain burger shop which deliberately builds its stores for discomfort. It crowds its patrons and provides no coat hangers so as to get the coffee-gulpers out as quickly as possible and thereby increase its turnover. (The company's president told me that only by making the customer less comfortable could it afford to sell good burgers and coffee at a modest price.)

Some commuter railroads are no more accommodating. Stuffy terminals, seatlessness, discontinuance of train service, rough tracks, and other irritations may drop business a bit, but some railroads feel that the case for federal aid will be strengthened by the discomfort. Railroad and bus terminals have few seats to discourage loitering, and the battle fatigue it brings to their customers is viewed as incidental. A bench at a bus stop with a canopy to keep the customer dry might convenience the weary traveler, but lack of it will fend off the weary street pilgrim, and this is thought to be all to the good. The museums and libraries that exact the climbing of a long flight of steps to reach the entrance place pomp above comfort, although a ground-floor store window baited with a Picasso would draw more patrons into the interior.

The architecture of discomfort appears on streets, parks, and public places. A comfort station living up to its name is still to be found in America. Public privies of any kind, comfortable or otherwise, are absent in most cities—a somber tribute to the fortitude of the American bladder.

The same philosophy of discomfort governs in public housing as in public toilets. If the poor were given doors on their closets, it would be too good for them. It might also compete with what private enterprise produces. Subsidies, interest rates, and maximum costs per unit are therefore set at levels that assume a low standard as good enough and a 40-year project life as long enough.

All large private projects, when assisted by government, should be joint private-public ventures in which public contributions to the area complement the private builder's amenity-bare structures. Profit-making may be the builder's main concern, but the neighborhood affected should be the public's concern. A small park or playground and a social center (either within a private project or nearby) should be part of every major private improvement, whether or not it is government aided. The city could even rent space for the facilities (a play space, community center, library, etc.) from the builder and by doing so make it profitable for him to install them. But there is a rigid separation of function between private and public contributions that prevents this.

Until better architecture is embraced as part of the public purpose and the inducements are provided to make it possible, mediocrity will continue on our urban horizons.

2. Utilize the Natural Features of Cities and Reclaim Them Wherever Possible

The era in which a city is born conditions its current and future appearance. Most American cities were originally blessed with good landscapes and waterscapes. They were far seemlier in their natural endowments than most of the European cities we envy. Much of these blessings were destroyed or shrouded during the industrial surge. Lakes, rivers, and streams were polluted, blocked off, or harnessed into industrial use; old trees were felled and hills leveled for factories, houses, piers, or speculative developments. If a city's natural features were retained (as in San Francisco), it was not because of planning wisdom but because the terrain would not yield.

Instead of blending their new works with the old vistas, officials have bisected the vistas with highways or hidden them with housing cordons that make them inaccessible to the general public. In less than a quarter of a century, Manhattan's lobe on the East River has been so walled in by housing projects that no one thinks any longer of Manhattan as an island. Taking a walk along the East River means taking one's life in his hands while crossing the busy highway. The old cluster of interest at the city's Battery Park was destroyed by the ruthless demolition of the Aquarium, and Coney Island's recreational value has been dwarfed by turning Luna Park into a housing site. Louisville's Ohio River has been obscured by an industrial slum. Boston's old waterfront along Atlantic Avenue, once the bustling scene of commerce, was left to decay as its loosening piers became floating hazards in the harbor.

Sometimes, as on Boston's waterfront, a few restaurants, chandlers, and a fish market have held out courageously; and some small remodeling operations have begun to convert a few abandoned warehouses into studio apartments. But the area remained cut off as a source of recreation for decades, although within a stone's throw lie the downtown office center, Faneuil Hall, and other old monuments which call up history at every crossing. At the northern extremity a solvent Italian section leads to Paul Revere's house, Cobbs Hill, and other mementoes. The area at sunset provides a panorama of sea, sky, and ships, blending into a silhouette melodized at pleasing intervals by sea-borne sounds. But as night falls the area remains sad and abandoned. The reintegration of this section into the life and substance of Boston would help maintain the solvency of existing businesses as well as of the Boston area as a whole. Fortunately, the site has been chosen for urban renewal, but despite the insistence of the planners that the emphasis be recreational, Boston's citizenry insisted that it also produce property tax revenues of at least $1 million more than it presently yields. The result was a compromise. It will salvage at least part of the values[2] for recreation while providing 2,000 dwelling units.

All too often, however, the tendency is to think mainly in terms of *new* revenues and *new* private developments, when the reinforcement of *existing* urban assets and *existing* revenues should also be put on the scales. Revenues from apartments need not be the only gain—the stabilization of existing urban assets should have a prime place in official calculations.

[2] See Charles Abrams, *Boston's Waterfront—Some Ideas for Study,* a report to the Boston Chamber of Commerce, April 1961. Some of these values will be built into the Boston site, thanks to Kevin Lynch, author of *The Image of the City,* Technology Press and Harvard University Press, 1960, who is planning the site.

Proper planning of city waterfronts can combine specific revenue-producing improvements without sacrificing the scene. Marine sales centers and nautical operations could fit a site's aquatic orientation. Fish markets and seafood restaurants can draw gourmets as well as revenues. A heliport, a hydrofoil base, a marina, a commercial amusement center on the water or an interesting recreational addition could create new values as well as conserve the existing values.

Water has been the age-old magnet for people—the Roman bath, the fountain, falls, village well, beach, spa, and more recently, the resort swimming pool. Yet while preservation of natural access to water has been the pride and stabilizing force of great cities, American cities have been relinquishing their waterways so recklessly that the last vestige of the aqueous will soon be the laundromat.

California provides another example of prodigality with nature's gifts. By 1980 twice as many new homes as presently exist will punctuate California's horizons—some 5 million in all.[3] Whether California's future environments will be slum, "slurb," or a decent aggregation of neighborhoods and where its future homes will be located hinge largely on what is done today. Yet one giant urban complex is being allowed to form in the north from Monterey Bay to Sacramento and another in the south from Los Angeles to San Diego. Outside the central cities, new subdivisions carved out of agricultural lands are linking these two complexes in scattered developments. Three million acres of productive land will soon succumb to the bulldozers, and much of California's most valuable resource—its great natural landscape—will be turned into building lots. Its unique vineyards, pasture lands, and orchards will be a memory; for by 1980, the present farmland in these areas will be gone and its most virginal terrain will be cut up into building plots.[4]

In 1963, a commission appointed by Governor Edmund G. Brown

[3] On a rough estimate, one-quarter to one-fifth will probably be replacements of existing properties (Donald L. Foley, Wallace F. Smith, and Catherine Bauer Wurster, "Housing Trends and Related Problems in California," *Housing in California: Appendix,* Governor's Advisory Commission on Housing Problems, 1963, p. 172).

[4] *Ibid.,* pp. 35 ff.

outlined a series of objectives to guide California's future development. But the pressures of builders and savings and loan associations to allow business to go on as usual will see California's rare remaining gift of nature go the way of others in the deteriorating American environment.[5]

3. Multiply the Number of Trees, Parks, and Green Spaces

Street trees and small parks, strategically placed, supply reprieve from the steel and cement facades dominating the cityscapes. The human being can accept the unrelenting Bastilles of the industrial era if respite is nearby. But most of our big cities have never redressed the ravages of the industrialization that denuded them of their verdure. No greenbelts or wedges run through American cities as they do in Copenhagen. There are a few surviving public greens as in New Haven, an occasional square for a courthouse or a common such as in Boston. But these are exceptions. The small parks that run through London or the green walks of Paris have not often been duplicated in America.[6] The use of ivy or creepers on buildings is rare and an air conditioner with a place for flora or fauna to relieve its ugliness is still to be manufactured. American attitudes have too often placed the jackpot ahead of the flower pot. The best use of a tree is for manufacturing billboards.

Trees are more than aesthetic props; they provide ventilation and shade and absorb noise and dust.[7] A city with properly laid out green areas will provide an improved neighborhood climate,[8] and in

[5] *Report on Housing in California,* Governor's Advisory Commission on Housing Problems, 1963, pp. 1, 4.

[6] *Trees in Town and City,* Ministry of Housing and Local Government, London, 1958.

[7] "A city of monumental buildings . . . needs trees to interrupt the reflected light. The landscape architect uses trees to soften hard building lines and accentuate vertical or horizontal devices. The home owner plants trees to give scale and proportion to desired features. . . ." (Irving C. Root and Charles C. Robinson in *The Yearbook of the Department of Agriculture,* 1949).

[8] Erich Kuhn, Director of Institute for City and Regional Planning of Techniche Hochschule, Aachen, in *Medizin and Stadteban,* reprinted in *Landscape,* Spring 1959.

some cities a difference of 30 per cent in humidity has been measured
between its green areas and its downtown sections.

A city's environment should encourage its inhabitants, particularly
those from crowded areas, to walk or remain outdoors for reasonable
interludes. The presence of trees in a pleasant atmosphere or a small
retreat of green will not only draw people from their houses but
provide an essential contrast to the world of cars, signs, wires, metallic
sounds, and gases that permeate our streets. But most cities are
unconcerned. Small clusters of treed areas with benches and a small
playground are easily created, but they too are not common. The
shambles of grim enclosures in the backs of houses could be turned
into pleasant refuges for the occupants if there were a movement to
unfence and replan them as tenant commons, but this is also a rarity.

Cambridge, Massachusetts, plants street trees and maintains them
without charge, and the lush trees of Brattle Street have helped zoom
the section's value, but its stately elms on Memorial Drive are scheduled
to be sacrificed to a highway. In Los Angeles, San Jose, and Berkeley,
the cities plant trees on the petition of 75 per cent of the property
owners; but while Beverly Hills is well treed, there are few walkers
because there are few sidewalks for walking. A few cities have shade
tree commissions, and Washington spends about $100,000 a year for
street tree maintenance, while the Japanese have given it a line of
cherry trees which have survived the example ascribed to the city's
founder in his precocious youth. But most city officials are unconcerned.

The attitude of officialdom was illustrated for me in 1960, when
I sponsored a bill in New York City which would have given the
borough president the right to require installation of trees on any block
on which more than 50 per cent of the owners agreed to plant or had
planted trees. The aim was to have all the owners who benefited from
the planting do their share. When the bill came before the City Council,
a councilman objected that "trees encourage juvenile delinquency"
(presumably small trunks provide ambush for muggers). Another
councilman objected that "trees break windows" (presumably trespass
by inconsiderate branches). Others argued that the proposal would

violate due process. It got no support, and New York City's streets remain mostly treeless.

Similar attitudes cause resistance to small parks in the city's crowded
sections. Small parks add both to aesthetic and real estate values. The
dearth of such parks in New York has made the small Washington
Square Park the most crowded in the nation. It is the areaway for
towering apartment houses, a campus for New York University, a
much needed series of playgrounds for children of all ages, an open air
chess club, a singing and concert center, and a dog walk, among other
uses. It was barely saved from being turned into a major throughway,
as well.

The near sacrifice of this smaller park to a roadway only highlights
the public indifference to the city's larger parks as well. The larger
park should exist in every city, not only for passive enjoyment and as
a place of natural beauty, but also for the more active sports and
recreational forms—picnicking, boating, long strolls, baseball, tennis,
football, riding, skiing, bicycling, and other activities that the smaller
park cannot supply. New York City's Central Park, composed of 840
acres in Manhattan's heart of which 185 acres are devoted to lakes
and ponds, has long been one of the city's blessings. But by default,
officials and citizens have allowed the park to be closed to them after
dark, a time when it should be serving its most useful purpose. Because a few muggers, delinquents, and homosexuals have taken it over
at night, no citizen dares any longer to walk alone through its pleasant
paths. (The city's real estate director has even proposed that it
be turned into another real estate development.) The case of Central
Park manifests not only a lack of official imagination but the indifference of citizens to one of their most precious heritages. Yet if five
hundred New Yorkers would organize a walking club, whose members
would amble through it in groups at given hours nightly, other walkers
would follow, the police would be bound to give them the necessary
protection, and the park would soon be reclaimed for the city's people.
A few more strategically placed chess centers with coffee served to the
players, more Shakespeare and off-Broadway productions, more concerts, well-organized square dancing, and other well planned evening

recreation would help, too. But this calls for citizen action and the harried New Yorker has become indifferent and inert.

In Europe, the surge of industrialization saw the development of both large and small parks for the growing urban populations; and at the beginning of the twentieth century, Berlin already had about a hundred such open spaces within the city limits. Paris not only had a similar number but owned about 200,000 acres of park area. Park squares are almost indigenous to areas of Spanish orientation. But while our colonial past showed a concern for neighborhood scale, beauty, and landscaping, industrialization and urban growth have harnessed all possible space to profit operations. Federal concern in parks is recent, and it was not until the end of the nineteenth century that the federal government was granted the right even to acquire land for park reservations. Parks were not considered a "federal concern."[9] Though the housing acts now authorize a federal advance to local governments for a fifth of open space cost, this usually is assigned to the spaces outside city limits. If our city neighborhoods are to be properly rebuilt, federally assisted park programs are as essential within cities as are road programs and open spaces outside them. Urban renewal can be a useful tool for appropriating more space for parks and playgrounds within and around the developments, while public acquisition of areas for small parks and playgrounds can capture for the cities some of the attributes of suburbia which lure people from our crowded cities.

4. Make the City More Attractive for Tourism, Diversion, and Leisure

When the American breadwinner decides to spend his earnings on a vacation in his own country, he generally points his auto compass toward the exurban mountains, lakes, or national parks. When the same vacationer has saved enough to go abroad, his ticket will read

[9] *U.S.* v. *Gettysburg Electric Railway Co.*, 160 U.S. 668 (January 27, 1896). The case granted the right to the federal government to acquire the site of the Gettysburg battlefield as a park memorial partly under the war power, i.e., the memorial would inspire youth to defend their country!

Paris, London, or Rome. New York, San Francisco, Miami, Las Vegas, and New Orleans still draw customers; but few vacationers ever pick Buffalo, Detroit, or Pittsburgh for their two-week splurge. In the United States a domestic vacation is generally an escape from the city, not to it.

Tourist figures tell the story. United States tourist traffic to foreign ports doubled between 1954 and 1961, and about half the 8,260,000 travelers were repeat visitors. While Americans traveling abroad in 1960 spent more than $2.6 billion, the collective visitors from every part of the world to the United States spent only $1.08 billion. The disparity widened in 1961.[10]

Tourism is a vital element in the life of societies. H. T. Buckle, the nineteenth-century historian-philosopher, coupled tourism with the discovery of gunpowder and political economy as the three principal agents responsible for lessening the love of war.[11] While this might be stretching it a bit, the fact is that tourism not only enhances culture but is also one of the best devices for promoting understanding. It exposes a nation's people to others in their own native environment. Tourism from the Communist countries would do more to advance the democratic image than the stentorian Voice of America. But if so many of our own folk go abroad and fewer foreigners come here, it is partly because foreign cities have more to offer than our own. The price we pay for it is misunderstanding and antipathy.

Alarmed by the flow of money abroad, President Kennedy in 1961 sought to revise the unfavorable balance by setting up a "Visit USA" project. After spending $2.5 million to print posters and promote trips by foreigners, the nation's hotelmen hopefully printed their menus in foreign languages, taught their doormen how to say "good day" and "thank you" in four languages, and began offering cheap packaged deals. But neither the cheap jet journey nor the menus and brochures succeeded in whetting foreign appetites for American urban scenes. A

[10] *Britannica Book of the Year,* Encyclopaedia Britannica, Inc., 1962, p. 677.
[11] F. M. Oglivie, in *Encyclopedia of the Social Sciences,* Macmillan, 1937, XIV, 661.

visit to Paris or a slow auto trip through suburban France or Italy are still far more alluring prospects than a trek through America's cities or suburbias.

The dearth of foreign tourists is not due entirely to the differentials between American and European incomes. It is due also to our growing urban and suburban dullness. The biggest slice of tourist spending is by our own 106 million vacationers who pour some $16 billion annually into tourist travel. But about 90 per cent of it is by automobile and except for the few bright spots, the cities are little more than stopovers enroute to the open spaces. One city looks too much like another and many have three things in common—a waning Main Street, a cavalcade of gas pumps, and tedium. With few exceptions, the American city is still the place to earn a living, but it is losing its attraction as a place to spend the evening, a vacation, or one's leisure hours.

Our collective governments have let dullness happen. Their contributions have been a few housing projects, the statue of a forgotten hero and more and more freeways that bypass the city. Ignored are the devices for renewing the city's spirit and providing more room and inspiration to move the citizen's body. Thus bicycling in the city has been replaced by slendercycling, walking by motor gunning; figure rejuvenation has been turned over to the Body Culture Institute; diet has supplanted body movement; and the sunlamp is depended on to add the veneer of health.

The picture looks somber despite the increase in leisure time and leisure activities. Given more time to do nothing, Americans are bursting with energy to do something. Some have taken to ice skating, skiing, cookouts, and archery, but more have taken to bridge (40 million, or about double the number in the 1930s) and to miniature sports cars (a $25 million hobby). Though bowling has gained as an urban and suburban pastime (30 million bowlers), it is exurban recreation that has benefited most from the leisure-time extension. Thus water sports gained new heights while skin diving and spear fishing had 5 to 8 million "aquaticians" in 1962. More than 7.2 million recreational boats wallowed in our waters, including some floating lodges or houseboats rented under a drive-it-yourself housekeeping plan. Mobile homes in 1963 accounted for about a tenth of all housing starts and a de luxe Rolls Royce camper can be bought by those with the wherewithal for $18,627. (A super-de-luxe domestic model that can be opened with the press of a button into a 1,000-square-foot sanctum costs twice that.) Camping areas increased to about 20,000 to accommodate one quarter of a million campers.

All this is fine for the vacation period or the long weekend. But in a society that has become urban and in which the city should be the main haven of continuing pleasure, the city dweller keeps looking mostly toward the outside and does so only during his two-week fling. He tends to run from his city as though it were a company town. It is not surprising that despite the recreational explosion nationally, gross receipts of the hotel industry and city clubs have fallen.

Better in-city recreation[12] is a *sine qua non* for city survival and human renewal. And one of the most important of the environments for recreation—and the most neglected—is the city street. A city street is the main scene of urban interest. Here one is free to look and be seen. It is the landscape of humanity revealing the houses people live in, the clothes they wear, their probable station, their smiles and frowns, and the wares of tradesmen luring the passer-by. It is the living room of the overcrowded poor, the playground of their children, the Louvre of living art for all walks of life. Interesting streets should be among the city's best assets—for walking, recreation, and diversion. But Americans are insensitive to a building's unique history or to an unusual facade, while a newspaper or television station that takes the trouble to publicize it is the rare exception. Nor have cities done more to make their streets more interesting. As for the federal government,

[12] According to the *Encyclopaedia Britannica,* recreation has been variously characterized by different writers as "any activity engaged in voluntarily just for the pleasure it brings to the participant, whether through relaxation, refreshment of strength after toil, renewal of spirit, the opportunity for self-expression, relief from boredom, release of emotional tension, the provision of an outlet for repressed impulses, the testing of one's powers, the attainment of a sense of achievement, the forgetting of one's worries, sheer fun or the strengthening of the ego that comes from feelings of adequacy and self-esteem" (1961 Edition, XIX, 15).

it pays 90 per cent of the cost of interstate highways, but it does nothing to improve the city streets for people.

Recreation in cities is another important asset. It is big business. Amusements (indoor and outdoor, urban and exurban) hold eighteenth place among the nation's industries.[13] The theater, the dance hall, and night club are urban operations; and to survive, their cash registers must be fed not only by urban customers but also by suburbanites and tourists. But while some smaller night clubs have kept their doors open by catering to limited audiences with folk sings, belly dancing, and avant-garde raconteurs, the number of customers in night clubs and dance halls is a pittance compared to the 40 million recreational boaters, or those who point their cars annually toward the open spaces and their purses toward the gas station and motel. Both should be available for the customer's choice. But too many large supper clubs served their last supper in the 1960's and with the larger night clubs gone, the big stars now tour college campuses or make one-night stands in public auditoriums.

The art boom has seen more galleries go up in the big cities, and it exemplifies how a nation that for more than a century took no interest in art can burgeon almost overnight into the world's great art market. Tax incentives for gifts are not the main explanation, though a good stable of paintings can yield profit with honor. Another reason may be that we have moved from the status symbols and honorific values of stud horses and dogs to name paintings. (A New York City multiple dwelling is no place to raise a pair of wolf hounds, and a Picasso does not have to be taken for a walk three times daily.) Whatever the other reasons, the art millenium suggests the still-uncharted potentials for the city renaissance.

The theater, though suffering from finance fatigue, still goes on in New York with an occasional tryout in Boston, Philadelphia, Los Angeles, Washington, D.C., or San Francisco. A *My Fair Lady* can still enrich its backers, but the juke box is still more popular than the theater box.

The restaurant allays hunger but can also be a rich man's salon or,

[13] *Britannica Book of the Year,* 1962, p. 615.

as in France or Greece, a retreat for workers with nothing more to spend but an hour and some change. Both types should be available on every mainstreet. The restaurant business employs one out of every six people engaged in the retail trades. Good food and drink in a good environment draw people with money to spend, but the restaurant enterprise in the United States is no longer a place of interest. While in some cities (especially New York, San Francisco, and New Orleans) they have held their perilous own, many others that deserved survival have gone into the soup. Loss of the old proud pros, a dearth of talented chefs, high prices, and low returns are among the causes.[14] The Prohibition period snuffed out some of the best taverns, though a few survived by settling with the prohibition agent.

The restaurateur's major problem is that, despite our greater leisure time, one takes fewer minutes to eat and when he does, it's a TV dinner. Our creative culinary handiworks have given way to the snack pots and steam tables. Our dining salons are counter restaurants, chuck wagons, and cafeterias that depend on fast turnover rather than good food. (The cafeteria can be operated with fewer employees, and customer movement per seat is 3½ times greater than in a service restaurant.) A prefabricated meal is wolfed down in ten minutes— often at a steering wheel.

Officialdom must share the blame. Sales taxes, overrigid zoning laws, and lack of public parking spaces are among the reasons for the restaurateur's troubles. The ceilings on expense-account spending damped down the enthusiasm of salesmen in search of tax-deductible junkets. Officialdom is responsible also for discouragements to other recreational forms. Sunday laws permit baseball and bar hopping but not bookstore browsing. Censorship has often leveled the public taste to that of the official arbiters of decency, while Shakespeare was barred for a time from showing in New York's Central Park as an intrusion on the park's greenery. The vibrant little-theater movement in Greenwich Village was almost strangled at the start when the police

---

[14] Sometimes rising rents have been a factor in the decline—it should not be more than 7 per cent of gross sales—but rents are less of an item than rising wages and cost of construction.

refused a pioneer group the right to operate a theater-in-the-round except under a cabaret license, which would have required liquor to be sold at every show. Since the sponsors would not gamble on showing Eugene O'Neill's *The Iceman Cometh* to a drinking audience, the theater group demurred. After a hard fight, it got the license. The off-Broadway movement buzzes today not because of official encouragement but despite official discouragements.

European countries have long supported the opera, maintained orchestras, and launched festive occasions. Tivolis are publicly sponsored. Some have national ballet, dance companies, and folklore performers; and, thanks to the Ford Foundation, George Balanchine and his ballet troupe will survive. But the programs and funds of our own state and federal agencies have been given over mostly to exurban recreation. (The principal federal agency for recreation, for example, is the Outdoor Recreation Resources Review Commission which pays little attention to urban or indoor forms.) As for the city, it usually sees recreation as a few uninspiring playgrounds, an athletic field, and an occasional community center. Foregoing another housing project on New York's Polo Grounds site in favor of a Negro cultural center with a museum and a jazz stadium would have shown more imagination and helped make isolated Harlem a part of New York. But imagination in recreation has never been an official virtue. The theater and allied enterprises not only get no public aid and encouragement, but are regulated and levied upon drastically. The theory behind the tax on admissions to entertainment (20 per cent, finally reduced to 10 per cent) is that entertainment is not a necessity and that those who spend for it have more than ordinary taxpaying ability. When New York City's tax on admissions was dropped after 1960, the art movie business saw a small spurt in theater building—only to face a new 5 per cent city tax on leasehold rents in 1963. This, coupled with the exorbitant demands of film distributors, undid some of the benefits of the admission tax repeal. It was not long before further building was curtailed. Sales taxes, difficult and expensive parking, and traffic troubles are other impediments to in-city excursions.

Yet the main cause of the American city's decline as an entertain-

ment center is not the taxes, nor the loss of the upper-bracket population, nor the arrival of Negroes, Puerto Ricans, and Mexicans. A main
trouble is the decline of the urban spirit, the lag in the initiative of
the American people, and their waning interest in their urban culture
and leisure and in the environment that nourishes them. The federal
and state unconcern with cities is only one of the factors responsible.

The world's cities are the birthplaces of sophisticated entertainment.
They have created new traditions and opportunities for mass entertainment, both recreational and educational. Ancient Rome launched
its games to make the citizen's life bearable and allay unrest. In the
Orient, the city is the seat of the sporting events, competitive games,
mass spectacles, and celebrations, and the road to elective office often
lies in the organization of entertainment on the city's streets. But in
American cities, the city's streets are viewed as the domain of the automobile, and the sidewalks as the prospects for curb cuts. With indus-
trialism, the old yeoman outdoor sports disappeared and have never
been replaced.

Ideas are born in the city if people have the opportunity and the
scene in which ideas can be spawned. An example is the theater in
New York City's slum streets, started in 1962 by Patricia Reynolds on
less than a shoestring. It proved that *The Bear* by Chekhov can
compete with its counterpart in the zoo. The slum kids remained
glued to their seats as the romance unfolded, and they cheered when
the widow accepted her suitor's offer. When, during the play, the suitor
cried for water, a hoodlum delivered a bag of it from a tenement roof,
but this was the only interruption, and the show went on. When 300
rented chairs were set up on the street, cynics were convinced they
would disappear with the audience. When the performance was over,
there were 306 chairs on hand. The audience helped put them on the
truck and pleaded for more performances.

One of the opportunities ignored by our officials is competition
among cities. No sport has made the American male more conscious
of his city than his professional baseball team. But where are the
officially sponsored intercity contests in the multiple sports? The
Olympic game idea among cities is an unexplored frontier.

Urban recreation and urban entertainment need urban recreation commissions that could give the same encouragement to urban and indoor recreation that has been given to public outdoor forms. Since culture and recreation are kin, and since culture and cities have always gone together, such an enterprise might lift the American cultural level, too. If, as proposed by the Rockefeller Brothers Fund report of March 8, 1965, on the performing arts, the National Council on the Arts would help strengthen existing federal arts programs, show a greater awareness of their cultural implications, and provide federal matching grants for cultural facilities, it would help considerably.

The passions and aspirations, the dreams and desolations of millions of city souls are still hinged to the cities. So is the social solvency of the suburb. The asphalt may seem hot and barren, yet within these cities there still lies a wellspring of creativity that needs a chance to start flowing. A little thought, a little help, a little money, and, above all, imagination and concern, might make the difference.

5. Salvage the Central Business Districts

Part of the fuel that makes a city flicker is its central business district or downtown.[15] Downtown is the museum of style, the change of scene, the confluence of diversities, and the escape to anonymity. It is the city's main taxpayer, generating from a quarter to a third of its local taxes, and it accounts for a substantial portion of the city's jobs. It is the scene of political action, of marriage license bureaus and divorce courts, doctors, dentists, psychoanalysts, and lawyers. It is the place in which the deeper human problems are exposed and allayed, where a man can meet a lady without being accused of having a rendezvous. It has become the locus of the great modern institution of Lunch, where a businessman can negotiate a sale or a loan over the coffee cup. It is the nub that draws the masses and that the masses have made. Without downtown there is only the neighborhood, and with only the neighborhood there is no contrast and no alternative, no easy

---

[15] Downtown is the city's hub or hubs, on which people converge for business, trade, shopping, etc. The term is often used interchangeably with central business district, even when it is uptown.

escape and no real freedom of movement. The cities with pulsating downtowns are the cities that thrive. Those without them are headed for desuetude.

The tourist who confronts Rome's grandeur, ambles through the never-ending surprises of London, or sips a Cinzano on the sidewalks of Paris remembers them for their downtowns. The human animal has always required a central area to which others of his species will gravitate to exchange glances, boasts, confidences, or protests. The human concourse in India's hinterlands is the village well; in tribal West Africa it is the village center or "mammy market." In the metropolis, it is the downtown.

Trade usually follows where people convene, and where trade follows, more people arrive. The initial concourse may have been the square, the religious center, the town hall, the trading post, crossroads, bazaar, or guild area. One of the historic forerunners of downtown was the fair, but by the dusk of the eighteenth century, it had given way to fixed shops and markets, banks and exchanges. These sections salvaged some of the flavors and excitements of their antecedents. With the expansion of modern enterprise, downtowns became not only the unassailable market places of urban life, but the refuges from provincialism, the new cores of urban activity and influence. They have outlasted wars and revolutions in Europe and stand steadfastly as the focal points of tourism, trade, and interest.

Availability of raw materials, power, transport, and labor as well as orientation to the market and a kindly attitude toward investment are some of the reasons for the city's existence. Proximity to education, officialdom, to other trades, finance, and to centers of talent and research are other reasons. But if a city is dull, the inducements of profit, subventions, and cheap labor are not enough to make it sparkle.

Executive wisdom is essential to city growth, and one of the most unfaltering influences on the executive (and therefore on the location of industry) has become the executive's wife. She will not settle for a suburban house and a television set unless there is a humming downtown nearby. Climate, department stores, beauty parlors, servants and cooks, a bridge club, the prospects for the teen-agers, bazaars, and a few good friends may make the difference with this sphinx of the trade routes. A study in depth of her motivations could yield one of the hidden secrets of industrial location. Downtown is her escape from boredom, the place where she can spend the day shopping and come back with only a new can opener and be happy. Variety in a city is indispensable, and it is a thriving downtown that holds it for her. If we all come to depend on mail order catalogues and television advertising to tell us what to buy without stirring from our chairs, our urban culture will grow dreary indeed.

More recently the downtowns of our cities, like the old fairs and bazaars, have been threatened. The "For Rent" signs are going up in what was once the old 100 per cent block. A downtown that could once boast a draw of 300,000 people has lost it to an outlying market on Route 6A where wives have found it easier to drive and park. In the retail sections of 45 metropolitan areas, retail sales rose 32 per cent; it gained only 1.6 per cent in central business districts.[16]

Hackensack, New Jersey, had a population of only 29,000 in 1950, but its downtown area had a retail trading radius of 393,000 people. Real estate men rated it as one of the nation's three best trading centers of its size, and chain stores were continuously on the hunt for available space. Hackensack's downtown real estate sold at a yield of only 5 per cent.

Then department stores like Alexander's and Korvette settled on the outskirts. Markets and other retail trading shops competed for space near the big stores and formed huge self-contained shopping hubs on the highways. Soon Hackensack stores lost not only the trade of the out-dwellers, but the custom of many in-dwellers. A downtown store with 22 feet of frontage which rented for $12,000 annually before the new competition had its rent reduced to $3,600. A Main Street property which had sold for $220,000 in the 1940s could not support a $50,000 mortgage and in the 1960s was surrendered to the mortgagee.

[16] Address by William L. Slayton, "Achieving the New Downtown through Directed Urban Change," at New York State Association of Urban Renewal Officials, May 13, 1963.

The once humming downtown center of Newburgh, New York, which housed its department stores and chains, is today an abandoned street. About 90 per cent of Water Street's stores are vacant. With downtown streets too narrow for expansion or adequate parking space, a new shopping center developed on a wider street, and thereafter mushroomed in the county outside. The old downtown was soon surrounded by slums. A property which had sold for $100,000 free and clear of mortgage in the 1940s had almost no value at all in the 1960s and was turned back to the city because it could no longer pay even its real estate tax.

Similar developments are occurring in dozens of other old cities where the big chain stores are deserting their downtowns by the scores. Some communities have tried to meet the competition by installing parking areas, but they were too often too late. The competitive shopping centers had already been built, and the new shopping habits had firmed.

Disparity of interests, segmentation of lots, lack of regard for the city's traffic headaches, sales taxes, and the failure to view a business street as a common concern have brought many a downtown section to its present decline.

A downtown area lives or dies as a whole. The decision of its department store to leave the area can start an epidemic of other move-outs and foreclosures. Similarly, one good store that gives the customer a break can boom business on the whole block. But why should one landlord cut rent to invite an attractive tenant when the main dividends will go to others? Why should one owner let his property be taken for a parking lot to benefit the rest? The suburban shopping center in single ownership has no such problem; the owner apportions space on the basis of over-all benefit, cuts rent to a minimum so as to woo Sears, Roebuck, J. C. Penney, or a department store as its magnet. It then makes up for the "loss" by increasing the rent of the other stores that benefit.

With urban renewal, some cities have tried to peg their downtown areas. By acquiring a large plot within the urban area, providing parking, and running the highway to the new center, they hope to meet the competition. If they can get the main department stores and chains to stay, they may succeed, but in too many cities, the efforts still lag.

One trouble with the downtowns is that they become places to get into and out of as quickly as possible. The suburban workers pour into the offices and businesses at 9 A.M. and are disgorged at 5. The city is where they spend their working hours to pay for the berth in which they spend their sleeping hours. The shoppers converge all at once for the special sale and lumber out as fast as their aching feet can reach their accelerators. The parking meter is set for half an hour. Speed and turnover have become downtown's objective. But people today are looking for more interesting combinations. The sidewalk cafes are what help make Paris exciting. The London club is available for the well to do and the intellectual elite. The afternoon siesta exists in Italy and Spain. But there is no retreat for the average mortal in America's downtowns, no alternative but the quick purchase (sales tax added) and the long journey home.

If downtown is to live, the city must cater to the pedestrian as well as the driver. It must aim to be a night city as well as a day city. It must be planned as a place to spend a day, not an hour, a place where a suburban worker can also spend an evening and not just his working hours. Frequent buses on express lanes, monorails or other forms of transport to and from its downtowns should make it easy to come and go. Commuting by rail and bus should be made an interesting and even entertaining experience, and federal highway programs should make it easy to get into the city's center rather than skirt it. There should be more tearooms, street cafes, retreats inside and outside department stores, pleasant roofs for shoppers, some free television corners and benches. There must be more clubs that proletarians can join as a family and where each member can find an interest. Libraries and art galleries should have more comfortable seats and be accessible at street level. There should be music rooms and more diversions for the kids. In short, a city, like a play, must have an absorbing setting, good stagecraft and direction, and a plot that draws interest and holds it. Just another row of stores and a pedestrian walk are not enough.

Every downtown should have a center where a mother can deposit a child for safe care during a shopping tour and where the child can have a gay time while waiting. Tokyo's department store roofs, where a child can go on rides or play games under the supervision of a matron, are an example. Universities which are adjuncts of downtown can lure adults to pleasant leisure as well as to exhibits and to adult education.

Downtown's surrounding area must be made interesting, too. More people will come if there are also engaging sections in neighborhoods near to downtown. London, Paris, Rome, Hong Kong, and a host of other cities abroad exemplify how they can be both interesting and shopworthy. The city should be giving people a series of choices, not just a shopping tour. If one cannot get into the theater, there should be the concert, night club, bowling alley, or just an interesting walk. Since variety in a city is its stock in trade, variety in neighborhoods is indispensable. The same cooperation that periodically spurs business corporations to finance a city fair should spur them to finance the lasting well-being of downtown. They can rent stores not only for displaying their wares, but with noncommercial attractions that will draw families cityward.

Our strict immigration quotas have helped not only to make our downtowns dull but our cities dull as well. In the United States there are all too few Chinatowns and too few Chinese—only 237,292 in 1960. The United States and Canada tend to look upon Chinatown as a slum or ghetto instead of an entertaining neighborhood. Canada leveled two of her Chinatowns and Boston reduced hers with a highway, while New York's demolition scheme was luckily halted by the protesting Chinese themselves. Cities have all too many package stores and too few sukiyaki restaurants, too many banks that are dark at night, and too few foreign specialty shops that stay open at night. Smuggling in some good chefs might violate the immigration laws, but not the laws of urban growth. Cities and their businessmen should seek out the world's great cakemakers, tailors, and craftsmen, and guarantee them a place on the Main Streets. A nation of vitamin pills and chemical bread might find relief as well as better bread with a few more foreign bakers and their wives.

Our Main Streets were rarely planned and mostly grew. In the course of growth, they began to yield some of the secrets of success as well as some of the reasons for frustration. Many downtowns were unplanned, yet proved fascinating and solvent. They became so through the headaches and heartaches of hundreds of storekeepers. Ousting these people without providing them with alternatives—as urban renewal is often doing—is a wanton destruction of a vital asset. Their investments, talent, and perseverance should be utilized wherever practical in the renewal undertakings. The city should seek the cooperation of as many of the owners as possible in the regeneration of a downtown site. A corporation might be formed to hold the property in single ownership with existing owners given stock for their holdings, or cash if they refuse. The area should then be replanned, added to, or rebuilt as a unit with proper parking and adequate space for the stores. Help in financing the operation should be given by government. Where cooperation of enough owners cannot be secured, a rebuilding of the area may be the only alternative.

Yet building a downtown without revitalizing the city itself will not perform the miracles for which the planners are looking. Revitalizing of the urban downtowns will succeed only when the federal government, the states, and the cities themselves are ready to grapple with the city's physical, economic, and social problems as a whole instead of relying on a few public housing and renewal projects for the solution.

6. *Build upon Existing Values of Neighborhoods Rather Than Destroy Them*

American neighborhoods include the good and the miserable. But housing conditions should not be the sole determinant of what deserves to stay or be torn down. Nor is a neighborhood of bad houses always made better by leveling it and reshuffling the inhabitants. Too often this is not slum clearance but slum transference. Many old houses have better standards than the new private and public multiple dwellings that replace them. After identifying what is valid, it should be reinforced. Sometimes a paint job with a varied and interesting color-scheme can spark life into a whole block of flats. What a neighborhood may need is not physical improvement but the addition of key amenities that can bring out its hidden values or generate new ones.

A neighborhood is a voluntary formation of people, each of whom has his own good reasons for electing to live in it. The reasons may include proximity to friends, parents, or work, a rent that fits the budget, the right church, the proper playmates for the children, or just plain sentiment. When Mrs. Stanley P. Jadwin, a gracious and discerning widow who left $27 million to Princeton University, chose to live out her life with her seven servants in the declining South Williamsburg section of Brooklyn, New York, it was not because she would not be welcomed in Greenwich, Connecticut, but because she felt happier living where she did. Demolition of a functioning neighborhood nullifies these choices, disrupts associations and institutions, destroys what the people have added to the neighborhood and the attributes that drew them to it in the first place. It means the forced withdrawal of children from school, the dispersion of those who attend its churches, settlements, and synagogues; the disappearance of its stores which are a vital ingredient in the neighborhood life.

Poorer people can create interesting environments if given the chance, and the low quality of the dwellings or the physical environment may be compensated for by what the people themselves have brought to their neighborhoods. Nor is every slum the precinct of misery. It can be a dull slum or an interesting slum like New York's Lower East Side. Slums are not devoid of values when they provide an easy journey to work, a greater latitude to do what one wants, living with less concession to the higher social pressures (including wearing one's best clothes on Sundays only), and living with one's own culture while providing access to the city's more diverse cultures.

Nor is the much maligned ghetto always a dispensable slum. A walking tour from the bagel belt to Chinatown and the pizza complex in New York City can be a rewarding experience, and it would have been officialized vandalism to sacrifice such areas for dull housing projects as was so often proposed. The engineer and architect are not always the final arbiters of environment—the Ukrainian beekeeper who sells homemade honey on New York City's East Seventh Street and McSorleys a few steps east are more gratifying to the eye and nose than the lifeless and supersanitary Cooper Union annex put up a stone's throw to the west; the open markets and humming old stores on Orchard Street lend more life to the landscape than the stiff, storeless housing projects a few blocks north.

Customs and traditions play a part in the Little Italy, Germantown, or the neighborhood with Spanish, Russian, or Finnish inflections. Their shops boast the native traditions and are the magnets for tourism and trade as well as the museums of Old World cultures. Here the street has values not found along the nation's dull Park Avenues.

Italian sections are particularly interesting for their espresso shops, block parties, and cheese pendants. They have provided good soil for the settlement of artists and poets in both San Francisco and New York. Chinatowns are a joy for their Old World contrast, while the eat shops and delicatessens run by Jews—a people who in the Old World had to make the cheaper fish and meat discards tasty and edible—have helped to dissipate the dullness of America's palate.[17] Poles and Ukrainians have their own formations but are more clannish, while the Puerto Rican is too recent an arrival to forecast that his *bodega* will branch out into a more engaging mart.[18]

The Negro migrant contributed much to American music, dance, and humor. His failure to emerge into a storekeeper, however, is not in-born as some whites claim, and this is confirmed by the "mammy-traders" of West Africa. Destroying the Harlem ghetto, as some reformers and Negro leaders have urged in order to achieve citywide integration, would neither achieve it nor would it be welcomed by the

[17] When I took Lord William Holford, London's famous city planner to Katz' delicatessen on New York's lower East Side, his comment on the hanging salami and like renderings was that the best decoration of a store was the arrangement of the provisions themselves. Good smells and inviting food are better designs than anything the industrial designers can conjure up. Delicatessen may not always be delicate, but it is tasteful.

[18] At dinner with President Muñoz Marin, I brought up the point that a few good Puerto Rican restaurants would help dissolve the fiction that there is no Puerto Rican culture. "I'll ask Moscoso to do it," he promised. But Moscoso went over to the Alliance for Progress. Puerto Rican enterprises nevertheless are beginning to sprout in New York City.

Harlem Negroes themselves. Though Negroes in New York will and should diffuse their settlements, Harlem is destined to remain as the capital of Negro America. Instead of leveling all of Harlem, amenities should be added to it which would make it an interesting place to live in and to visit. This means, among other things, adding appropriate cultural and educational institutions that will induce the Negro to be proud of his community and his culture and which will tempt the whites to venture more visits to it.

Destruction is not always the answer, even in the depressing skid rows. A little imagination can father a neighborhood revival without displacing the skidrowers who would, if evicted, probably form a worse skid row elsewhere. Skid row's cheap rents and good location might support an interesting restaurant, a reminder of the gay nineties, a thriving flea market, cheap art studios, and speciality stores that draw bargain hunters despite the presence of the skidrowers. Allen Street in New York City is a bargain center for antiques, the Bowery a low-priced market for electrical fixtures, while one of San Francisco's old areas has become the thriving bazaar for wares from Europe and the Orient.

In old sections with cheap rents, one might also find bargain centers for pottery, antiques, jewelry manufacturing, furniture making, and other crafts that benefit from the location and cheap rentals. Every big city in fact needs a well-located cheap rental area, and even the business of collecting old paper, refuse, and junk must find some place in the big city. To tear the buildings down without proposing an alternative for the lost services and jobs shows a feeble awareness of a big city's needs.

Many of the aging will be found in older sections, too, and a good landlady may be a good shepherd as well as a slumlord (or slumlady) —her furnished room may be better than the best ward in a public institution or the choicest unit in a public housing project. As 75-year-old Miss Elizabeth McGovern put it when an urban renewal project threatened to displace her from the $65-a-month flat she had occupied for thirty years: "It was a fine neighborhood in the old days. We'd have tea in one another's flats and we'd go to the neighborhood socials.

Oh, it's still a good neighborhood, what's left of it. It's changed in some ways, but people are still kind to one another in times of trouble."[19]

The old sections offer the aging their friends and the social communion which they cannot often recapture after ouster. The old church, the presence of people and faces, the friendly dog or cat (which many public housing projects forbid), the proximity of relatives and doctors, the miscellany of life and the familiarity of scene to dimming eyes are values more precious than rubies. Here *all* the values must be weighed against *all* the failings, and the slum may be only a single digit in the total calculation. Here too, the addition of a few values could make the section worth keeping for those for whom it has meaning.

Because the United States is less than two centuries old, it has not yet acquired a sense of heritage, and rarely will a good old piece of architecture escape the steam shovel when there is profit to be made. To escape rent controls, New York builders demolished Mark Twain's house and some other period pieces. (This recalls Twain's device for saving a man atop a burning building: to throw him a rope and pull him down.) Some big businesses like Lever Brothers and Pepsi Cola will build good buildings because it helps prestige or sales, but New York Central and the Pennsylvania Railroad, which once built for the same motivations were quick to destroy their contributions in the interests of higher rent revenues.

Programs to preserve historic sites are mostly inadequate and often nonexistent. The grant of partial tax exemption to owners on condition that the buildings are retained, improved, and tagged might be one device to save a homestead where Washington slept or Tom Paine polemicized. The city could be granted an option to buy as a condition for the exemption, or an agreement could be made that the tax rebate be repaid if, after the city declines to buy it, the property is destroyed. Landmark preservation should qualify for renewal grants. Cities should have funds for purchase and exercise eminent domain where essential. In Philadelphia, architectural and historic examples have been acquired by a good-citizen nonprofit corporation. They are resold to

[19] *New York Times,* April 20, 1961, p. 35.

buyers who agree to preserve or improve them. But most other cities either lack the right legislation or are unwilling to pay the price of effective preservation. If they rely on restrictions only, the buildings will be shunned and will decay rather than be preserved.

Home ownership in slum areas would increase the incentive to improve, and a federal program to make purchases by slum tenants feasible can often elevate standards without a complete physical overhaul.

7. *Leave Room For the People to Contribute to Their Own Environment*

Many current projects, because of their sheer size, impose a neighborhood straightjacket. The people in the neighborhood have neither the chance to add their own appointments nor to create something reflecting their own contributions and personalities. The project is destined to remain as cold as when it was built.

The large-scale project approach derives from the theory that slums always spread and blight always creeps, while the self-contained project is thought to guarantee its own environment forever. Yet big public housing projects or even private projects like Stuyvesant Town do little for the surrounding areas. Stuyvesant Town embedded its own row of towers into the slum without becoming part of the functioning neighborhood around it.

The needs of a neighborhood cannot all be known in advance. More property should therefore be acquired for a project than is required for its immediate improvement; after the buildings are erected, some of the undeveloped land can be devoted to needs as they arise—a community or social service center, another playground, a library, a private or public school, or whatever improvement or service blends with the initial improvement and fulfills it.

Where land costs are low, small buildings can be projected (or rehabilitated). They provide more opportunity for embellishment by the individual. Such a project built in the scale and scheme of the surrounding environment will add life to the neighborhood just as the existing neighborhood may add life to the project. (The small groups of low-cost dwellings in Philadelphia's Whitman renewal area are an example.) The human being is himself an unproclaimed architect and if given the chance, will demonstrate it (usually for better though sometimes for worse). He will do so within his own shelter or outside it—in the design or arrangement of the shops, the particular decor on the buildings, the back yard, the flower pot, ivy, or tree. He often improves his own estate when he is inspired by pride, personal gain, or a neighbor's example. He tends to sponsor or join a nearby club, a settlement house, or a church that add to the neighborhood's value. In these instances, the touch is of a hundred hands applied over a long time span. The total product can have variety, originality, individuality, and the patina of humanity that is rarely achievable by the massive architectural superimposition. (This human quality is noticeable even in an occasional squatter area in Asia and Africa where a makeshift composite of individual contributions sometimes compensates for the grimness and poverty of the general scene; and when security of tenure is given, a remarkable regeneration is almost suddenly accelerated.) The big rental project too often lacks the potential for the human contribution.

Public additions to a neighborhood are as important as the individual's. But it need not always be a housing project. It might be a school, a library, or a center for recreation or culture. It might even be a combination of a housing improvement and a school in the same building. The trouble is that the main emphasis of public housing and urban renewal is rental housing, and it is bigness and respect for the balance sheet that dictate their scale.

8. *Give People a Sense of Belonging in Their Neighborhoods*

The urban planning profession is still in embryo, and social architecture and social planning (the science of creating socially functioning neighborhoods) have not yet matured.

The public housing project provided an opportunity for experimentation with social architecture, but income limitations and tenant turnover have made the average tenant's stay too short. Fear that a neighbor might reveal one's income has made for distrust; the promotion and pay raise which should have been the tenant's boast becomes the family secret. Tenant organizations which bring people together have been often discouraged for fear they might give the management trouble.

The main difficulty has been that brick and mortar have assumed the dominant role in the creation of human settlements. How to make people feel part of the area in which they live remains a vacuum in the planning curricula and a void in government thinking.

When a family chooses a neighborhood, its decision usually implies that it belongs in it or wants to be part of it. It is this feeling of belonging that finds parents becoming involved in school or church affairs, in politics and community life. The big city is a tough place to get to know one's neighbors, and one may not even know the folk next door—many do not want to know them, which is their privilege. But socially solvent neighborhoods are those with institutions or organizations that are intrinsic parts of the neighborhoods themselves. In London's Elephant and Castle section, Peckham Center (which unfortunately closed its doors when, during the period of postwar reconstruction, it was denied national support) supplied an interesting example of the type of institution our neighborhoods should have. The family joined as a family with a nursery provided for the infant and with each family member having available to him an interest for his particular age group. Activities were centered around a swimming pool (the water magnet). The swimmers were viewable from a balcony equipped with tables for games and tea. The center encouraged infamily as well as interfamily interests.

The public school could serve a multiple function—not only as a place for educating children but as a social meeting place, a theater, dance center, or a forum. Some cities have done this, but the usual city schoolhouse is as frigid as a bank at night.

The church has always served as a binding force, but its members and leadership are heading toward suburbia when they should be performing their most important functions where they are.

The university in the city could provide both the education for community life and the leadership that stimulates it. It has or can have the facilities and the people for research in the neighborhood's needs and desires. Such research projects could combine study with the actual effort to make the neighborhood part of the campus and the campus part of the neighborhood. This is done in smaller communities but rarely in the large city, where the university's presence is announced only by the inflow and outflow of its students. At nightfall it becomes the neighborhood tomb.

When urban renewal came onto the scene, some universities treated it simply as a prize opportunity to expand their real estate holdings instead of a chance to integrate their facilities with the neighborhood. But often the concern of the university and the city coincide, as when former Mayor Charles Farnsley, acting on behalf of the University of Louisville, sought to bring the three elements (the university, the renewal program, and the neighbors) into a common program for neighborhood uplift.

More sponsored theater performances, concerts, and forums would help also. If the university took more leadership in grappling with the problems of the local public school and the school system, it would endear the university to local parents. Opening its libraries and facilities and taking down the "No Trespass" signs on the walks would be welcomed. Guided tours of the university for the neighbors, greater leadership in community functions, and recreation on and off the campus would also help.

9. Encourage "Commercial Clustration" and Reinforce Existing Clusters

The limitations of human locomotion and the convenience of concentrated bargain hunting influence a convergence of certain enterprises toward defined city sections. These sections become the focal points for the purchase of wares, entertainment, or services. Many also evolve into important concourses of human interest.

A commercial cluster of interest can be a concentration of department stores, food marts, fish stores, secondhand bookshops, insurance enterprises, jewelers, coffeehouses, textile or leather merchants, antique shops, art dealers, chandlers, theaters, bargain shops, furniture stores, vitamin markets, stock exchanges, radio and television shops, flower markets, flea markets, or discount houses. An hour's walk through Manhattan's Lower East Side, starting at Manhattan Bridge in New York City, reveals the jewelry cluster (where the ring can be bought), then moves one into the bridal gown cluster (for the wedding), the raw wool cluster (for the baby), and the bargain counter cluster on Orchard Street for the household goods of every variety.

A cluster can be a wholesale or retail center, a homogeneous cluster (selling the same wares) or a heterogeneous cluster. It can also be an ethnic cluster like a string of Chinese shops in Chinatown. The cluster formation may be deliberately planned as it is in a regional shopping center or it may follow out of initial activity by a few businesses (usually the leaders) at a strategic point which then draws others and ultimately becomes a magnetic hub. It may be the center for professional buyers, for women in search of marked-down woolies, or for amateur numismatists in search of Cleopatra's tetradrachmas. In the larger cities, restaurants, night clubs, and hotels will go where the theaters or cinemas are, which may give rise to an entertainment cluster; or there may be several such clusters, some catering to the pedestrian and some to the carriage trade.

Clustration can be one of the most effective devices for revising neighborhoods. In New York City, a builder named George Backer persuaded leaders of the textile industry in the 1920s to establish showrooms around Fifth Avenue and Thirty-first Street. The concentration helped stabilize an area on the downgrade. Other clusters in New York City which have buoyed up lagging sections are the toy industry on Twenty-third Street, the antique industries on Second and Third Avenues, and the secondhand bookshops on Fourth Avenue. The replacement in 1927 of a small slum by an art movie on West Eighth Street and some live stores next to it activated the section and made it one of Greenwich Village's most walkable clusters. A similar cluster for entertainment sprouted on McDougal Street with the mushrooming of coffeehouses.

Clustration widens the choices of buyers, browsers, and bargain hunters within a compact area. The presence of many has been found to yield more benefit than the competition discourages. The bigger the city, the better the chances of commercial clustration.

Incipient or functioning clustrations are sometimes broken up by government action. Because a section seems alive and strategic, the Post Office Department or a Port Authority (as in the downtown radio, television, and flower section in New York City) often drop their heavy hands on a cluster and disintegrate it. Public buildings are generally massive, dull, deadly at night and can snuff out not only the life of an incipient cluster but of the surrounding sections. Areas that have a chance of growing into live clusters should be strengthened. Instead of tearing down a whole section, urban renewal should acquire the dormant plots that deter cluster expansion and add carefully selected enterprises that will complete or enliven it.

One of the impediments to cluster formation or cluster expansion is the diffusion of lot ownerships. Urban renewal has the tools to assemble the land. The owners of an area can be convened, their advice listened to, a plan drawn that will fulfill the section's needs in parking and traffic as well as through the addition of the essential stores that will invigorate the area. Sometimes it may be advisable to cover the cluster with a skylight (this might be appropriate for Orchard Street, Manhattan), provide a rest area, widen a sidewalk, add a parking area, or reserve a street for pedestrians only. More owners will be found willing to comply with a sectional improvement than the urban renewers think. But some lack the capital and others the plottage essential for expansion. A few parcels may have to be acquired for rehabilitation or enlargement of plots.

The trouble is that renewal programs are too often geared to all-or-nothing actions and to ownership and operation by the successful bidder looking for an FHA bailout. They raze what should remain and which might grow if given a little help. Commercial renewal should emphasize commercial reinforcement, not just demolition for apartment houses. As the sole owner of his acreage, the builder of the regional center can plan his clustration and, after he has committed his main tenant, mark out the stores for the satellite tenants.

Planned clustration in an area of multiple ownerships is more difficult. It calls for the same expertness possessed by the knowledgeable shopping center entrepreneur plus the power to assemble land and replan the store locations.

10. *Make the City the Great Center of Adult Education*

Four factors have combined to highlight the role of the central city in the education and re-education of adults: (1) the reduction of working hours and the availability of more free time, (2) the extension of the life span and the need for utilizing the talents of older people with useful years, (3) the mass displacement of workers through automation and the need for retraining, and (4) the preparation of married women for useful tasks after their children are grown.

In little more than a century the on-the-job labor effort of Americans has been halved. In the three decades 1930–1960 the average length of life has been stretched ten years. Automation is eliminating clerical, bookkeeping, and assembly-line jobs by the tens of thousands while those hardest hit are the poorly educated.

The still unmet imperatives in education of adults are continuation studies and corrective education to compensate for deficiencies in earlier education. The need for intellectual growth in either general or special fields is essential for improving personalities, training the specialists, or preparing for job changes. The best insurance against unemployment and social inadequacy is better schooling, and the theory that separates cultural from vocational education is fast losing its force.

The city is better equipped for training and education than the suburb. It has the pool of institutions, the university, the trade schools, the libraries, and the museums. In the city, a wider range of motivations can be served, more specialties and more vocational and cultural subjects taught, a better and a greater variety of teachers hired. Suburban travel, which often consumes two hours a day for the work journey, leaves little time or energy for adult education and re-education. But though in 1964 the need for adult education was emphasized by the national drive on poverty and unemployment, neither cities nor their institutions have risen fully to the challenge. Saturday schools are infrequent and should be expanded. A pioneering effort in adult education like the New School for Social Research in New York City has received little foundation support and in 1963 was almost extinguished for lack of funds at a time when it was operating to full capacity as a teaching institution. Though improvement of its adult education facilities would give the city a more important status, adult education and extension programs in most cities have been poor in quality, short in duration, dependent on improvisations, and too often employing the same techniques for adults as for children. Ample federal grants for tuitions and for expansion of training facilities would help. Assumption of responsibility by industry for retraining people in cooperation with schools would also help.

11. *Develop a Realistic Mass Transportation Program*

When the present 70 million cars go to 100 million in 1980, many a city will look like the still of a giant ant heap. Some do already. Cities are becoming suburbia's mammoth garages as well as its crossways and throughways. Los Angeles—"the freeway city"—is already using two-thirds of its downtown area for freeways, streets, and off-street parking, and America's current car pilots are only the outriders of the invasion to come.

Disfigurement, congestive fevers, and land shortage will not be the only consequences. Some twelve to eighteen lanes will be needed by 1980 to carry traffic from Washington, D.C., to suburban Wheaton. The inner loop in Washington, D.C., will call for fourteen lanes. In Atlanta, Georgia, the northern portion of the expressway already has traffic to warrant sixteen lanes, and by 1970 the need will have jumped to thirty-six lanes. To keep pace, New Jersey by 1975 will require 821 miles of freeways into every county of the state.[20]

Automobiles and air both fill vacuums; but governments keep spending billions, creating more vacuums to be filled. As the Depart-

---

[20] *Urban Mass Transportation—1962,* Subcommittee of the Senate Committee on Banking and Currency, 87th Cong., 2nd Sess., April 24, 25, 26, and 27, 1962, p. 55.

ment of Commerce concedes: "Merely adding highways which will attract more automobiles which will in turn require more highways is no solution to the problems of urban development."[21] But what the department concedes is ignored by departmental policy.

So many cars feed into the city that some cities are getting fed up. As Mayor Raymond Tucker of St. Louis, president of the American Municipal Association, put it:

The plain fact of the matter is that we just cannot build enough lanes of highways to move all of our people by private automobile and create enough parking space to store the cars without completely paving over our cities and removing all of the . . . economic, social, and cultural establishments that the people are trying to reach in the first place . . . Even if we could do it physically, the costs would bankrupt the combined resources of the city, state and federal governments.[22]

A 15-mile strip in Washington, D.C., is estimated at $300 million, a 22-mile highway through Philadelphia along the Delaware River at $300 million, a 12-mile turnpike into Boston's downtown area at $180 million, a little more than one mile in Manhattan at $100 million. All this does not include access highways, local street systems, and parking costs.[23] Under the Newtonian law of motion applied to politics, more and more taxpayers' money will continue to go into more and more highways, byways, freeways, and throughways.

One reason for the decline of cities and the rise of suburbs has been a national propensity to help the new and ignore the old. This applies to fledgling industries as it does to the fledgling suburbs. When the railroads cut across the plains in the 1860s and 1870s, states bought their stock, guaranteed their bonds, gave liberal loans and tax exemptions, provided huge areas of land and ample supplies of convict labor. The railroads were also the darlings of the limited federal sovereignty which after 1850 gave them liberal land grants. But when, a century later, the federal sovereignty was virtually unlimited in its

[21] From "Rationale of Federal Transportation Policy," cited in *Urban Mass Transportation—1961,* Subcommittee of the Senate Committee on Banking and Currency, 87th Cong., 1st Sess., March 20, 21, and 22, 1961, p. 43.

[22] Helen B. Shaffer, "City Traffic Congestion," *ibid.,* p. 44.

[23] *Urban Mass Transportation—1962,* p. 53.

powers and more lush in the distribution of its bounties, the old railroads were left to their own devices. The new airlines were subsidized; and the new automobile, new highways, and new suburbias became the federal favorites.[24] If the railroad had not been invented until after the airplane and automobile, the probability is that a good portion of the subsidies now provided to the plane and road would be poured into the development of the infant railroad enterprise.[25]

A big city's main line of defense against automobile glut is mass transportation. As long as the central city can hold a fair share of jobs and purchasing power, it can survive even if it no longer grows. But the railroads are no longer giving the city the passenger service of twenty years ago. Hurt by competition from private cars, buses, and planes, passenger runs generally mean a loss. (The Pennsylvania Railroad says it loses $13 million annually on its suburban service and has lost $675 million on all passenger traffic since World War II.) While railroad passenger traffic has dropped drastically, passenger highway traffic has increased by 144 per cent since 1946, and air carrier traffic, by 404 per cent. To cut losses, the railroads have raised fares, reduced runs, abandoned stations, and continued using equipment ripe for the junkyard. This hardly proved a way of turning losses into profits—cutting commuter runs only increased the number of tires rolling into the cities.

Other mass transit operations are also in trouble. In 1962, the urban transit industry consisted of 1,247 operating companies of which 1,217 were exclusively buses. Heavy traffic impedes bus opera-

[24] By comparison with the money given for highways, the land grants to railroads were a pittance. Only about 8 per cent of the route mileage had the benefit of land grants-in-aid for construction.

[25] If the railroads had shown any ingenuity, they might have bid for a place in the urban renewal program. They were real estate-oriented at their beginnings, hold important real estate today, including developable air rights, and have eminent domain powers. Being regional in the scope of their operations, they could serve as regional instruments for overcoming boundary and jurisdictional snarls in regional development. (Japanese railroads develop residential settlements to increase the number of their customers, but American railroads have not thought of doing this since land grant days.) With 100 per cent financing, the railroads could still become a medium for regional renewal operations, either on a contract or entrepreneurial basis and secure some cash profits to offset some of their losses.

tion, and the competition of the automobile has not helped. The number of passenger trips on all forms of transit dropped from 19 billion in 1945 to 7.6 billion in 1959; 119 transit companies ceased operations between January 1, 1954, and September 1, 1959.[26]

Meanwhile, despite expressways, street widenings, one-way streets, traffic lights, parking meters, and other improvisations, movement of passenger cars and trucks is steadily being slowed to a crawl. Public parking lots cost $3,000 or more per space; and even where the city is prepared to spend it, it cannot find the spaces. Though 40 per cent or more of the land in the central areas of some cities is already often dedicated to the needs of automotive traffic, there seems no dimming of the call for more. With the automotive and the suburban ages only at their beginnings, the cities face the choice of abandoning the vehicle owners to their collective inconveniences or continuing to improvise more and more stopgaps.

The transport problem is not exclusive to the older cities. From 1920 to 1960, the Los Angeles metropolitan area gained in population by 570 per cent compared to 70 per cent for the nation. With two-thirds of downtown Los Angeles occupied by freeways, streets, and off-street parking, this sample city of the automobile age, which sent its first crate of oranges to the East in 1877, is making desperate efforts to attract around-the-clock customers for its sprawling business districts. Inveigling the Dodgers to abandon Brooklyn has not been enough. A new civic center, a medical center, a textile mart, a convention hall, and tall office buildings (New York cut) are depended on for the additional enticements to lure in the trade. Mass transportation (also New York cut) is now looked to as the great redeemer. But as long as automobiles can come in without too great an inconvenience, and as long as Los Angeles keeps making it less troublesome to come in by creating more and more roads and parking lots, it will sacrifice more and more land and become a duller and more polluted place in which to gasp.[27]

[26] Shaffer, *Urban Mass Transportation—1961*, p. 43.
[27] Air pollution attributable to automobiles is estimated at 65–70 per cent for Los Angeles and 40 per cent for New York City.

The transport problem highlights the still unsettled confusion over the roles and responsibilities of our three governments. Transportation is as much a federal obligation as housing or urban renewal, if not more so. Mass transportation is at least as urgent as interstate highway building, to which the federal government contributes 90 per cent of the cost. A good argument can also be made that in-city transit connects to railroad transport and is therefore within the interstate commerce responsibility. Since the movement of people and goods does touch the national welfare and cuts across state lines, the federal government need not depend on the state or the suburban entities within any region to give their consent to federal intervention or allow them to superimpose their judgments on the national government's.[28]

The reliance upon "coordination" or "stimulation" within each metropolitan area, as called for in a joint memorandum of the Secretary of Commerce and the Administrator of the Housing and Home Finance Agency, was therefore simply another invitation to the age-old frustration of states rights and local autonomy shibboleths. So is the reliance on more state surveys and more interstate compacts. If the federal government has the jurisdiction, it should assume it, and assumption does not mean only "research," a few pilot projects, or half-way regulation by an Interstate Commerce Commission. More research (which everybody seems to advocate) can only be meaningful if the gravity of the problem is conceded and the political responsibility assumed where it belongs. Research could then be action-oriented.

Yet up to 1965, the only action taken by Congress was giving the Housing and Home Finance Agency a small appropriation to undertake studies, make a few loans, and finance a few experiments. It was as if the whole transportation problem were involved with HHFA's

[28] In the classic decision of *Gibbons* v. *Ogden*, 9 Wheaton 1 (1824), Chief Justice John Marshall early laid down the rule that "the authority of Congress is at all times adequate to meet the varying exigencies that arise, and to protect the national interests by securing the freedom of interstate commercial intercourse from local control." (The Interstate Commerce Commission has fixed fares not only on interstate but also on intrastate traffic.)

housing and renewal operations to the exclusion of other causes of
city decay including commuter problems, rising fares, decrepit equipment and terminals, inefficient service, labor problems, inadequate
road and connective networks, lack of new transportation techniques,
tax and jurisdictional headaches, and the numerous other vexations
of the metropolitan transportation maze.

When the federal government appropriates huge funds, as it has
done since 1933, for roads and highways, it has an obligation to view
the impact these appropriations have on the central cities. It is obliged
to plan not only roads but the housing and commercial developments
at strategic points such as the exits. Here is one frontier for the rarely
used power of excess condemnation and for planning and building new
neighborhoods within a metropolitan framework.

An efficient mass transport system should have a place as an adjunct
of any major road program.[29] The government should not devote
funds and efforts mainly to one form of transportation—road building
—to the exclusion of others. Extravagant aid to the automobile has
been one of the main causes of mass transportation's troubles as well
as of the metropolis's problems.

An assortment of remedies has been proposed: making travel more
convenient and comfortable; more trains and buses; separate bus
lanes; better stations and terminals and lower fares; better feeder and
transfer services to airports and commuter rail services as well as
coordinating schedules; providing fringe area parking; coordinating
mass transit with new highway networks; putting taxi and similar
services to better use as feeders; examining new types of mass transit
and locomotion; and better land planning.

All or some of these proposals will doubtless help in some cities.
But Congress has been chary of making any constructive money commitments. The state and federal governments, which are willing to
spend for highways, expect transit and suburban rail facilities to be
self-supporting. Though millions of corporate dollars go into auto-

[29] Auto movement at 20 miles an hour requires from 6 to 45 times as much
road space per person as does a transit bus, and from 10 to 90 times as much
as does a multiple-unit rail car (Lyle C. Fitch *et al., The Urban Transportation
Problem and Public Policy,* Chandler, 1964, p. 14).

mobile research, private research for transit and traffic control amounts
to a pittance, mainly because the railroads are less able to invest
the money. Not only is little being done to convenience present populations, but little thought is being given to the problems of future
growth.

No program and no Congressional legislation can be meaningful
unless it is viewed within the context of regions, unless jurisdictional
resistance and boundary autonomies are superseded, and unless land
use, highways, and transportation are not only effectively programmed
but also implemented by a regional agency. Transportational rationalization should be one phase of a regional, not a local, renewal program and the responsibility should be assumed directly by the federal
government, where state cooperation would be lacking or would be
futile.

One trouble is that Congress sees mass transport as a problem only
of the largest metropolitan areas, and Congressional representation
what it is, there is little prospect of the support necessary for a real
program for such areas. Nor will states consent to federal hegemony
over their regions, and if federal aid were to be funneled through
states, the central cities would be bound to come off second best.

Assuming that better mass transportation is provided to and from
every metropolis, some pertinent questions will still remain un-
answered. Though it may be easier to get to the city, why should
one go there? Will better mass transport to and out of the city do
more to push the suburb further outward than to prop up the central
city? Better and cheaper mass transport is essential to get people to
where they want to go, but will they want to go there if the city provides no incentive for going?

In short, better mass transit and better local transport can help
some metropolitan areas. Those it will help are those that already
have something to offer and to which more people would come if
they were made more accessible. But the problem can no more be
viewed in isolation than can housing or urban renewal. Part of the
package must be a city worth living in, worth seeing, worth coming
to, and traversable when one gets there. Other parts of the package
are suburban communities located near enough to the city to humanize

travel to the city. Unless suburban land is close to the city, city schools are improved, the city's neighborhoods made attractive, and the interest in the city restored, easy access to it will neither be enough nor good enough.

12. *Enhance Walkability*

Urbanization in America has reduced the scenes and enticements that encourage walking. The peripatetic is a waning breed. Even the word "pedestrian" has become an ugly adjective describing the dull, commonplace, and unimaginative, while the word streetwalker now describes a less honorable exercise. Yet though almost half the nation's people do not drive—either because they do not want to, do not need to, are too old, too young, or too poor—the automobile's demands now dominate planning as well as city rebuilding. The boulevard and promenade are losing their place in the city scene. Sidewalks are being narrowed and trees cut down to make room for more cars, and the residue is being cluttered with driveways, vault openings, ashcans, traffic signs, pumps, parking meters, mail boxes—in fact everything but trees and benches.

Fortunately, one of the surviving charms of our older cities is their still walkable sections, which were built when foot travel was respected and when neighborhoods had to be near each other for communication. Pilgrimages are still made to these old areas by the discriminating, commerce is personal, and the hard lines of the city's concrete are softened by the presence of the human element. Apprehensions in a city subside when the number of automobiles diminish; interests focus on people and objects, the air gets better, and there is a general relaxation of tensions.

We now take the automobile for granted, but there is still something arrogant about a driver propelling a contrivance fifteen times the human weight and ten times its size, past other human beings at a speed a dozen times their capacity to dodge it. It is a thousand times as arrogant when a thousand such contrivances whiz in and out of our main streets, forcing other chaps to take cover and taking the life of one human target every fourteen minutes. If it were found that cranberries took only a fraction of this toll, cranberries would be banned overnight. But automobiles are not cranberries. They are, moreover, here to stay. But since they are, their separation from the pedestrian is the least that can be done.

Venice (Italy), Dubrovnik (Yugoslavia), and Fire Island (New York) have demonstrated that the automobile is not indispensable for the good life, and one has rarely seen people more human and friendly than when a great snow storm has immobilized all automobiles, or when the Easter Parade takes over New York's Fifth Avenue. The busiest shopping centers are Japan's *ginzas* which are no more than old alleys too narrow for automobiles and therefore safe for shopping and walking. The areas most attractive to Singapore's shoppers are the closed pedestrian arcades. The knowledgeable architect of the shopping center may plan it to lure the automobile trade, but he also provides an interesting ambulatory inside. San Francisco's downtown renewal project will remove all transit vehicles from the Market Street renewal project and substitute a 20-block-long pedestrian mall with a few intersecting plazas. Providence, while providing for a freeway to downtown, will also have a pedestrian mall, and Chestnut Street, Philadelphia, may be given over to walkers too. Mass and other transport to the walkways will be provided both in San Francisco and Philadelphia.

With all our intramural entertainments, the individual still finds it necessary to get out of the house and look for alternative activities. In the more highly urbanized centers, the largest proportion of outdoor activities is conducted in or near the urban environment.[30] The more concentrated the area and the more the population is subjected to urbanism as a way of life, the more it walks for pleasure. One sees on foot what is merely a blur through a windshield. In metropolitan areas of 1 million or more persons, 45 per cent of the population walked for pleasure in the summer of 1960—only 33 per cent did so in areas of less than 1 million.[31]

[30] Philip M. Hauser, "Demographic and Ecological Changes as Factors in Outdoor Recreation," *Trends in American Living and Outdoor Recreation,* Outdoor Recreation Resources Review Commission, Study Report 22, U.S. Government Printing Office, 1962, pp. 27 ff.

[31] *Ibid.,* p. 49.

Yet despite Harry Truman's walking press conferences and President Kennedy's plug for walking as a device for gaining "vigor," more walking as a national objective has been subordinated to more cars. Even the great open spaces are reserved for those with a car that can reach them. Pedestrianism is not only a forgotten art but a forgotten word.

If some courageous mayor would appoint a Commissioner of Pedestrians to guard their rights against the incursions of the Traffic Commissioner, he would set an example that could enhance the cultural and recreational life of the nation. The new Commissioner of Pedestrians could think of ways to link walking to mass transport, change a few downtown streets into no-way streets, create some interesting pedestrian islands, raise downtown sidewalks to second-floor levels free of automobile traffic or provide safe crossings over the traffic and help redeem the city for its unremembered strollers. Pedestrian planning would be reborn and a part of the billions spent for road programs might even be earmarked for urban walkways.

With the restoration of pedal mobility must also come a new attitude toward density in big city office buildings. These buildings can accommodate a large number of people within a compact area provided they are near enough to mass transportation to be reached by foot. They should also be near well-planned residential areas of multiple dwellings reachable by walking or a short bus or train ride.

Contrary to general belief, high office buildings do not generate much horizontal car traffic. Their elevators can quickly disgorge large masses of people who can walk to the mass transportation that should be provided. The verticality of the human animal (in contrast to the automobile's horizontality) and his easier maneuverability facilitate the efficient use of the elevators, while the use of sidewalks diminishes traffic concentration on the pavements that must bear the bulkier and longer forms of transport.

One of the unsung virtues of these office concentrations is the business efficiency and social climate they make possible. The executive's luncheon appointment is kept by foot, his loan is negotiated from his banker across the street. The stenographer can keep a lunch or cocktail rendezvous a block away. The desirability of mass office concentrations is reflected in the high rent paid in the office cluster despite the availability of cheaper space outside it.

The efficiency of the triform (pedal, vertical, and mass horizontal) journey from desk to home is exemplified in the two great central hubs of New York City, i.e., the Grand Central and the Wall Street areas. Some planners have fought to limit the heights of office buildings in these areas on the mistaken notion that all high-density buildings clog the streets with automotive traffic. Their most recent target was the Pan-American building at Grand Central Station. It has many faults, but its concentration of people in a single compact area close to mass transport is not one of them.

If the working population of the Grand Central area were horizontalized as many planners would have wanted it to be, the mass transit would be no less crowded, for the workers would have to reach the same terminal by other forms of transit (subway, bus, or taxi), while the population that now walks to the Grand Central Terminal from the tall buildings would add to the strain on all forms of heavy horizontal transport, mass, taxi, and automobile. The obvious answer is to improve the commuter service and the mass transit facilities without zoning down the office concentrations. The same theory applies to the Wall Street concentration, one of the heaviest on earth. Despite its tall buildings and narrow streets, it is not as victimized by street traffic as one might expect. It could be otherwise if the tall buildings were used for purposes that generate traffic, as in the case of the projected Port Authority building which proposes to park 2,000 cars. What brings heavy traffic on horizontal streets is not the high density of buildings per se but the type of businesses. A section that depends on heavy trucking of goods will burden its streets even if the buildings are only two stories high.

A similar logic applies to multiple dwellings within the city. Many of these buildings should be placed within walking distance of the city's main job centers or at least within easy transport distance. Such accessible land exists in most cities and is either underdeveloped or not developed for its most useful purpose. There is nothing wrong with multiple dwellings of high density for small families, single persons, aging families, families with grown children, or wealthy families with children who can compensate for their shortcomings with weekend and summer places, servants, etc. Urban renewal can assemble land for such dwellings and minimize the load on transportation within the city itself. On the other hand, public housing for families with children should be built at lower densities and on cheaper land in other parts of the city or on its fringes.

13. *Make Cities More Livable for the Female*

A vital component in the city's social (as well as economic) base are the women, and one reason for the trek to suburbia is that the city has ignored their needs. They are the walking museums of fashion, but cities have cut down on the masonry on which they can walk, much less radiate.[32] They are the main buyers of goods and the supports of the downtowns, but cities have made it hard for them to get there. Though Alexis de Tocqueville attributed the growing strength of the American people to the superiority of their women,[33] the city gives them little chance to exhibit it.

The city inhibits female prospects as often as it enhances them. For all too many it has become the desolate land of the lonely heart. If the big city has lost population, it is partly because it is losing the confidence of the female—as one seeking love, as a wife, a career woman, and a mother.

The Social Environment for Love

Three elements are vital to the successful mating and reproduction of any species of life: convergence (the coming to the same point from different directions), selection (the choice of a variant in preference to others), and courtship (the wooing process). None of these

[32] It hath been thus since Isaiah the Prophet: "For the daughters of Zion are haughty, and walk with stretchedforth necks and wanton eyes, walking and mincing as they go, and making a tinkling of their feet" (Isaiah, 3:16).

[33] *Democracy in America,* Century, 1898, II, 262.

elements has been given even honorable mention in the planning texts.[34]

The urban mechanisms for convergence have become defective and the opportunities for boy meeting girl fewer. The newcomer to a city may never meet her neighbor, much less a suitor. The taboos on easy dating are still sacred. "The newcomer should particularly avoid forcing herself on her neighbors. . . . A smile to the passing acquaintance, the friendlier the better, is never out of place, but after smiling she should continue on. Never grin weakly and cling. A really well-bred person is as charming as possible to all but effusive to none. Enthusiasm should, of course, be shown to friends, in contrast to the more impersonal courtesy displayed to strangers."[35] This advice may ultimately produce a rendezvous in the hinterlands or in suburbia, but it is a tough routine for a busy city street.

Meetings in the city do take place in other ways. Walking a dog may facilitate exchanges between dog lovers. A girl may bring along an extra companion for her boy's friend (provided of course the girl is not too pretty or clever to lure her own friend away). There are parties—if one gets enough invitations—and if there are enough residual boys and girls who are not paired, a selection may result. Meetings in offices and at bowling parties also take place, but, except in the smaller offices, protocol forbids the boy in a superior position to date a subordinate—it threatens office discipline.

The debutante or coming-out party is known in the higher social circles but nowhere else. The church and the "Y" operate to a limited

[34] In interviewing an architect in 1948 who was then planning the Cleveland zoo, I was struck by the quantity of research that goes into the study of animal habits. The general instructions to the architects were to retain the natural values of sites, simulate the natural habitats of each animal, and guarantee freedom from unnecessary distractions as well as absolute privacy for copulation. Specialists from all over the world were consulted on the eating, sleeping, and mating habits of each species, and the findings were reduced to detailed reports which were carefully studied before a line was drawn. No comparable studies, to my knowledge, have ever been made on the human animal in its urban surroundings nor are we even as much concerned as the zoo architect about the human habitation. The sciences of urban anthropology and human nidology, particularly as they bear on the human female, are not even at their beginnings.

[35] Emily Post, *Etiquette,* Funk and Wagnalls, 1960, p. 274.

extent for others. The most strategic opportunity for convergence and selection is the college, and many a parent's hopes are raised with the matriculation. But if this filtration point for kindred souls is passed up, no better one will come along easily. Only about 40 per cent of the youngsters 18 to 21 years of age go to college anyway. The rest must either angle in the small provincial pools in which they were reared or head for the difficult waters of the metropolises.

The exurban summer resort and its social director are also depended on for convergence. There is more informality and more prospects to choose from for a dance or a stroll. But in the two weeks of one's vacation, one must quickly deploy one's armament for the encounter, and here, too, only a small percentage succeed; the rest return disconsolate. Nor, considering the cost of a two-week vacation or some of the tours for "singles only," can every boy or girl afford the junket, let alone the sea journey to Europe or even the economy trip to San Juan. Ski camps and music festivals are good theaters of action, though they are outside the city. A recent in-city expedient for meeting and mating is the political club,[36] and the common effort to nominate and elect a young candidate brings together the workers for the common cause. This quest for tryst in fact contributed to the downfall of District Leader Carmine De Sapio in 1963. It is the buttress of the political reform movement in New York City.

The limitations of city life are a boon to some employers. The qualifications for the job of hostess on the nation's airlines require the candidate to be single or divorced, be the right age, have the right weight, legs, teeth, complexion, and be the "banker's daughter type"; the probabilities of winning a passenger are embraced in the pay. A young stenographer who can land a job in the right university has achieved a tour de force. A plant or office with an excess of young males is certain to draw a ready flow of females, and wages are often adjusted to the prospects of alliance. A company social policy that facilitates meetings guarantees a ready supply of workers, and the cost is a deductible contribution to good employee relations. Labor unions

[36] The uptown Lexington Democratic Club, where the sons of some of the wealthier folk are members, is reputedly a choice assemblage for those in the know, according to a reliable female informant.

have also entered the social competition and run camps, barbecues and dances to hold members, compete with the company union, or reap the fruits of companionship. But somehow all these are no longer enough to fulfill the biological wants and needs in the big city.

A tough problem is selecting the mate after convergence and the date. All sorts of restrictions are at work to discourage serious companionship, e.g., religious and social differences and even variations in size, personality traits, or language. The recent increase in the Negro population has made the problem tougher for white females; nor is the growing proportion of the aging in cities a solace for the young in heart.

There are fewer males than females (the 1960 ratio was 97.1 males to 100 females) and though the numbers are almost equal at ages up to 34, the prospect of marriage dips distressingly after the early twenties. After the twenty-eighth year, the statistics are frightening enough to drive a *femme seule* into cutting corners with a hacksaw. Her marriage prospect, which was 91 per cent at 21, drops to a terrifying 64.4 per cent at 28. (The male, whose prospects were 92.3 per cent at 21, slips only to 80.3.)

In the effort to fill the need, thirteen firms in Manhattan list themselves in the "yellow pages" as social encounter institutes, matrimonial bureaus, and introduction services. There are hundreds of other part-time marriage brokers and unlisted "consultants." In most other cities, there is not a single listing; and even in New York, the law frowns on the brokerage business and will not enforce collection of a fee for consummating a merger. The state, however, does nothing itself to provide a substitute service.

Improvisation to effect convergence after the budding years have budded appear in the form of "28 Clubs." Two pages in a Friday edition of the *New York Post* will advertise a "reunion" for bachelors and "bachelorettes" only; a "dansant" for "business and professionals 28 and over" with a Saturday get-together that guarantees "equal guys and girls at tables." There are groups for "singles only," "membership clubs" and affairs "ladies free up to 9 P.M., gents $1.50" and a "young college graduates club, proof of college degree required." There is

"Vera's exclusive party for professionals, college grads, and socially select singles," while an "Indoor-Outing" is offered that promises a "feast on toasted marshmallows" with an option to "have a waiter serve you or find some fair maid or gallant Galahad to do the honors" (the waiter often has the better entree to conversation and may even prove the best catch in the pool).

In a big city these meet-marts have a function and sometimes work but their brashness keeps the verecund from venturing. The night club with telephones at each table has all the ugly and risky aspects of the pickup; the burgeoning professional houseparties at $3.00 per head are embarrassing—there is rarely a surplus of males and more of them are apt to be prowlers than prospects. The professional dance studio is big business and costly but, like the dancehall, it holds dubious opportunities.

What is missing in all these enterprises is the existence of the honorable purpose or cause, and for cause-value, there is nothing that can hold a candle to the Communist movement that flourished between 1932 and 1939, or the Spanish loyalist parties (later infiltrated) in 1936. (Had the anti-Communist cause entered the competition with similar social opportunities, it might have drawn some of the innocent young fellow travelers into the more honorable fold.) More recently, the art show openings are providing the semblance of purpose, though few of the invitees ever see the art. The civil rights movement spawned out of the Negro revolution carries a cause and provides the opportunities for fraternization, protest meetings, marches, and sit-ins. But usually the healthy motivational factor in the convergence process is lacking; it highlights one of the big defaults in our new urban age. Neither the church nor adult education (employing the social occasion or purpose) has as yet filled the gap. What exists not only invites personal humiliation, frustration, and futility among the young, but gives opportunism and coarse commerce free play to move into the breach.

Assuming that the processes of convergence and selection have been mastered, the problem of courting in a city will challenge the most tenacious suitor. The automobile affords ample opportunity in the suburb, and the motel has become the oasis for premarital activities. In the city, where the automobile is less in use, there is greater safety from seduction (carlessness prevents carelessness). But the price is also lack of space for the decent privacy of love. The chances for convergence, selection, and courtship are becoming fewer.

In the city's new multiple dwellings, the contest for space and the rising building costs have reduced the number of available rooms per apartment so that even the multiples built by public housing and urban renewal provide little or no room for privacy. Public housing projects with their maximum income limits automatically disclose the poverty of the parents before the daughter has had a chance to be wooed on her merits. Selection within the project is limited for the white girl by the large proportion of Negroes and in any event, promises no breakthrough to higher economic status.

Sharing apartments to pay the high rents in good sections has some advantages but is limiting for both occupants. The parlor with an age-old tradition for human contiguity has been taken over for family television. The fireplace that warms hearts has given way to the radiator that only heats rooms. Large parks have become dangerous to stroll in, and small safe parks as in London are rare. The growing lack of protection in unpoliced city areas has made a girl's walking alone after dark or venturing toward a decent meeting place a dangerous adventure. With the surge in land prices and the need for maximum use of urban sites, the front porch has gone, eliminating one of the hallowed areas for decent caressing. The urban cinema survives, but is expensive and hardly a satisfactory trystorium.

In the more sizable projects both public and private, better opportunities for convergence and selection can be planned with more communal rooms for dance, talk or semiprivate television in a subdued environment where the young need not always be in the presence of the elders. The techniques of good, soft-colored lighting can be applied to the private open spaces as well as the park, and make a girl look as attractive on a park bench as in a glamour-lit night club. Provision of a few darker spots properly sited need not be an invitation of defloration. More neighborhood social settlements, common in the old

immigrant areas, can bring more teenagers and post-teenagers together for healthy fun. The common sing has spontaneously sprung
up without benefit of the park commissioner (and even over his initial
opposition) in Washington Square, New York. The open-air concert
where a couple can lie on the grass need not increase the incidence
of illegitimacy. This and other planned retreats might even restore
the conversational art to a generation to whom the ear-rending band
and the amplified discothèque and juke box have dispensed with the
need to converse.[37]

The provision of supervised social activities in the larger parks can
make their evening use more constructive as well as safer. Square
dancing, for example, sanctions hand-holding, and not all the dancers
are squares. Better planning and more use of school buildings for
evening recreation, the provision of Spanish-style park-squares for
convening in neighborhoods, the block party, more theater in parks,
and the organized use of now-deserted waterfronts are only some of
the potentials that have been ignored in the renewal process. A few
well-run tearooms and coffeehouses launched with the help of civic-
minded citizens would provide healthy competitors for the roadside
bars. Organized dancing would enhance neighborhood life. More
vision is needed than supervision, although the availability of understanding people trained in doing the honors can help bring more boys
and girls together. The churches and synagogues could render a service
by acting more imaginatively where they now are anchored instead
of thinking of how to take wing to suburbia. "The Exit," an interdenominational specialty club in St. Louis, featuring jazz, dancing
and talk, is a good start.

The trouble is that no one in authority gives much thought to these
simple human needs. The Commissioner of Commerce is not com-
missioned to encourage commerce between sexes. The highway commissioner thinks of cement, the FHA of mortgages and cul-de-sacs,

---

[37] The owner of Greenwich Village's Village Barn, who has seen the shifts
in nightclub entertainment over the last thirty years, is my authority for the
statement that boiler-room music is drawing more customers today primarily
because it relieves one of the need to talk—a kind of "entertainment of discomfort."

the park commissioner of fences around his pollinating flowerbeds. Urban renewal administrators have not yet thought of revitalizing the human spirit.

The City and Motherhood

The central city brings more complications when the mother faces the problem of child-raising. The big city, though tolerable when the baby is born, is not good enough for the growing years. The abbreviated living unit in the city's multiple dwelling is far from the last word in family livability. Except in a very few large developments, there are no communal facilities to help lighten the mother's chores. Giving the apartment-housed nursling an airing means dressing it for the outdoors; preparing the carriage and maneuvering it from apartment to street; wheeling the baby five or ten blocks to a park; watching it on the cement and keeping it from being hit by a swing or a ball; caring for the baby's other functions along the route; wheeling the baby and the carriage back to the apartment; and finally undressing the baby and preparing it for the new temperature. (The carriage garages that have cropped up in neighborhood stores are few and costly.) With a built-in open balcony, a mother might perform many a household task while the baby is sunning nearby. But in the United States, the balcony is provided for the wealthy who have summer places and don't need it, while the poor and middle class must do as best they can with the fire escape—if there is one. For the child that has become ambulatory, the city provides its unimaginative and often dangerous play apparatus as well as the dirtbox. The crowded kindergartens and schools, poor air and traffic dangers then turn the mother's attention to the periphery and the single-family home with a garden space. Home ownership asserts its lure, and since the flushing of a neighbor's toilet can never compete with the murmur of a suburban brook, suburbia is apt to win the contest.

If the city has shortcomings for motherhood, it does have some advantages for wifehood, thanks to its versatility of attractions and the husband's shorter work journey. It holds an advantage for the working mother in the variety and proximity of its employment opportunities, although the houses available rarely suit her needs, and what she would have to pay for a better apartment or a maid to look after the child may consume most of her salary.

The spurt to suburbia does not mean that it is the final answer to the needs of women and families. The choice is being made not because it is the best of all possible worlds, but because it is the better of two, both of which are deficient. The city still has advantages for some families and would for more if it were bettered. The suburb has fewer of the city's defects but lacks many of its benefits. In fact, the suburban choice is less a disengagement from the city than a hyphenization. Both city and suburb must be made better for families if the decision to stay or move is to be more like a preference than a compulsion.

A good middle-income housing program financed by cheap money could help keep many middle-class families in the city and make it more tolerable for those already living there. But not only must the houses be cheap enough; they should have day care centers, and nurseries, good schools and recreation within easy distance. They should offer a better environment for life and be planned for the larger family as well as for the childless family for which most of the new housing inventory is built. But planning for the large or even average families is still an unbroken frontier in the United States—for the poor as well as the middle class. It will remain unbroken until the balance sheet of private enterprise is merged with the social balance sheet and an accommodation made.

The big city resumes its magnetism for the woman after the children have been emancipated. The extension of the life span and the progress of cosmetics find her still looking young and often ready to engage the talents she had laid aside during child rearing. The greater availability of jobs for women gives her a better chance of resuming a career or preparing for one at the city's schools. "Grandma Goes to College" is no longer a movie farce—it is a routine occurrence.[38] But

[38] I have taught grandmas in a number of university courses and thousands are found in adult education courses.

whether she looks to a career or simply to an expansion of her horizons
or pleasures, the central city provides the better environment to engage the hours once spent on raising the child. Now the apartment
competes with the suburban home, grown too large and too much to
care for.

The city thus plays its role for womanhood, but only during part
of the life cycles. Its main task is to try to embrace more of the cycles.
Planning each neighborhood to include not only the school, but the
child-care center, the small park, and the community house would
help. So would projects planned for working mothers as in Sweden,
and subsidized middle-income projects with the right facilities. But
the city's main task is to sustain its interests and enlarge them where
it can. The city can still boast more people, more jobs, more drama,
more surprises, more culture, more night life, more streets and
churches. What it lacks is more understanding, more imagination,
and a greater interest in cities and city life than it has won to date.
Not the least of the needs is an understanding of how it can function
better for womanhood in all its stages.

14. *Improve the Central City's Public Schools*

The sad state of the city's public school system is one of the big
reasons for its decline. The number of recent studies dealing with the
problems of the city's schools would fill several bookshelves. Emphasized and re-emphasized are the shortage, low pay, and abnormal
turnover of teachers, the dearth of classroom facilities, the impact of
slums and poverty on the children, the slum child's reading deficiencies, and the extraordinary number of dropouts among the minority
children.

Yet the single most important development responsible for the
decline of the city's educational system has been the massive Negro
in-migration into cities and the segregation it has brought to the public
school system. The nation has had segregation and segregated neighborhoods before, but they were more dissolvable through forces implicit in their character—it was a segregation of white immigrants
whose children could be absorbed into the cultural milieu in a single
generation or, at most, two.

The segregation that exists today in the central cities is one mostly of an identifiable and therefore a more easily excludable minority group. The segregation of Negro children in the schools is far greater than is represented by the Negro's numbers. In Manhattan, New York City, where the Negro population is 23 per cent, 42 per cent of the elementary school students and 40 per cent of the junior high school students were Negro in 1965 (in addition, 35 per cent were Puerto Rican in the elementary schools and 33 per cent in the junior high schools).[39] The number of elementary schools considered segregated by the Board of Education in March 1965 rose from 63 in 1957 to 148 in 1964. In Washington, D.C., where the Negro population is about 55 per cent, 85 per cent of the school children are Negro.

Not only are the public schools being called upon to educate a growing number of culturally deprived children, many of whom are recent arrivals from the backward South, but many white families who have elected to remain in the cities have been withdrawing their children from the public schools and entering them into private schools. The greater the proportion of Negro children in the schools, the greater is the solidification of school segregation.

The situation is having a cumulative impact. It is driving more white families into the suburbs; it is making it more difficult to hire good teachers for the segregated schools; it is putting a greater strain on the finances of the cities in their efforts to meet the added social and economic burdens which segregation and poverty impose; it is depriving the Negro children of the benefits they would receive in a

[39] In a report by the New York City Superintendent of Schools (*New York Times,* March 8, 1965, p. 22), the ethnic composition of the school register as of January 15, 1965, was given as follows:

| | | Per Cent of Total | |
Citywide	Puerto Rican	Negro	Others
Elementary	20.7	30.1	49.2
Junior High	18.7	28.0	53.3
Academic	8.9	18.2	72.9
Vocational	24.2	28.6	47.2
Special Schools	28.3	40.5	31.2
GRAND TOTAL	18.2	27.3	54.5

racially integrated school system; it is confronting the cities with embarrassing demands to achieve an integration through devices that cannot possibly accomplish it; it is straining the relations between white and Negro families, and creating a moral claim among whites for the right to give their children an education in their own neighborhoods; in California, Akron, and Detroit, it has already won legislation to ban the future passage of antidiscrimination laws in housing.

The power to halt housing segregation rests with the states and the federal government. But the states have all but closed their eyes to their responsibility, while the federal government has been concentrating its efforts on breaking the segregation pattern in the South but ignoring the North and West, where the situation is equally if not more critical. The cities lack the power to stem the migrations, nor is it in their tradition to do so. But it is time that the people of the central cities exerted their concentrated political influence toward forcing the opening of the suburbs to minority families instead of looking mainly to urban renewal and public housing as the panaceas.

Better education and desegregation in the South would help the children of the new migrant families but, despite some gains, the stubborn barriers persist. The schools in which the educational capacities of students are reported the lowest and where tensions between whites and Negroes are greatest are generally those with the heaviest influx of southern youngsters. It is these very schools and neighborhoods that need the most attention by social workers as well as the best teachers. Except for some token demonstrations, they get neither.[40]

If the Negro child is to have an equal chance to advance, and if the middle classes are to be kept from leaving the city and withdrawing their children from the public schools, not only must conditions be improved within the slum areas but the new and better areas must be opened to poor families, and this calls for state and federal subsidies that would make it possible for the minority families to move there.

[40] James B. Conant, *Slums & Suburbs,* McGraw-Hill, 1961; A. Harry Passow, ed., *Education in Depressed Areas,* Columbia University Teachers College, 1963; Charles E. Silberman, *Crisis in Black and White,* Random House, 1964; and *Urban Education Requirements,* Government Consulting Service, Fels Institute of Local and State Government, 1964.

Enforced desegregation may work occasionally but it is not solved by sending a few Negro children on long bus rides to white schools or white children to Negro schools. Nor is antibias legislation enough. Negro families must also be given the right to live where they choose and where they can find work, in the city or the region, and to buy or rent housing in either place at costs they can afford. Only this type of program can dilute the compulsory urban concentrations in which malice and bitterness presently fester. There can never be equal opportunity as long as only white families can enjoy a better education and environment. Nor can the promised end to poverty be achieved as long as the barriers to free movement persist.

15. *Concentrate More Effort on Improving the Environment for Children*

When social concern for the city child manifested itself in America, it took three forms: child labor legislation, compulsory education, and judicial supervision. Child labor was outlawed, but no one gave thought to how to make the child's new-found freedom more creative. Compulsory education sought to take the child off the street, but it was not seen that the child spends only a fifth of its waking time in school and that the street, where he spends much of his after-school hours, would be assigned to the insatiable motorcade. Judicial supervision concerned itself only with "the case"; and when it was supplemented by other activities such as care of dependent, handicapped, and delinquent children, the emphasis continued on the problem child instead of on the problem environment. The few underpaid, untrained, and overworked social workers and the few underfinanced settlement houses were depended on to do the rest.

Not often mentioned is that the American city was never planned for the growing child. What was installed for his use, recreation, and play came after the city's configuration had been fixed. The pavements and sidewalks became play spaces because they happened to be there. A few playgrounds were added with the spurt in traffic tolls, but in the over-all shuffle and reshuffle of priorities, the child's needs were forgotten and the space left to him was withered and assigned to other claimants. The bicycle disappeared from the streets, the roller skate became impractical on the ill-suited walks, and curb cuts and civic clutter reduced the space for sidewalk games near the home. A fenced-in sidewalk extension onto the paved area would make more room for hopscotch or jacks and would wrest parking space from only one or two cars. Demolition of one or two buildings in every neighborhood would make room for some "finger playgrounds." But this costs money. Even the few streets withdrawn from traffic have been left as they were without amenities.

Environment enters subtly into the life of the child from birth and becomes more important with growth. It generates personal associations and conditions attitudes and emotions. The lack of play room, the absence of a place in the social stratum and of constructive influences in shaping the child's attitudes and behavior all have impacts that are felt through life. The home is one of the most important aspects of the child's environment. But the city apartment and tenement too often lack the space for privacy and study. The extra room costs money. The yard which might have afforded freedom from street dangers is just a light shaft.

Not all slums are equally bad, and not all are alike. But the neighborhood and the streets of the slum areas filled by the recent in-migrations are hardly the best an affluent society can provide. Certain social conditions correlate with such slum areas: high population density; high death rates; high proportion of illiteracy; high proportion of women employed; high juvenile delinquency rates; high rate of sex offenses; high rate of gambling arrests; more multifamily dwellings; large average family size; small proportion of owner-occupied homes; high proportion of relief cases; more unemployment; more poverty; high rates of nonsupport cases; high rates of illegitimacy; high rates of venereal disease; high rates of alcoholism; low proportion of males married; high suicide rates; high rates of various mental disorders and mental deficiency; low marriage rates and greater instability of the relationship; low average educational levels; high residential mobility.

Many children escape the effects of such neighborhoods, and much can be done to build buttresses that might offset their influences within the neighborhood itself. But as long as the emphasis is on tearing neighborhoods down, instead of building morale up, it can only be expected that most of the families will drift to other areas, where the same problems and the same syndromes will reappear.

Juvenile disorder is the tocsin that summons officials to action. When the newspapers seethe with stories of juvenile outrages, gang wars, and teen-age murders, conferences are hastily convened, officials blast the parents, churchmen blame lack of religion, and federal crime officials denounce citizen indifference. The usual "remedies" are teen-age curfews, more frequent use of nightsticks, more work camps for delinquents, or "the creation of a moral climate—by parental example, love, and moral guidance."[41] A youth program may be generated, but officials are not concerned with the more costly and continuing remedies such as the social renewal of neighborhoods. This would take time, money, and effort. Quick, painless, and inexpensive pilot programs are needed to mollify public indignation, and this is usually what the public gets.

Almost every aspect of city planning dealing with environment has emphasized the house while ignoring the neighborhood. Both must be improved. Despite the serious social consequences of housing and neighborhood disorder, the federal housing handbooks are saturated with talk about interest charges, amortization periods, depreciation rates, maintenance technicalities, and other passwords of the trade. The slide rule has become the principal yardstick of slum economics and of public as well as private housing production.

The appearance of the minority problem has added a new dimension to the problems of city children. Any new group that enters an alien environment plagued by poor and overcrowded housing conditions is bound to suffer. The child is often handicapped in doing his homework; overcrowding forces the minority children into the streets; family controls are weakened; with cultural dislocation and social disorganization, the gang organizes as a form of excitement, predatory exploitation, or social or physical defense.

---

[41] These were among the proposals after the juvenile outbreak in New York City in 1959. The quotation was Governor Rockefeller's proposal.

The problems of the new in-migrant Negro child are more serious than those of the immigrant youngsters of yesterday. His greater identifiability and enforced social segregation are among the new elements that must be dealt with. Feeling the bias of the whites, prevented by confinement within cities and in his overcrowded slums from having contact with white children in schools and sometimes encouraged by his elders to blame the whites for his condition, his resentments solidify. Poverty and unemployment, the flight of white neighbors, the lack of jobs and training for life, the dearth of institutions in cities, the wholesale dislocations by slum clearance operations with no better alternative offered to the evicted family, and the inferiority of schools in Negro neighborhoods combine with lack of proper parental controls to slow the development of a sounder community life.

A substantial easing of the problem may take a generation or more. It is certain, however, that a *rapprochement* will never occur under the enforced exclusion practices that presently prevail in suburbia. It is equally certain that the cities cannot undertake the immense task of social acculturation as well as the sorely needed neighborhood and institutional improvements without federal help and without a broader, stronger, and more realistic federal stand on the discrimination and segregation issues in city and suburb.

Thirty years ago, environment was the product of a congeries of individual decisions made by a diverse group of investors in the pursuit of profit. What was known as "the community" or "the neighborhood" evolved thereafter out of the in-movements and out-movements of people, associations, institutions, investments, and physical formations.

But today, government has expanded its powers, particularly in the areas of housing, planning, and environment. It insures risks in housing, acquires huge acreage for demolition and rebuilding, restricts and subsidizes private real estate operations, and moves people in and out *en masse*. Officialdom is, for the first time, posed to affect environment and has, in fact, become the main influence in its creation. It must share the blame for what eventuates.

There have been a few heroic demonstration projects like New

Haven's special assistance programs, sponsored by the Ford Foundation, and New York City's All Day Neighborhood School Program, providing after-school group work facilities, teachers for reading improvement, and other assistance to the slum child. The Economic Opportunity Act (Poverty Program) has proferred a job corps analagous to the New Deal's Civilian Conservation Corps, work and training programs for youngsters 16 to 21 years of age, projects to help them obtain a higher education, urban and rural community action, and other pilot undertakings. Some of the assistance supplements existing programs; other programs are new. The program has been hailed as the opening gun in what is being called a "war on poverty," the aim of which is to "eliminate the paradox of poverty in the midst of plenty in this nation by opening to everyone the opportunity for education and training, the opportunity to work, and the opportunity to live in decency and dignity."[42]

The dedication is a mighty one and federal assumption of responsibility for eliminating ignorance and poverty is a step long overdue. But the program can hardly be called a War on Poverty when the total initial appropriation for the country, in rural and urban areas combined, is no more than $800 million. It is more nearly a series of unrelated skirmishes. The poverty program can have only minor significance in improving the city's school system, the environment in which children of the poor spend most of their formative years, the economic conditions of their parents, or the neighborhoods in which they live.

If the city is to be a better place for the child, it must be made a better place for everybody, black and white—in schools, playgrounds, and in every aspect of its environment. Such proposals do not make headlines. They must be laboriously organized and fought for. But they hold the only real answers to the welfare of the city child in the long run.

[42] *Public Law 88–452*, 88th Congress, S.2642, August 20, 1964.

Chapter

14

The City Faces the Future

EVERY INDUSTRIALIZING NATION must go through a period of slum formation, and the United States is no exception. Every nation with a pride in its environment has been moved to renew its cities, and the United States faces the prospect for the first time in its history.

After referring to "the blighted cities and bleak suburbs" in his State of the Union Message on January 4, 1965, President Johnson proposed that "we launch a national effort to make the American city a better and more stimulating place to live." Pointedly, the President said: "The Great Society asks . . . not only how fast we are going but where we are headed." The President did not answer his question, but the answer is that we have been edging about in many directions but are not yet off the ground. As matters stood in 1965, Congress' promise of "a suitable living environment for every American family" and the President's hopes for "communities where every member has a right to belong" were almost as far from realization as ever.

One reason for the chasm separating promise from performance is an ambivalence in the national attitudes. An American sense of morality has generated a sensitivity to slum life in cities, but our slums cannot be cleared without a housing program, and no adequate housing program has either been proposed by the President or emanated from Congress.

A similar sensitivity has prompted some federal aid for education, relief of poverty, and improved transportation, but the programs operate in isolation. They lack a unifying aim, and the amount of money allotted for the central cities where the problems are concentrated is a token.

We have similarly committed ourselves to renew our cities, but the authorized funds for renewal are no more than a gesture compared to what a real commitment would entail. No real renewal of our cities can, in fact, be accomplished without easing the gigantic financial burdens which the urban society has imposed upon them, and this, too, appears unlikely for the present. In less than forty years, said President Johnson in his message to Congress of March 2, 1965, urban population will double and city land will double. "It is as if we had forty years to rebuild the entire urban United States," he warned Congress, but in another part of the message, he conceded that "we are still only groping toward solution" and he dedicated ten of those forty years as "a time of experimentation." What we spend, create, and build during the first experimental decade will, of course, condition what we can do thereafter.

The anticity and antiminority forces and the political blockade at the state level are still too formidable to permit a meaningful federal aid program to cities that will pull them out of their ruts. The historic coolness of the rural sector toward cities has not changed with the rise of urbanization, and the flight to suburbia has only contributed another faction to the anticity coalition. The influx of Negroes into cities has linked racial fear and bias to city life (one can more readily admit to a prejudice against cities than against Negroes though the emotions are intermeshed). The image of planlessness, slums, crime, and social and physical distortions has not produced many champions for the big city's regeneration, nor has the mobility of its people and industries brought to the side of its cities a broad-based, stable citizenry with a pride in place and a stake to protect and improve.

Yet with the rise of the federal government as the primary force in the creation and re-creation of environment, the city's destiny is at the mercy of federal policy. In 1902, for example, the combined tax revenues of federal, state, and local governments were less than $1.4 billion, but by 1964 they exceeded $158 billion, of which the federal share was more than two-thirds. The huge federal resources available for credit, public improvements, defense, and services and the influence they have on environmental development are so great that they can generate population inflows or draw them elsewhere, help or hurt cities, make or break them.

If we are to know where "we are headed," therefore, the nation's first task is to bring the national perspectives, political powers, influence, and resources more in line with the responsibilities of an urban society—by consensus, if possible, or by taking the issue to the people, if necessary. While the federal power to act in the general welfare should embrace the welfare of its urban people and its central cities, the federal political structure is still geared to its agricultural origins. The political gap between the society of 1865 and of 1965 is still to be bridged. Direct federal aid to cities for housing and community development, for example, was only $400 million in 1963 compared to $7.7 billion spent by the Department of Agriculture. Such urban aid was less than one per cent of total federal budget expenditures. Though there is a cabinet office for agriculture, Congress up to 1965 had refused to give the President a cabinet office for urban affairs, and if it does under President Johnson's prodding, its power over urban affairs will be meager.

Funds for public housing are minuscule compared to the need. Though the deteriorating public schools of cities have been an important cause of poverty in the cities and the flight to suburbia, there is no sign of real aid to the city school systems—up to 1965, only about $1.3 billion of federal funds were available annually for education of all kinds in rural, urban, and suburban areas. Insistence on more subsidized housing in suburban areas as well as cities would help equalize the city's burden of maintaining its poorer people and dissolving its Negro concentrations. It would make possible for the first time the demolitions and displacements which cities must inevitably undertake for their essential beautification, recreation, housing, services and utilities, and for their conversion into places where people can work and live decently. More open space within cities would give their people more room to breathe but most of the federal government's open-space spending is outside, not within, the cities. More playgrounds would be a boon, but this has not even been accepted as a federal concern. Efforts to solve the problems of air pollution are hardly at their beginnings, nor can they be meaningful without regional cooperation. Except for the nominal appropriations for urban renewal, public housing, and parts of the poverty program, there has been no national acknowledgment that an urban society demands a federal program of direct dealing with cities and direct aid to them, as the federal government is doing in the case of farms, savings and loan associations, private builders, and other enterprises.

If we discount political rhetoric dealing seasonally with the plight of city living and poverty, and look at the actual impact of national policy in the last three decades, not only has the federal government not aided existing cities but it has been a contributing cause of their deterioration.

To cite a few examples:

• Since the end of World War II, local governments have increased their debt more than fivefold, while the federal debt per capita has declined. The central cities have been straining their resources to meet their growing social problems. As state aid to cities failed to keep pace with their needs, the cities were left to bear their burdens almost alone. Although population migrations and racial problems, poverty, ignorance, and urban environment are the concerns of a federal government with a welfare power, its assistance to the cities which have been bearing the main weight of these problems has remained nominal.

• By offering cities cheap mortgage money and adequate housing subsidies for their middle-income families, the federal government could have encouraged central and suburban development simultaneously and given the cities a more equal chance to compete for the fruits of the immense growth the nation was experiencing. Instead, its policy under the Federal Housing Administration, Veterans Administration, and other agencies has encouraged and emphasized suburban development. Capable of creating distinctive environments that might have been the envy of the world, federal policy made it easy for middle- and upper-class families who needed help least to buy homes in our mushrooming suburbias, while it left to their own devices the low-income families who lived mostly in the cities. It is still doing so.

• By openly and deliberately advocating racial restrictive covenants in its suburbs between 1935 and 1950, the federal government put its weight behind racial discrimination, virtually influencing a whole generation of suburban families, firming a lasting division of classes between its cities and its suburbs, lending an ethical base to an unethical practice, and establishing a new social milieu that was not only repugnant to its faith but difficult to alter after the Supreme Court had condemned the practice. Although President Johnson has done much to expand the Negro's political rights, his program has done little to regain the ground in housing that was lost after 1935. Housing discrimination is still being openly practiced in the suburbs and the Negro is still confined to his ghettos in the central cities.

• Having assumed the general welfare power after 1934, the federal government could not only have helped build new cities but salvaged the old ones, regenerated the transportational links between them, and made both part of a functioning whole. It could have done this through private enterprise, the states, or both. If the states demurred, it could have conditioned its aid upon state cooperation. Or it could have elected to build housing for needy families directly in suburbs and cities as indeed it did during the New Deal days. But having won the power in the courts to do so,[1] it renounced it and again surrendered its welfare power over cities to the states. While devastated Europe had to rebuild its cities under the pressure of homelessness and disorder, the federal government could have helped rebuild our own cities with predeliberation and purpose. But while it helped Europe rebuild, it let its own cities fall away.

• By concentrating major federal expenditures on road building after 1935, the federal government stimulated employment during the depression years; but long after the economy had recovered everywhere but in its ailing cities, it accelerated the road program, in-

[1] See Chapter 11, Appendix A, p. 238.

creased the subsidy to 90 per cent of road cost, and drew more hordes of middle-class families from the cities. In 1964 it increased its highway aid almost sixfold over 1954, the largest percentage increase in federal aid for any purpose during this period.

There are no easy roads to the better city—and it is in fact easier to build roads than cities, which might be one explanation for the direction of federal policy. But no society can be a great society without great cities. And a nation of ever-widening suburban enclaves thrusting outward from bankrupt cores is no pathway to a great society or even a middling one.

With more than half of the people who live in metropolitan areas still living in the central cities, and with some 320 million people destined to live in urban areas fifty years hence, there is no development plan, no philosophy of urban progress, no program for stemming city decay—only a fortuitous concourse of patchwork programs, most of which reflect the successful lobbying power of a particular pressure group and most of them working to the detriment rather than to the benefit of existing cities.

"We have been called upon," said President Johnson, "to build a great society of the highest order, not just for today or for tomorrow, but for three or four generations to come." Yet unless something more relevant and more comprehensive is offered, we shall see in the very first generation acres of speculative sprawl controlled by a myriad of jurisdictions, each of them armed with governmental powers over their environments that are superior to that of the federal government itself; our central cities will steadily fade as solvent communities; new cities composed of arteries without souls; cities for the poor and cities for the better-situated; and some cities that are little more than workshops, deserted at nightfall by all but the poor and the transients— like the nation's capital which, planned and built by a young and hopeful government, is now inhabited mainly by the Negro while most of the white working population flees into the dormitories of three states with each twilight.

Unless our policy changes, we shall be leaving to the "generations to come" a millstone, not a milestone—a long procession of suburbias made up of the same straggling subdivisions carved out of whatever patches of land the developers happen to pick up; the development of such land will entail the same astronomical burdens for follow-up roads, schools, water, recreation, and services. As each farm and orchard is consigned to the steam shovel, the only vestige of nature will be the little greenbelts preserved to separate the blackbelts from the whitebelts. For a look at a decent city in this age of cities, our people will have to look abroad.

There is another alternative: better planned communities surrounding the cities and with interests linked to them. They can be built on land acquired by public authorities, with schools, services, and utilities provided in advance and with the land developed by private and public builders for families of all classes and incomes. This would mean no more than extending the urban renewal concept to open land, as indeed was its original concept, and harnessing it to a vital public purpose.[2]

Simultaneously, we can make our existing cities worth living in by replanning and rebuilding their slum sections realistically and with adequate provision for rehousing their people. We can provide a small park as the focus of every neighborhood. We can revitalize the city's business centers and link them to the highways that now spread only outward to the suburban centers; we can provide more open spaces, recreation, and better schools, and make them available to families at all social and economic levels. But without a firm federal position, this will never happen.

A New Philosophy for Cities

Yet simply planning new cities and pouring money into the old ones will neither make the new urban formations live nor make the old

[2] Although this recommendation was made to Governor Edmund G. Brown by his Advisory Commission on Housing Problems and by President Johnson in his message to Congress of March 2, 1965, it is noteworthy that California by 1965 did not adopt the recommendation. Similarly, the Johnson proposal was rejected in committee.

ones spring to life. There is a dearth of ideas and, thanks to our long unconcern with the problems of cities, there has also been a diversion of the talent for generating such ideas. Our great capital pools stand aloof of any responsibility to invest in city rebuilding. The younger generation with the imagination has been siphoned off into building the machines for industry and ignoring the machines for living; our gifted people are concentrating their attention more on systems planning than on neighborhood planning; on target values rather than human values. We have succeeded in extending the duration of life but in housing we have learned only to extend the duration of mortgages. Compare the skills and endowments going into the physical sciences with those into city planning, or the advances made in assembly-line production with those made in house production, or the progress made in the conquest of outer space with the progress in the use of space on our own planet.

It is late but not too late to alter the stream of events. But it will require a change in the nation's philosophy.

• The new philosophy must acknowledge that there are values worth preserving in cities as there are in suburbs; not only because they are where most of the people in urbanized areas live but also because they provide an essential contrast to suburban life; they are still a vital influence in national life and the market places of trade, experimentation, and ideas; they are the main forums of civil rights and the soils on which our democratic principles will receive their most crucial tests. The cities are history, havens of interest and contrast. They offer variety in life's chances, and if they fail to suit the needs of all, they are the desired environments for many. They are still one of our frontiers—for the poor whom the suburb shuns, for those who choose them as their initial anchorages, for the enterprising young in search of new horizons, for the elderly when the suburb no longer satisfies their needs. If the city is not the only environment, it must remain one of the essential electives in a society which has always boasted a diversity of environments in which to live, work, and raise one's family.

• The new philosophy must acknowledge that the central city and suburb are an entity. They depend on each other for job opportunities, services, recreation, escape, variety, and progress. The city shapes and supplies the future recruits for the suburbs, and the suburban character in turn depends on the training and education the city's people receive and on the environment in which they grow. The suburb is a new form in the history of human settlements and must still be tested in the crucible of time. It is as unique to America as is the decline of its cities. It may have to cope with the racial problems the cities are facing. As it spreads out farther onto the millions of acres which it will consume, the limits of travel may be reached and the suburbias may decline just as the older cities have declined. A suburb requires an urb and one reason for the growth of the fringe is that the cities survive at the core. If the central city dies, new central cities will have to be created out of the satellites, and it is by no means certain, with all of the imperfections of the present cities, that the new ones will be better or that they will serve the needs and accept the social responsibilities which the present cities are doing.

• A third aspect of the new philosophy would redefine state and federal functions in fulfilling the general welfare. The partitioning of the welfare responsibility with no definable lines of jurisdiction between the states and the federal government impairs the effectiveness of both jurisdictions. It creates billions in new tax-exempt obligations, an increasing proportion of which are monuments to financial legerdemain; it duplicates levying powers, confuses the responsibilities of both governments and threatens to impair the federal capacity to borrow for its needs. Where jurisdiction is divided, there will be sterility, not progress. When as presently, there are two sovereignties concerned with the general welfare, one must be the paramount power in that area.

Federal assumption of the welfare power should not bar the state from its traditional lawmaking powers or those affecting intrastate affairs. But in the history of democratic governments, men's devotions have long leaned toward their nation and their city. The nation has been their shield, their local community the seat of their homes, jobs, pleasures, and interests. The state in the United States has become the tertiary form of government toward which personal affections are least drawn and sacrifices least made. It is now the limited not the supreme sovereignty—it has never acquired the logic of the province and has lost its luster as a tradition. State sovereignty is being asserted in the South mainly as the shield for white supremacy, and in the North as a means of maintaining boundary lines and status concepts that lost their logic a century ago. With the nation's urban population doubling in the next forty years, and with thirty million people to be added to our urban areas in the next fifteen years, state lines, city limits, and suburban border lines have become largely meaningless. A realistic redefinition and re-allocation of state and federal functions would make both sovereignties stronger and effect a giant step toward the great society. And it need not mean a lasting concentration of federal power or a surrender of state and local autonomy on matters not touching the general welfare.

• A fourth aspect of the government philosophy should be to assure to citizens the right to live where they choose. As the historic refuge, the city's doors must be open to all. The same rule must apply to the suburb. But to achieve this right, executive orders and civil rights laws are no longer enough. Unless the federal government enforces its orders and provides the subsidies that can make it possible for the poor to live where they choose and in homes that are decent, the right to move is a shell. A city, whether new or old, large or small, is by definition a community of people of every status or fortune and every level of aspiration. Neither a city nor any governmental entity, old or new, can function as the enclave of a single class or race. Where federal funds are dispensed to create cities or suburbs or build roads leading to them, they must not only be conditioned upon the right of all to move into the area but federal housing programs must be devised to make the right meaningful.

• A fifth aspect of the new philosophy should be that low-income families are entitled to the opportunity to own homes and to own them without fear of losing them when unemployment, illness, or death supervene. The present housing programs, which offer them rental housing only and confine them within cities, must be broadened to guarantee every family a home near its work, in city or suburb, and on terms that make it safe and feasible. If the government made it possible for all workers to own or rent homes near their jobs, the racial problem would be reduced to insignificance and school segregation would disappear.

• A sixth aspect of the new philosophy should be that poverty is a national concern. Though the federal government has moved to relieve poverty, its power to do so is still viewed as subject to state consent. Because poverty exists mostly in the cities, the cities as well as poverty must be part of the national responsibility. The poverty program must be expanded from a demonstration to a comprehensive program. The main burdens for relieving poverty cannot be left on the shoulders of the cities alone, nor can federal intervention be conditioned on a local government's refusal to cooperate. The central cities, which are the havens of the poor, must be made better cities with better environments, more opportunities for jobs, educational facilities, and recreation. It means, in short, that the federal government must take on many of the obligations that the old city can no longer bear and which the state is no longer posed to do. This entails a re-examination of the nation's tax system, its re-adaptation to the needs of an urban society, and the re-deployment of revenues to meet the needs and responsibilities of people wherever they live.

Once these principles are built into the national philosophy, we can be poised to prepare the relevant laws, policies, and programs. Educational aid, poverty, transportation, and other programs affecting urban welfare could be integrated and directed toward a common goal and be the concern of a cabinet office. The housing programs would be expanded and varied, and be made regional in scope. The urban renewal program would encompass not only slum demolition but also rebuilding of cities and suburbs; it would embrace transportation renewal, recreational renewal, downtown renewal, environmental renewal, public services renewal, and also a political renewal that acknowledges the existence of a regional city and not a collection of political enclaves pegged around a beleaguered core. Every major city would be the sound and functioning epicenter of its region.

In an urbanized society, neither the city nor the suburb serves its purpose when there is constant strife between those who live in the city and those who dwell at its edges; when there is fear or prejudice among those who should share common interests; when there are better schools and teachers for one class or race and not another; when poverty, ignorance, and slums are the lot of one class, while the rest of us all but close our eyes and hearts to it.

In the division between city and suburb and in the dual jurisdiction over national welfare, the nation has become more divided against itself than it was before the Civil War. We have become a nation of a thousand Mason-Dixon lines—in the North as well as the South—and they are spreading daily with each sprouting suburb. The influence of city life on the national culture is fading. Love of city is disappearing as it did in the cities of Greece and Italy before the Roman conquest and later in Rome itself before its decline and fall. People in the United States are losing their ties to their own older cities and their faith in them—not only because the cities are failing to meet all their needs, but also because neither the states nor the nation seems concerned with providing for such needs.

The main virtue of the American system has been that it has been able to adjust itself to political and economic change. But while it has taken the industrial revolution in stride, it has not yet coped with the urban revolution that came in its wake. Only when it has done so can it demonstrate that democracy can be as valid a faith, as sound a political system, and as practical a way of life in our new urban society as it was in the society that has passed.

Index

Former chairman of the New York State Rent Commission and the State Commission against Discrimination under Governor Averell Harriman, CHARLES ABRAMS has been described by *Architectural Forum* as "perhaps the foremost housing consultant in the United States." Of his most recent work, *Man's Struggle for Shelter in an Urbanizing World,* which the *London Economist* has called "remarkably wide-ranging and cogent," the *New York Times* has said that this "authoritative study . . . has the interest and excitement of being a pioneering work."

Now chairman of the city planning department of Columbia University, Mr. Abrams was visiting professor of urban affairs at MIT and an adviser to the United Nations and the Agency for International Development. He has been called upon by governments around the world to guide their city planning, housing, and urban renewal systems.

His first book, *Revolution in Land,* was cited by Lewis Mumford as the first really important study on land problems since 1879. *The Future of Housing* was a Book-of-the-Month dividend, and *Forbidden Neighbors* has been recognized as a "landmark" in the study of housing segregation.

Format by Sidney Feinberg
Set in Linotype Times Roman
Composed, printed and bound by The Haddon Craftsmen, Inc.
HARPER & ROW, PUBLISHERS, INCORPORATED